SATAN'S SECRET DAUGHTERS

SATAN'S SECRET DAUGHTERS

The Muse as Daemon

Robert Savino Oventile

The Davies Group, Publishers
Aurora, Colorado

Library of Congress Cataloging-in-Publication Data:

Oventile, Robert Savino.
  Satan's Secret Daughters : the Muse as Daemon / Robert Savino Oventile.
    pages cm
  Includes bibliographical references.
  ISBN 978-1-934542-33-0 (alk. paper)
  1. Demonology in literature. 2. Influence (Literary, artistic, etc.) 3. Inspiration in literature. I. Title.
  PN56.D465O94 2014
  809'.9337--dc23
                        2013047135

Selections from *Moby-Dick* appear by permission of Northwestern University Press: Melville, Herman. *Moby-Dick*, ed. Hershel Parker and Harrison Hayford. Evanston: Northwestern University Press, copyright © 1988 by Northwestern University Press and the Newberry Library.

From THE ILIAD by Homer, translated by Robert Fagles, translation copyright © 1990 by Robert Fagles. Used by permission of Viking Penguin, a division of Penguin Group (USA) LLC.

Selections from *The Tree of No* appear by permission of Action Books: Florian, Sandy. *The Tree of No*. Notre Dame, IN: Action Books, copyright © 2008 by Sandy Florian.

Printed in the United States of America
Published 2014. The Davies Group, Publishers

1 2 3 4 5 6 7 8 9 0

Table of Contents

Preface

For the wages of sin *is* death.
—Paul the Apostle

Who is responsible for the origin of death,
and what is the nature of the resurrection?
—Harold Bloom

I will carry your song, as old as god,
through the gates of death.
—Horacio Ferrer

About a reality entirely unavailable to experience, Harold Bloom writes, "Dying comes to all, but 'death' to no one."[1] All readers undergo dying eventually, yet of their own deaths readers encounter nothing. Besides each reader, the foregoing holds for each writer, even for poets of the finest sensibilities. Rather than *As I Lay Dead*, William Faulkner wrote *As I Lay Dying*. Perhaps for all, whether poets by vocation or not, dying inescapably solicits imagination. No one finally escapes the call to become a poet, even if for only a moment. Imagine a poet imagining a muse accompanies the self, even to dying's utmost verge. Imagine a poet imagining this moment. This imagining may occur at any point in the poet's chronological existence. In excess of the chronological, this moment with the muse remains open to imagination at any moment, though to persist in the moment with the muse, to forgo irreversibly any relapse into the chronological, would be wholly to immerse in that moment as the final moment, though really ever the only moment, with the contingently last encounter as much involved with imagination as any encounter.

Such imaginings people the moment with personages who may come to the poet at the very edge of demise, and depending on the strength of the imagination, these personages hover just on that edge, as distinct from the poet yielding to nihilism by aberrantly positing the nothing and no one beyond as something and someone, as if the poet were to encounter the poet's own death, an aberrance turning the poet from the muse who comes to the poet when and where nothing and no one are. In the poet's catachresis "death," the reader would find the poet's idiomatic failure of imagination. If for the imagination entirely to forgo such aberrance defines the impossible, then sublime poetry approaches the impossible.

Imagine the edge in question abuts the blankest and most adamantine of walls. Might the imagination stay with dying and refrain from skipping into a beyond or to a reifying and personifying catachresis of nothingness, always an aberrant leap? Even Melville's Ahab dreams of punching through the wall, but Ahab partially recovers by speculating behind the wall exists nothing. About Athena, the Oracle at Delphi warns, "Be ever watchful, wanderer, / For the eyes that gaze into yours at the bend of the road / May be those of the goddess herself."[2] The distinction between peopling solitude and positing something/ someone beyond corresponds to the distinction between staying with the muse to what Melville's Ishmael calls the endless end and abandoning or fleeing the muse, as if the poet were to lose Athena or shy away from confronting the goddess, forsaking her or yielding attention to the Medusa her shield bears. Then the poet would indeed see the Gorgon, turn stone mute, and become "responsible for the origin of death," forgetting Athena's shield bears the Gorgon only because from Athena the Gorgon knows destruction. The "nature of the resurrection" would be a rising from the poetic weakness of losing the muse in petrifaction before the Gorgon-bearing shield, a rising into poetic strength, into a fluid burgeoning with the muse: to meet here, to meet now, at just this turn in the path, the gaze of Athena. The impossible would come to the poet who evades surrendering the moment with the muse to "death," the poet who forgoes sacrificing this moment to a nothingness become idol, with this resurrection from "death" preceding the culmination of demise so the poet knows an overcoming of nihilism. In the moment with Athena, the need to justify existence vanishes.

A muse almost as overwhelming and as challenging to contemplation as Athena may accompany the poet at the edge, and this accompaniment may define resurrection. Consider the following lines by the Sufi poet Sa'dī:

> If the sword of your anger puts me to death,
> My soul will find comfort in it.
> If you impose the cup of poison upon me,
> My spirit will drink the cup.
> When on the day of Resurrection
> I rise from the dust of my tomb,
> The perfume of your love
> Will still impregnate the garment of my soul.
> For even though you refused me your love,
> You have given me a *vision of You*
> Which has been the confidant of my hidden secrets.[3]

Thinking of demise as brought in anger by the beloved, the poet wavers. Yet as the poem proceeds, and the poet imagines a "Resurrection" in which the "perfume" of the beloved's love "Will still impregnate the garment of [the poet's] soul," then the poet works toward an imagining in which what the poet calls "Resurrection" becomes an event of imagination peopling the poet's solitude. Into this solitude the poet carries the "perfume" of the beloved's "love," the love the beloved had "refused" the poet. In the "perfume" inheres a *"vision"* of the beloved. And this *"vision"* or imagination bears the poet's secrets. The poet imagines the *"vision"* (metonymic of the "perfume," the "love," the "beloved") will accompany the poet in the poet's utmost secret moment, the poet's "Resurrection." As having been given the *"vision"* promises to trump having suffered the refusal of "love," the resurrection will trump the "death" brought by the "sword" or the poison cup. The *"vision"* having been an intimate "confidant" of the poet's "secrets" promises the *"vision"* will accompany the poet toward the most entirely secret of secrets. This "confidant," this *"vision,"* this "perfume," this "love," this "beloved" attends the poet's solitude in the abyssal secrecy of the resurrection. The unsearchable secrecy goes with the fathomless intimacy, in excess of paradox.

The poet welcomes an event of imagination enacting the only resurrection. The beloved becomes the muse of this resurrection and so of a desire whose predicate of dying associates desire taken to the end with dying's culmination. Such muses are to die for. *Satan's Secret Daughters* tracks various journeys toward and with such muses. These muses function as what Homer in the *Iliad* describes Athena to be: a daemon who, with force and dynamism, possesses Achilles and draws him toward the limit of mortality so as to exalt him toward an ecstatic fulfillment tied to imminent perishing. As Diotima explains to Socrates in Plato's *Symposium*, the daemonic exists between the mortal and immortal realms, and daemons mediate between mortals and immortals.[4] Homer tends to use the vocabulary of the daemonic to refer to the gods and goddesses, but especially as a god or goddess interacts with a mortal toward the mortal's exaltation. A daemonic muse inspires the wanderer to dodge any norm and to disdain any compromise diverging from that mortal's fate or singular and irreversible going under. Asking readers to love their fates, Nietzsche, or his Zarathustra, urges them to go under to become who they are: "I love him who has a free spirit and a free heart: then his head is simply the entrails of his heart, yet his heart drives him to his going-under."[5] Daemonic muses inspire or drive their votaries to become who they are. The fragment of Heraclitus, *ethos anthropoi daimon* ("character is fate"[6]), stands as an incisive reading of the relation of Athena to Achilles in the *Iliad*. The daemon Athena drives Achilles toward realizing his character through his fate.

In the Gospel According to St. John, Christ insists on distancing himself from the daemonic, if only because John presents Christ as the only legitimate mediator between mortals and an upper realm, all other such mediators or daemons then becoming demonic. John exemplifies the Christian demonization of daemons. In the Middle Ages, rejection and dismissal of the muses became a Christian commonplace.[7] The concern of this study is with daemonic muses, their demonization, and their return in particular works of literature. How did the blurring of the Greek notion of the daemonic with the Christian notion of the demonic shape what a muse became in English and American literature, or at least what a muse became for specific authors in specific works? And, in these works, does the return of a daemonic muse herald the realization or the overcoming of nihilism?

Straying from literature written in English, chapter one takes Henrik Ibsen's play *The Master Builder* as a paradigm case of the daemonic muse-at-the-end. Chapter two celebrates Athena as the daemonic muse inspiring Achilles in Homer's *Iliad*. Chapter three meditates on the Wisdom of Proverbs as Yahweh's muse who undergoes demonizing abjection in the New Testament and then an ambivalent rehabilitation in Gnosticism and by Boethius. The remaining chapters treat of daemonic muses in William Shakespeare's play *Othello*, John Milton's epic poem *Paradise Lost*, Herman Melville's novel *Moby-Dick*, and Sandy Florian's novel *The Tree of No*. To elaborate briefly:

Chapter One: Introduction: Ibsen's Hilda as a Daemonic Muse

In Ibsen's *The Master Builder*, Halvard Solness feels his prominence as an architect under threat, his career perhaps about to pass its meridian as his days approach a nihilistic impasse. Just as this crisis looms, the young Hilda Wangel enters his life. Rather, she uncannily returns to his existence: Halvard, she claims, had kissed her ten years ago, promising her a kingdom in a decade's time. She has come, she tells him, to claim her kingdom. Halvard protests he has no memory of the kiss or the promise, but, with a daemonic force of purpose, Hilda soon persuades him of the interlude's actuality. Somewhat demonically, Hilda inspires Halvard to climb the scaffolds enfolding his latest edifice, all the way to the top of the building's tower. There he is to place a wreath in celebration of the structure's achievement, a ritual that would echo the climb Hilda reminds him she witnessed him make ten years before on another tower, sparking her self-exultation through her vision of his greatness. Halvard rashly climbs again, and only falls to his death after, to Hilda's eyes and ears, he titanically grapples at the tower's pinnacle with a divine antagonist to the sound of transporting music. Ibsen's play anatomizes the topic of *Satan's Secret Daughters:* the muse as ambiguously daemonic and demonic and inspiring a once illustrious artist (or Moor, or archangel, or whaling captain) now facing ruin to attempt the impossible. Hilda exclaims of the entowered Solness just before his fall, "Yes, it *is* the *impossible* that he's doing now!"[8]

Chapter Two: Athena, Achilles's Daemonic Muse

In the *Iliad*, Athena acts as a muse who assists and inspires Achilles in his agonistic strivings. His agonistic drive compels Achilles toward his choice to reenter the battle at Troy (and die sooner rather than later) so as to win immortal fame. Besides a trading of mortality for fame, Achilles's *agon* entails a sharp realization of erotic loss and allegorizes Homer's aesthetic ambition, as Longinus implies. Chapter two explores the connection of the muse figures in the *Iliad* with this confluence of mortality, the erotic, and the aesthetic.

Chapter Three: Yahweh's Daughter and Her Metamorphoses

Satan's secret daughters find an antecedent in Yahweh's daughter, the sprightly Hokmah who, in Proverbs, inspires Yahweh to let the creation burgeon into existence. The King James Bible (KJB) names Hokmah Wisdom. Chapter three reads Wisdom as a muse and examines her inspiring force in relation to the seductive and destructive Folly against whom Proverbs sets Yahweh's darling. Both Wisdom and Folly remain creatures in excess of the creation, and their calls are indistinguishable, so the wanderer never can be sure whether inspiration comes from Wisdom or from Folly, insuring a terrible or thrilling ambiguity of the muse.

In the Septuagint translation of Proverbs into Greek, and in Middle-Platonic thought, Hokmah undergoes a metamorphosis into Sophia, a daemonic *logos* mediating between human creatures and their deity. However, as Daniel Boyarin persuasively argues, the Gospel of John's definition of Christ with the Logos or "Word" sidelines Sophia to insist that, in the beginning, not Yahweh's daughter but God the Father's son was the "Word" facilitating creation.[9] The apostle Paul precedes John in spiriting away

Sophia to replace her with Christ. Chapter three suggests this solidification of the mediating *logos* as Christ corresponds to an abjection and demonization of Sophia as muse, as evident in the career of Sophia in Gnostic Christianity. In Boethius's *Consolation of Philosophy*, this demonization entails an equation with evil cast as nothingness. Instructive in this context is early Islam's satanic verses episode (contemporary Islam denies the episode altogether) demonizing the attribution of daughters to Allah, the daughters (Al-Lāt, Al-'Uzzā, and Manāt) whose abjection and erasure resonate with the Christian demonization of muse figures. In Plato-inflected Abrahamic traditions, a logic of nihilism became entangled with demonized muse figures, articulating a complex of nothingness, satanic will or rebellion, and aesthetic inspiration, setting the stage for a play like *Othello* and a character like Iago.

Chapter Four: The Nihilistic Muse in Shakespeare's Othello

Chapter four argues that in *Othello* Shakespeare achieves the most lucid articulation of the fate of Sophia, Athena, and the muses in their demonization. Cassio's praise of Desdemona exalts her as a daemonic *logos* redemptive of the world, but Iago, from nothing, births from Othello a demonic Desdemona, a seductress of the world. Though in love with Desdemona as mirroring all of himself he most dreads losing, or perhaps because of this love, Othello succumbs to Iago's drive for annihilation. In exploring the wondrous and terrible potentials of the daemonized/demonized muse, Shakespeare sets the standard for subsequent authors.

Chapter Five: Milton's Paradise Lost: *Sin's Ambition, Eve's Flight*

In *Paradise Lost*, exalting a muse and falling converge for Satan in his relations with Sin and Eve. In heaven, Lucifer, becoming Satan, burns with inspiration, and his muse Sin births forth from his head. Homer's daemonic Athena becomes demonic, the daughter of Satan. As Athena inspires Achilles, so Sin inspires Satan. Milton rewrites the relationships between Zeus and Athena and Achilles and Athena as the relationship between Satan and Sin. In

Sin, Satan finds an image of his unfallen self. Satan's exalted form Milton refers to as female, the very form Sin mirrors or embodies while remaining a distinct entity pursuing her own ambitions. If, inspired by Sin, Satan could storm heaven, he might regain his unfallen form. But Satan must work by guile to take revenge on God by way of seducing Eve into eating the forbidden fruit and by her fall delivering the new creation over to his daughter Sin. Sin's ambition flames as she anticipates becoming her father's queen to reign with Satan over the earth. Chapter five explores the crossings of Wisdom and Folly in *Paradise Lost* to trace Sin's career as a muse to Satan, Satan's career as a muse to Eve, and Eve's career as a willful wanderer.

Chapter Six: Melville's Moby-Dick: *Sin Finds Her Throne*

In Melville's *Moby-Dick,* contrary to appearances, among the *Pequod's* crew sojourns a woman, the drastically internalized muse of Ahab, whom he follows to his destruction. Ahab finds inspiration in the muse he exalts as his "queenly personality." In Ahab's exaltation of this regal lady, Milton's Sin finds her throne. At once the concentrated center of Ahab's self and a limitlessly infinitesimal point of nothingness, Ahab's muse also reincarnates Iago's inexistent Desdemona. In love with the Othello named Queequeg, Ishmael reincarnates the Desdemona who sought adventure at sea. Chapter six explores the influence of *Othello* and *Paradise Lost* on Melville's Ishmael and Ahab.

Chapter Seven: A Daemon Writes: Florian's The Tree of No

In an uncanny extension of and reply to the tradition of the daemonic demonized muse, Sandy Florian returns from and to that tradition, as though to allow the daemonic muse finally to have a say and a kingdom, or at least a city. As slyly humorous as it is sublimely poetical, Florian's novel *The Tree of No* rewrites *Paradise Lost* and riffs on biblical stories from Genesis to Revelation to trace the career of a narrator who, unhesitant to go under, ventures forth from Eden to pursue meditations on imagination, quirky civic projects, and an odd love affair with the enigmatic Montgomery, all the while struggling toward a resolute affirmation of the earthbound self. Drawing *Satan's Secret Daughters* to a close, this last chapter explores Florian's novel as both an epitome of and a counterstatement to the muse tradition in question.

One

Introduction:
Ibsen's Hilda as a Daemonic Muse

Henrik Ibsen's play *The Master Builder* dramatizes a muse scenario in which daemonization defines the encounter of artist with muse. The play confronts the playgoer or reader with a daemonic muse who goes by the name Hilda Wangel. Or a trollish muse: Ibsen thinks of the daemonic by way of trolls. The play opens with an aging architect, Halvard Solness, late one workday letting his anxiety about a young architect in his employ, Ragnar Brovik, blossom into a general fear of youth. Not only will some upstart architect seek to knock Solness from his pedestal as the town's "Master Builder," but also the town's youth, Solness fears, will one day collectively march to his door and demand he step aside. When Ragnar's father Knut Brovik, a former architect also in Solness's employ, suggests to Solness that he relinquish a commission so Ragnar can take it on and start a career of his own, Solness insists he will never give way for "younger men": "Never of my own free will" (15). Later the same evening, at the insistence of his wife Aline, Solness converses with Doctor Herdal, physician to the Solness family and friend to Aline. The two men get onto the topic of youth, and Solness explains he worries his "luck *will* turn" under the pressure of youth seeking change (47). He cries out, "I know it—I feel the day approaching" (47). This change will come from youth marching on Solness:

> Someone or other will take it into his head to say: Give *me* a chance! And then all the rest will come clamouring after

him, and shake their fists at me and shout: Make room—
make room—make room! Yes, just you see doctor—presently
the younger generation will come knocking at my door—(47)

No sooner has Solness finished his rant and Dr. Herdal given
a brief reply ("Well, and what if they do?" [47]) than there is a
knock on the door. Solness says, "Come in" (48). And in steps the
divine, nay, the daemonic Hilda Wangel.

In a stage direction, Ibsen describes Hilda as attractive,
tomboyish, and dressed to signal her previous appearance in
Ibsen's play *The Lady from the Sea*.[1] When she arrives at Solness's
door, the *"supple"* and slightly *"sunburnt"* Hilda is wearing *"a
tourist costume, with skirt caught up for walking, a sailor's collar open
at the throat, and a small sailor hat on her head. Knapsack on back, plaid
shawl in strap, and alpenstock"* (48). In *The Lady from the Sea*, Hilda is
the stepdaughter of Ellida, wife to one Dr. Wangel. Ellida grew up
where a sublime fjord empties into the open sea. Before marrying
Dr. Wangel, Ellida, wild for the ocean, had been passionately
in love with a sailor who had to flee because he murdered his
captain. The sailor returns to claim Ellida, who wavers, yet she
decides to stay with Dr. Wangel. With this heritage at her back,
Hilda knocks on Solness's door.

Hilda arrives at the architect's door because, ten years
earlier, in Hilda's town, Solness had built a church with a very
high tower. Solness had climbed the scaffolding still around the
newly built tower, to the very top, there to hang a wreath on the
weathercock, a tradition in celebration of a building's completion.
The town's schoolgirls had attended, dressed in white and
carrying flags, among them Hilda. In wonder, Hilda had gazed
up. She explains her memory to Solness, and her transport
comes back, causing her to imagine the past as if it were present.
Suspending chronology midsentence, she speaks as if she were
again standing below the tower: "It was so wonderfully thrilling
to stand below and look up at you, Fancy, if he should fall over!
He—the master builder himself!" (62–3). In recounting her
wonder in transport, Hilda suddenly collapses the distinction
between past and present. Such switching from speaking of the

past as past to speaking of the past as present Longinus notes as a technique for intensifying the sublime by putting the auditor or reader right into the action.[2] Solness agrees that he certainly might have fallen: "For one of those white-frocked little devils,— she went on in such a way, and screamed up at me so—" (63). Reliving her transport, Hilda interjects the cry Solness recalls, as if she were again at the base of the tower: "'Hurra for Mr. Solness!' Yes!" (63). After Hilda's cry, Solness continues to describe the actions of the little devil he saw below: "[She] waved and flourished with her flag so that I—so that it almost made me giddy to look at it" (63). With significant emphasis on the first-person singular pronoun, Hilda replies: "That little devil—that was I" (63).

In several regards, Hilda resembles the Sin of *Paradise Lost*. In heaven, Sin's birth from Satan's head surprises the archangel, who soon after falls from the heights. After his fall, Sin again surprises Satan upon his meeting her at the gates of hell. When Satan encounters Sin at the gates, he at first does not recognize or remember her from their escapades in heaven. She has to remind him. Hilda tells Solness that when he was standing gloriously atop the tower, he sang. This act Solness does not remember: "I've never sung a note in my life" (64). Hilda insists: "Yes, you sang then. It sounded like harps in the air" (64). Solness remembers the day he climbed the tower, and he does remember how, standing atop the tower, the enthusiasm of the "little devil" below "almost made [him] giddy" and could have brought him to fall. He does not remember singing. This surprises him, as does Hilda: "This is very strange—all this" (65).

Hilda has another surprise in store for Solness, something he also does not remember. Hilda reminds Solness that, after the triumph of his tower climb, a banquet was thrown in his honor. This he remembers. And then he was invited to visit the Wangel household for supper, says Hilda. This Solness remembers. But what Hilda recounts next Solness does not remember. Hilda says that, arriving at the house and finding her alone, Solness had spoken to her. Hilda: "You said I was lovely in my white dress, and that I looked like a little princess. [...] And then you said that when I grew up I should be *your* princess" (66). Solness wonders aloud if he indeed said that. Hilda to Solness:

> Yes, you did. And when I asked how long I should have to wait, you said that you would come again in ten years—like a troll—and carry me off—to Spain or some such place. And you promised you would buy me a kingdom there. (67)

Anticipating her father bringing her to the new creation, Sin says to Satan: "I shall reign / At thy right hand voluptuous, as beseems / Thy daughter and thy darling, without end" (2.868–70).[3] Sin would reign over a kingdom where all are subject to her. Hilda too craves a kingdom ("I want my kingdom" [77]), and Ibsen has Solness name her kingdom a kingdom of sin. When Hilda knocks on Solness's door ten years to the day after Solness promised he would return and bear her off to her kingdom, Hilda tells Solness he had even named the kingdom he would provide: "Orangia," or, as the translator notes, in "the original [Dano-Norwegian] 'Appelsinia,' 'appelsin' meaning 'orange'" (67). A passable reader of English, would Ibsen have read "apple sin" in "Appelsinia"? Joyce did, or so *Finnegans Wake* evidences.[4] Ibsen wrote *The Master Builder* in the Norwegian city Christiania (now Oslo), a name in counterpoint to Appelsinia.

Solness asks Hilda, after promising her a kingdom, what did he do next? Hilda is particularly incensed that Solness has forgotten what he did next. Hilda tells Solness what his next action was: "You came and kissed me, Mr. Solness" (68). Solness, incredulous: "*I* did!" (69). Hilda, insistent: "Yes, indeed you did. You took me in both your arms, and bent my head back, and kissed me—many times" (69). A topic Solness had raised with Dr. Herdal before Hilda uncannily arrives is whether a person, by wishing and willing some event strongly, might bring about the event. Solness has in his employ Kaia Fosli, fiancé to Ragnar. On first meeting Kaia, Solness had wished ardently to himself that she would become his employee, in part as a strategy to bind Ragnar. Solness explains to Herdal that, without stating his thoughts aloud, but only by his wishing and willing Kaia would hear them, Kaia did hear his thoughts or believed she had, and returned the next day to ask for work from Solness.

Hilda too exercises will. As the play opens, Solness is about to finish construction on a new house for himself and his wife. This house includes a high tower. Solness admits to Hilda his susceptibility to vertigo. Yet she wills Solness into deciding to climb the scaffolding to the top of the tower to place a ceremonial wreath, just as he had done ten years before to Hilda's rapture. Or does Solness will himself into the act having unconsciously willed the return of Hilda? Do Hilda and Solness share in a will, as if they share a paranormal, daemonic connection? Though they have both given up reading, Hilda and Solness admit to each other of having read the "old sagas," the tales of Vikings (145). In *The Master Builder,* Hilda derives her name from the Valkyrie of Norse saga Brunhilde.[5] Hilda associates with flight, agreeing with Solness when he calls her a bird of prey (148). In the sagas, the Valkyries decide which warriors will die in battle and which will live. Riders of flying horses, the Valkyries bring their fated dead in the afterlife to Valhalla. In Wagner's *The Ring Cycle,* the Valkyrie Brunhilde sings out to her father Wotan, "Who am I, then, if not your will?" Wotan replies, "I am only thinking to myself when I speak to you."[6] In *Paradise Lost,* extreme intimacy bordering on a telepathic connection characterizes Satan's relationship with Sin, and such intimacy characterizes the relationship between Solness and Hilda. With no other character in the play besides Solness does Hilda enjoy such a connection, and the arc of their relationship plays out a kind of sublime and ecstatic *folie à deux.*

In this madness, Solness, through Hilda, wills himself to climb the tower. The attempt involves the impossible, not just in the sense that the vertigo Solness suffers from should preclude such climbs for him. In the climb Hilda proposes the impossible beckons. Elevating Solness from the human realm toward the realm of the gods, the climb would take Solness up toward the daemonic. In the play's last scene, Ragnar and Hilda watch Solness climb. Seeing Solness attain the top of the tower, Hilda exalts, "At last! At last! Now I see him great and free again!" (224). Ragnar says, "I feel as if I were looking at something utterly impossible" (224).

Hilda in response: "Yes, it *is* the *impossible* that he's doing now!" (224). Hilda asks Ragnar if he sees anyone else atop the tower with Solness. Ragnar does not, but Hilda insists, "Yes, there is one he is striving with" (224). Hilda sees Solness atop the tower wrestling with a numinous being. Hilda asks Ragnar if he hears music; he does not. Yet Hilda insists, "*I* hear a song—a mighty song!" (225). The music she heard ten years before again sounds on the wind, the "harps in the air" (227). She sees Solness standing at the top of the tower as she saw him ten years prior and as she held him in her imagination over that decade: "So I have seen him all through these ten years" (224). The ecstatic moment exceeds chronology.

Seeing Solness wave down to those gathered below, and wanting to wave back, Hilda grabs Aline's white shawl from Dr. Herdal and begins to wave it. As she had done ten years before, Hilda shouts up to Solness: "Hurrah for Master Builder Solness!" (225). Fearing Solness will fall if distracted, Dr. Herdal insists Hilda stop, but the gathered townspeople and workers take up Hilda's cry, and the gathered ladies wave their handkerchiefs. Are the audience members to feel as Dr. Herdal, anxious to forestall disaster, or are the audience members to join in ecstatically cheering Solness atop the tower? After Hilda's cry and the general outbreak of cheering, all the spectators suddenly go silent as Solness falls from the tower down into the rock quarry below. The architect is soon reported dead, his skull crushed on impact.

When Solness reaches the top, places the wreath, and waves, Hilda states she and the spectators should wave back: "Oh, wave, wave back to him! For now it's finished" (225). Hilda's words "For now it's finished" resemble Christ's last words on the cross: "When Jesus therefore had received the vinegar, he said, It is finished: and he bowed his head, and gave up the ghost" (John 19.30).[7] After Hilda waves and cries out, "Hurrah for Master Builder Solness!," and after her cry and wave are taken up by the crowd, Solness falls and dies. This death counters, is a contesting reply to, Christ's death on the cross. Christ dies and then resurrects. Finding his lost moment of triumph again, Solness resurrects and then dies. This departure from the standard Christian pattern defines an aspect of the impossibility of the ultimate moment ravishing Solness, his attainment to glory, if only in Hilda's eyes, and so in his own. Exactly with whom and with what does Solness wrestle in Hilda's final vision of him? The wrestling only does happen in her vision, as the music only does sound in her audition. Though Ragnar has the impression of the impossible, this is perhaps mainly in terms of seeing a man subject to vertigo climb high. The other aspects of the impossible are unavailable to Ragnar's perception. Ragnar has eyes, yet he sees not, ears, yet hears not.

Hilda brings Solness to his end. Through her, he achieves in undergoing finality a transport, a sublimity. None of the other characters in the play offer Solness this gift. And none of the other characters even understand or can cognize the gift Solness receives from Hilda, much less what she receives from him. Yet Ibsen would draw the audience into experiencing an intimation of this gift. Or the audience may understand and even sympathize with Aline, Dr. Herdal, Knut Brovik, Ragnar Brovik, and Kaia Fosli. These characters interact with Solness in relation to the cares and worries of workaday routines, where fending off or mitigating change often defines success, as if any such fending off or mitigation ever occurs. Before dying, Knut Brovik wants to see his son Ragnar start upon a career. Through compulsive adherence to what she calls "duty," Aline seeks to overcome her guilt at the death of her twin boys from a fever she transmitted to them by insisting, though ill, upon performing the duty of nursing them.

Before Hilda arrives, the members of the Solness architectural firm and household welter in various deadlocks. Knut has been declining for some time, imploring Solness to release Ragnar into his own career, yet Solness grimly holds to his refusal to write an endorsement on Ragnar's architectural drawings. Though she has been engaged to Ragnar for years, Kaia is held by Solness as his office worker with Solness encouraging her in revering him and believing herself to be irreplaceable for him. Aline lives in perpetual grief, bitterness, and sullenness. Hilda undoes these various deadlocks. She exalts exercising what she calls a robust conscience, a conscience sturdy and remorseless in support of her being a creature in flight, traveling light and shrugging off binding conventions. How Solness appeared to Hilda in climbing the tower a decade before, Hilda now appears to Solness: beautiful, strong, and free.

Pragmatically, Solness finds the Hilda who shows up at his door to die for. In so finding Hilda, does Solness exercise wisdom or folly? For the audience, apprehending the play's action from the perspectives of the salvation-hungry world groaning for mitigation and the ecstatic domain of the Solness–Hilda *folie à deux*, what seems wise from one perspective may seem foolish from the other and vice versa. Reviewing a London production of *The Master Builder*, Henry James states that by her uncanny arrival and precipitation of Solness's "destiny," Hilda opens a play within the play: "The mingled reality and symbolism of it all give us an Ibsen within an Ibsen."[8] Which "Ibsen" contains which James does not specify: does the daemonic opera for two between Solness and Hilda contain the fourth-wall realist theater of Solness, Dr. Herdal, Aline, Kaia, and the Broviks? Or vice versa? James displays accuracy in finding *The Master Builder* to involve distinct realms, a static and an ecstatic, yet his "within" perhaps strays. *The Master Builder* juxtaposes divergent realms quite fully incommensurate, though through Hilda the ecstatic invades the static.

Climbing up to the top of the tower, Solness enters into the nameless, where the harps in the wind play a rhapsodic Dionysian music and the wrestler with a divine being undergoes an irreversible crossing, a traversal the only return from which could be a fall. Solness falls when, seeing him hail her below, Hilda hails him there above. The impossible: to wrestle with and win out against the interpellations of the world wishing for mitigation, the interpellations calling toward hesitation, toward economizing against catastrophe, toward carrying about "death" like a wearying pig of lead weighing always upon the wanderer's back. Yet this weight always there just is a kind of nothing, conjured up by anxious thought. There is the giddiness that might unbalance Solness and cause him to fall, a fearful vertigo dragging him off the tower, yet there is also the giddiness of his sloughing the weight off from his back, allowing him to climb up lightly like a bird ascending. Such flight is Hilda's swift movement through her days, yet she needs Solness, she needs her vision of his exaltation, as a countersignature to her transport.

The engagement with the impossible Solness undergoes also involves his insistence he never will again build a church. A decade previous, Hilda had seen Solness climb the tower of the church he had built. When Hilda again meets Solness ten years later, he has long vowed never to build another church. The title *The Master Builder* translates the Dano-Norwegian title *Bygmester Solness*. In the English translation used here, where Hilda addresses Solness as "Mr. Solness," the original has her addressing him simply as *Bygmester*—Master Builder. The appellation "master builder" appears in the letters of Paul. In laying the foundation he claims Christ to be, Paul calls himself a master builder: "According to the grace of God which is given unto me, as a wise masterbuilder, I have laid the foundation, and another buildeth thereon" (1 Corinthians 3.10). In the New Testament Ibsen would have read, Paul's "masterbuilder" is "bygmester." As a self-proclaimed *bygmester,* Paul explicitly precludes any other foundation than Christ: "For other foundation can no man lay than that is laid, which is Jesus Christ" (1 Corinthians 3.11). This declaration of Paul's comes amidst 1 Corinthians 1.17–3.23, where Paul complexly appropriates, displaces, and spirits away Wisdom, as this book's third chapter will detail. Paul declares the foundation must be the Father as incarnate in the Son: Christ. The foundation must be of this father-son relationship and none other, not to mention a foundation-subversive father-daughter relationship, such as between Yahweh and Hokmah (Wisdom) in Proverbs 8. Paul says fire will test every building built upon the foundation:

> Every man's work shall be made manifest: for the day shall declare it, because it shall be revealed by fire; and the fire shall try every man's work of what sort it is. If any man's work abide which he hath built thereupon, he shall receive a reward. If any man's work shall be burned, he shall suffer loss: but he himself shall be saved; yet so as by fire. (1 Corinthians 3.13–15)

The fire will test any structure built on the foundation. Though the structure burn down and the builder "suffer loss," the builder will be saved by the fire.

This fire shows up in *The Master Builder*. When fire destroyed Aline's ancestral home, where Aline and Solness lived with their twin infant sons, Solness got his chance as an architect: the land the fire cleared of the house Solness parceled into lots on which he built homes. This fire Solness attributes to his will as influenced by demonic agency. Solness believes he willed the fire, imagining the fire to be his own and demonic, trollish, and thus related to Hilda rather than Paul's Father and Son. And in Proverbs, rather than the Son of the Christian Father, the daughter of Yahweh, Wisdom, bears the appellation "master builder." When Paul claims this title for himself, he is shoving Yahweh's daughter aside, and ultimately Paul is shoving aside the Yahweh who lets the creation burgeon. Paul shoves this Yahweh aside in favor of the Father who through or as the Son, through or as the Word, fiats a cosmos into existence and order.

Would to claim that atop the tower Solness wrestles Paul be too much? Perhaps. Yet Solness attempts to exalt himself in Hilda's eyes, to be the master builder his title declares him to be, as if Solness were the Yahweh of Proverbs 8 whom Wisdom inspires to let the creation flourish: this dynamic of retrieving Wisdom from oblivion puts Solness into an *agon* with Paul. For the Son, Paul spirits Wisdom away and John shunts her aside, processes chapter three will examine. To struggle with the logics of Paul and John to bring Wisdom back: with this effort the encounters between Hilda and Solness pulse. In Solness's wrestling with the divine the reader might even find a wrestling of Yahweh with Paul. That is, in Solness flickers the Yahweh who exalts in creation through Hokmah's inspiration. This is the Yahweh Paul abjects in denigrating Yahweh and Hokmah's creation as a fallen cosmos good only for escaping. Who is the *bygmester*, Yahweh or Paul, Wisdom or Christ?

In *The Master Builder* an *agon* with Paul operates, or at least an *agon* with the logic by which Paul displaces Wisdom in favor of Christ, spiriting Wisdom away in the process. This struggle owes something to Ibsen's familiarity with Nietzsche's thought.[9]

In Nietzsche Ibsen would find a call to take Paul as the antagonist, and so the antagonist of any retrieval of Wisdom, and also as the antagonist of the forces the play associates with the sagas. No clergyman appears in the play, unless Dr. Herdal counts, and he does so insofar as, in league with Aline, the doctor presses Solness toward a normalizing acceptance of deadlock and toward learning contentment within routine sadness. To conduct with Solness a conversation of preachy admonishment Aline has invited Dr. Herdal over to visit.

Paul claims to be a master builder. In Proverbs, Wisdom boasts that title. As Yahweh creates or builds the creation, Hokmah, that is, Wisdom, delights beside him, cheering him on or even, as a kind of apprentice, participating in the labor. The KJB translates the ambiguous Hebrew to emphasize her role as inspirer:

> When he prepared the heavens, I *was* there: when he set a compass upon the face of the depth: When he established the clouds above: when he strengthened the fountains of the deep: When he gave to the sea his decree, that the waters should not pass his commandment: when he appointed the foundations of the earth: Then I was by him, *as* one brought up *with him:* and I was daily *his* delight, rejoicing always before him[.] (Proverbs 8.27–30)

The Hilda who cheers at Solness climbing to the top of the tower, both ten years ago and in the now of the play, resembles Hokmah in Hokmah's exuberance. In the KJB, "one brought up with him" translates Hebrew (*amon*) that can also be and has been translated as "master builder." So the verse could be rendered as Hokmah exulting, "Then I was by him, as a master builder." With this translation, are readers to think of Hokmah as being or as being with the master builder? The second option resonates more with how Hilda and Solness share the qualities that allowed Solness to attain the status of master builder. So whenever Hilda addresses Solness as "Bygmester," she would be calling to what in him corresponds to what in her makes for exaltation. She wants to see him great and free so the vision will confirm or countersign her greatness and freedom.

In the Geneva Bible (1560), the gloss on Proverbs 8.30 takes what belongs to Hokmah and gives it to Christ, disappearing Wisdom into Christ as his "prefiguration." Regarding the translation of *amon,* the gloss informs the reader: "Some read a chief worker: signifying that this wisdom, even Christ Jesus, was equal with God his father, and created, preserved and still works with him, as John 5.17." Consider Hokmah in relation to Nietzsche's slogan, "*Dionysus versus the Crucified*": Paul and John variously disappear Hokmah in their presentations of Christ, and her joyful exaltation in and with Yahweh aligns her rather more with the reveling and ecstatic Dionysus than with the Crucified.[10] For Yahweh to will for Hokmah to suffer and die on a cross—that's unimaginable. As Yahweh and Hokmah energize each other as allies in the creation, Solness and Hilda share a Dionysian gusto none of the other characters in the play can participate in or understand. One place to find the topic of secrecy in the Hebrew Bible is in the relation between Yahweh and Abraham, when Yahweh commands Abraham to sacrifice Isaac and Abraham keeps the command in entire secrecy from Sarah, Isaac, and so on. Jacques Derrida argues the fearful burden of this secret and its keeping by Abraham hint toward the enigma of literature.[11] But another place to find the topic of secrecy in the Hebrew Bible is in the relation between Yahweh and Hokmah. *Amon* may also translate as "confidant": Hokmah stands by Yahweh as his confidant, as she who holds his secrets, say the delight he partakes of with her, yet this delight she also brings to the creatures made in Yahweh's image in the "habitable part of the creation": "Then I was by him, *as* one brought up *with him:* and I was daily *his* delight, rejoicing always before him; Rejoicing in the habitable part of his earth; and my delights *were* with the sons of men" (Proverbs 8.30–31). This "delight" she brings comes to each in confidence, as a kind of secret. Another reason to translate *amon* as "master builder" would be that Proverbs describes Hokmah as an architect, a builder: "Wisdom hath builded her house, she hath hewn out her seven pillars" (9.1).

The links between Hokmah and Hilda complicate the interpretation of the stance Solness takes toward church building.

To read his rejection of building churches, houses for the Christian god, as setting his character simply in antagonism to the Christian Bible becomes doubtful. Rather, Solness finds himself in antagonism with the Pauline thread, and this thread itself exists in complex tension with the Hebrew Bible. Paul's division between the letter and the spirit can stand as shorthand for this tension. The wrestling Solness takes part in atop the tower Hilda witnesses; Knut's son Ragnar sees only Solness atop the tower. What differences between Hilda and Ragnar might account for these divergent perceptions? Hilda does admire and believe in Solness in a way Ragnar does not. More importantly, Hilda resembles a daughter, almost the Gnostic Sophia who kicks down the traces to know her father, whereas Ragnar is a son embodying for Solness an attempt to displace and erase his ecstatic priority and singular distinction.

After the master builder's fall and death, Ragnar concludes about Solness and his attempt to scale the tower, "So, after all, he could not do it" (227). Hilda counters, "But he mounted right to the top. And I heard the harps in the air" (227). And then Hilda again waves the shawl and calls out, "My—my Master Builder!" (227). These words end the play. Standing on stage as the curtain comes down, does Hilda still envision Solness atop the tower? When he had mounted the tower, Ragnar says he "feel[s] as if [he] were looking at something utterly impossible" (224). Ragnar experiences an affect "as if" he "were" viewing the "impossible." A split divides the affect Ragnar must acknowledge from what he sees or is willing to acknowledge he sees. In response to Ragnar's "as if" declaration, Hilda affirms, "Yes, it is the impossible that he's doing now!" (224). Ragnar's statement implies a split between affect and vision. In contrast to Ragnar's "as if," Hilda states emphatically "it is." The impossible Hilda expects and welcomes Ragnar rebuffs, and Ragnar quickly and with smug resentment concludes: "he could not do it." In contrast, Hilda ends the play in a reverie, holding before herself in imagination the event of the impossible.

In her inspiration of Solness to climb the tower, with Solness then falling to his death, Hilda resembles the Athena who inspires Achilles to reenter the battle with the Trojans and slay Hector, only at the price of Achilles's mortality following hard upon. Hilda's inspiration comports with little to nothing of preserving existence; rather, this inspiration transports Solness into an ecstatic moment. In his concern for his son's career, Knut understandably worries about continuance into the future. The climb Solness makes brings ecstatically into the now a moment of transport in which Hilda would live on. Reveling in flight, Hilda shakes off the weight of the future and of the past. She brings Solness into a moment entirely without sequel. In this moment, a glory and a sublimity happen—or at least they happen within the *folie à deux* Hilda and Solness share. An inspiration antithetical to merely going on: such inspiration Hilda brings to Solness. Or she brings back to Solness what he, knowing not what he did, had brought to her. G. Wilson Knight argues the fondness of Ibsen for the following scenario: in dying, a protagonist attains a revelation and a glory through a femme fatale.[12]

In relation to Solness, Hilda acts as a daemon. She achieves in Solness his daemonization: when Solness climbs the tower, he attains to the daemonic, standing midway between the earth of the mortals and the skiey heights of the gods. In their conversation upon her arrival, Solness speaks of Hilda as a "little devil," but he later explains to her that "there are devils innumerable abroad in the world": "Good devils and bad devils; light-haired devils and black-haired devils" (144). The "troll in one," says Solness to Hilda, "it's *that* that calls to the powers outside us" (144). These "powers" are devils that "one never *sees*" (144). So the problem with these devils, says Solness, is that they are indistinguishable: "If only you could always tell whether it's the light or the dark ones that have got hold of you!" (144). If he could tell which type of devil called before responding to the call, says Solness, "Then it would be simple enough!" (144). He would respond when one type called, and not respond when the other type called. But the calls are indistinguishable.

With this indistinguishable quality of the devils, Solness confronts a dilemma Proverbs articulates by giving Folly and Wisdom identical calls to hail the young man wandering the street: "Whoso *is* simple, let him turn in hither" (9.4, 16). As chapter three will explore, Folly and Wisdom speaking the exact same words to say "come hither" to the young man introduces such an ambiguity as Solness discusses with Hilda: when a devil calls, say even Hilda, does Folly or Wisdom call? Is Hilda among the "light" or the "dark" devils? Solness wishes he could see and sort out the devils prior to acting on their suggestions, as if he would look before he leapt.

Hilda urges him just to leap. Hilda would divert the anxious problematic of sorting out devils by suggesting to Solness another way to make things "simple enough." Rather than futilely and in hesitation trying to sort out the devils, Hilda suggests to Solness that he act: "Or if one had a really vigorous, radiantly healthy conscience—so that one *dared* to do what one *would*" (144). This suggestion of Hilda's steers their conversation from the biblical provenance of devils toward the sagas of the Vikings and their penchant to act without anxious hesitation. After her statement about a "radiantly healthy conscience," Solness asks Hilda if, like he, she has read the sagas, and the two go into a reverie about Vikings carrying away women and treating them with utmost trollishness, Hilda finding the prospect "thrilling" (146).

To think of Hilda as simply unbiblical, as the bearer in the play of only a Nietzschean healthy conscience, would be to miss her connections to Wisdom or especially to Wisdom and Folly in their being indistinguishable in their calls. Hilda inspires Solness to act, and this inspiration culminates in his fall, and this fall happens only when Hilda calls to him. Thomas J. J. Altizer argues the Christian god's act of creation and this god's opening himself to his own death, the crucifixion, are two dialectical sides of one kenotic coin.[13] Solness finishes his creation by his placing a wreath atop the tower and falls to his own death. Hilda brings about both the climb and the fall. Solness ends; Hilda goes on.

In Hilda something of the Viking returns, yet so does something of Hokmah, especially as Hokmah describes herself as an exuberant creature of "delight." Neither the Athena Hilda, nor the Viking Hilda, nor the Hilda of Hokmah's "delight" are compatible with Paul's spiriting away of Wisdom, not to mention

John's exclusionary displacement of Wisdom by Christ. If Solness wrestles atop the tower with aspects of Christianity, he wrestles with Paul. Paul's spirit/flesh rhetoric sets aside or precludes or renders inadmissible Hokmah's "delight." The return of this "delight" in Hilda Wangel sets Paul at defiance.

In each chapter of this study there will be a Hilda: in chapter two, the Athena of Homer's *Iliad*; in chapter three, Hokmah herself and her metamorphoses; in chapter four, the Desdemona of Shakespeare's *Othello*; in chapter five, both Sin and Eve in Milton's *Paradise Lost*; in chapter six, the "queenly personality" of Ahab in Melville's *Moby-Dick*; and finally, in chapter seven, the gender-anonymous narrator of Sandy Florian's *The Tree of No*. So too will there be a version or aspect of Solness: Homer's Achilles, the young man of Proverbs, Milton's Satan, Melville's Ahab, and, in *The Tree of No*, Florian's Montgomery.

Two

Athena, Achilles's Daemonic Muse

Does not Homer introduce a daemon or genius,
whom he calls Minerva, checking the rage of
Achilles?
—J. B. Ottley paraphrasing Maximus Tyrius

Homer's *Iliad* belongs to Achilles, but Achilles belongs to Athena. Homer leaves no doubt as to this goddess's exalted status: "Athena first in glory, third-born of the gods."[1] Athena epitomizes glory. More than the aura of a victor, the glory blazing forth from Achilles signals the hero's daemonization by Athena. To Athena Achilles attributes his defining act, his killing of Hector. As the last moment of their clash nears, Achilles declares to Hector, "Athena will kill you with my spear" (22.319). When the epic reaches its climax, Hector is "struck down at Achilles' hands by blazing-eyed Athena" (22.524). The "girl with blazing eyes" brings to Achilles his final and fateful glory, his fate being to die soon after killing Hector (24.30). Undergoing inspiration by Athena, the warrior receives a daemonic fire he must welcome if he is to realize his fate. Attempting to defuse and evade the influence of the *Iliad*, Ovid, in his *Metamorphoses*, has an unnamed muse tell Minerva she would be a great candidate for musehood except her higher martial calling precludes that destiny.[2] In Boethius's *Consolation of Philosophy*, Lady Philosophy, a Neoplatonically Christianized Athena, turns her fiery eyes on the muses of poetry, chasing them away, again suggesting a rift between the goddess and the Muses.[3] Yet Homer's Athena very much acts in the *Iliad* as Achilles's daemonic muse.

A dispute over a daughter the Achaeans had plundered from a town loyal to Troy opens the *Iliad*. This woman the Achaeans gave to Agamemnon as a battle prize: Chryseis, daughter of Chryses, a priest to Apollo, an immortal and ally of the Trojans. The epic begins with Chryseis's bereaved father entering the Achaean camp to plead for his daughter's return. All the Achaeans agree, and Achilles insists: Agamemnon should heed Chryses, who implores: "Just set my daughter free, my dear one . . . here, / accept these gifts, this ransom. Honor the god / who strikes from worlds away—the son of Zeus, Apollo!" (1.22–24). In the priest's daughter, Apollo's honor abides: to violate the daughter dishonors her father and through him Apollo. Yet Agamemnon too considers honor to be at stake, his own. Therefore, with hubristic disrespect for the immortals and callous disregard for paternal affection, Agamemnon rejects Chryses's plea, which pathetically expresses a father's desperate concern yet assertively invokes the due process of ransom. After the rebuffed Chryses's indignant prayers bring Apollo's deadly arrows of plague upon the Achaeans, and after the Achaean seer Calchas reveals to Achilles and his comrades Apollo's anger and the god's demand for Chryseis's return without ransom, Agamemnon states a condition of his compliance: "But fetch me another prize, and straight off too, / else I alone of the Argives go without my honor. / That would be a disgrace" (1.138–40). For Agamemnon even to voice the possibility of yielding Chryseis back implies a compromise of his will and a voiding of the honor to which she in his possession testifies. So, when his compatriots simply imagine Agamemnon acquiescing, he imagines Chryseis already gone: "You are all witness, / look—*my* prize is snatched away!" (1.140–41). Implicitly, should the Achaeans return Chryseis to her father, for Agamemnon a nothingness would be left testifying to her absence and his disgrace. For the Achaeans to provide Agamemnon another woman as a prize would satisfy him. "But if they give me nothing / I will take a prize myself," Agamemnon declares (1.161–62). Agamemnon proposes to take Achilles's prize Briseis in recompense for Chryseis. To take Chryseis from Agamemnon absent another prize is to "give [him] nothing" because, imaging his honor and glory, Chryseis stands for everything: Agamemnon's sense of being a commander. Once Agamemnon threatens to take Achilles's prize, Briseis, in exchange for Chryseis, the warriors' dispute quickly becomes a contest over nothing, over who bears nothing, over who must submit to being nothing, over who will lose everything.

Achilles castigates Agamemnon for disprizing the sacrifices Achilles has made to regain Helen and so to take Agamemnon's "honor / back from the Trojans": "What do *you* care? Nothing. [...] / And now you threaten to strip me of my prize" (1.187–90). Already feeling "disgraced" just by the notion of yielding Briseis to Agamemnon, Achilles announces his intent to leave the battle and head home for Phthia (1.198–202). In reply, Agamemnon: "Go home with your ships and comrades [...] / You *are* nothing to me—you and your overweening anger!" (1.212–13). Achilles accuses Agamemnon of regarding the presence and effort of Achilles at Troy as "[n]othing," and Agamemnon echoes and affirms this nullification: "You *are* nothing to me." In both cases, constructions with negation are involved. In the first ("What do *you* care? Nothing."), "nothing" translates *ou ti, ou* signaling negation and *ti* being an indefinite pronoun encompassing anyone and anything. No thing whatsoever, no one whomsoever: *ou ti* here suggests a devastating negation resulting in an encompassing nullity. Achilles warns Agamemnon (the son of Atreus, so here called Atrides) that after he, Achilles, departs along with his martial prowess, "a yearning for Achilles will strike / [...] But then, Atrides, / harrowed as you will be, *nothing* [*ou ti*] you do can save you" (1.281–83). Any and all action on Agamemnon's part will become *nothing*, leaving the Achaeans helpless.

Achilles notes that Agamemnon, not the Trojans, "brought [him] here to fight": "The Trojans never did *me* damage, not in the least [*ou ti*]" (1.179–80). The Trojans have done nothing to Achilles. Relinquishing Chryseis, Agamemnon orders Talthybius and Eurybates to Achilles's camp to take Briseis. When the two arrive, full of fear, Achilles reassures them: "You have done nothing [*ou ti*] to me" (1.395). They and the Trojans have done nothing to Achilles, but Agamemnon *does* do nothing to Achilles, does affront Achilles with nothing, in taking Briseis: Agamemnon would bring to Achilles the sense of nothingness the two wrestle over, each attempting in speech and action to pin the other in the position of nullity.

Briseis is led away from Achilles's quarters. Seated and weeping before "the endless ocean," broken to a childlike despair, Achilles laments his loss in a prayer to his mother, an immortal, the sea nymph Thetis: "You gave me life, short as that life will be, / so at least Olympian Zeus, thundering on high, / should give me honor—but now he gives me nothing" (1.415, 417–19). As does Solness in Hilda and Othello in Desdemona, Achilles finds in Briseis the image of his glory, just as Milton's God in *Paradise Lost* finds in Christ the "radiant image of his glory" (3.63). And, just as Othello, mistakenly believing Desdemona lost to Cassio, declares his warrior existence void ("Othello's occupation's gone"[4]), Achilles, with the loss of Briseis, faces "nothing," his martial glory coming to naught. This nothingness or evacuation of being leaves Achilles before the seemingly limitless expanse of the relentless ocean.

Similarly, after Agamemnon brutally denies Chryses the return of Chryseis and orders the priest away under threat of death, Chryses flees the Achaeans' camp in humiliation and walks along the desolate shore where endless waves crash: "The old man was terrified. He obeyed the order, / turning, trailing away in silence down the shore / where the battle lines of breakers crash and drag. / [...] over and over / the old priest prayed to [.../...] Apollo" (1.38–43). The ocean's constantly incoming and receding surges become the compulsive "over and over" of Chryses's prayers to Apollo, suggesting a symptom of trauma.

When Agamemnon first threatens to take Briseis, Achilles struggles within himself whether to contain his rage or to kill Agamemnon then and there, pinballing between the two alternatives. But "just as he drew his huge blade from its sheath, / down from the vaulting heavens swept Athena," who, grabbing Achilles by his hair, answers his astonished question as to the purpose of her sudden appearance: "Down from the skies I come to check your rage" (1.228–29, 242). In *Paradise Lost*, Sin checks the rage of Satan when he moves to combat his (grand)son Death; absent this checking, a titanic battle would occur between Satan and Death, but the Satanic journey to earth and Satan's despoiling of humankind would not take place. Should Athena not check Achilles's rage, a drastic *mêlée* encompassing Agamemnon and Achilles would take place but the long course of the repression of Achilles's rage would not, nor would the uncanny and daemonic clash between Achilles and his own armor as worn by Hector occur. Athena serves as Achilles's daemonizing muse, as Sin does for Satan.

Athena's delay of the enactment of Achilles's rage lasts nearly the entire *Iliad*. Achilles keeps himself away from the siege's battles until his friend Patroclus comes to displace Briseis as the bearer of Achilles's pride in self, and, with Patroclus's killing by Hector, Achilles's rage can find a target outside the Achaean camp. But Achilles ultimately focuses his rage on an ambulatory casting of his unwilling dross: Hector in Achilles's armor. The complex and uncanny turn of Achilles's rage from Agamemnon toward Hector, and the two champions' combat, in which Hector wears the armor of Achilles Patroclus was wearing when Hector slew Patroclus, plays out with sublimity the confrontation with nothingness shaping the conflict with Agamemnon.

The extremity of Achilles's *agon* for the sublime of glory, its all-or-nothing rhetoric, also appears when Homer invokes the muses to assist him in pronouncing the grand list of the Achaeans who have gathered at Ilium:

> Sing to me now, you Muses who hold the halls of Olympus!
> You are goddesses, you are everywhere, you know all things—
> all we hear is the distant ring of glory, we know nothing—
> who were the captains of Achaea? Who were the kings?
>
> (2.573–76)

The Muses "know all things," including the Olympian realm. Absent the Muses' inspiration and aid, Homer hears only "the distant ring of glory," and in suffering this separation from glory, from the battle we hear only as a "distant ring," "we know nothing." Homer needs the muses to inspire him to imagine being in the midst of the siege, of the battles, of the strife between and among mortals and immortals. The echo of Achilles's confrontation with nothingness in Homer's suggests Achilles's eventual return to battle and martial apotheosis allegorize the epic poet's drive toward aesthetic grandeur. Perhaps registering this allegorization of the poet's daemonization in the hero's, Longinus insists that Homer, in composing the sublimities of the *Iliad*, enters into the world of epic struggle he narrates. The poet of the *Iliad* "is wont himself to enter into the sublime actions of his heroes": "In truth, Homer in these cases shares the full inspiration of the combat" (Longinus 82). However, as a poet, Homer would be no Agamemnon but an Achilles, who plays the lyre and sings of heroes' deeds (9.223–28). The "full inspiration of the combat"— for Achilles, that inspiration comes finally from Athena.

However agonistic Homer shows himself to be in striving for the sublime, he knows he should give to the Muses all praise for any such achievement: "The mass of troops I could never tally, never name, / [...] unless you Muses of Olympus, daughters of Zeus / whose shield is rolling thunder, sing, sing in memory / all who gathered under Troy" (2.577–82). These daughters of Zeus, the Muses, brook no challengers. As Homer relates in the catalogue he implores the Muses' aid to recite, when Thamyris "boast[ed] to high heaven that he could outsing the very Muses, / the daughters of Zeus whose shield resounds with thunder" fiercely and with finality "stopped the minstrel's song": the Muses "were enraged, they maimed [Thamyris], they ripped away / his voice" (2.687–92). This action between the Muses and the doomed singer also parallels the action in battle Homer narrates, the voice the Muses tear from the singer being analogous to the breath a soldier tears from an enemy. A Trojan seer insists his two sons never enter battle, but, despite their father's foresight, "the forces of black death drove them on" to become soldiers, and in battle the Achaean and favorite of Athena Diomedes "stripped them of life breath" (11.385–89).

Death, fate, and the daemonic mingle in Athena's inspiration of Achilles, who faces a choice of destinies: he may either choose to return home and live a long life or return to the battle at Troy and win immortal fame at the price of his prompt demise. As Thetis has told him, two possible "fates bear [him] on to the day of death":

> If I hold out here and I lay siege to Troy,
> my journey home is gone, but my glory never dies.
> If I voyage back to the fatherland I love,
> my pride, my glory dies . . .
> true, but the life that's left me will be long,
> the stroke of death will not come on me quickly.
>
> (9.499–505)

Achilles's long hesitation before willing his fate not only results from the contrast between a long life without glory and a short life eternal glory crowns. Achilles also must wrestle with the nihilistic despair the taking of Briseis reveals within him. Brooding over her loss, Achilles begins to sound like Ecclesiastes or the Hamlet of his play's fifth act: "The same honor waits / for the coward and the brave. They both go down to Death" (9.386–87). This collapse of distinctions before mortality brings Achilles to soliloquize, "And what's laid up for me, what pittance? Nothing—" (9.389). Both the "man who hangs back" and the "man who battles hard" undergo the common fate, dying into oblivion (9.385–86). While the narrator can call Agamemnon "the great field marshal," Achilles finds him to epitomize the "man who hangs back," denouncing Agamemnon as "always sulking behind the lines," waiting to appropriate the plunder Achilles wins in battle (10.3, 9.402). Being a "[k]ing who devours his people," consuming them as a means to reap plunder, Agamemnon stands at a distance from the battle (1.270). So rather than facing mortal risk, from a distance Agamemnon "can see death coming," a localizable, visible, avoidable thing (1.267). But Achilles appears to Agamemnon as death: "Let [Achilles] submit to me! Only the god of death / is so relentless, Death submits to no one" (9.189–90). Agamemnon imagines undertaking an effort to rule death, as if, with the great earthen defenses he orders built around the Achaeans' ships, death could be kept out and overmatched. Achilles will welcome daemonization from a goddess, Athena, who, donning the helmet of death, becomes invisible, and whose inspiration Achilles in no way controls.

By hacking through Achaeans to kill Agamemnon and regain Briseis, Achilles would stymie or waver back from both his fates. By acting on his urge to kill Agamemnon, Achilles would turn neither toward the peace of homecoming nor toward the glory of battling the enemy Hector. He would lose his antithetical distinction from Agamemnon. For Achilles traitorously to kill his commander Agamemnon over Briseis would reduce Achilles to Agamemnon's symmetrical counterpart, another avaricious king valuing a prize of battle over being in battle, valuing things battle undergone by others might bring over being in battle like no other, Achilles's daemonic fate. Achilles's urge to slaughter Agamemnon Athena must repress to keep Achilles on the path toward his fate of triumphing over Hector, winning glory, and meeting his death sooner rather than later. Achilles presents himself as antithetical to Agamemnon. Only by persisting as antithetical to Agamemnon's stance does Achilles remain or become who he is, Achilles.

With his invocation of fire as the primal source, his equation of strife with justice, and his nomination of war as the king of all, Heraclitus arguably learned from the *Iliad* to think: the ethos of a man is his daemon (*ethos anthropoi daimon*). A man's character spurs him on as his destiny. Here, the Greek term *ethos* bears little to no moralistic connotation. Rather, the daemon's inspiration drives a poet toward his fate, in the process relentlessly discarding or bringing to destruction every version of the self that wavers from the poet's character. Heraclitus's fragment, Bloom suggests, ultimately treats of the aesthetic, of the sublime, rather than any societal or moralistic concern.[5]

Athena emerges in the *Iliad* as daemonic in her driving of the Achaeans toward their fates. When Odysseus wavers between two potential actions in battle, Athena moves him toward the action in accordance with "the gallant Odysseus' fate" (5.774). When Athena checks Achilles's rage, she drives the warrior away from an errant deviation, from any turn diverting him from his fate.

Being so remorselessly destructive of versions of the self hesitant before or in retreat from fate, the daemon brings an antithetical force virtually indistinguishable from yet the overcoming of any suicidal longing for death. Consider the following: early in the *Iliad*, in the course of rallying the Achaeans for yet another assault on Troy, Agamemnon tests their resolve by saying aloud what many hope for yet fear to speak, a call to abandon the campaign and return home. When many of the Achaeans, confusedly agitated at the prospect of retreat, hectically begin to prepare the ships for the homeward journey, Hera calls upon Athena to act: "And now they might have won their journey home, / the men of Argos fighting the will of fate, yes, / if Hera had not alerted Athena" (2.181–83). That the Achaeans here fight "the will of fate" and so act out of character Homer emphasizes by describing them as "shaken," as in "alarm," and as uttering "Shrill shouts / hitting the heavens" (2.173, 174, 178–79). By appearing to Odysseus and urging him to persuade and admonish the troops back into a fighting mood, Athena seeks to reverse the turmoil and doubt among the Achaeans Agamemnon's stratagem unleashes. Nestor and Agamemnon join this effort, but the successful reorientation of the Achaeans toward their fate waits upon the more direct intervention of "fiery-eyed Athena," who plunges down from Olympus and out among the amassing soldiers:

> Her shield of lightening dazzling, swirling around her,
> headlong on Athena swept through the Argive armies,
> driving soldiers harder, lashing the fighting-fury
> in each Achaean's heart—no stopping them now,
> mad for war and struggle. Now, suddenly,
> battle thrilled them more than the journey home,
> than sailing hollow ships to their dear native land.
>
> (2.532–38)

The alternatives the soldiers waver between are those of Achilles writ large: to return home or to return to the battle. In this episode, Athena functions for the mass of soldiers as she does for Achilles, as a daemonic and daemonizing force antithetical to any slackening from their fate and fateful character.

In the lines immediately following Athena's turning of the Argives toward battle, a simile of the kind thrilling for Longinus takes a vast perspective on an overwhelming natural force as revelatory of the quality of the Homeric heroes in the vehemence of their more than natural, really their contra-natural, passion for combat:

> As ravening fire rips through big stands of timber
> high on a mountain ridge and the blaze flares miles away,
> so from the marching troops the blaze of bronze armor,
> splendid and superhuman, flared across the earth,
> flashing into the air to hit the skies.
>
> (2.539–43)

The natural fire figures the antithetical fire Athena brings, she of the "fiery" eyes and "shield of lightening." Though seemingly not the most Homeric of writers, Samuel Beckett, at the end of *Krapp's Last Tape*, has the title character listen to a recording of his earlier self declare: "Perhaps my best years are gone. When there was a chance of happiness. But I wouldn't want them back. Not with the fire in me now. No, I wouldn't want them back."[6] These words finish the play, Beckett's stage directions stating: "*Krapp motionless staring before him. The tape runs on in silence.* CURTAIN" (28). With the forlorn, year-poor Krapp listening to his prior self's boast, Beckett may undercut the sentiment exalting the fire and dismissing the lost years, yet Krapp does select this triumphal tape segment as his last to hear before his play's end, before his end. For Krapp, the antithetical fire exalts a self fully willing to spurn any prior version merely content with happiness. In the *Iliad*, Athena gives such fire to her votaries. So the Achaean Diomedes might "win himself great glory," Athena "set the man ablaze, his shield and helmet flaming" (5.3–4). With this "fire," Athena "drove" Diomedes into the heart of the battle (5.7–8). Bearing the fire of Athena, Diomedes becomes daemonized. Dangerously exceeding Athena's initial council to fight no deity but Aphrodite head on, Diomedes attacks Aeneas, "though what he saw was lord Apollo himself, / guarding, spreading his arms above the fighter" (5.497–98). In his clash with the god, Diomedes charges Apollo "like something superhuman," the English "like something superhuman" translating the Greek *daimoni isos,* meaning "equal to a daemon" (5.504). Apollo underscores this daemonization when, complaining to the war god Ares about Diomedes, the archer god says about the Achaean: "like something superhuman [*daimoni isos*] he even charged at *me!*" (5.528). After the confrontation with Apollo, the daring of Diomedes in battle mounts, with Athena fighting directly by his side and guiding his spear to wound Ares. The god goes to complain to Zeus about Diomedes, Ares saying, "*Athena* spurred him on to rave against the gods. / First he lunges at Aphrodite, stabs her hand at the wrist / then charges me—even me—like something superhuman [*daimoni isos*]!" (5.1020–22). Here, the god of war directly cites Athena as the daemonizing agent.

The fire from "Pallas Athena / driver of armies" spurs Diomedes toward the battle line where fate and death intermingle, whether for an Achaean or for a Trojan such as Hypsenor: "red death / came plunging down his eyes, and the strong force of fate" (13.151–52, 5.91–92). A reader begins to understand why, in response to the Athena of the *Iliad*, Milton would invent Sin, who births Death into the world. Homer links the *Iliad*'s Athena to what the poem repeatedly laments as the cause of all the casualties at Troy, Paris's abduction of Helen. The ships Paris sailed on his journey to abduct Helen were made by the Trojan Phereclus. His "hands / had the skill" to make ships "since Pallas Athena loved him the most, her protégé / who had built Paris his steady, balanced ships, / trim launchers of death, freighted with death / for all Troy" (5.65–70). During a battle in which Ares fights for the Trojans, Athena has the advantage of death's invisibility: "Athena donned the dark helmet of Death / so not even stark Ares could see her now" (5.976–77). A reader could reasonably ask: what is the difference between Athena and death? Perhaps this: within the instant of glory, of Athena's inspiration, perishing arrives. Though distinct from death, Athena provokes a desire realizable only through a will to perish. When the immortal's daemonic inspiration comes, the mortal undergoes the sharpest realization of mortality. Athena is to die for. Agamemnon takes honor and glory as concomitants of battle's aftermath, as prizes accrued later, with the conflict safely in the past. For Achilles, honor and glory ultimately occur only in a battle with death alone following hard upon.

Achilles only forgoes his rage over Briseis when a greater rage comes to overwhelm him, his rage over the death of Patroclus. Briseis's imaging of Achilles's honor only intensifies in Patroclus's imaging of Achilles in arms. Patroclus's fated death nears when Nestor asks Patroclus to persuade Achilles to let Patroclus don Achilles's armor and enter battle so that the Trojans, mistaking Patroclus for Achilles, will fall back from the Achaean ships. In tears over his gravely wounded friend Eurypylus, Patroclus approaches Achilles to propose Nestor's plan. Achilles exclaims, "Why in tears, Patroclus? / Like a girl, a baby running after her mother" (16.7–8). While Achilles had wept at the shore to his mother, here Achilles himself figures the mother, as he does in Patroclus's complaint after Patroclus explains his tears' source. Patroclus: "But *you* are intractable, Achilles! / Pray god such anger never seizes *me*, such rage you nurse" (16.32–33). Achilles agrees to Nestor's plan, insisting to Patroclus that the prophecy of his fate does not balk him from returning to battle, only the loss of "[t]hat girl," Briseis (16.64). Yet given the closely proceeding troping of Patroclus as a girl and Achilles as her mother, a mother who nurses "rage" (Patroclus continuing the daughter/mother figurations), Patroclus substitutes for Briseis and takes over her reflection to Achilles of his glory. This mirroring becomes more abyssal as Achilles then exhorts Patroclus as follows: "[W]in great honor, great glory for me / in the eyes of all the Argive ranks, and they, / they'll send her back, my lithe and lovely girl" (16.97–99).

Overlapping Patroclus with the female who images his glory, agreeing to send Patroclus out as himself to win that glory: no wonder Achilles mounts in his rhetoric to a solipsistic vision of triumph in which he and Patroclus could ruin Troy together yet in a limitless solitude. Achilles to Patroclus:

> Oh would to god—Father Zeus, Athena and lord Apollo—
> not one of all these Trojans could flee his death, not one,
> no Argive either, but we could stride from the slaughter

so we could bring Troy's hallowed crown of towers
toppling down around us—you and I alone!

                                                    (16.115–19)

Patroclus complains to Achilles that, in his rage, Achilles turns
his back on his obligations to the Argives. Echoing Agamemnon's
comparison of Achilles's relentlessness with death's, Patroclus
imagines Achilles as having been born not from his mother
Thetis impregnated by his father Peleus but from an anonymous
existence bereft of human relation: "The salt gray sunless ocean
gave you birth / and the towering blank rocks—your temper's
so relentless" (16.39–40). This "gray," "blank," anonymous being
defines the existence Achilles imagines he and Patroclus would
enter as, in a world empty of any other mortals, the two would
bring down Troy's towers. As those who bring death to all yet
walk away from "the slaughter," Achilles imagines himself and
Patroclus massacring their way back to an anonymous existence
where being in glory would also be a state of being alone yet not
alone, the paradox of "you and I alone!"

     Achilles's fate of glory requires the hero's willingness to die.
However close Achilles's vision of "you and I alone!" brings the
reader to the state of Achilles in the final enactment of his fate, still
Achilles speaks this dream to Patroclus out of his unwillingness,
his words stating that, while no one else, no other combatant,
Trojan or Argive, "could flee his death," he and Patroclus
"could stride from the slaughter." This vision again aligns with
Agamemnon's, being a reverie in which glory arrives after and
beyond a battle, solitude before death having been avoided, rather
than in a battle and with the solitude of dying the only future.
The brothers Agamemnon and Menelaus siege Troy together.
The brothers Hector and Deiphobus defend Troy. By appearing
to Hector as Deiphobus ready to fight Achilles, brother seconding
brother, Athena tricks Hector into his final battle; when Hector's
time to die arrives, the goddess as faux brother vanishes, and, in
solitude before his opponent, Hector realizes his fate looms upon
him. Confronting fate, the agonist stands alone. Marching toward
glory, Achilles, like Melville's Ahab, moves toward a fate no one

else can share. Wearing Achilles's armor, Patroclus marches into battle and Hector kills him. Only with the death of Patroclus does Achilles become willing to meet this fate.

About Patroclus's death, Achilles declares, "There is no more shattering blow that I could suffer" (19.382). No other mourning will ever so sharply cut him. His mourning the loss of Patroclus outpaces his previous mourning of the loss of Briseis, whom Agamemnon returns to Achilles. Briseis imaged the honor of Achilles, yet then Achilles's investment in her shifts to Patroclus, who dies in the armor of Achilles, dies as if Achilles. With the loss of Patroclus, Achilles mourns an irreversible passing into death, and his mourning foreshadows his own death. As when a dying soldier falls to the ground with "the dark [...] swirling down to shroud his eyes" (6.13), so, on hearing the news of Patroclus's death, a "black cloud of grief came shrouding over Achilles": "Overpowered in all his power, sprawled in the dust, / Achilles lay there, fallen . . ." (18.24, 28–29). Mourning Patroclus, Achilles mimes his own perishing, and so his grief over his friend also addresses his own oncoming demise. This death to come, however, is one Achilles willingly hails.

The willingness of Achilles (Hamlet: "The readiness is all" [5.2.222]) both resembles yet remains utterly distinct from a suicidal gesture. The distinction appears first in the initial moments of Achilles's mourning when Antilochus takes Achilles's hand, fearful Achilles "would slash his [own] throat with an iron blade" (18.38). But, rather than attempt suicide, "Achilles suddenly loosed a terrible, wrenching cry," which his mother Thetis hears, "and she cried out in turn" (18.39, 42). Rather than rip away from his own "throat" the life breath, from that throat Achilles lets his voice speak out.

Thetis's echoing of Achilles's cry of mourning is soon followed by Athena's war cry seconding Achilles's, again with a suicidal dynamic hovering in the background yet being displaced. Having decided to return to the battle, where the Trojans and Achaeans fight a gruesome tug of war over Patroclus's body, Achilles is prompted by the goddess Iris to reenter the fray. Iris urges Achilles to "[d]efend Patroclus" by preventing the Trojans from taking and violating Patroclus's corpse (18.200). Achilles asks Iris how he can do so with no armor. She tells him to stand at the earthen defenses bordering the ships so the sight of him might frighten the Trojans, giving the Achaeans a chance to secure the dead Patroclus. Achilles agrees. As he mounts the earthen rampart, Athena slings her shield on his shoulder "and crowning his head the goddess swept a golden cloud / and from it she lit a fire to blaze across the field" (18.238–39). Athena's glorious and fearful fire helmets Achilles: "from Achilles' head the blaze shot up the sky," and, sporting Athena's "tremendous storm shield," "he rose and loosened an enormous cry / and off in the distance Pallas shrieked out too" (18.247, 237, 251–52).

Forming a chiasmus of self-immolation, the simile describing Athena's fire crosses with the simile describing the cry of Achilles, the cry the goddess echoes. Homer compares Athena's fire blazing out from Achilles's head to the signal fires a besieged island town lights in hopes neighbors will sail to the town's aid (18.240–46). Yet then Homer describes Achilles's cry as "[p]iercing loud as the trumpet's battle cry that blasts / from murderous raiding armies ringed around some city" (18.254–55). Are Athena's gifts like a fire gathering aid for a "town" under siege or are they like a "battle cry" rallying "murderous raiding armies" against a "city"? A city alit with a signal fire would show the enemy the way. The gifts of Athena are both: they signal Achilles's daemonization, his willing his fate, his *amor fati*, his decision to fight and to die. Achilles's cry of mourning and even more so the hero's battle cry, inspired by Athena, do confirm Longinus's claim about Homer: in his *agon* to achieve a sublime utterance (the *Iliad*), Homer shares the combatants' inspiration to enter battle.

The Trojans strip the corpse of Patroclus of Achilles's armor, which Hector then dons. To go into to battle, Achilles needs new armor, which Hephaestus forges, including a new shield. Though Longinus does not examine Homer's description of Achilles's shield, this originative instance of *ekphrasis* connects to the force of Homer's voice, confirming the reductiveness of definitions of *ekphrasis* as merely the verbal replication of a visual artwork. The shield Thetis asks Hephaestus to make Achilles functions as a part of the *Iliad* representing the whole, an element of the poem's world itself depicting an entire world, a cosmos the war deities Ares and Pallas oversee. On the shield, the totality of the *Iliad*, or more precisely a totality of the type the *Iliad* projects, finds depiction within the work. So in Homer's founding instance of *ekphrasis*, the words replicating the shield act out in little the attempt of the *Iliad*'s words to replicate a world. Perhaps Longinus avoided this episode as too mired in the representational, as the composition of an orderly whole Longinus contrasts early in his treatise to the sublime's overpowering, uncontrollable outbreak of force, like a lightning bolt.[7]

But Longinus should have considered how, in Homer's *ekphrasis*, more than the mimetic comes to the fore. Also, the dynamic force coursing through existence manifests in the shield, so the true miracle of the shield is less its mimetic encompassment of a cosmos and more the shield's embodiment of the cosmos's burgeoning *physis*. If any poet and poem merit being called "forces of nature," Homer and the *Iliad* do because the contemporary cliché implies something of the dynamic, order-shattering, exalting quality of the sublime. That quality does capture Longinus's interest but indicates the limit of the cliché, the sublime involving an extra-natural force. The shield carries this force only because Homer's words allow the reader to imagine the dynamic *physis* as somehow inhering in what narrow theories of *ekphrasis* would contemplate: a mimetic and static shield.

But the reader of the *Iliad*, before reaching the *ekphrastic* exercise in question, has been trained by the poem to think of a grand shield as an overwhelming, oncoming rush of turbulent wind, rain, and thunder, Zeus's "storm shield," which Athena appropriates, the shield Athena places on Achilles's shoulder when he makes his grand war cry. So should Aristotelian formalists have the last word on Achilles's famously *ekphrastic* shield?[8] Not at all: in the *Iliad*, *ekphrasis* touches on *ekstasis*.

The *ekphrastic* shield embodies *physis* only because Homer's words do. In Homer's words differential, amimetic force vibrates or finds voice. The Greek term *ekphrasis* derives from *ek* (out) and *phrasis* (speak).[9] To speak out the totality of the work, to create by voice a world at war embroiling mortals, immortals, and their context of cosmic nature: the *ekphrastic* shield suggests what Homer's voice achieves, but this voicing implies Homer's Longinian *ekstasis*. If, as Longinus prompts readers to consider, the course of Achilles's daemonization allegorizes Homer's, then in Achilles's war cry Homer offers the reader an image of his own ecstatic voice.

Achilles's decision to return to battle and slay Hector courts the suicidal. Book one narrates Achilles mourning Briseis, with Thetis alone attending him by the shore. Book eighteen exorbitantly restages this scene as Achilles's mourning of Patroclus. In this second scene, Thetis arrives with every Nereid in tow, the mourning sea nymphs gathering in their droves around Achilles at the shore. Achilles declares to Thetis that she will never again "embrace him" on his triumphant return "home":

> My spirit rebels—I've lost the will to live,
> to take my stand in the world of men—unless,
> before all else, Hector's battered down by my spear
> and gasps away his life, the blood-price for Patroclus,
> Menoetius' gallant son he's killed and stripped!
>
> (18.104–09)

Thetis reminds Achilles that "hard on the heels of Hector's death [Achilles's] death / must come," in reply to which Achilles declares, "Then let me die at once" (18.112–13). Note the seeming paradox: simultaneously, Achilles's "spirit rebels" and the hero loses "the will to live." Achilles now finds himself willing to meet his fate, to kill Hector: "For my own death, I'll meet it freely" (18.137). Yet in this fate Achilles hopes for his apotheosis in glory: "I'll lie in peace, once I've gone down to death. / But now, for the moment, let me seize great glory!" (18.143–44).

Readers seeking confirmation for the interpretation of Achilles as a wrestler with a kind of nihilism should consider Shakespeare's rewriting of Achilles in *Hamlet,* or really the dramatist's complex shattering of Achilles and refracting the shards into King Hamlet (the overwhelming warrior and [via Patroclus's ghostly appearance to Achilles] the grieved-over, armor-wearing motive for revenge) and into Prince Hamlet (who checks his rage for revenge, delays his action for nearly the entire play, and takes action only when, done mourning kingship's finitude, he accepts his fate, going into the duel to kill and be killed). Listening to the first player recite "Aeneas' [tale] to Dido" of how Achilles's son Pyrrhus avenges his father's death by killing the Trojan king Priam, Hamlet may contemplate himself as Pyrrhus and the dead King Hamlet, his noble father, as Achilles (2.2.446). In Shakespeare's *Troilus and Cressida,* Falstaff's creator treats the *Iliad* with mockery, yet *Hamlet* responds to the sublime Homer with an answering achievement. The fury of satirical debasement toward the *Iliad* Shakespeare manifests in *Troilus and Cressida* contrasts with the revisionary appropriation of Achilles in *Hamlet* entailing implicitly Shakespeare's reading of the epic's hero as suffering from yet overcoming nihilism. Because Achilles undergoes his long-delayed yet irreversible transition from devastation and despair to affirmation and exaltation-toward-perishing, Shakespeare can dramatize Hamlet's move past "[t]o be or not to be" and toward "let be," apotheosis, and silence (3.1.55, 5.2.224). The relation of Achilles to Hamlet spurs Milton to achieve in his Satan a combination of Homeric warrior-hood and Hamletian brooding.

The translator of the *Iliad* Alexander Pope, in his verse "Essay on Criticism," says of Longinus what Longinus says of Homer, that Longinus "is himself that great sublime he draws."[10] "All the Nine inspire" Longinus, "bless[ing] their critic with a poet's fire" (675–76). In the *Iliad,* Athena takes on the role of a muse, bringing a daemonic fire to Achilles. The hero aflame becomes daemonic, "superhuman," "like inhuman fire raging" (20.506, 554). In chasing Trojans toward and killing them in the river Scamander, Achilles becomes like a "rushing fire" (21.14). In the process, Achilles heaps scorn on the river as unable to aid or save the Trojans who have so faithfully offered sacrifice to it. Incensed by these taunts and by Achilles choking his flow with Trojan corpses, Scamander rears up, "taking a man's shape" to confront Achilles (21.239). Achilles refuses to stop his slaughter, the river appeals to Apollo to stand by the Trojans, and, enraged by this, Achilles charges into the river, which rises against him. Achilles attempts to outrun Scamander, which he does only because of Athena "pumping enormous strength deep down Achilles' heart" and because, fearing the river might overwhelm him, Hera commands her son the god of fire Hephaestus to direct his "inhuman blaze" against Scamander (21.346, 389). The god's fire pushes back and dissuades Scamander, in the process "devour[ing] / all the dead" and burning away trees along his banks (21.396–97). Again Achilles associates with a fire threatening to consume all in its path, all of nature (the trees) and any simple dying into nature (the corpses).

In the advent of full daemonization, Achilles strains toward his fate and so toward an unsharable moment, if only a moment ever about to be. In this moment, from the encompassing cosmos drops away any significance his interactions with his fellows determine, leaving Achilles before existence as the incessant strife from and in which a warrior wins a name; the strife itself remains utterly and irreducibly nameless. This strife finds figuration as waves: "As a heavy surf assaults some roaring coast, / piling breaker on breaker whipped by the West Wind, / [...] / so wave on wave they came, Achaean battalions ceaseless, / surging on to war" (4.489–96). Another example: Achilles orders the Myrmidons to feast and then prepare the grand funeral pyre for Patroclus, and they all "hung on his words, complied, / [and] rushed to prepare the meal," yet Achilles turns from them: "But along the shore as battle lines of breakers / crashed and dragged, Achilles lay down now, / groaning deep from the heart" (23.62–63, 67–69). He mourns for Patroclus before the incessant "breakers" that figure "battle lines," the figuration echoing "the battle line of breakers" Chryses, bereft of his daughter, wandered along in silence after his rebuke by Agamemnon and recalling "the heaving gray sea" Achilles faced bereft of Briseis (1.40, 414). This background of the nameless intrudes in the poem when in extremities of battle a character nears or chances death. So, when the river Scamander seems about to overwhelm and drown Achilles, above him the hero sees "the arching blank sky" (21.307). As the Trojans and Achaeans fight desperately to secure the body of Patroclus, armor and arms clashing, "the iron din went rising up / to the bronze sky through the barren breathless air" (17.491–92). Consider the simile describing Hector's slaughter of Achaeans in which Zeus bestows the fighter with "glory" (11.349). Hector kills Achaeans "like the West Wind battering soft shining clouds / the South Wind wafts along—in deep explosive blasts / it strikes and the great swelling waves roll on and on" (11.355–57). The hero gains glory only from entering into a battle touching on an anonymous and relentless flux of strife waves again figure.

Only the without-name solicits events of nomination. To win glory, a name, requires the warrior's submersion in nameless strife, a descent down and out into the anonymous. The erotic's asemantic, starkly nameless sensations precipitate cries of nomination. Thus, when Hector desperately accepts his fatal battle with Achilles, the Trojan's thoughts race to an erotic analogy: "No way to parley with that man—not now—/ not from behind some oak or rock to whisper, / like a boy and a young girl, lovers' secrets / a boy and a girl might whisper to each other . . ." (22.151–54). Why should a woman, in her beauty, image martial glory? Why should Briseis be the image of Achilles's glory? Because in her beauty something Achilles experiences in combat finds an analogy. Mortality and sensuality find odd juxtapositions in the *Iliad*. The Trojan corpses "sprawled across the field" the narrator describes as "craved far more by the vultures than by wives" (11.187–88). Boasting that his killing spear drops a man to the ground, Diomedes describes how the victim "rots away himself—/ more birds than women flocking round his body!" (11.464–65).

The *Iliad* dramatizes throughout contests over beauty. The beauty contest among Aphrodite, Hera, and Athena backgrounds the war. Hera and Athena's siding with the Achaeans against the Trojans Aphrodite supports continues the antagonism among the goddesses sparked when Paris chose Aphrodite's bribe of beauty (Helen) over Hera's bribe of kingship and Athena's bribe of wisdom. Judged less beautiful than Aphrodite, Hera and Athena suffer a wound to their pride. In stealing Helen from the Achaeans, Paris wounds their honor, sparking the war, a titanic struggle over the possession of the mortal exemplar of female beauty. Arguing over Briseis, in appearance comparable to "golden Aphrodite,"

Agamemnon and Achilles pursue a contest over beauty (19.333). In this contest, Briseis images Achilles's glory. When Patroclus comes to substitute for Briseis, he takes on this aura of glorious beauty. Patroclus becomes in appearance as "vivid as a god," and Iris reminds Achilles of Patroclus's "soft, tender neck" to rouse the hero's concern for the fate of Patroclus's corpse should the Trojans capture the body (11.762, 18.205). This aura encompasses Patroclus as he wears Achilles's armor in battle until Hector, the "prince of beauty," dons this armor, only in his defeat and death to have Achilles tear off the armor to reveal his "marvelous, lithe beauty" (17.162). When the Achaeans and Trojans fight a tug of war over Patroclus's corpse, an anonymous Achaean cries out that to win or lose glory depends on winning or losing this body (17.481–86). Achilles agrees. After the Achaeans secure Patroclus's body and ready it for burial, Achilles commands, "Down to the ships we march and bear the corpse on high—/ we have won ourselves great glory" (22.462–63).

The shield Hephaestus crafts for Achilles manifests the beauty in glory toward which Athena drives her "brilliant" warrior (22.257). No one but Achilles can face this shield "in all its blazoned glory" (19.16):

> A tremor ran through all the Myrmidon ranks—none dared
> to look straight at the glare, each fighter shrank away.
> Not Achilles. The more he gazed, the deeper his anger went,
> his eyes flashing under his eyelids, fierce as fire—
>
> (19.17–20)

Achilles "thrilled his heart with looking hard / at the armor's well-wrought beauty" (19.22–23). On an irreversible path toward his fate, his eyes aglow with Athena's daemonizing fire, Achilles alone shows himself willing to confront the beauty in glory his apotheosis will entail, Achilles's "exulting" in contemplation of Hephaestus's "shining gifts" presaging Achilles's triumphal vaunting over Hector's body (19.21). In the armor, in the shield, Achilles encounters a glorious beauty only manifest to him as he makes his way toward his death, which, his glory won, will rush to him as if without interval, Achilles being, Thetis's hyperbole states, "doomed to the shortest life of any man on earth" (1.603). Narratively, Achilles cannot die before the poem ends, his existence being constitutive of the world Homer invents. Affectively, Achilles's transport of beauty in glory and Achilles's perishing belong to a single (the single) fleeting moment. Declaring himself "doomed at birth, cut off in the spring of life" (24.630–31), Achilles refers to his fate but also to the overwhelming sense of brevity with which he wrestles, again Hamlet articulating an analogue: "And a man's life's no more than to say 'one'" (5.2.74).

In Longinus's *On the Sublime*, the critic admires the orator Demosthenes. To justify his leadership and those who followed it, "inspired by heaven," Demosthenes pronounces an "oath by the champions of Greece" (88). Longinus quotes Demosthenes's oath: "assuredly ye did no wrong; I swear it by those who at Marathon stood in the forefront of the danger" (88). In this oath, Demosthenes "deifies his ancestors" in bringing forth the implication "that we ought to swear by those who have thus nobly died as we swear by gods" (88). To die at the farthest pitch of battle amounts to an apotheosis. An image of plunging toward fate fascinates Longinus: a chariot, the rampant horses leaping forward, the charioteer urging them onward toward destiny. From a lost play of Euripides, the *Phaethon*, Longinus cites passages in which Helios to no avail advises his offspring Phaethon to drive the solar chariot with caution, the reckless and inexperienced youth driving on to a high and wild flight ending disastrously. About these passages, Longinus comments: "Would you not say that the soul of the writer enters the chariot at the same moment as Phaethon and shares in his dangers and in the rapid flight of his steeds?" (87). The poet, achieving sublimity, imaginatively shares the drive toward fate the poet's poem dramatizes.

Set on an unwavering flight toward finality, the steeds of Emily Dickinson's "Because I could not stop for death" capture the resolute drive toward the irreversible characterizing Longinus's chariot teams. With the poet, Death, and Immortality aboard, Dickinson's carriage "paused" before a grave and tombstone: "Since then—'tis Centuries—and yet / Feels shorter than the Day / I first surmised the Horses' Heads / Were toward Eternity—."[11]

Dismissive of Homeric *agon* ("We passed the School, where Children strove / At Recess—in the Ring—" [9–10]), Dickinson would separate her uncanny team's one-way journey from passionate strife, she asserting the "Civility" of her kind visitant and fellow carriage passenger "Death" (8). In contrast, Longinus exalts "the spirit of contention," "the eagerness of mutual rivalry and the emulous pursuit of the foremost place" (95, 101). The struggle to attain the foremost place in poetry Longinus finds analogous to the drive to win the glory of being in the foremost place in battle. In this analogy, Longinus offers an interpretation of how Homer allegorizes his drive toward apotheosis as a poet in narrating Achilles's drive toward apotheosis as a warrior. To be foremost among poets becomes analogous to being foremost in battle.

Longinus evokes the daemonic in quoting a simile from the *Iliad* describing the horses drawing the chariot Hera gathers Athena into for their plunge earthward into the midst of battle. Noting the carnage Ares is bringing to the Achaeans, Hera requests permission from Zeus to enter the battle. Zeus replies: "Leap to it then. Launch Athena against [Ares]" (5.879). In this episode, argues Longinus, "Homer magnifies the daemonic," that is, Hera and Athena in sublime flight out from Olympus and down into strife, by way of the following simile from the *Iliad:* "[A]s far / as a man's glance can pierce the horizon's misting haze, / a scout on a watchtower who scans the wine-dark sea—/ so far do the soaring, thundering horses of the gods / leap at a single stride" (81, translation modified; 5.885–89). Longinus offers this *Iliad* quotation following what evidently is Longinus's quotation or mention of Homer's personification of strife as a goddess, "Strife, [who is] only a slight thing when she first rears her head / but her head soon hits the sky as she strides across the earth" (4.513–14). While a lacunae interrupts *On the Sublime* at this point, evidently Longinus aligns Homer with the goddess, stating that her stature encompassing "the distance from earth to heaven [...] might well be considered the measure of Homer no less than of strife" (81). Then, quoting a passage from the *Iliad*'s "Battle of the Gods" in which the strife among the deities threatens to rend the earth, laying bare for all to see the realm of the dead, Longinus comments: "[A]ll things together—heaven and hell, things mortal and things immortal—share in the conflict and the perils of that battle!" (81). Strife pervades the Homeric cosmos.

To praise Plato's *agon* with Homer and the poetic "struggle for the crown of glory," Longinus writes: "For, as Hesiod says, 'This strife is good for mortals'" (86). Homer wrote the *Iliad*, Longinus argues, "at the height of his inspiration" (82). The "action and conflict" this inspiration allows Homer to depict become themselves conditions for that inspiration (82). Homer can write of strife because he commits himself to strife. He "enter[s] into the sublime actions of his heroes" (82). The inspiration of entering into strife unto the death becomes Homer's: Ajax seeks "a death worthy of his bravery, even though Zeus should fight in the ranks against him. In truth, Homer in these cases shares the full inspiration of the combat" (82). The poet attains the sublime in struggling for the foremost place, and this struggle can sustain analogy to being in the foremost place in battle insofar as both struggles take the agonist toward an irreversible fate. To commit fully to the poem the poet must commit fully to perishing. Or, in Achilles's case, for the hero to commit fully to his attainment of glory, he must commit fully to his death in battle. The muse of this commitment, Athena, associates with the Gorgon. In an erotically tinged passage, Homer describes Athena gearing up for battle:

> Then Athena, child of Zeus whose shield is thunder,
> letting fall her supple robe at the Father's threshold—
> rich brocade, stitched with her own hands' labor—
> donned the battle-shirt of the lord of lightening,
> buckled her breastplate geared for wrenching war
> and over her shoulders slung her shield, all tassels
> flaring terror—Panic mounted high in a crown around it,
> Hate and Defense across it, Assault to freeze the blood
> and right in their midst the Gorgon's monstrous head,
> that rippling dragon horror, sign of storming Zeus.
> (5.841–50)

This shield bearing the Gorgon's visage Athena slings onto Achilles before he gives the war cry to scare the Trojans away from Patroclus's body.

How does Athena's shield bearing the Gorgon's head relate to the *ekphrastic* shield Hephaestus forges for Achilles? Athena bearing her shield faces her opponent with the Gorgon, freezing her opponent with fear into stone with the prospect of a death born unwillingly. When Achilles dons Athena's shield and gives his battle cry, he brings such fear to the Trojans. But in donning this shield, Achilles accepts his fate to reenter the battle, willing his mortality. In giving the cry, he takes on Athena's daemonic energy and stands outside of any version of his self that diverges from his fate. In donning her shield, Achilles gives himself over to his mortality as his daemon drives him toward his fate. Sounding his Athena-inspired war cry, Achilles breaks with the stasis of waiting in hesitation away from the battle line and begins to move toward an *ekstasis* only available at the forefront of the danger in the act of a moment, his killing of Hector while wielding the *ekphrastic* shield.

In contrast to the Gorgon's effect of freezing the viewer into a stone statue, static in space and withdrawn from time, the *ekphrastic* shield burgeons with *energeia*, with the turbulent dynamism of a cosmos everywhere in motion and wholly given to transience.[12] Bearing the *ekphrastic* shield to confront Hector, Achilles entirely immerses in yet ecstatically steps beyond this *energeia* in his moment of daemonization. In this moment, the entirety of his cosmos, depicted in Hephaestus's *ekphrastic* shield, becomes at stake in the infinite, acosmic arena for his attainment of glory. Only in this moment does Achilles act, or in this moment alone does his long-delaying pale cast of thought give way to an action worthy of the name. In the final confrontation with Hector, Achilles acts within the world of the siege yet in an ecstatic triumph irreducible to that world, just as Hamlet both plays out the ghost's revenge plot yet as an actor wholly detached from the rancid and absurd world of Ellsinore. When Hamlet lets himself become willing to act, he steps toward an undiscovered country from which no swordsman returns or toward a silence. So does

Achilles in embracing his fate. In *Hamlet's* closing duel of Hamlet and Laertes, Shakespeare collapses the mutually fatal duel of Achilles and Hector (afterwards Achilles only lives posthumously awhile, as Hamlet does after his duel) into the nonfatal games for prizes Achilles orders staged after Patroclus's funeral. Homer and Shakespeare attempt to follow their heroes into an arena of last gestures. Writing as if from that arena defines fiction.

The hero undergoing apotheosis (Hamlet) or daemonization (Achilles) in such an arena gains a perspective on the arena. Being in excess of the world of the siege, and even of the encompassing cosmos, Achilles carries a shield mimetic of that world and cosmos, the shield scholars define as an originary example of *ekphrasis.* The shield offers a mimesis of the entirety of world and cosmos. Achilles fully gives himself to his fate in the world and cosmos by an act he undertakes only through his *ekstasis* vis-à-vis the world and cosmos. To depict an act in excess of the entirety available for mimesis defines Homer's sublime ambition, yet, as Longinus implicitly teaches, another such act is Homer's speaking out the *Iliad.* Driving toward the super-mimetic, Homer attempts to represent the ecstatic condition productive of the *Iliad,* his triumph in epic representation.

This super-mimesis engages the temporal *ekstasis* of the sublime Bloom proposes: the ever-more-about-to-be.[13] At the opening of Nietzsche's *Genealogy,* Nietzsche ponders the inverse asymptote of recounting moments in a moment ever about to be recounted yet never finally recounted.[14] An account of existence assumes a moment, the existing moment, will remain always in excess of the account, which always, in its mimesis, tends toward a travesty of the moment. The super-mimetic would provide a mimesis of the moment any mimesis can only travesty. Achilles's armor animate with Hector mimes Achilles. A super-mimesis only happens in an *agon* with the travesties of mimesis, an *agon* whose triumph remains ever about to occur. Any self spoken of presumes the speaker, who remains ever about to be spoken.

Or rather: magnetizing the poet toward the abyss of fate, the muse beckons. The ethos is the daemon: this apothegm implies a parallel structure. Achilles becomes who he is by letting go of or struggling with evasions of his fate, his self as fate-enacting only coming to the fore in defeating versions of his self as fate-evading. The final agonistic opponent of Achilles is Achilles, or his self as unwilling dross, or Hector parading in Achilles's original armor. Consider Achilles's declaration to Hector: "Athena will kill you with my spear in just a moment" (22.319). Achilles speaks toward a "moment" in which the realization of his fate, the apotheosis of his character, happens as his daemon's action. In no way a static, sculptural entity, the *ekphrastic* shield Hephaestus makes Achilles in no way merely represents but embodies the energy of the cosmos at war. Taking up this shield, Achilles carries into battle a synecdoche of the cosmos Homer speaks out in achieving the *Iliad*. The poet brings this world into mimesis only by partaking in a daemonic energy, the fire of Athena, burning away the mimetic as travesty and flaring up in the poem's episodes of super-mimesis. Patroclus in Achilles's armor represents the hero; Hector in Achilles's armor confronts Achilles with his own travesty, and in destroying Hector, Achilles enacts a finality of overcoming the travesty by his irreversible giving over of himself to fate and toward the ever-about-to-be fusion of ethos and daemon.

Achilles belongs to Athena. As the gods look down on Achilles chasing Hector round Troy's walls, Zeus grieves for Hector and floats the option of saving him. Ever the remorseless partisan of fate, Athena sharply objects to relieving from death "a mere mortal, / his doom sealed long ago" (22.213–14). Zeus quickly denies making the proposal "in earnest" and unleashes his daughter: "Do as your own impulse bids you. Hold back no more" (22.219, 221). Zeus lifts his scales to weigh "two fates of death," Achilles's and Hector's; the "day of doom" of Hector pulls down the scale, "and god Apollo left him. / Athena rushed to Achilles, her bright eyes gleaming" (22.250, 253, 254–55). The goddess had previously checked Achilles's rage. Now, "winging orders," she urges Achilles on: "At last our hopes run high, my brilliant Achilles—/ Father Zeus must love you—/ we'll sweep great glory back to Achaea's fleet, / we'll kill this Hector, mad as he is for battle!" (22.256, 257–60). "So Athena commanded /

and he obeyed, rejoicing at heart": in obeying Athena, Achilles knowingly welcomes his own death, doing so joyously (22.267–68).

Consider the following case of a chariot plunging into battle. To engage Ares, Athena hijacks Diomedes's chariot, drawing the mortal into a fearful clash of deities. Deftly tossing out the chariot's driver Sthenelus, Athena boards, "blazing to fight beside the shining Diomedes": "The big oaken axel groaned beneath the weight, / bearing a great man and a terrifying goddess—/ and Pallas Athena seized the reins and whip, / lashing the racing horses straight at Ares" (5.968–72). Here again "Pallas Athena / driver of armies" brings a mortal to a pitch of intensity in conflict (to fight the god of war himself) said mortal would neither achieve nor dare absent Athena's daemonic inspiration (13.151–52). With "her eyes afire," standing immediately adjacent Diomedes in the chariot, Athena stabs into Ares the spear with which Diomedes lunges at the god, the action of the goddess and the action of Diomedes fusing (5.985–89).

In the traditions of literature, Bloom finds the *Iliad* in an agonistic struggle with the Hebrew Scriptures and the Abrahamic tradition more generally. Given English literature's divergent ancient Greek and Judaic heritages, argues Bloom, what Homer's Achilles might be for readers today remains inseparable from what Genesis's Joseph or 2 Samuel's David might be for them. Bloom cites Friedrich Nietzsche and Simone Weil as thinkers whose writings work out a stance toward the *Iliad* only insofar as they also work out a stance toward the Abrahamic tradition. Bloom follows suit, thinking out his assessment of the *Iliad* by way of comparisons to the Hebrew Scriptures. Especially through their most imaginative threads, argues Bloom, the Hebrew Scriptures have usurped forever the imagination of belief as tied to a vision of the human enjoying Yahweh's blessing, more life into a time without boundaries. Involving a "time dimension, *olam*, unknown to Homer," the blessing is the "highest good" in the Hebrew Scriptures, while in the *Iliad* victory, agonistically to achieve the foremost place, is the highest good.[15] The "radical otherness" of Homer's heroes, "particularly that of Achilles, is fated to remain the essence of poetry for us, and the essence of unbelief. Achilles' final and most poetic greatness is that he keeps no covenant, except with death" (*Ruin*, 34–35). These last sentences show Bloom exemplifying how, in thinking about the *Iliad*, an Abrahamic vocabulary ("covenant") inevitably intervenes. So why would a covenant only with death define poetic greatness?

In *The Anxiety of Influence*, Bloom contrasts two stances: the acceptance of a deity wholly outside the self versus an insistence on the self and a deity overlapping. The relation between Yahweh and Abraham resembles more the first option, while the relation between Athena and Achilles is more like the second. While Yahweh stands in a relation of "shocking incommensurateness" to his warriors, Athena and Achilles can exchange "battle shouts in mutual support" in Homer's "magnificent antiphony between man and goddess."[16] Yahweh could never drive Moses toward a fate epitomizing Moses only by turning him toward his death as an unconditional finality. Achilles's daemon Athena drives Achilles toward a triumph with a consequence of death the hero embraces, while even as Moses dies, Yahweh allows him to look into the promised land where the Israelites will realize the blessing of more life into a time without boundaries. If the *Iliad* takes on a nihilistic cast for Bloom, it does so at least partially because the critic, along with any contemporary reader, cannot help but think of the epic by way of and in contrast to the Hebrew Bible.

Another perhaps useful contrast would be with the Apostle Paul. Though Paul describes the effort toward awakening into the life with Christ as a competition, a foot race, Paul also argues that the final opponent is death. Triumphing over mortality and so entering the realm of the spirit where death is no more, through the gift of grace the follower of Christ subdues and subsumes the flesh, that is, the "I" as the fallen captive of sin. Thus the Christian overcomes the world. To claim, as does Bloom, that Achilles keeps no covenant except with death articulates an aspect of the *Iliad*'s agonistic divergence from Pauline thought. For Paul, the wages of sin is the death the "I" brings to itself. In contrast, Achilles holds fast to his fated death to assert heroically his "I" in fidelity to the earth. Or so suggests Longinus in linking Homer and the

Iliad to rifts in the earth and citing a play by Simonides in which Achilles stands on his grave to salute the Achaean ships leaving Troy for home (81, 85, 87). And, in the *Iliad* itself, consider again the daemonic Achilles, taking a stand for Patroclus's body, towering on the earthen battlement adjacent the trench in the ground encircling the Achaean ships. This Achilles knows the nameless strife amidst anonymous *energeia* through which names are won or lost. This arena for glory's out-flaring Paul can only abject as the "world," as the realm of sin and death. By wresting a phrase away from the *Iliad* scholar Simone Weil, the narrator of Sandy Florian's *The Tree of No* sounds a Homeric assertion of the "I" complexly through, with, and against the Pauline legacy, the narrator triumphantly closing the work with: "The sin in me says I."[17]

The splendor won by the agonist Achilles in battling to his death, that is, to his irreversible, unavoidable fate: this beauty taken up into the sublime, this glory, only comes to the hero in his daemonization. The glory betokens the hero's achievement of the foremost place, the battle line but also the cusp of his fate where daemon and self mingle, where Athena through Achilles kills his enemy, his travesty: any avatar of the hero in flight from the hero's fate. In terms of a display of valor in the service of the Greek cause at Troy, Ajax's defense of the Achaean ships against the Trojan onslaught perhaps merits more praise than does Achilles's triumph over Hector. In Ovid's *Metamorphoses*, Ajax falls on his sword, having lost in debate the prize of the dead Achilles's armor to Ulysses, Ajax's suicide proving only Ajax could overcome Ajax (13.1–95). No gesture could be farther from Achilles's defeat of Achilles's armor as animated by Hector. Only in his daemonization does Achilles overcome Achilles, through embracing his fate rather than by a futile attempt to escape or evade fate by self-slaughter. To direct destructive force away from the hero and toward anything or anyone potentially blocking the daemon's triumph in the hero's accession to fate: this gesture the *Iliad* exalts.

In the *Iliad*, when Apollo spurs the Trojans to their nearly decisive assault on the Achaean ships Ajax heroically defends, Apollo becomes Hector's daemon: "Hector charged head-on at

Ajax," yet "Hector [could not] burst through and ignite the hull
/ nor [could] Ajax drive him back—a god [*daimon*] drove Hector
on" (15.486, 488–89). When, in Achilles's armor, Patroclus fights
his way toward the city walls, he "might have taken Troy," except
Apollo, "blazing with death for him but help for Troy," beats
Patroclus back (16.816, 820). Mounting to the daemonic, on his
fourth assault Patroclus charges "like something superhuman
[*daimoni isos*]," prompting Apollo to fear a deviation in fate:
"Back—/ Patroclus, Prince, go back! It is not the will of fate / that
the proud Trojans' citadel fall before your spear" (16.824, 825–27).
When two daemonic forces clash, fate hangs in the balance.

"[B]ent on glory," Achilles charges Hector "like something
superhuman [*daimoni isos*]," though Apollo thwarts this attack
(20.498, 506). Depicting Achilles's frenzy for battle, Homer returns
to the simile of the Athena-inflamed warrior as a raging forest
fire:

> Achilles now
> like inhuman fire raging on through the mountain gorges
> splinter-dry, setting ablaze big stands of timber,
> the wind swirling the huge fireball left and right—
> chaos of fire—Achilles storming on with brandished spear
> like a frenzied god [*daimoni isos*] of battle trampling all he killed
> and the earth ran black with blood.
>
> (20.554–59)

Homer associates the daemonic with the determination of fate.
With nightfall suggesting a halt to the conflict until the next
morning, Hector declares, "We'll fight again tomorrow, / until
some fatal power [*daimon*] decides between our two armies" (7.334–
35). Priam and Idaeus reiterate this notion, the formulaic phrase
suggesting a common recognition of the daemonic as a bringer
and decider of fate (7.434–35, 458–59). Chasing Diomedes, Hector
threatens him, telling Diomedes he will never in victory cart
Troy's women off captive: "I'll pack you off to the god of darkness
[*daimona doso*] first!" (8.189). Richmond Lattimore's translation of
the same line brings out the association of the daemon with fate:
"I will give you your destiny."[18]

Achilles's "covenant with death": mocking the Abrahamic covenant promising more life into a time without boundaries, how does this promise relate to Athena, who wears "the dark helmet of Death"? Achilles's fidelity to the goddess, the hero's acquiescence to her as his daemon, becomes the paradox of adhering to the self only in rejecting any prudential care for the self. Or the defense of the poetic self toward sublimity can only manifest as a disregard for the self of prudential calculation. If to the Hebraic promise of more life Achilles remains irreducibly other, and if in covenanting with death Achilles sets the paradigm for poetic greatness, then what Bloom calls the poetic sublime seems inevitably to entail a kind a nihilism. In Achilles's daemonization toward fate, sublimity breaks out where nihilism and nihilism's overcoming cross. The apotheosis of Achilles places him on a threshold where he both abandons and achieves himself and where existence contracts to a moment of glory bordering mortality, as distinct from extending as more life into a time without boundaries. Here the reader might revise Keats's statement about Milton ("Life to him would be death to me"[19]): what is an apotheosis for Achilles, his moment of glory, for Milton is idolatry.

Achilles's shield betokens the entire cosmos of interhuman encounters the hero strays from, out and down, in an extravagant moment of glory. This moment estranges him from Achaeans and Trojans alike, from any relation the shield-depicted cosmos organizes. The fate of Achilles takes the hero toward a moment in excess of the mores and ways of both his comrades and his enemies. The episodes of the *Iliad* after Achilles's killing of Hector show the hero organizing funeral rites and athletic contests and recognizing the social good of returning Hector's body to Priam: these episodes imagine an Achilles reintegrating into the interhuman, but the poem ends with a reminder of the moment suspending or even mortifying the domestic, civil, and ritual relations for which Hector gave his life: "And so the Trojans buried Hector breaker of horses" (24.944).

Just as Achilles, in his daemonization, becomes a force unbound, so Athena in acting as his daemon strays magnificently into wildness. Priam's son the seer Helenus commands Hector to order his mother Hecuba "to gather all the older noble women together / in gray-eyed Athena's [Trojan] shrine" (6.103–04). There, the women are to join the priestess in offering a superb robe to the statue of the goddess and to promise the sacrifice of a dozen heifers in the hope of inducing Athena to "pity Troy, / the Trojan wives and all our helpless children" (6.111–12). Athena is to exercise this pity by "hold[ing] Diomedes back from the holy city—/ that wild spearman, that invincible headlong terror!" (6.113–14). Note Helenus's figuration of Diomedes as "wild" and galloping "headlong." Athena loves raging chariot horses galloping headlong. A breaker of horses, Hector would discipline unruly forces for orderly use; Helenus's plan would tame Athena. Hecuba dutifully carries out her son's command, approaching the temple "with a file of noble women rushing in her train" (6.351). Hecuba and the women walking in obedient "file" bring a fine robe to the goddess's temple. There Theano, "the horseman Antenor's wife / and Athena's priestess," spreads the robe "across the sleek-haired goddess' knees" and commands Athena: "Now shatter the spear of Diomedes! That wild man—" (6.354–55, 358, 361). Hector orders women to order Athena to take pity on women as passive nonwarriors. Should Athena accept and don the robe, a garment for women in domestic life, Athena would perhaps become attentive to orders. But in her preparation to inflame Diomedes and rouse his chariot team wildly to plunge headlong into battle, Athena lets "fall" from her body "her supple robe" so she can don her father's "battle-shirt" (5.842, 844). A warrior on a rampage, Athena rejects the domestication Hector tries to arrange: "Athena refused to hear Theano's prayers" (6.366).

The Athena on the loose in battle with Diomedes, who inspires Diomedes to wound Aphrodite and challenge Ares and Apollo; the Athena who first orders Diomedes not to challenge gods but then exclaims gleefully to him, "Forget the orders," her own orders; the Athena no one quite controls, even her father: this is the Athena whom Ares calls Zeus's "senseless daughter," a "murderous curse" who is "forever bent on crimes!" (5.954, 1012–13). And this Athena defies Zeus, prompting Iris to stammer at her: "You, / you insolent brazen bitch" (8.485–86). Only this rather spirited Athena becomes the daemon of Achilles. Rather than a domesticating robe, Diomedes and Odysseus offer Athena armaments stripped from an enemy's corpse (10.528–35). The Athena figure Boethius exalts, Lady Philosophy, wears a fine robe, never defies her father, Boethius's Neo-Platonic god, and could hardly be Achilles's daemon.

To offer praise of Odysseus's martial ability and enthusiasm for combat, Diomedes exclaims of Odysseus, "Athena loves the man" (10.287). Outside and after the *Iliad*, Helenus, who orders Hector to order women to give Athena orders, becomes the seer who prophesizes that as long as the statue of Athena remains in her Trojan temple and the rituals pacify the goddess into harmony with the routines of Trojan life, the city will stand. Once Odysseus steals his way into Troy, removes the statue from its ritual location, and takes it to the Greek camp, Troy is doomed. But this tradition only imagines Athena again as primarily a goddess at the disposal of her votaries by way of her statue. The episode in the *Iliad* of Athena rejecting the gift of the robe shows her to shrug off taming.

The untamable Athena, in becoming a muse for Achilles, becomes a muse of nihilism and the overcoming of nihilism, with the overcoming a moment of aesthetic ecstasy. In *The Queen of the Air*, a prose rhapsody to Athena, John Ruskin notes that the "first word of the Iliad, Menis, afterwards passes into the Latin Mens [mind]; is the root of the Latin name for Athena, 'Minerva,' and so of the English 'mind.'"[20] In the name "Achilles" a student of Greek like Ruskin can hear "*achos,* 'ache, pain, grief.'"[21] Ruskin calls the *Iliad* Homer's "mighty" song "of the Menis, mens, passion, or zeal, of Athena, breathed into a mortal whose name is 'Ache of heart,' and whose short life is only the incarnate brooding and burst of storm" (15). Claiming his own "art-gift" came to him from "Athena's will," Ruskin finds that "[t]hroughout the *Iliad* Athena is herself the will or menis of Achilles" (114, 41). Questing for this *menis* as alit in aesthetic sensation, Ruskin insists Athena's eyes are an intense pale blue, the Greek word translated as "gray" in the epithet "gray-eyed" actually "standing for a pale or luminous blue" (95). Ruskin's Athena overtly stands as a muse of sublimely beautiful or glorious sensation, of the sky's blueness as a "blue fire" that "cannot be painted" (95). This blue's synesthesia fuses fire, light, and vibratory air. Manipulating chemicals, gases, and a prism to produce and observe blueness, the scientist John Tyndall exclaimed he had replicated "a bit of more perfect sky than the sky itself!" (v). Against Tyndall's scientific reduction and laboratory replication of Athena's synesthetic blue incandescence, Ruskin cries out, "Ah, masters of modern science, give me back my Athena out of your vials" (vii). The lab can only replicate for the scientist's observation at a reifying distance the blue Ruskin would encounter in the common air and sky, hoping again to find the blue of Athena's eyes. The "queen of the air," Ruskin's Athena acts as the goddess of breath, both "bodily breathing" and "mental breathing or inspiration," so Ruskin's muse would be the very air Ruskin breathes (13). Athena brings and courses through "the vibratory power of the air to convey sound" (39). While the music of Apollo embodies the orderly patterns of measure, to the music of song Athena inspires belongs "whatever is impulsive and passionate," and so she displays a "constant strength of voice or cry (as when she aids the shout of Achilles)" (49). Ablaze with Athena's fire and sounding a cry reverberating through Athena's air, a cry the goddess joins: Achilles, in Ruskin's terms, undergoes an aesthetic epiphany or flowering. The fire of the heart the breath voices (61): this gift of Athena Ruskin associates with a flower in epiphanic, ecstatic, transient bloom, the plant's "time of peculiar and perfect glory" and "moment of […] intensest life" (66, 67).

Three

Yahweh's Daughter and Her Metamorphoses

> And thus Enthymesis (thought) was the passion;
> for she was thinking of things impossible.
> —Irenaeus

In the Hebrew Scriptures, Proverbs introduces two women: Wisdom and Folly. The feminine Hebrew noun *hokmah* refers to prudence, shrewdness, or discernment. In Proverbs, the noun names a woman: Hokmah. In the third century BCE, the Septuagint translators rendered her name in Greek as Sophia, and in the seventeenth century CE the King James translators followed the Geneva Bible in bringing her name into English as Wisdom. Anxious commentators admonish readers to interpret Hokmah merely as a personification of Yahweh's wisdom, yet Proverbs 8.22–31 dramatizes Hokmah as Yahweh's daughter. In the beginning, prior to the creation, amidst the void waste of waters and wind, Yahweh gave Hokmah birth from himself, and then she became his inspiration, co-conspirator, and confidant in letting the creation burgeon and flourish. Genesis opens with, "In the beginning" (1.1). The Hebrew of Genesis 1.1 the KJB translates as "In the beginning" reappears in Proverbs when Hokmah speaks of her origin: "The Lord possessed me in the beginning of his way, before his works of old" (8.22). Here, "possessed" translates a Hebrew word meaning to create or to give birth.[1] Hokmah continues: "I was set up from everlasting, from the beginning, or ever the earth was. When there were no depths, I was brought forth; when there were no fountains abounding with water" (8.23–24). "Set up" translates the Hebrew referring to creation by pouring out or to semen pouring out, and "brought forth" translates the Hebrew for a woman writhing in childbirth (Penchansky 54).

Hokmah is Yahweh's daughter. In the beginning, she was there with Yahweh in the time before time and the space before space. She was with Yahweh amidst the chaos of waters and wind prior to any of the structuring differentiations by which Yahweh created, by which he let light be and separated the light from the darkness, by which he let the dome of the sky be and separated the waters from the waters, and so on. As Hokmah says, "Before the mountains were settled, before the hills was I brought forth: While as yet he had not made the earth, nor the fields, nor the highest part of the dust of the world" (8.25–26). The structuring differentiations Yahweh let happen occurred through Hokmah's inspiration. When Yahweh did begin letting the creation proliferate, Hokmah was there with him, inspiring him in his work, herself a master builder:

> When he prepared the heavens, I *was* there [...] When he gave to the sea his decree, that the waters should not pass his commandment: when he appointed the foundations of the earth: Then I was by him, *as* one brought up *with him:* and I was daily *his* delight, rejoicing always before him.
> (8.27, 29–30)

The Hebrew the KJB renders with the words "as one brought up with him" allows for various translations: "like a master worker" (NRSV) or "as a confidant." In "rejoicing before" Yahweh and being "*his* delight," Hokmah too was a master builder, a daughter taking after her father, a daughter to whom he could entrust his secrets. The joy and delight she gave him she also brought to the creatures made in his image: "Then I was by him, [...] Rejoicing in the habitable part of his earth; and my delights *were* with the sons of men" (8.30–31).

Besides Hokmah, besides Wisdom, Proverbs introduces Folly. She leads the unwary down and out from the creation, to the place of dissolution, the gray, anonymous Sheol, which the King James translators problematically render as "the depths of hell" (9.18). The word "hell" connotes a domain of punishment and suffering;

in Sheol, dissolution into naught prevails for all. As Ecclesiastes explains, in Sheol nothing of the creation happens: "for *there is* no work, nor device, nor knowledge, nor wisdom, in the grave [Sheol], whither thou goest" (9.10). Because some grave or another awaits everyone whomsoever, "grave" translates Sheol much better than "hell." Only "under the sun," amidst the creation, are knowledge, work, and wisdom available for enjoyment (8.15). The dupe of Folly abandons the creation, all life's burgeoning, all work, and all the structuring differentiations, and enters Sheol, where, amidst chaotic entropy, any turn only furthers the passing away of structuring differentiations. This entropic void strangely echoes the pretropy "without form, and void" Yahweh and Hokmah occupy in the beginning prior to their turns toward letting the creation's structuring differentiations happen (Genesis 1.2). Like Wisdom, Folly associates with secrecy. Folly says, "Stolen waters are sweet, and bread *eaten* in secret is pleasant" (Proverbs 9.17).

Yahweh would never confuse Wisdom for Folly or Folly for Wisdom, would he? Proverbs tells how a young man walks a street and hears Wisdom and Folly call to him to enter their respective domiciles. The paternal narrator admonishes the young man to distinguish Wisdom from Folly. The young man should heed the call of Wisdom and reject the call of Folly, turn toward Wisdom and turn away from Folly. However, these two women, Wisdom and Folly, resonate uncannily with each other; their calls sound virtually indistinguishable. In English literature, the perplexing yet intriguing and energizing way each appears as the other has become proverbial.

Consider an example from Herman Melville's *Moby-Dick*. Stubb overhears Flask musing on the doubloon Ahab nailed to the *Pequod*'s mast as a reward for the first sailor to spy the white whale. About Flask's words, Stubb asks himself, "Shall I call that wise or foolish, now; if it be really wise it has a foolish look to it; yet, if it be really foolish, then has it a sort of wiseish look to it" (433). Stubb wrestles with an ambiguity: should Flask's words about the doubloon "be really wise," they would then have a "foolish look," yet should these very same words "be really foolish," they would manifest a "wiseish look." Each state of being,

being wise, being foolish, upon approaching complete actuality, gives the appearance of the contrary state. Wisdom appears as folly, and folly appears as wisdom, to the end of reckoning. Stubb contemplates a bottomless abyss (or an unsearchable height) of counter-resemblances, with wisdom and folly each withdrawing in the appearance of the other. The very same words, Flask's, may be wise or may be foolish, yet in their phenomenality, these words dissimulate wisdom as folly and folly as wisdom, so any decision Stubb might make to read the words as wise or as foolish would entail a leap of interpretive faith on Stubb's part with Stubb having no way to know whether that leap would land him amidst wisdom or amidst folly. In Shakespeare's *Othello*, Iago comments sardonically on the difficulty of distinguishing wisdom from folly, and Milton in *Paradise Lost* has Adam comment on how Wisdom may appear as Folly. By dramatizing the perplexity of moments when Wisdom and Folly each seem to offer the other's face to the baffled, Shakespeare, Milton, and Melville show themselves to be attentive readers of Proverbs.

Proverbs carefully parallels the calls of Wisdom and Folly. As does the Geneva translation, the King James translation brings to the reader the quite startling realization that, for the young man walking the street, the hailing words of Wisdom and Folly sound indistinguishable. Calling down to the street, Wisdom hails the passerby: "she crieth upon the highest places of the city, Whoso *is* simple, let him turn in hither" (Prov. 9.3–4). Now consider the "foolish woman" or Folly: "For she sitteth at the door of her house, on a seat in the high places of the city, To call passengers who go right on their ways: / Whoso *is* simple, let him turn in hither" (9.13, 14–16). To say, "Come hither," Wisdom and Folly use exactly the same words: "Whoso *is* simple, let him turn in hither." The auditory phenomena are indistinguishable. For the young man wandering the street who hears Wisdom or Folly call, in the very moment of the call, the hailing invitation, the call of Wisdom is indistinguishable from the call of Folly and vice versa. How might the young man discern who calls? In the crucial moment of hailing, in the moment when the young man must decide how to respond, the auditory phenomena offer him no guidance whatsoever. Listen: "Whoso *is* simple, let him turn in hither." Does Wisdom call or Folly? Have I just quoted the one or the other? Can I even know which I have quoted, once the words through quotation wander from Proverbs 9.4 or from 9.16?

In the moment of the call, the young man can only take a decision as an utter risk: if the young man decides to "turn in hither," he may be giving himself to Folly, yet if he decides not to cross the threshold, he may be withholding himself from Wisdom. What is a decision in a situation where any criteria for deciding withdraw? Kierkegaard knows the moment of decision as a moment of madness. Kierkegaard writes, or rather his Johannes Climacus asserts, "[T]he moment of decision is *foolishness.*"[2] The English "foolishness" here translates Kierkegaard's noun *Daarskab,* folly, so Kierkegaard's apothegm both captures and sidesteps the moment of madness in decision the young man of Proverbs undergoes. The young man cannot know whether in his mad moment of decision he engages in folly or in wisdom. In calling that moment "foolishness," Kierkegaard implies he might know, might be able to distinguish in the moment of decision folly as distinct from wisdom.

In deciding to turn or not to turn in response to the call ("Whoso *is* simple, let him turn in hither"), the young man traverses a moment when all guardrails fall away and he must gamble. By leaving his residence and walking on the street, he already gambles on hearing "Whoso *is* simple, let him turn in hither," and hearing those words, he must either step toward or away from the doorway or threshold the call calls him to cross: "turn in hither." In this moment, however he decides, whether to step toward or away from the threshold, he cannot help but act as someone entirely "simple": wholly unknowing, utterly naïve. Both Wisdom and Folly call to a young man who "wanteth understanding" (9.4, 16). In the moment of decision, he has no way to know, whichever choice he makes, whether he acts wisely or foolishly. Therefore, heedlessly to apply Kierkegaard's apothegm and describe the moment as one of foolishness prejudges the moment as Folly's and so shies away from the depthless perplexity of the moment. The moment of decision may take the young man toward either Wisdom or Folly, yet the moment itself participates in neither foolishness nor wisdom but madness. The very same madness in the moment of decision may lead to Wisdom or to Folly. To intend folly would be madness, yet such madness would precisely resemble the madness of a decision taken with the most ardent intent to find wisdom. The one madness resembles the other uncannily, indistinguishably, an abyss: in his moment of madness, does the young man court Wisdom or Folly? He has no way to know.

On a first reading, the two fates the young man madly courts in his moment of mad decision would arguably appear starkly opposite or completely distinct, as separate as parallel lines which will never cross regardless of how far the young man might travel along either. Wisdom associates with life, Folly with death. Wisdom associates with fidelity, Folly with infidelity. The fatherly narrator of Proverbs wants the young man ever to cleave toward Wisdom and never to cleave toward Folly. However, what if Proverbs finally gives credence to one of William Blake's "Proverbs of Hell": "If the fool would persist in his folly he would become wise"?[3]

The words "turn in hither" sound, and a threshold beckons. Should the threshold be Folly's, it leads to Sheol. Should the call be from Folly, and should the young man choose to "turn in," he would be unknowingly choosing to join the dead: "But he knoweth not that the dead *are* there; *and that* her guests *are* in the depths of hell" (9.18). Wisdom says, "all they that hate me love death" (8.36). Yet if the young man hears "turn in hither," and should the threshold be Wisdom's, and should the young man choose to turn, this choice also entails his fully giving himself over to the unknown, to luck, to the chance of his own demise. Even if the threshold should turn out to be Wisdom's, the commitment in choosing to "turn in" and cross the threshold entails the very same anxiety as does crossing a threshold that turns out to be Folly's. The threshold of Wisdom leads to life: "Forsake the foolish, and live; and go in the way of understanding" (9.6). Yet the decision that turns out to be toward life and understanding involves the selfsame madness as the decision that turns out to be toward death and ignorance. Only through undergoing the trial of this madness does the young man "turn in hither." The beginning or Sheol, the time and space prior to time and space or the dissolution of time and space: walking amidst the creation, the young man, gambling on a threshold, gambols toward women active in the creation's doing (Wisdom) and undoing (Folly).

As he approaches Wisdom, as he approaches Folly, what phenomena confront the young man? Or are they themselves, Wisdom and Folly, Folly and Wisdom, the phenomena? If the phenomena offer contraries, if amidst the phenomena every contrary admits of encounter, would bookworms then have a way to read the ambiguity the young man faces, Wisdom and Folly being both at stake in the moment of the young man's response to the call? Or are the phenomena radically ambiguous because the young man only encounters any phenomenon through the risk of answering the call, with Wisdom and Folly never appearing as such? Stubb comments about how, when Flask's words approach giving the appearance of being wise, they take on a foolish cast, and when they approach giving the appearance of being foolish, they take on a wise cast. Neither wisdom nor folly ever appears as such or *per se*, the phenomenon ever carrying ambiguity and doing so without bottom (or top).

Each of the two women affiliates with a state distinct from the creation: Wisdom with the beginning, Folly with Sheol. In these states, the distinctions of light from darkness, the waters above from the waters below, and so on, are yet to happen (the beginning) or have gone missing (Sheol). While the young man only goes to his encounter amidst the creation, both women, Wisdom and Folly, remain irreducible to the creation, somewhat in the manner Emerson ascribes to the friend in his essay "Friendship": all phenomena only become available in their intensity through the friend, the friend the sojourner encounters amidst the phenomena, yet the friend remains irreducible to the phenomena. And the friend inspires the sojourner toward an *ekstasis* undergone in agonistic striving. So the Emersonian friend takes on the stigmata of a daemon.

Wisdom and Folly too resemble daemons situated as it were between the creation-gambling youth and the nonrealms in excess of the creation. In the moment of answering the call, the moment of madness, the young man undergoes exposure to the beginning and to Sheol and so fully immerses in the creation, the creation only burgeoning in relation to the beginning and to Sheol. This moment of mad decision thus entails the ecstatic. Does this ecstasy intimate a transport immersive in the creation and touching on the beginning or a transport immersive in the creation and touching on Sheol? To determine beforehand the orientation of the ecstasy remains impossible: toward the beginning, toward Sheol, or somehow toward both? The young man only undergoes the ecstasy through madly risking this utter disorientation, and in this disorientation, *ekstasis* brings intuitions of the beginning and of Sheol, though which is which remains ambiguous. As the narrator of *Paradise Lost* might wonder in his poetic transport: am I being drawn toward Wisdom and God in Heaven or toward Sin and Satan in Hell? Consider also Satan's topic of hells becoming heavens and heavens becoming hells. In driving toward the final confrontation with Moby Dick, does the *Pequod* regain the beginning, a chaos of waters fostering origination, as Ishmael exultantly hopes, or does the *Pequod* plunge toward a watery hell, a Sheol of drowning toward dissolution, as Ahab exultantly despairs? The *Pequod* voyages into a realm of phenomena allowing for both readings of her journey, and the Stubb who meditates on the wisdom/folly ambiguity at the start of the voyage acts in a dream as "a blazing fool" only to then encounter a "badger-haired old merman" who mutters over and over, "wise Stubb, wise Stubb" (131, 132). Stubb concludes the dream has made him a "wise man," though of this dream Flask says, "it seems a sort of foolish to me" (132). In the world of *Moby-Dick*, where the only female is Ahab's "queenly personality," the "merman" appears to be Wisdom, or so Ishmael intimates in his narration of the visions Pip undergoes while almost drowning: "the miser-merman, Wisdom, revealed his hoarded heaps" (414).

Proverbs narrates a city with streets. Through these streets the young man wanders, and along these streets women beckon. A woman who may ally with Folly is "the strange woman" (2.16). She "forgetteth the covenant of her God" (2.17). She "flattereth with her words," and to be seduced by her speech would lead the young man to Sheol: "For her house inclineth unto death, and her paths unto the dead. None that go unto her return again, neither take they hold of the paths of life" (2.16, 18–19). In apparent contrast to the paths of the "strange woman" are the paths of Wisdom: "Her ways *are* ways of pleasantness, and all her paths are peace. She *is* a tree of life to them that lay hold upon her: and happy *is every one* that retaineth her" (3.17–18). After Adam and Eve, how can anyone "lay hold" of a "tree of life"? Having followed Eve's lead and eaten the fruit of the tree of knowledge, the two mortals, Adam and Eve, may well reach out to eat from the tree of life and gain immortality; for this reason, "the Lord God sent him forth from the garden of Eden," sent Adam and Eve out from Eden and onto a path of mortality and so a path toward Sheol (Genesis 3.23). As a "tree of life," Wisdom associates with a place, Eden, from which Adam and Eve's progeny are radically estranged, a place where the tree of life was within Adam and Eve's unruly grasp. The verse in Proverbs immediately following the verse calling Wisdom a "tree of life" states Wisdom partakes of what remains strange or foreign to any creature, the beginning: "The Lord by wisdom hath founded the earth; by understanding hath he established the heavens" (3.19). The young man may encounter the "strange woman" in the street. But, "in the city," "in the openings of the gates," he may also encounter Wisdom: "Wisdom crieth without; she uttereth her voice in the streets" (1.21, 20). The voice in the street may come from the strange woman or from Wisdom. By bringing death, a culmination toward Sheol, the strange woman associates with a nonplace uncanny for the creature. Just so, in bringing life and being a "tree of life," Wisdom associates with a lost place, Eden, and with the beginning, a place prior to place uncanny for the creature. In the street, a woman's voice calls: to Sheol, to the beginning?

An author confronting the depthless intrigue at work in the call, "Whoso *is* simple, let him turn in hither," confronting in the call a bottomless ambiguity, might stay with the fecundity of the phenomena, the phenomenon the call is, to invent further variations. Consider Samuel Johnson's riff on the Wisdom/Folly *aporia* and bring in Melville's Stubb to offer a reading. Johnson: "Love is the wisdom of the fool and the folly of the wise."[4] Rather than attempting to sort out Wisdom from Folly or Folly from Wisdom, through his words Johnson lets their intrigue draw in love, so the encounter with love too becomes an event Stubb could read as caught up in a perplexing irony or Kierkegaard could read as calling for a mad decision. Johnson writes from the rich ambivalence of affect the call solicits, remaining with the exposure to the contrary yet complementary impingements of the beginning and of Sheol.

Rather than staying with (and straying with) the phenomena, writers may respond or perhaps react to Wisdom and Folly's zero-point of indifferentiation in Proverbs by attempting to set the two women in a polar opposition by way of contrasting "values." Yes, the prevalent narrator of Proverbs 1–9 would have the young man cleave toward Wisdom and away from Folly, but these chapters leave the young man to decide without any guardrails to guide him or to prejudge his decision. By culminating in the depthlessly ambiguous call, chapters 1–9 even render the narrator's value judgments moot in relation to the young man's mad decision. If through abstract values the decision had a guiding, prejudging guardrail, the phenomena would become lost; the intimations of the beginning and of Sheol and the immersion in the creation would fail to happen. Such a value-driven opposition of Folly to Wisdom occurs in Cormac McCarthy's novel *The Road*. An interpretation of *The Road* might come down to reading the novel's narration of two women, one who speaks foolishly and one who speaks wisely.

The novel depicts a perpetually gray-skied wasteland, every tree burnt dead, the ash-laden consequence of some unspecified but human-caused disaster. Amidst this wasteland a man walks along a road with a boy. Toward the start of the novel, the reader learns of the late wife of the anonymous man. As the back-story relates, in the early days of the disaster, she gave birth to a son, presumably her husband's. Some months later she killed herself, unable to cope with the nonworld of environmental and civilizational devastation she, her spouse, and her son inhabit. In this novel of extremely spare diction and characterization, this woman comes across as urbane and sophisticated in her brief appearances via the back-story the narrator provides. In her despair over the ashy nonworld and in her terror of rape and cannibalization, she says to her husband, "You can think of me as a faithless slut if you like. I've taken a new lover. He can give me what you cannot."[5] To this the husband replies, "Death is not a lover," yet she counters: "Oh yes he is" (57). Very much Folly inviting her husband to join her on a quick path toward Sheol and to bring her son along, she says, "As for me my only hope is for eternal nothingness and I hope it with all my heart" (57). Though she has killed herself before the narrative starts, the husband spends almost the entire novel fighting the urge to turn toward her, to join her, to take up her advice to give himself death after giving his son a death she would have called a mercy except she believes in nothing. Despite the unrelenting circumstances of hopelessness, dire want, and hideous danger, the husband refrains.

In his final days, dying, he tells the son to continue to speak with him after he has passed. In desperate anxiety confronting his presumptive father's imminent death, the son asks about a boy: "But who will find him if he's lost? Who will find the little boy?" (281). In his last reported words, the father says: "Goodness will find the little boy. It always has. It will again" (281). The two fall asleep, but the son wakes to find the father dead. After three days, a stranger appears. Learning from the stranger that he eschews cannibalism and lives with others, including a boy and girl, the son agrees to accompany him. The stranger leads the son to a woman who offers her embrace: "The woman when she saw him put her arms around him and held him" (286). While his urbane sophisticate of a mother had refused to say goodbye to him previous to cutting herself to bleed to death (58), this woman who embraces him expresses her joy at his presence: "Oh, she said, I am so glad to see you" (286). This woman associates with the wind or breath that was there in the beginning: "She would talk to him sometimes about God. [...] She said that the breath of God was his breath yet though it pass from man to man through all of time" (286). This woman speaks to the son of the delights of the creation prior to its devastation: "Once there were brook trout in the streams in the mountains. You could see them standing in the amber current where the white edges of their fins wimpled softly in the flow" (286). These trout associate with the beginning, with the time before time prior to the human: "On their backs were vermiculate patterns that were maps of the world in its becoming. [...] In the deep glens where they lived all things were older than man and they hummed of mystery" (287). But notice how these words place the burgeoning of the creation into a past collapsed onto the beginning. In the now of the narrative, the rich, fecund phenomena of the creation are lost in an increasingly gray dissolution. Yes, the plot presumes this gray waste to be the result of a human-caused environmental catastrophe. But the moralist stance of McCarthy toward Proverbs gives the fiercest energy to the novel, working beneath and trumping the environmentalist frame and message of his plot.

Walking a path ever further into a gray void of a nonworld ever more like Sheol, the husband remembers his wife in daydreams of "siren worlds," memories of his past with her, say at a "theater [...] listening to the music" (18). In relation to his death-inviting wife, "siren" is a very loaded term. For survival's sake, he must only focus on the grim moment he and his son occupy, and so he fights these daydreams. To succumb to his daydreams would be to turn to folly. In telling the son of the pre-disaster mountain stream, the embrace-offering woman offers a counter daydream, and this vision gleaming with intimations of the beginning ends the novel.

"Goodness will find the little boy": the woman who speaks of the beginning the novel tags as embodying goodness. The mother who abandoned her son to his fate the novel tags as contrary to goodness. McCarthy has her say of herself, "I am done with my own whorish heart," though he also has her say about her son, this carrying a morally suspect cast too: "My heart was ripped out of me the night he was born" (57). The moralistic polarization of Folly and Wisdom in *The Road* comes down to the opposite attitudes toward the son shown by the woman at the start of the novel in the man's back-story and by the woman at the end of the novel after the man has passed: the first woman, the despairing mother, rejects her son and his continuing life, while the hope-bearing woman embraces the son and his continuing life.

About the son, his presumptive father says in the novel's first pages: "If he is not the word of God God never spoke" (5). The "word of God," the Logos, Christ: in the nonworld of the novel, "[b]arren, silent, godless," the man imagines the son as incarnating the divine Christian Word (4). The man imagines the boy to be messianic, his hair worthy of "some ancient anointing": "He sat beside him and stroked his pale and tangled hair. Golden chalice, good to house a god" (74, 75). The son would be a god undergoing the irreversible kenosis of incarnating into an utterly fallen world. The son calls attention to what seems a snowflake falling down: "He caught it in his hand and watched it expire there like the last host of christendom" (16). In the novel's context of father and son, of a dying father and a son who lives on toward perishing in a perishing world, a context evoking the dying of God the Father through his kenotic incarnation as the Son, Folly and Wisdom must separate fully. The call of Folly, the urbane mother's call to give oneself death, must sound as distinct from the hope-bearing woman's call to persist in life. The call toward Sheol and the call toward the beginning must sound different, or so the novel's value judgments demand. In *The Road*, McCarthy demarcates Folly from Wisdom by rewriting the two ladies from Proverbs as in no way confusable, Folly at the beginning of the novel calling toward an end and Wisdom at the end of the novel calling toward a beginning.

A segregation of Wisdom and Folly such as *The Road* narrates, or at least a separation between two types of women, appears in the final chapters of Proverbs. These chapters collect sayings and poems older than and distinct in authorship from chapters 1–9, the chapters that culminate by staging the uncanny call, "Whoso *is* simple, let him turn in hither." In the last chapters of Proverbs, the reader can find such sayings as: "Whoso loveth wisdom rejoiceth his father: but he that keepeth company with harlots spendeth *his* substance" (29.3). And the final chapter of Proverbs includes a poem extolling the "virtuous woman," an obedient and chaste wife who can in no way double as a cunning prostitute (31.10). In chapters 1–9, the chapters of more recent authorship, Proverbs enacts the fecund ambiguity of Wisdom and Folly, their being indiscernible in the call calling for a mad decision. This fecund ambiguity and maddening call bring into question the verses that appear in the final chapters that seem recuperative of the maddening call and suggest an erasure of the fecund ambiguity, such as the verses narrating the bad prostitute and the good wife as simply distinct and clearly distinguishable. These verses are in the chapters of earlier authorship. Perhaps readers should peruse the collage of texts titled Proverbs backwards, from the last chapters to the first chapters. Something like this seems to have been the practice of authors like Blake and Melville, who work from the ambiguity of Wisdom and Folly.

Among the progeny of Adam and Eve, the men and women who manifest the image of Genesis's god, Enoch and Elijah alone bypass Sheol. After vigorously participating in the begetting the deity urges on the animals and then on men and women ("Be fruitful, and multiply" [Genesis 1.22, 28]), that is, the fruitful multiplication participant in the burgeoning letting be of the creation in the beginning, Enoch exits the creation otherwise than via Sheol: "And Enoch walked with God: and he *was* not; for God took him" (Genesis 5.24). Elijah enjoys a similar privilege: "Elijah went up by a whirlwind into heaven" (2 Kings 2.11). With the exceptions of Enoch and Elijah, every man and woman ultimately ends in Sheol, and even Enoch and Elijah were procreated. In the Hebrew Scriptures, moral judgment bypasses the fact mortals find their ultimate start, via procreation, in the beginning, and moral judgment bypasses the fact mortals find their ultimate end in Sheol. Indeed, down the generations procreation carries the blessing given men and women upon their creation: "And God blessed them, and God said unto them, Be fruitful, and multiply" (Genesis 1.28).

Rereading the Hebrew Scriptures as "the old testament" (2 Corinthians 3.14), Paul revalues the fruitfulness Genesis associates with the beginning. Paul writes, "For the wages of sin *is* death" (Romans 6.23). Paul applies a moral stigma both to the origin of men and women in procreation and to the end of men and women in death. That is, mortality *per se* becomes for Paul a moral stigma because Paul reads an otherwise immortal Adam as committing sin, a sin all Adam's progeny then inherit and pass on: "by one man sin entered into the world, and death by sin; and so death passed upon all men, for that all have sinned" (Romans 5.12). From Paul, the early Church fathers learned to define sin as passing from generation to generation via procreation, and from Paul and these fathers Augustine developed his doctrine of original sin.

When Paul writes of Wisdom and Folly, he does so by way of his flesh/spirit and related distinctions. Reading Hokmah through these distinctions, Paul revalues her as what he calls "spirit," as prefiguring Christ, and as opposing the wisdom of what Paul calls "the world." Paul's attempt at a variation on the *topos* of wisdom crossing with folly and folly crossing with wisdom appears in 1 Corinthians 1.17–3.23. Or rather, with his Middle-Platonist distinction between the worldly (the apparent yet false) and the godly (the unapparent yet true), with his negative valuation of the worldly and his positive valuation of the godly, Paul narrates himself as in control of the wisdom/folly ambiguity, as able to sort out amidst the phenomena wisdom from folly and folly from wisdom. This control he would assert by mapping folly and wisdom across an antithesis between "the world" and "God." This world-versus-God value dichotomy becomes the alibi or prejudgment by which Paul claims to adjudicate between wisdom and folly. The factor of control ties with Paul's positing his god as a self-presence transcendent of the world yet, as Christ, manifesting in the world as spirit devoid of flesh, as a word sounding without rhetoric, as a phenomenon wholly empty of the phenomenal.

In seeming paradox with the declaration of Paul that he proceeds disarmed of rhetoric, of the sophistic "wisdom of words" (1 Corinthians 1.17), the structure of a chiasmus operates in 1 Corinthians 1.17–3.23. Through this chiasmus, wisdom and folly show up doubled and divided between the worldly and the godly: what the worldly hear as folly the godly hear as wisdom, and what the worldly uphold as wisdom the godly cast down as folly. By having the identical speech or *logos*, his "preaching [*logos*] of the cross" (1.18), complexly speak both wisdom and folly, Paul does pick up on how in Proverbs both Wisdom and Folly say, "Whoso *is* simple, let him turn in hither" (9.4, 16). And as does Proverbs, Paul invites his readers to a decision. But while the words in Proverbs ("Whoso *is* simple, let him turn in hither") perform an abyssal ambiguity drawing the young man into the creation via his mad decision, Paul situates the *logos* he evokes (the "preaching of the cross") in a sublating dialectic. This dialectic would spirit the sojourner away from the "world" and offers a prejudgment to guide and guarantee the sojourner's decision. By deploying value-marked oppositions (world versus God, flesh versus spirit, and so on), this dialectic would mitigate if not defuse the anxiety the young man's decision entails in Proverbs. For Paul, those who become "perfect" unambiguously know Wisdom, Wisdom as Christ (1 Corinthians 2.6). In Paul's dialectic, perfection results from the Christ-follower etiolating or sublating the flesh to become more and more of spirit and then, ultimately, "[i]n a moment, in the twinkling of an eye," to become perfectly of spirit (15.52). Perfect entrance into spirit entails this "twinkling of an eye" jump-cut that happens via the flesh's crucifixion, even to death on the cross. What is crucifixion for Paul but *his* circumcision of the flesh? As Paul writes, "For we are the circumcision, which worship God in the spirit, and rejoice in Christ Jesus, and have no confidence in the flesh" (Philippians 3.3). By emulating Christ crucified, the perfect know godly wisdom as wholly spirit.

For the godly, worldly wisdom seems folly. For the worldly, the message of the cross, godly wisdom, seems folly. Paul sorts out these appearances by aligning the elements of his chiastic wisdom/folly trope with salvation and perishing. Thus, while the chiasmus in structure displays the symmetry of four elements (wisdom worldly and godly; folly godly and worldly) among which figurations circulate, these figurations polarize across Paul's flesh/spirit opposition, the flesh moving the wayfarer toward perishing, the spirit moving the wayfarer toward salvation. The worldly, the fleshly, are given over to perishing: "For the preaching [*logos*] of the cross is to them that perish foolishness" (1 Corinthians 1.18).

However, to those of spirit, to the "saved," this very "preaching of the cross," this very *logos*, manifests power and wisdom: "But we preach Christ crucified, [...] Christ the power of God, and the wisdom of God" (1.23–24). Those who decide for the world undergo irreversible perishing. Those who decide for God can anticipate salvation: "For the preaching of the cross is to them that perish foolishness; but unto us which are saved it is the power [*dynamis*] of God" (1.18). Paul parallels "the power of God" with "the wisdom of God" (1.24). To the "saved," the "preaching of the cross" voices God's "wisdom," God's "power." To the "perishing," this very "preaching" voices "foolishness."

Paul distinguishes between two related types of perishing individuals. The first consists of the perishing of "this world" who remain outside the Corinthian network of Christ-followers. The second consists of those who, though inside the community, bring division and strife, being partially of "this world," fleshly, imperfect, and so among the perishing. Distinct from both types of perishing are the "perfect," though Paul finds none of the "perfect" among the Corinthians. Or rather, all the Corinthian brethren might be "perfect" if only they would give themselves over to Christ completely and become wholly of the spirit. This giving over would require the entire humbling or emptying out of the Christ-follower, an entire imitation of Christ, who "humbled himself, and became obedient unto death, even the death of the cross" (Philippians 2.8). In 1 Corinthians, Paul's "preaching of the cross" implies each Christ-follower, to enter perfection, must undergo such a kenosis. The KJB uses the word "perfect" to translate the Greek *teleios* (brought completely to its end, finished), an adjective Paul substantivizes. *Teleios* derives from *telos* (end, purpose). In the "perfect," the world and the flesh have been fully overcome, completely spirited away, so the perfect are wholly in Christ, one in Christ without division or strife. The Corinthian Christ-followers would finally enter oneness with themselves if only their remaining worldliness could be overcome, and Paul writes his letter to the Corinthians toward that end, purpose, or *telos*.

Following Christ all the way to the end, becoming fully of spirit, a Corinthian would attain knowledge of Wisdom but Wisdom as Christ. The Wisdom of Proverbs 8.22–31, to whom Yahweh gave birth and with whose inspiration Yahweh created all that he created, Paul reads as Christ, as prefiguring Christ. Though Paul's authorship of Colossians remains in dispute, that letter, under Paul's name, thinks of Christ through Wisdom. Colossians describes Christ as having been there in the beginning, "the image of the invisible God, the firstborn of every creature: For by him were all things created, that are in heaven, and that are in earth, visible and invisible [...] And he is before all things" (1.15–17). A similar evocation of Christ as he through whom all things were created appears in 1 Corinthians: "But to us *there is but* one God, the Father, of whom *are* all things, and we in him; and one Lord Jesus Christ, by whom *are* all things, and we by him" (8.6). A more direct allusion to the Wisdom active in the beginning occurs when Paul tantalizes his imperfect Corinthian addressees about his speaking the *logos* of the cross amidst the "perfect." A Christ-follower who enters perfection, who wholly enters the spirit, may know God's wisdom, that is, Sophia, yet Sophia as Christ or assimilated to Christ in prefiguring Christ:

> Howbeit we speak wisdom among them that are perfect: yet not the wisdom of this world, nor of the princes of this world, that come to nought: But we speak the wisdom of God in a mystery, *even* the hidden *wisdom,* which God ordained before the world unto our glory: Which none of the princes of this world knew: for had they known *it,* they would not have crucified the Lord of glory. (1 Corinthians 2.6–8)

As Paul states, "before the world," that is, before the creation, God "ordained" "wisdom": Wisdom, Sophia, Hokmah. Any Christ-follower who enters perfection may know God's Wisdom, and in knowing Sophia, the perfect gain knowledge of a secret unknown to the world. From the "world," God's wisdom has been "hidden," a "mystery." Those of the flesh, "the princes of this world," by following the wisdom of the world, finally arrive at their own inexistence. They "come to nought"; they perish into oblivion. Those Christ-followers who enter perfection will attain God's wisdom and know the secret, hidden wisdom God "ordained" in the beginning.

Thus Paul draws into his discourse and revalues the realms (the beginning and Sheol) Wisdom and Folly associate with in Proverbs. His revaluation of these realms Paul enacts by assigning them valuations. In Proverbs, the beginning and Sheol *per se* remain value neutral, an origin and an end for all and tingling intimations for the young man who undergoes full immersion in the creation. However, when the dissolving null oblivion of Sheol becomes for Paul the "nought" the "princes of this world" perish toward, this inexistence takes on a negative valuation as the destination only for the worldly, the fleshly; in a corollary valuation, the Wisdom there in the beginning becomes unworldly; the beginning becomes the otherworldly preexistence the perfect alone know. And the creation undergoes revaluation as "the world," the *kosmos*, the domain of "fleshly" activities generally.

The Hebrew Scriptures compare idolatry to adultery. Idolaters stray from Yahweh to other gods after having promised the Israelite god fidelity, so idolatry resembles adultery. Conversion too resembles adultery: the convert leaves one god for another. The apostle to gentiles who believe in various gods, Paul seeks their conversion. The *logos* of the cross solicits conversion. Christ crucified, the Logos on the cross, calls through Paul's preaching, Paul's *logos* of the cross. Christ the Logos through Paul's *logos* calls on Paul's readers to turn. Proverb's call "Whoso *is* simple, let him turn in hither" becomes in 1 Corinthians 1.17–3.23 the call of the Word, of the Logos on the cross, of Christ crucified. Paul sounds this call in his "preaching [*logos*] of the cross." In Christ on the cross, in Christ crucified, in "the preaching of the cross," does wisdom call or folly? The listener's answer reveals the listener as either worldly or godly. Attaining to perfection, the Christ-follower finds the wisdom of the world folly and persists in God's wisdom however much the worldly find God's wisdom foolish.

The "power of God," "the wisdom of God," Paul sets against the fleshly: "For ye see your calling, brethren, how that not many wise men after the flesh, not many mighty, not many noble, *are called*" (1 Corinthians 1.26). Rather than the "wise," "mighty," and "noble" of the world, God chooses the foolish, the weak, and the base:

> But God hath chosen the foolish things of the world to confound the wise; and God hath chosen the weak things of the world to confound the things which are mighty; And base things of the world, and things which are despised, hath God chosen, *yea,* and things which are not, to bring to nought things that are: That no flesh should glory in his presence. (1.27–29)

The "foolish" of the "world" "confound" the "wise" of the world; the "weak" of the "world" "confound" the "mighty" of the world. The Greek the KJB translates as "confound" can also refer to shame. The "wise" and "mighty" shame the "foolish" and "weak," but here those who shame undergo shaming. The KJB's "despised" translates a Greek word deriving from a word meaning to consider someone or something as nothing. The "noble" despise the "foolish" and the "weak" as "base." Assuming themselves something, the noble consider the base nothing. Yet, "chosen" by God, these "things which are not [...] bring to nought things that are": the noble who usually negate undergo negation by those the noble negated, the base. "[T]hings which are not [*ta me onta*]" "bring to nought things that are [*ta onta*]." What does "not" have being brings to "nought" what has being. The negated negate their negation in negating their negators. The flesh belongs to the *kosmos*, to being; introducing a void in the *kosmos*, this dialectic of negations wholly spirits away the flesh: "That no flesh should glory in his presence." To the voided worldly glory of the flesh Paul contrasts an unworldly glory, and this glory shows Christ becoming wisdom: "But of him are ye in Christ Jesus, who of God is made unto us wisdom [*sophia*], and righteousness, and sanctification, and redemption: That, according as it is written, He that glorieth, let him glory in the Lord" (1.30–31). The Christ-followers may glory, only not as the flesh or the world glories. Any flesh glorying "in his presence" would disturb "his presence."

Paul's dialectic of negations would insure "no flesh" will "glory in his presence" (1.29). What is the relation between "his presence" and the negation of the "things that are" by the "things which are not"? This "presence" of God is a state of sameness. The theme of establishing sameness pervades 1 Corinthians. After his opening salutation and thanksgiving, Paul implores the Corinthian Christ-followers to become the same: "Now I beseech you, brethren, by the name of our Lord Jesus Christ, that ye all speak the same [*to auto*] thing, and *that* there be no divisions among you; but *that* ye be perfectly joined together in the same [*to auto*] mind and in the same [*te aute*] judgment" (1.10). Paul's variations on the phrase "the same" all include versions of the Greek word *autos*. This word as a pronoun is reflexive: himself, herself, itself. The word combines with others to name states or actions that turn back on themselves: *automatos* means self-moved, automatic, and *autokatakritos* means self-condemned. The Greek New Testament the KJB translators worked from was the edition later known as the *Textus Receptus*, the "Received Text" deriving from the editorial work of Erasmus. Thus, from the *Textus Receptus* the KJB 1 Corinthians 1.29 "in his presence" translates *enopion autou*, more literally "before him." Given Paul's chiming on how the Christ-followers should speak, judge, and think "the same" (*to auto, to auto, te aute*), when Paul refers to God as *autou* (a variation on *autos* meaning "him"), the theme of self-sameness again rings. For any "flesh" to "glory" before him, *enopion autou*, would disturb his presence or self-sameness, would disturb him. Rather than from boasting flesh, rather than from the "mighty" or "noble" who are of the world, that is, rather than from those who *are* ("that are [*ta onta*]"), God only accepts wisdom from himself as a self-presence at a remove from the world however much in the world as Christ or like a word at a remove from rhetoric however much sounding amidst words operating persuasive force. Only in this godly wisdom should Christ-followers glory. In the beginning, as Yahweh did his creating, Hokmah was there, "rejoicing always before him" (Proverbs 8.30). As wholly kenotic or "perfect," in Christ manifest as Wisdom, Christ-followers may glory before the Lord as Wisdom did in the beginning, however, only Wisdom read as the preexistent Christ.

In the *Textus Receptus*, 1 Corinthians 1.29 ends with *enopion autou* (before him), and 1.30 begins with *ex autou* (out of him), so the Greek chimes a version of *auto: enopion autou ex autou*. Before him those who are must become "nought" so out of him those who are not may glory in Christ, whom God makes Wisdom for the Christ-follower. God chooses

> things which are not, to bring to nought things that are: That no flesh should glory in his presence [*enopion autou*]. But of him [*ex autou*] are ye in Christ Jesus, who of God is made unto us wisdom [*sophia*], and righteousness, and sanctification, and redemption: That, according as it is written, He that glorieth, let him glory in the Lord. (1 Corinthians 1.28–30)

God's choosing the "base" who "are not" to bring to "nought" the "noble" who "are" leaves before God, before God's presence, nothing worldly, nothing fleshly, a void, a void empty of any flesh glorying in worldly wisdom. Being becomes nothing so in the resulting void self-presence may glory. This voiding premises any perfect Christ-follower's glorying "in the Lord." Christ-followers may glory before the Lord "in Christ Jesus," whom God "made unto [them] wisdom." The "perfect" may know Sophia, "even the hidden *wisdom*, which God ordained before the world unto our glory," but only Sophia as Christ, Christ become Sophia.

Christ becomes Wisdom only by Wisdom becoming Christ. To read the daughter as prefiguring the Son spirits Wisdom away. In Christ as Wisdom, the Christ-followers would attain to perfection: completely of spirit, completely the same, completely one. The Christ-followers would overcome all strife were they in Christ as Wisdom. However, the Corinthian Christ-followers have yet to attain this oneness: "For ye are yet carnal: for whereas *there is* among you envying, and strife, and divisions, are ye not carnal, and walk as men?" (1 Corinthians 3.3). Paul addresses them in his letter precisely because, in their factional and interpersonal strife, the Corinthians show themselves to be of the flesh. They have yet to crucify the flesh completely and undergo the jump-cut into spirit. When Paul came to them, he had hoped to know amidst them Christ crucified: "For I determined not to know any thing among you, save Jesus Christ, and him crucified" (2.2). Paul would not know among the Corinthian Christ-followers anything of the flesh: any of their lingering participation in the world. He would know in them their perfection, their entire crucifixion of the flesh, even unto death. In this kenosis, foolish and weak to the worldly, the Christ-followers would show themselves wise and strong: "Because the foolishness of God is wiser than men; and the weakness of God is stronger than men" (1.25). But Paul finds the Corinthian Christ-followers at strife with one another, the strife worldly entanglements fuel. So these Corinthians, insofar as they remain worldly, must pass through the dialectic of negations to become wholly unworldly, to become nil, even unto death, so their flesh's dying in crucifixion may allow their spirit's living in salvation.

Notice how Paul emerges as the teacher to Hegel of the gathering up into self-present spirit by way of negations of negations. Encountering Paul's dialectic, Nietzsche cried out for fresh air. Paul's dialectic by which the active being in the world of the "noble" undergoes a reactive voiding by the nonbeing in the world of the "base" Nietzsche tags as a logic of resentment and a resentment against and hoping to leave existence, a nihilistic resentment. Besides through Paul's introduction of a void or nothingness, the nihilistic workings of Paul's dialectic emerge in Paul's revaluation of the creation as the "world" (1 Corinthians 1.21). Here, the KJB English "world" translates Paul's Greek word *kosmos*, cosmos. The god of Genesis sees his creation as good. Paul defines the "world" as Satan's realm. What for the Hebrew Scriptures belongs to the creation for Paul belongs to the world. The procreative creature active in the blessing to engender life in the creation becomes the flesh active in sin to engender death in the world.

To cease completely being of the world, the Christ follower must crucify the flesh entirely. Angered by advocates of circumcision among the Christ-followers in Galatia, and disputing rumors that he himself opportunistically preaches circumcision, Paul dreams of the castration of those he opposes: "And I, brethren, if I yet preach circumcision, why do I yet suffer persecution? then is the

offence of the cross ceased. I would they were even cut off which
trouble you" (Galatians 5.11–12). The Greek the KJB translates
as "cut off" can refer to castration, specifically to self-castration.
As Nietzsche might conclude, in imagining the self-castration
of those who "trouble" the Galatians, Paul reveals something of
himself: he inadvertently hints at what troubles him. This Paul
who hopes for a cutting off dreams of entering the oneness where
the trouble of sexual difference ends: "there is neither male nor
female: for ye are all one in Christ Jesus" (Galatians 3.28).

In Paul's wisdom/folly chiasmus, which polarizes wisdom
between worldly and godly, Christ-become-Wisdom spirits away
Wisdom's sexual difference. When the Son becomes the daughter,
an androcentric suspension of sexual difference occurs. Such
erasure of sexual difference operates when Paul addresses all
the Corinthian Christ-followers, male and female, as "brethren,"
brothers, *adelphoi* (1 Corinthians 1.10). The title "brethren" speaks
to the overcoming of the world as the realm of sexual difference.
Paul calls Christ God's "power," *dynamis*, and this power manifests
in God's Wisdom. This power paradoxically operates via "the
weakness of God" that is "stronger than men": the nothing, the
not that brings to naught what is so that "no flesh should glory in
his presence," including the Wisdom of Proverbs in her pleasure
towards the earth. That is, in spiriting Wisdom away, Paul splits
Wisdom between the godly and the worldly, the spirit and the
flesh. Proverbs calls Wisdom Yahweh's "delight," his pleasure,
and this pleasure Wisdom brings amidst the creatures: "I was
daily *his* delight, rejoicing always before him; Rejoicing in the
habitable part of his earth; and my delights *were* with the sons of
men" (8.30–31). This Wisdom who brings pleasure to Yahweh and
to the "sons of men" and who rejoices in the earth, the earth that
burgeons and brings forth creatures, never could glory before
Paul's god. Only Wisdom as Christ can so glory, the Wisdom on
the godly side of Paul's spirit/flesh division.

To the flesh belongs the wisdom of the world armed with the
"excellency of speech" Paul claims to forgo (1 Corinthians 2.1). In
speaking his Word-sounding word, his preaching of the cross,
Paul claims to have forgone any seducing pleasure of words:

And my speech and my preaching *was* not with enticing [*peithos*] words of man's wisdom, but in demonstration [*apodeixis*] of the Spirit and of power: That your faith should not stand in the wisdom of men, but in the power of God. (2.3–5)

The adjective *peithos* relates to the verb *peitho*, to persuade. An alternate translation would thus be: "not with persuasive words." Any such worldly eloquence would annul Paul's preaching: "For Christ sent me [...] to preach the gospel: not with wisdom of words, lest the cross of Christ should be made of none effect" (1.17). Were Paul's words to be enticing or persuasive, they would annul the *logos* of the cross and render ineffective the Logos on the cross. The "cross of Christ" the Corinthians are to take up, the "Christ crucified" whom Paul urges the Corinthians to imitate, signals the cessation of the self, the Christ-follower's complete kenotic emptying of self. Enticing or persuasive words exhibit rhetorical skill by enacting the rhetorician's self-enhancing purpose. To deploy such rhetoric wisely augments the self and strengthens the self's stance in the world, or so think those whom Paul calls worldly. For worldly users of rhetoric, say the "princes of this world," words soliciting a kenosis of the self would be precisely foolish and even unrecognizable as rhetoric.

In 1 Corinthians 1.17–3.23, the tropes Paul deploys include an elaborate chiasmus, paradox, irony, and rhetorical questions, for example: "where *is* the disputer of this world?" (1.20). This rhetorical question aligns the "disputer" or rhetorician with the world and asks where the rhetorician is. The question's implicit answer seems to contradict the rhetorical status of the question: the rhetorician is nowhere, both because "God [has] made foolish the wisdom of this world" and because, claims Paul, nowhere within him exists a self striving with words to exert its will via persuasion. Paul's rhetorical question about the rhetorician of the world must not be rhetorical. Rather than a persuasive argument asserting his self, Paul claims to speak selflessly, without will and without exercising persuasion. Paul denies he harbors any will to power: at this denial Nietzsche laughed. Despite the plethora of tropes his words enact, Paul claims, and indeed he must claim, that his words and their tropes in no way enact rhetoric or persuasion. Were they to do so, they would be words of the flesh and worldly rather than words of the spirit and godly. The "words which man's wisdom teacheth" speak from the flesh and to "the natural man" (2.13, 14). Here, the KJB English "natural" translates the adjective *psychikos,* referring to that which has the quality of or consists of *psyche.* The rhetorical words of the world address and are receivable by a Christ-follower's *psyche.*

Paul repeatedly claims his words are in no way rhetorical (1.17, 2.1, 2.4). About his words Paul implicitly wants to say what he says about his apostolic labors: "not I, but the grace of God which was with me" (15.10). Or perhaps: "I am crucified with Christ: nevertheless I live; yet not I, but Christ liveth in me" (Galatians 2.20). In his preaching of the cross, not Paul but the Logos on the cross, Christ crucified, speaks. Or manifests: Paul's words proceed "in demonstration [*apodeixis*] of the Spirit and of power" (1 Corinthians 2.4). *Apodeixis* refers to a making manifest, the showing forth of a self-evident presence. Everywhere in his words, Paul claims, not Paul but the spirit manifests, power manifests, the kenotic power of weakness, Christ crucified, the Logos on the cross. To the "perfect," those wholly of the spirit, Paul's words "speak wisdom," "*even* the hidden *wisdom,* which God ordained before the world unto our glory" (2.6, 7). This hidden wisdom, Wisdom as Christ, as the Logos, speaks through, manifests through, each of Paul's words, at least to the perfect or to the spirit in Christ-followers who might become perfect should they ever wholly crucify the flesh. In all Paul's words the Word speaks or manifests, so none of his words are rhetorical but they are all apodictic: immediate and certain manifestations "of the Spirit and of power," that is, "*even* [of] the hidden *wisdom,*" Wisdom, Sophia as the Word, the Logos. In each word the Word immediately manifests, at least to those perfectly of spirit. To the "natural man" or the *psyche,* Paul's words "are foolishness"; Paul's words must be "spiritually discerned" (2.14).

When the implications of words depend on their speaker, the words are deictic. In Proverbs, the semantic associations of the words "Whoso *is* simple, let him turn in hither" are entirely contingent on their speaker, Wisdom or Folly. These words are deictic insofar as their implications (the beginning and life? Sheol and death?) depend on the speaker: if Wisdom speaks them these words have very different resonances than if Folly speaks them. And yet these words, in themselves, precisely remain ambiguous as to their speaker. With his claim to *apodeixis,* Paul pushes the deictic ambiguity of Wisdom and Folly operative in Proverbs onto the side of *psyche* and the flesh. The "natural man" and those of the flesh confuse the wisdom of the cross for folly and the folly of the world for wisdom. Complete and final ascension to the spirit, the entrance into perfection, would allow the Christ-follower to know with full certainty, to know apodictically, the wisdom of the cross as wisdom and the folly of the world as folly. This position of knowledge comes through Christ. As in contrast to the "natural man," "he that is spiritual judgeth all things, yet he himself is judged of no man. For who hath known the mind of the Lord, that he may instruct him? But we have the mind of Christ" (2.15–16). Without ambiguity, in Christ the perfect have immediate access to Wisdom, Christ as Wisdom. For the perfect, in the words the Word manifests: the words become transparent to the Word.

The conflicts among the Corinthian Christ-followers involve given Corinthians taking the Word or Christ as relative to whoever baptized them or enunciated the Word to them, so that some declare themselves of Paul, some of Apollos, and so on. These Corinthians take the Word as deictic, as interpretable or as requiring an interpretation contingent on the Word's speaker. This reading of the Word as deictic threatens the semantic unity of the Word: "Now this I say, that every one of you saith, I am of Paul; and I of Apollos; and I of Cephas; and I of Christ. Is Christ divided?" (1.12–13). To approach the Word as caught up in *deixis* shows the Christ-follower to be of the flesh: "For while one saith, I am of Paul; and another, I *am* of Apollos; are ye not carnal?" (3.4). Paul insists whoever enunciates the Word, the Word manifests as apodictic and the same. Rather than at all exemplifying *deixis,* Paul insists the Word on/of the cross exemplifies *apodeixis* and renders all his words apodictic, at least to the perfect. The Christ-follower would receive the Word as apodictic were the

Christ-follower in no way fleshly but perfect. Each word of Paul manifesting the Word apodictically, none of Paul's words carry semantics, much less ambiguous semantics, contingent on Paul's self. Paul claims his words are entirely selfless. For the perfect, Paul's words would in no way involve *deixis* or any ambiguous contextual interpretation, say the mad interpretive leap the young man must make in Proverbs.

In a follow-up to his spiriting away of Wisdom, Paul takes her place. In Proverbs, Wisdom recalls how she stood next to Yahweh as a master builder herself when Yahweh laid the foundation of the earth: "when he appointed the foundations of the earth: / Then I was by him, *as* one brought up *with him*" (Proverbs 8.29–30). An alternate translation of the Hebrew "as one brought up with him" is: "as a master builder." In Christ, in Christ as Wisdom, Paul allows himself to think of himself as a master builder: "According to the grace of God which is given unto me, as a wise masterbuilder, I have laid the foundation, and another buildeth thereon" (1 Corinthians 3.10). The "foundation" Paul "laid" was "Jesus Christ" (3.11). The KJB English "wise masterbuilder" translates *sophos architekton*, a phrase Paul borrows from the Greek Isaiah 3.3 of the Septuagint and imports into his revision of Proverbs 8.29–30 in which he, Paul himself, becomes the master builder who lays a foundation. Having appropriated Wisdom to Christ, Paul takes her place as master builder to carry on his god's foundational work. Wisdom stood before Yahweh. Paul describes Christ becoming her while the perfect, in Christ as Wisdom, glory before Paul's god. Paul then replaces her. As chapter four will detail, Shakespeare echoes this replacement in *Othello*. Before Othello stands Desdemona. Iago demonizes her, splitting her in Othello's jealous imaginings between flesh and spirit. Iago then replaces her, espousing himself to his general: "I am your own for ever" (3.3.479). What Paul brings to Wisdom, her spiriting away, Iago brings to Desdemona. Iago manages to shift Desdemona from a fruitful partaker in the beginning to a divided being whose flesh Othello extinguishes to save her spirit. Shakespeare's recasting of Paul as Iago draws out the nihilistic violence toward Wisdom Paul's splitting of her across the spirit/flesh divide entails. Writing *Othello* brought Shakespeare to realizations almost too painful to bear, or so his later play *Cymbeline* implies, in which Shakespeare lets Desdemona live again and live on as the delightful Imogen. Shakespeare in *Cymbeline* diminishes Iago to Iachimo, a seducer who ultimately fails to ruin Imogen, who, vital and unitary like Desdemona, never suffers murder by a deceived and jealous lover raving of her division between "spirit" and "flesh."

Along with Paul's spiriting away of Wisdom in 1 Corinthians 1.17–3.23, the other major conjuration, revision, and exorcism of Wisdom in the New Testament takes place in the Gospel According to St. John, the gospel presenting Jesus as the incarnate Word, the Logos coeternal and consubstantial with the god John evokes. John calls his god "the Father," and the Word who becomes incarnate John calls the "Son" (1.14, 18). In John's gospel, parallels between the Word and Wisdom are extensive.[6] These parallels are most evident in John 1.1–18, the gospel's prologue, but such parallels are also evident in John's subsequent narrative of Jesus's career. The prologue describes the Word as existing in the beginning with the Father prior to the creation and as the agent by whom all of the creation was created (1.1–3); Proverbs describes Hokmah as existing in the beginning with Yahweh prior to the creation and as the agent inspiring Yahweh to do all his creating (8.22–23, 30). John has Jesus describe how he "proceeded forth […] from God," with the English "proceeded forth" translating Greek that can mean "born from" (8.42; see also 16.28). Hokmah says, "I was brought forth," that is, from Yahweh (Proverbs 8.24): "brought forth" translates Hebrew referring to a woman in the throes of childbirth. The Word brings life (John 1.4); Hokmah brings life (Proverbs 8.35). Through incarnation in the flesh, the Word moves from being (with) the Father to sojourning "among us" (John 1.14). Hokmah dances from Yahweh to delight amidst "the sons of men" (Proverbs 8.31). In John's narrative of Jesus's path to crucifixion, the Son describes himself and his relation to his Father in ways reminiscent of Hokmah and her relation to Yahweh. Praying to the Father, the Son says, "thou lovedst me before the foundation of the world" (John 17.24). Earlier in the same prayer, the Son asks,

"And now, O Father, glorify thou me with thine own self with the glory which I had with thee before the world was" (17.5). As Hokmah explains, "The Lord possessed me in the beginning of his way, before his works of old. [...] when he appointed the foundations of the earth: Then I was by him" (Proverbs 8.22, 29–30). As Hokmah was with Yahweh before the creation, the Son was with the Father "before the world was."

Yet John stages these various parallels only to replace Hokmah with the Word. And a separation and segregation of Folly from Wisdom, of her call from hers, of her words from hers, happens in John's gospel. Through this separation, Yahweh's daughter Hokmah disappears and the Father's Son appears, taking the place of the daughter, and, in taking her place, dividing her place: the delighting continuity of the beginning with the creation in Proverbs 8.22–31 John splits between a serene realm of being, home to the Father and Son, and a realm of becoming and desire, where the Son confronts the devil. In the beginning, Hokmah stands beside Yahweh as he lets the creation burgeon and proliferate, a burgeoning proliferation Yahweh initiates by birthing Hokmah, this birthing in effect the first instance of the "Let there be." In John, the Word operates qua fiat; through John, the "Let there be light" of Genesis stills into the *fiat lux*, a fiat standing above and beyond a cosmos prone to fallenness and given over to the devil.

Rewording Genesis 1.1–3 with reference to Proverbs 8.22–31, John insists that in the beginning, the Word, the Logos, was with the Father: "In the beginning was the Word [*logos*], and the Word was with God, and the Word was God. The same was in the beginning with God. All things were made by him; and without him was not any thing made that was made" (1.1–3). *Hokmah* is a feminine noun, *logos* a masculine. Proverbs states that, in the beginning, Yahweh's daughter was with Yahweh, and through her inspiration Yahweh created all that he did create, she being a master builder, like father like daughter. John states that, in the beginning, the Word was with the Father and was the Father, and by the Word all was made that did get made. Giving the Word, the Son who is the Father, all command over making, John precludes the feminine from the creation process, shunting Wisdom aside.

In Proverbs, Hokmah states she was there "in the beginning" with Yahweh. John insists "the Word" was there in the beginning: "The same was in the beginning with God." The god John invokes has one offspring only, a son, none other, much less a daughter: "And the Word was made flesh, and dwelt among us, (and we beheld his glory, the glory as of the only begotten of the Father,) full of grace and truth" (1.14). Besides the Son, the Father has no other offspring, no daughter at all. In the process of rewriting Genesis 1.1–3, of rewriting the beginning, John alludes to Proverbs 8.22–31 only to write Hokmah out of the beginning and to write the Logos into the beginning. Rather than a father and a daughter who were distinct, in the beginning were a god and a *logos* who were one. The Logos incarnates as Jesus, the Son. The Word incarnate manifests the Father amidst the world, with the Son a weird reverse periscope or ambulatory spy camera for the Father, who looks out upon the cosmos from the Son's eyes. John's Jesus states, "And he that seeth me seeth him that sent me" (12.45). Upon his incarnation, amidst the cosmos he created, the cosmos that fails to recognize him as the creator, the Word insists on his oneness with his father: "I and *my* Father are one" (10.30). John has Jesus repeatedly assert this oneness against the confusion and resistance of his interlocutors.

The KJB "only begotten" translates the Greek *monogenes*, which means more literally "of a single [*monos*] kind [*genos*]."[7] In translating *monogenes* as "only begotten," the KJB translators may have been following Jerome's Vulgate, which renders *monogenes* as *unigenitus* ("only begotten") to counter the Arian claim that the Son is a created being.[8] In response to the Arian notion of the Son as the highest creature, as the pinnacle of the creation the Father created, the fourth-century Nicene Creed reads John's *monogenes* as stating the Son's oneness with the Father:

> I believe in one God the Father Almighty; Maker of heaven and earth, and of all things visible and invisible. And in one Lord Jesus Christ, the only begotten [*monogenes*] Son of God, begotten of the Father before all worlds, [...] begotten, not made, being of one substance [*homoousios*] with the Father; by whom all things were made [...].[9]

The "one Lord Jesus Christ" was "begotten of his Father before all worlds," prior to the creation's creation, prior to the ages. The Creed thinks of this begetting as occurring amongst and never departing from the "one substance" the Father and the Son are. The Creed's somewhat odd alignment of a begetting with an eternal sameness does capture how John assimilates Yahweh's precreation birth of Hokmah to the preexistence of the Word with the Father, of the Son with the Father. Yet in this assimilation the fatherly-motherly process of some passion and passivity by which Yahweh births Hokmah in Proverbs gives way in John to an all-male, ever active assertion of being. In Proverbs, Hokmah reports, "The Lord possessed me in the beginning" (8.22). To state again: the English "possessed me" translates Hebrew referring to birth. "I was set up from everlasting" (8.23): "set up" translates Hebrew for creation by pouring, as by generative semen. "I was brought forth" (8.24): "brought forth" translates Hebrew referring to the writing of a woman in childbirth. This birth process, an event Yahweh lets happen to himself, suggests reading the various "Let there be" statements in Genesis 1 as indeed entailing a letting be, a relaxation into a fruitful eventfulness rich with surprise. Yahweh takes "delight" in Hokmah. Her "delight" in the creation and the men and women of the creation carries a playful, sportive connotation. The birth of Hokmah resembles the birth of Athena from Zeus at least insofar as in Athena's birth something happens to Zeus. And, in this regard, the birth of Hokmah even more resembles the birth of Sin from Satan in *Paradise Lost:* Sin's birth overtakes the archangel with surprise.

But in John, the Son's birth from the Father and the begetting of the Son by the Father must occur as entirely unsurprising to both, passional for neither nor events either passively undergoes. Rather than with a letting be, the birth and begetting of the Word comport with the "I am" assertions John has Jesus utter. In these assertions, Jesus repeatedly attempts to speak of his preexistent being to those blindly weltering in the cosmos or world, the realm of becoming. As Frank Kermode usefully explicates, in the three "was" statements of John 1.1, "In the beginning was the Word" and so on, "was" translates the Greek *en,* in John a word denoting eternal and unchanging being, whereas the words "were made" in John 1.3 ("All things were made by him") translate the Greek *egeneto* or "became."[10] In crossing from being (with) the Father to becoming incarnate in the world, the Word crosses from being into the becoming the Word made, though this realm of becoming does not recognize the Word (445). The being/becoming distinction of John 1.1–18 formats the narratives of the rest of the gospel: "the *ēn/egeneto* axis of the Prologue is also the armature of the stories and of the larger story" (452). Thus, in the various small narratives that make up the narrative of the gospel, Jesus often finds himself asserting the priority of his being over the cosmos of becoming where he sojourns as the incarnate Word. These assertions involve the famous *ego eimi* or "I am" declarations of John's Christ. The most startling of these declarations is: "Verily, verily, I say unto you, Before Abraham was, I am [*ego eimi*]" (John 8.58).

Jesus makes this statement in the course of his increasingly vitriolic statements "to those Jews which believed on him" (8.31). These hapless "Jews" Jesus assimilates to those the gospel depicts as homicidal toward him. Or, rather, his answers to these "Jews" drive them from "believ[ing] on him" to attempting to stone him to death. John writes these answers to gradually reveal an irreconcilable distinction in paternity between Jesus, Son of the Father, and the Jews, children of the devil. The "Jews" Jesus speaks with declare themselves Abraham's progeny, yet Jesus works this declaration toward his accusation that the devil is their father: "I know that ye are Abraham's seed; but ye seek to kill me, because my word hath no place in you. I speak that which I have seen with my Father: and ye do that which ye have seen with your father" (8.37–38). Flustered by this statement, the "Jews" then declare, "Abraham is our father" (8.39). Jesus tells them if Abraham were their father, they "would do the works of Abraham. But now ye seek to kill me" (8.39–40). In contrast, Abraham did not seek to kill divine messengers, Jesus notes (8.40). In their murderousness, which Jesus is in the process of inciting, the "Jews" show themselves taking after their father: "Ye do the deeds of your father" (8.41). The exasperated "Jews" deny any idolatrous deviation from their covenantal relation and genealogy: "We be not born of fornication; we have one Father, *even* God" (8.41). Yet in response to the ever more insistently pious answers of the "Jews," Jesus offers ever more provocative follow-ups. When the "Jews" claim to "have one Father, *even* God," Jesus replies: "If God were your Father, ye would love me [...]. Why do ye not understand my speech? *even* because ye cannot hear my word. Ye are of *your* father the devil [*diabolos*], and the lusts of your father ye will do" (8.42–44). To look at Jesus's father is to see serene truth (*aletheia*), but to look at the father of "the Jews" is to see lust and lie (*pseudos*) entangled. Between the Father and the Son, between the Word that was with the Father and the Word that was the Father, a completely transparent unity inheres. Those unreceptive to Jesus's "word" are the devil's progeny. Rather than the serenity and truth of the oneness of the Father and the Son, the devil as father comports with desires ("lusts," *epithymias*, inordinate desires), violence, and untruth: "He was a murderer from the beginning, and abode not in the truth, because there is no truth in him. When he speaketh a lie, he speaketh of his own: for he is a liar, and the father of it" (8.44). The energies of desire Proverbs associates with Yahweh and Hokmah become in John the "lusts" the devil inspires in his children.

The Son who displaces and replaces the daughter preaches an exit from desire. In the Hebrew Scriptures, explains Robert Alter, when a man encounters a foreign woman at a well, the scene often functions as a type-scene, in the case of encounters at wells a type-scene of betrothal.[11] When readers read of a Hebrew man encountering a non-Hebrew woman at a well, they may expect a betrothal to ensue, with the well an oblique reference to the woman's body. By narrating the Israelite Jesus, also known as "the bridegroom," as encountering a Samaritan woman at Jacob's well, John evokes the conventions of the betrothal scene (3.29). However, rather than woo the Samaritan woman into a marriage, or at least marriage "in the flesh," Jesus speaks to her of an end to the desire he then gently scolds her for vigorously pursuing. Readers learn that, like Chaucer's Wife of Bath, the Samaritan woman has had many husbands. To the Samaritan woman he encounters at Jacob's well, Jesus says anyone who drinks water drawn from the well "shall thirst again: but whosoever drinketh of the water that I shall give him shall never thirst" (4.13–14). The water the well offers quenches thirst; the water Jesus offers ends thirst. That the return of desire after any quenching is a subtext of Jesus's comments becomes clear after the woman asks him, "Sir, give me this water, that I thirst not, neither come hither to draw" (4.15). She wants some of the thirst-ending water so she will "thirst not" and never have to come to the well again "to draw." In terms of betrothal, she has gone to the well often:

> Jesus saith unto her, Go, call thy husband, and come hither. The woman answered and said, I have no husband. Jesus said unto her, Thou hast well said, I have no husband: For thou hast had five husbands; and he whom thou now hast is not thy husband: in that saidst thou truly. (4.16–18)

In saying, "Go, call thy husband," Jesus signals his disinterest in marrying the Samaritan woman, but she perhaps takes him to be performing a verbal equivalent of checking if she has a wedding ring on her finger. In saying, "I have no husband," does the Samaritan woman hint she would not mind meeting a potential husband at the well, as the type-scene context might prompt the reader to think? But Jesus exposes how she indeed has no husband in two ways: she *had* five and the man she has now is not her husband. In her having had five husbands, the Samaritan woman exemplifies how she "thirsts again" after each of the five. Like the Wife of Bath, this woman thirsts; she is now with a man not her husband. Jesus would redeem her from the water that quenches thirst by offering her the water that ends thirst. In the type-scenes in the Hebrew Scriptures, after the encounter with a man at a well, the woman hurries off home to her family to tell about the man and then the betrothal is arranged. After her encounter with Jesus, who tells her he is Christ the messiah, the Samaritan woman runs off to tell the men of the city about the messiah. In doing so, she significantly leaves behind her "waterpot": "The woman then left her waterpot, and went her way into the city, and saith to the men, Come, see a man, which told me all things that ever I did: is not this the Christ?" (4.28–29). Having believed on Christ, this woman will never require her "waterpot" again; she will return to the well no longer. To thirst or hunger again after drinking or eating characterizes those who died or who will die, whereas, promises the Son, "I am the bread of life: he that cometh to me shall never hunger; and he that believeth on me shall never thirst" (6.35). To "the Jews" who eat and hunger again, Jesus argues the "true bread" he is ends hunger, "not as [their] fathers did eat manna, and are dead: he that eateth of this bread shall live for ever" (6.32, 58).

To act upon the lusts their father the devil promotes would show "the Jews" to be opponents of Jesus, the ender of desire. Jesus calls the "Jews" progeny of the devil (*diabolos*). These "Jews" in turn claim a daemon inhabits Jesus: "Then answered the Jews, and said unto him, Say we not well that thou art a Samaritan, and hast a devil [*daimonion*]?" (8.48). Jesus explicitly and specifically denies any daemon inhabits him: "Jesus answered, I have not a devil [*daimonion*]; but I honour my Father, and ye do dishonour me" (8.49). Jesus then tells his interlocutors, "If a man keep my saying, he shall never see death" (8.51). This declaration seems a bit too much for the "Jews," who reply, "Now we know that thou hast a devil [*daimonion*]. Abraham is dead, and the prophets; and thou sayest, If a man keep my saying, he shall never taste of death. Art thou greater than our father Abraham, which is dead? [...] whom makest thou thyself?" (8.52–53). Jesus says, "[Abraham] rejoiced to see my day: he saw it, and was glad," leading the perplexed "Jews" to ask, "Thou art not yet fifty years old, and hast thou seen Abraham?" (8.56–57). This last question draws from Jesus his bold statement: "Verily, verily, I say unto you, Before Abraham was, I am [*ego eimi*]" (8.58). Hearing this, the "Jews" attempt to stone Jesus to death, but he slips away. In this attempted stoning, the "Jews" exhibit the murderousness Jesus accuses them of harboring. Those enmeshed in becoming, progeny of the devil, attempt to murder he who embodies divine being, the divine being, the Father. And the devil's progeny attempt this murder specifically in response to Jesus's claim of being. In moving from the beginning into the cosmos, the Word crosses from being into becoming, where his manifestations and declarations of being meet with misunderstanding and violence.

In Proverbs 8, from the place before place of the beginning, the place of her birth prior to the creation, Hokmah moves easily toward and amidst the creation. She exists with Yahweh prior to his acts of creation, she cavorts before him during his creating, and then she rejoices with him and with "the sons of men": "Then I was by him, *as* one brought up *with him:* and I was daily *his* delight, rejoicing always before him; Rejoicing in the habitable part of his earth; and my delights *were* with the sons of men" (Proverbs 8.30–31). The Hebrew the KJB translates as "rejoicing" refers also to laughter, play, and dancing. The Hebrew translated as "delight" derives from a word suggestive of light-hearted sensuality. A continuity of rejoicing and delight extends from Hokmah standing before Yahweh through her sojourn to the "habitable part of his earth" and among "the sons of men." In traveling from Yahweh's side to the "sons of men," Hokmah crosses no divide between being and becoming or between spirit and flesh or between truth and lies, nor does she leave an esteemed realm for a disesteemed realm. The move from Yahweh to the sons of men entails no suffering on Hokmah's part. To the contrary, Hokmah goes from rejoicing and delight to rejoicing and delight.

In moving from being (with) the Father to being among men, the Word crosses a divide between being and becoming and moves from an esteemed realm of spirit and truth into a disesteemed realm of the flesh and lies. The incarnation of the Word already implies Christ's suffering unto death on the cross, though of all the gospels John minimizes this suffering or rather has Jesus on the cross declare he acts out suffering to fulfill scripture. On the cross he says he suffers from thirst, but with the implication that thirst, for example, never could afflict the Word as the Word (19.28). Mark's Jesus on the cross cries out, "My God, my God, why hast thou forsaken me?" (15.34). John's Jesus makes no such cry and remains much more in control: "When Jesus therefore had received the vinegar, he said, It is finished: and he bowed his head, and gave up the ghost" (19.30). A reader might ask, just how much passion does John's Jesus undergo in John's telling of the passion? Passion defines the states foreign to the Father the Son is, as much in the begetting of the Son by the Father as in the death of the Son on the cross. Rather, desires or "lusts" are of the devil and of the cosmos or world in its unredeemed state.

In John, the abjection of the passionate and passive aspects of "begetting," and the implicit pushing away of any such from the Logos except in crucifixion, gives insight into the Gnostic Christians' narrations of how, in moving from the *pleroma* (the realm above) to the *kenoma* (the realm below), Sophia undergoes misadventures with passion, begetting, and creation. That an abjection of Hokmah's delight, read as passion, runs through John as a subtext of the Son's promotion finds striking confirmation in Gnostic interpretations of and appropriations from John's gospel. In John, Jesus insists his father resides outside and above the cosmos while the father of the Jews ranges amidst the cosmos after its creation. The Gnostics interpretively elaborated this contrast as their distinction between the true father at home amidst a fullness, a realm of spirit the Gnostic writings call the *pleroma*, in contrast to the god of the Hebrew Scriptures, whom the Gnostics cast as the demiurge who made the fallen cosmos, what Genesis narrates as Yahweh letting the creation burgeon. In the complex Gnostic array of divine entities, Sophia appears as the last of twelve aeons or divine emanations, and she undergoes a splitting into an "upper" and a "lower" Wisdom the Gnostics allocate across the dualistic Gnostic cosmography. The aeons come in pairs. But, like Milton's Eve wandering away from Adam, precisely the aeon Sophia provokes a crisis, specifically by undergoing passion on her own, without her partner-aeon "the wished for."

Writing in about 180 CE, the proto-orthodox Christian Irenaeus, in his *Against Heresies*, reports the extravagant career of Sophia as detailed by Ptolemy, a student of the eminent Gnostic Valentinus. According to Ptolemy as reported by Irenaeus, the "only-begotten" alone is fully "acquainted with the ancestor," the Father, the true god resident in the *pleroma*.[12] The various aeons long to see the Father, but only Sophia, on her own, rashly attempts to force her way into his sight. She "charged forward and experienced passion without the involvement of her consort, the wished-for" (283). Though this "passion originated in the region of intellect and truth," it "collected" in Sophia (283). "The passion consisted of a search for the parent" (283). In seeking to "comprehend" the Father's "magnitude," Sophia recklessly sought "to accomplish the impossible" (283). Having plunged toward the Father, Sophia suffers repulse by the inner boundary encircling him, so she "turned back to herself" (284). In this turning back, Sophia puts off her thinking and passion, and these then become or become characteristics of her offspring, Achamoth. Sophia's thinking and passion, shunted outward and downward from the *pleroma*, become Achamoth's or become Achamoth, who then becomes separated from the *pleroma* by an outer boundary. Because her collision with the inner boundary results in the purgation from her of thought and passion, Sophia remains within the *pleroma*.

The generation from Sophia of Achamoth stages a revaluation and a reversal. The Hebrew book of Proverbs and Hokmah precede the Septuagint's translation of Hokmah into Greek as Sophia. However, Ptolemy imagines the reversal of this precedence. In Ptolemy's thought as reported by Irenaeus, the name Achamoth renders the Hebrew *hokmah* from Proverbs, that is, Hokmah. The Hebrew Proverbs and Hokmah enjoy an irreversible priority vis-à-vis the Septuagint, Sophia, and any Gnostic narrative of Sophia. However, in narrating his Sophia as existing prior to and birthing Achamoth, Ptolemy seeks in imagination what never shall occur in actuality: the priority of Sophia in relation to Hokmah.

Rather than as simply temporal, this priority Ptolemy imagines as the priority of the timeless and perfect in relation to the time-bound and imperfect. In the fullness, the *pleroma*, Sophia participates in perfection, at least until thought and passion recklessly break out in her. She regains her place in the *pleroma* when the inner boundary stops her in her ardent, solitary plunging toward the Father. This boundary repairs her: "By this boundary—they say—wisdom (Sophia) was purified, established, and restored to membership in a pair" (284). When the inner boundary halts Sophia, saving her from being "dissolved into universal essence," her thought and passion fall outward and downward from the *pleroma* into and as her offspring, Achamoth (284). Ptolemy's imaginings make explicit the abjection of Hokmah and her delight implicit in John. Achamoth and her passion undergo exile from the *pleroma*. What Proverbs exalts, Hokmah delighting before Yahweh and delighting him, Ptolemy revalues and revises as Sophia in passion falling at the Father and then her passion falling from the *pleroma* as the "lower" wisdom or Achamoth. Wandering past the outer boundary of the *pleroma*, Achamoth enters "a region of shadow and emptiness" where she desperately seeks after "the light that had left her" but that she cannot regain, being "prevented by the [outer] boundary" (288, 289). The "light," the "anointed," is Christ (289, 288). As the inner boundary prevented Sophia from gaining the Father and the innermost heart of the *pleroma*, so the outer boundary prevents Achamoth from gaining the Son and the outermost edge of the *pleroma*. Again, passion takes the blame: "[Achamoth] was unable to pass through the boundary since she was involved with passion" (289). Her situation only exacerbates her embroilment with passion: "left outside and alone, she became subject to every aspect of manifold and diverse passion" (289).

Halted by a boundary posing an impasse to her passion, Sophia turns back and undergoes repair while her passion then falls outward and downward. A boundary also halts Achamoth and poses an impasse to her passion, but this boundary multiplies her passion beyond a yearning to regain the *pleroma* and into grief, fear, and uncertainty (289). Like Sophia, Achamoth turns back. Sophia's turning back sends thought and passion from the *pleroma*. Achamoth's turning back has the disastrous result of bringing about matter and the offspring of Achamoth, the demiurge or "craftsman": "She— they say—accounts for the genesis and essence of the matter out of which this world came into being. For, the entire soul of the world and the craftsman had its origination in her turning back" (289). Here Ptolemy seeks another reversal. In Proverbs, the fatherly/motherly Yahweh gives birth to Hokmah, the master builder. Ptolemy has Achamoth bring forth the craftsman, the demiurge, that is, Yahweh: the Yahweh Hokmah inspired to let the creation burgeon. Ptolemy imagines *him* as *her* offspring. That Achamoth instigates the demiurge's making of the lower realm suggests Ptolemy reads the Hokmah of Proverbs as inspiring Yahweh in his letting the creation be. This demiurge builds the lower realm without any idea of what he is doing: "For he made a heaven without knowing about heaven, modeled a human being without being acquainted with the human being, and showed forth earth without knowing earth" (291). That is, in all his makings, the demiurge proceeds "unacquainted [...] with the ideal forms of the things he was making" (291). These quasi-Platonic "ideal forms" reside in the *pleroma* and together constitute the upper realm; the demiurge proceeds in ignorance of the "ideal forms" and so botches all his makings. Yet these botchings together are the creation Genesis narrates burgeoning through the Genesis god's lettings. Genesis narrating Yahweh letting the creation burgeon out into differentiation tells of an utterly non-Platonic event, thoroughly distinct from the relative formal and logical coherence of a changing realm below deriving solely from and dimly replicating the complete formal and logical coherence of a changeless realm above. Ptolemy's scorn of the letting burgeon Genesis narrates, Ptolemy's scorn for the creation and of the Yahweh whom Hokmah inspired to let the creation burgeon, ironically serves as a sharp reminder of how drastically inassimilable to Platonism Genesis remains. The demiurge and his botchings result from Achamoth's passions, and these passions and Achamoth derive from the passion of Sophia. Though the thinking Achamoth is does derive from an aeon, Sophia, and so is "a spiritual essence," this thinking, and so Achamoth and her passion, "had not comprehended anything. And—they say—for this reason it was a weak and female fruit" (285). Yahweh as the demiurge undergoes scorn and so does Achamoth and thus Hokmah.

In Proverbs, Hokmah associates with the beginning, and Folly associates with Sheol. Ptolemy reworks the beginning. Rather than telling how Hokmah stands by Yahweh, Ptolemy tells how Sophia kicks over the traces in an exorbitant attempt to see the Father, to be with the Father, a privilege Ptolemy reserves for the "only begotten." Imagining the abode of the Father and the "only begotten," John purges the beginning of the burgeoning fruitfulness the beginning entails when Yahweh births Hokmah. Ptolemy's beginning resembles John's, only even more Platonized: "Within invisible and unnameable heights there was—they say—a preexistent, perfect entity [...]. And it existed uncontained, invisible, everlasting, and unengendered" (281). As Sophia undergoes the purgation of her passion, Achamoth comes to resemble Folly, at least insofar as, when thrown out and down from the *pleroma*, Achamoth lands in a nonplace that resembles Sheol: "a region of shadow and emptiness" (288). Ptolemy's separating out Achamoth from Sophia would enact a version of separating Folly from Wisdom, separating her word from hers. Such a separation is implicit in John, say along the demarcation John presumes separates truth from lie, *aletheia* from *pseudos*. In John, while taking Hokmah's place, the Word as a word may never harbor the ambiguity of Hokmah and Folly's "Whoso *is* simple, let him turn in hither." However, the roles of Sophia and Achamoth in Ptolemy's sketch of the Gnostic myth do harbor some intriguing ambiguities. Sophia emerges as the most sympathetic character, and the reader tends to identify with her or her plight. Her bold attempt at the impossible, to know the Gnostic deity, makes her a heroine, a heroine of passion and passionate thought.

After Proverbs, Paul, John, and the Gnostics, Wisdom's path toward Shakespeare, Milton, Melville, and Florian goes through *The Consolation of Philosophy* by Boethius, who depicts Wisdom through Athena. In 523 CE, the Ostrogoth ruler of the Roman Empire's collapsed western half, Theodoric the Great, brought a dubious charge of treason against the renowned Christian scholar and eminent Roman statesman Boethius. Theodoric imprisoned Boethius and, a year or so later, ordered his torture and execution. While imprisoned in exile, Boethius composed *The Consolation of Philosophy*, a work to become highly influential on medieval thought and on European and English literature. In the *Consolation*, Boethius dramatizes his encounter as a prisoner with *Philosophia*, Lady Philosophy. The author Boethius has the character Boethius speak mournfully to Lady Philosophy about his unexpected and seemingly unwarranted fate at the hands of Fortune. Lady Philosophy speaks consolingly to Boethius of the "One Father" in whose providence all apparently unjust turns of Fortune's wheel find their justification: "All men on earth from one source take their rise; / One Father of the world all things supplies," including wisdom (50). This "One Father" would be the father of Lady Philosophy herself. In colloquy with the daughter, Boethius gleans the wisdom emanating from the father. Lady Philosophy manifests her father's wisdom to Boethius.

The encounter of Boethius during his imprisonment with Lady Philosophy, the intervention into his narrow, world-bound captivity of her overwhelming, numinous, superlunary yet sensible personhood, appears fantastic, an extravagant literary fiction Boethius sets in the *mise en scène* of his imprisonment to lend drama to his didactic effort to justify the ways of his Neo-Platonic god. Yet Lady Philosophy's embodiment for Boethius of the wisdom of the "One Father" finds a striking parallel in the sublunary, mundane world when Lady Philosophy evokes Boethius's wife Rusticiana and her father, Boethius's foster father the Roman aristocrat, statesman, and Christian Quintus Aurelius Memmius Symmachus. A year after the execution of Boethius, Theodoric executed Symmachus for treason.

To help persuade Boethius to acknowledge the "blessings" of his life despite his imprisonment, Lady Philosophy says to him: "Consider first the undiminished vigour of your father-in-law Symmachus, that glory of the human race beyond price. You would readily give your life to be that total personification of wisdom [*sapientia*] and the virtues that he embodies" (25). Foster father to Boethius and father to the wife of Boethius, Symmachus "embodies" the complete personification of wisdom, argues Lady Philosophy. And, Lady Philosophy insists, in Rusticiana Boethius may encounter the very image of Symmachus: "To sum up all her attributes in a single phrase, she is the image of her father [*patri similis*]" (25–26). The father gathers the traits and wholly embodies or personifies wisdom; in the total confluence of her "attributes," the daughter images the father, so in imaging the father, the daughter images wisdom. And since the father manifests wisdom, the father images the daughter. Boethius could hear from Rusticiana what John's Christ asserts: to see me is to see my father. Symmachus could say to Boethius: to see me is to see my daughter.

Through the daughter Lady Philosophy is, Boethius will come to know her father, the "One Father," and in him Boethius will find wisdom. To attain this apotheosis of wisdom ultimately requires Boethius to welcome perishing and indeed to perish, though the *Consolation* opens with Lady Philosophy chasing away the muses of poetry whom she finds gathering around Boethius and inspiring him to write melancholic verses, including a wish for death: "Alas, Death turns deaf ears to my sad cries, / And cruel, will not close my weeping eyes" (3). The yearning for his earthly existence to end never leaves Boethius; rather, this yearning undergoes revaluation. Rather than sorrow at his fate, Lady Philosophy would reason Boethius into perishing to the earth joyfully as a transition to the "One Father." From start to finish, the *Consolation* orients toward perishing. The dialog ponders how to perish: mournfully as toward an unjust and chaotic fate or joyfully as toward just and orderly providence? By demonstrating fate wholly conforms to providence, Lady Philosophy would collapse the first alternative into an illusory indulgence in theatrics.

The acceptance of life's end, the willingness to perish, as by state execution, orients both the small narrative of Boethius's identification with his father in law and the larger narrative of Boethius's destiny to unite with the "One Father," amplifying the uncanny echoes between the two cases of a daughter imaging her father insofar as he manifests wisdom, the case of Symmachus and his daughter and the case of the "One Father" and Lady Philosophy. Lady Philosophy points out that Boethius would "readily give [his] life to be that total personification of wisdom" his father in law is, just as the drift of Boethius's colloquies with Lady Philosophy moves Boethius toward reconciling himself to his impending death as the transition to joining the "One Father." Lady Philosophy acts as a daemon turning Boethius away from the melancholy the poetic muses foster and exalting him toward his proper end: the happiness of dying toward the "One Father" who is the highest good. In checking an affect orienting Boethius toward an ignoble end, Lady Philosophy does for Boethius what Athena does for Achilles.

Boethius's echoes of the *Iliad* tie Lady Philosophy to Athena. As with the immortals generally in the *Iliad*, the stature of Athena may vary drastically: she may manifest in proportions similar to a mortal's, but she may also tower. In this manner, Homer describes Strife, "only a slight thing when she first rears her head / but her head soon hits the sky as she strides across the earth" (4.513–14). Just so does Boethius describe Lady Philosophy in her divergent statures:

> Her height was hard to determine, for it varied; at one moment she confined herself to normal human dimensions, but at another the crown of her head seemed to strike the heavens, and when she raised it still higher, it even broke through the sky, frustrating the gaze of those who observed her. (3–4)

Boethius associates Lady Philosophy with armor and warfare, and of course Athena springs from Zeus's head a fully armed warrior (6, 7).

The *Iliad* describes Athena as "fiery-eyed" (4.510). Athena's eyes blaze when she wings down from Olympus to check the rage of Achilles: "Rearing behind him Pallas seized his fiery hair—/ [. . .] he knew her at once, / Pallas Athena! the terrible blazing of those eyes" (1.232–35). To check the despair of Boethius, and to prevent him from finishing the melancholic poem the muses of poetry inspire in him, Lady Philosophy wings down from the Father and stations herself above Boethius: "My dutiful pen was putting the last touches to my tearful lament, when a lady seemed to position herself above my head" (3). Boethius describes her as "most awe-inspiring to look at" due to "her glowing eyes" (3). As Athena is to Achilles, Lady Philosophy is to Boethius. The association of Boethius with Achilles finds confirmation when, in Greek, Lady Philosophy quotes the request Thetis poses to Achilles to explain his tears. At the shore before the endless waves, her son weeps over losing Briseis. Thetis to Achilles: "Tell me, please. Don't harbor it deep inside you" (1.429–30). Lady Philosophy to Boethius, with her *Iliad* quote in italics: "Why are you weeping, with the tears running down your cheeks? *Out with it, nor hold it fast within your breast*" (8). Achilles has lost Briseis to the fortunes of war, and he feels loath to recount the whole shameful business to his mother: "You know, you know, / why labor through it all?" (1.431–32). Just so, in answer to Lady Philosophy's request that he explain his tears, Boethius replies by asking if he must recount his losses at the hands of Fortune: "Do I need to keep reminding you? Is not Fortune's harsh and cruel treatment of me self-evident?" (8).

Both Athena and Lady Philosophy intervene to redirect their charges from an inauthentic to an authentic destiny. Boethius describes how Lady Philosophy has "come gliding down from the pole of heaven to visit [him] in the solitude of [his] exile" (6). From the heights where the immortals reside, Athena descends to the mortals' realm to check Achilles's rage so the hero may shun taking revenge on Agamemnon, reject the fate of returning home from the siege, and embrace the fate of battling Hector and dying soon after. The two fate-options of Achilles, to return home or to die soon after killing Hector, fuse in the *Consolation*. As an Athena, Lady Philosophy would teach Boethius to embrace a return home to the Father through dying.

To guide Boethius toward his home, Lady Philosophy must teach him to discern between the apparent chaos of Fortune, with demise a last sinking into fate, and the order of providence leading upward toward the Father, with the Father, his oneness, and his goodness a home beckoning from beyond death. Boethius must learn to distinguish between the immediate sorrows of his fate and the eternal happiness awaiting him. In the *Iliad*, so Diomedes may in battle discern between mortals and immortals, Athena removes a mist from his eyes: "Look, I've lifted the mist from off your eyes / that's blurred them up to now—/ so you can tell a god from man on sight" (5.140–42). In the *Consolation*, the muses of poetry help suffuse Boethius's eyes with tears ("Sad verses flood my cheeks with tears unfeigned" [3]). So Boethius may recognize Lady Philosophy, distinguish amidst fate's seeming randomness the orderly workings of providence, and through a Platonic anamnesis remember who he is and where his home is (with the Father as the highest good), Lady Philosophy clears the mist of melancholic poetic tears from his eyes. Lady Philosophy declares, "He has forgotten for the moment who he is, but he will soon remember once he has identified me first. To help him in this, I must spend a moment wiping his eyes, for the darkness of his mortal concerns has clouded them" (6). Boethius: "With these words she puckered her dress, and dried my eyes, which were bathed in tears" (6).

However much Boethius associates Lady Philosophy with Athena, he revalues and redefines Zeus's wild daughter in the process of refashioning her as Lady Philosophy. The *Iliad* mentions Athena's ability as a weaver (14.218). In the *Metamorphoses*, Ovid narrates Minerva engaging Arachne in a weaving contest (5.1–142). With her own hands, states Boethius, Lady Philosophy wove her own garment, a robe (4). A taming of Homer's Athena kicks in when Boethius describes Lady Philosophy as weaving and wearing a robe. The *Iliad* consistently portrays weaving as women's domestic work and associates the loom with the acquiescence of women to their subjection within domesticity (1.33–36, 6.542–46, 6.585–87, 13.497–500). In the *Iliad,* Athena refuses the gift the Trojans offer her: a woven robe significant of the constrictive situating of women in domestic life (6.338–66). Instead, Athena takes up her father's storm shield and revels in battle. When Boethius narrates his Athena, Lady Philosophy, as weaving and wearing a robe, he withholds from her the wildness of Homer's Athena. Something of this wildness shifts onto the poetic muses.

The *Consolation* begins with Boethius composing verses inspired by the muses of poetry who gather to stand resolutely by him: "Sad verses flood my cheeks with tears unfeigned; / The Muses who inspire me are blood-stained. / Yet they at least were not deterred by dread; / They still attend me on the path I tread" (3). Previous to his imprisonment, Boethius had "penned songs in happier days," and the poetic muses were with him (3). These muses stick with Boethius even as he walks toward his perishing as a prisoner falsely condemned: they cross a threshold of "dread" with him. Boethius indicates the muses stayed with him as he passed the border toward his irreversible fate; these muses "were not deterred by dread." The glory of his youth, his muses now stand by him as he undergoes his fate: "I gloried in them, in my youth's full spate; / In sad old age they now console my fate" (3). His muses will accompany him to the very end, the culmination of his fate in his execution.

Lady Philosophy too would inspire and accompany Boethius toward a final culmination, but this ultimately would be demise as a happy ending, a final and uplifting transit from the earthly to the heavenly: "Once earth is overcome, the stars are yours for taking" (96). Lady Philosophy must shift Boethius from his melancholic meditation on fate toward a sanguine awareness of providence. If she can achieve this shift in him, he will learn to fly above and beyond the earth: "For I have wings equipped to fly / Up to the high vault of the sky. / Once these are harnessed, your swift mind / Views earth with loathing, far behind" (72). To shift the prisoner's orientation from the mutable, fate-bound earth to the providential heights of the sky, Lady Philosophy must chase away the muses who draw melancholy song from Boethius. These muses are her antagonists, however puny they may appear when they flee her wrath. A source for the conflict between Lady Philosophy and the muses of poetry may be Ovid's narration in the *Metamorphoses* of a status distinction between Minerva and the muses. When Minerva visits the muses on Helicon, a muse tells her, "Had not thy valour, Pallas, led thee on / To greater tasks, thou wouldest be numbered with / Our company" (5.72–74). Ovid implies Minerva is higher than the muses.

Lady Philosophy sweeps down upon the poetic muses from above and interrupts them in their feeding of Boethius's melancholy. When, obedient to his muses, Boethius is about to complete his mournful, self-elegiac poem, Lady Philosophy appears *above:* "My dutiful pen was putting the last touches to my tearful lament, when a lady seemed to position herself above my head" (3). Lady Philosophy turns her fiery eyes upon the poetic muses: "Her eyes lit on the Muses of poetry, who were standing by my couch, furnishing words to articulate my grief. For a moment she showed irritation; she frowned, and fire flashed from her eyes" (4). A reader of Plato, such as the aspiring translator of Plato Boethius, might take the "couch" in question for that famous piece of furniture in Plato's *Republic* Socrates casts as the mutable sensible exemplar of the far distant and immutable *idea* "couch." The muses gather around the sublunary couch on which the prostrate Boethius directs his gaze down, earthward. Adjacent the couch, their feet on the ground, the muses ply Boethius with "words to articulate [his] grief." Lady Philosophy excoriates these muses as seducing mummers who supply Boethius with sweet but poisonous words: "'Who,' she asked, 'has allowed these harlots of the stage to approach this sick man? Not only do they afford no remedies to relieve his pains, but their succulent poisons intensify them" (4). Lady Philosophy accuses the poetic muses of crowding Boethius with emotions and stifling his reason: "These ladies with their thorns of emotions choke the life from the fruitful harvest of reason" (4). She is particularly upset with the muses for "seducing" someone who "has been nurtured on the learning of the Eleatics and of the Academy," the schools of Parmenides and Plato, respectively (4). Lady Philosophy then lays into the muses with fierce and condemning words. She denounces the poetic muses as "Sirens," beastly bird-clawed females with human faces who sing the unwary toward death as a dead end rather than as a transition toward an upper, higher, and eternal realm: "Off with you, you Sirens! Your charms entice men to their destruction. Leave him to be tended and healed with the help of the Muses that attend me" (4). Lady Philosophy will later quote from Euripides, who in his play *Helen* has Helen call upon the Sirens as muses for her mournful and bitter words, Sirens who will sympathize with her sadness, Sirens Helen calls "deathly Daughters of the earth."[13] Euripides's Helen thinks of the Sirens very much as Boethius's Lady Philosophy thinks of the muses of poetry. The earth-bound melancholy the muses of poetry cultivate in Boethius Lady Philosophy defines as a seduction outward from reason, downward to the passions, and ending in dissolution. In relation to passion, these muses resemble the lower wisdom of the

Gnostics, while Lady Philosophy resembles the upper wisdom, Sophia cleansed of passion.

The melancholic Boethius praises the resolve of his muses, their courage to accompany him despite "dread." Yet these very muses abandon him when Lady Philosophy rebukes them as shameful panderers of passion. Even death these muses could walk toward, yet chastised by the fierce Lady Philosophy, they shamefacedly skulk away from Boethius: "At [her] rebuke the band of Muses rather gloomily trained their gaze upon the ground, and blushes proclaimed their shame as they dejectedly left the chamber" (4). Lady Philosophy exercises an "imperious authority" in chasing the muses of poetry away to supplant them with the "Muses that attend" her (4). Boethius here reworks the distinction Plato has Socrates make in the *Republic* between muses beholden to pleasure and muses beholden to reason and truth. In discussing Homer as an educator, to Glaucon Socrates insists, "And if you admit [to the city] the sweetened muse in lyrics or epics, pleasure and pain will jointly be kings in your city instead of law and that argument which in each instance is best in the opinion of the community."[14] Lady Philosophy will seek to prevent Boethius from allowing the pleasures and pains subject to fortune to guide his thinking. Plato calls the muse of lyric and epic poetry "sweetened." Lady Philosophy declares the elegiac or tragic words the muses of poetry offer Boethius sweet ("dulcibus") yet poisonous. As an alternate to the "sweetened muse," Socrates evokes "the true Muse accompanied by arguments and philosophy" (548b). Rather than any female companions, the only muses accompanying Lady Philosophy are her "arguments and philosophy," and especially those arguments achieving in Boethius a work of memory or anamnesis, the recollection by the soul of the knowledge of the highest good the soul forgot upon its birth into the body and the sublunary realm. Lady Philosophy states "Plato's Muse" inspires such anamnesis: "Indeed, if Plato's Muse sounds forth the truth, / What each man learns, forgetful he recalls" (65).

Lady Philosophy's denunciation of the muses of poetry as "harlots of the stage," as *scenicas meretriculas*, carries a Platonic resonance. English translators have variously rendered Lady Philosophy's phrase *scenicas meretriculas*. Chaucer translates the phrase at generous length: "comune strumpettis of swich a place that men clepen the theatre."[15] In her translation, Queen Elizabeth the First prefers concision: "stagis harlotz."[16] W. V. Cooper gives the reader "seducing mummers," a mummer being a roving, farcical, and costumed pantomime.[17] That a mummer might mime all moods or persons, however disparate, acting a sanguine milkmaid in one scene and a choleric queen the next, would upset Plato by fostering a taste for fluid, divergent manyness rather than a reasoned preference for stable, unitary oneness. In the phrase *scenicas meretriculas*, Lady Philosophy denounces the muses as devious seducers, as females of multiply layered surfaces, simulacra upon simulacra. A painted woman even before donning any theatrical mask or theatrical makeup, a harlot manipulates deceptive sensations, as do the muses of poetry, their words tasting sweet yet being poisonous. As "Sirens," these muses exhibit "charms" but only to "entice men to their destruction" (4). Now locate these "harlots" on a "stage," an arena for simulations, and contemplate these muses, already deceptive appearances, traipsing about a theatric *mise en scène:* in Lady Philosophy's phrase *scenicas meretriculas* sounds the Platonic denunciation of the stage as promoting desire's proliferation. The hapless who wander into the theater view copies of copies, mutable and multiple, far removed from and dissembling ideas or forms, not to mention leading the theatergoer further away from the good: the unchanging, one, and highest form. The muses of poetry as theatrical harlots indulge and reinforce the part of the self or soul vulnerable to passions and desires. A kind of hydra, this part of the soul Socrates calls "beastly," a "many-colored, many-headed beast" in which "all the desires, pains, and pleasures" throng and which must be "held down by force" and "ruled" (571c, 588c, 606d, 606a, 606d). Lady Philosophy must chase away the muses of poetry if she is to help Boethius to rule the passion-receptive aspect of his soul aware of Fortune's turns as only cruel caprices. Once Lady Philosophy drives the poetic muses away, she may teach Boethius again to embrace the aspect of his soul open to reason; Boethius can then follow her reasoning up toward the realm of the One and gain the perspective revelatory of providence working through fortune.

Confronted with Lady Philosophy's scornful words, fiery eyes, and command to be gone, the muses of poetry walk meekly and ashamedly away, their eyes directed to the ground, to the earth. His melancholic words gone silent with his abandonment by the muses of poetry, Boethius too looks downward: "I was struck dumb, and with downcast eyes I began silently to await her next course of action" (4). Where the muses of poetry were, standing about Boethius's couch, now Lady Philosophy is: "Then she drew nearer, and sat at the foot of my couch" (4). While the muses of poetry fed Boethius's melancholy, and in effect drew his gaze more and more earthward, Lady Philosophy, observing the downward gaze of Boethius, laments rather than reinforces his corresponding mental state: "She gazed on my face, which was heavy with grief and bowed to the ground with sorrow, and she lamented my distress of mind in these lines" (4). The lines of Lady Philosophy's first poem bewail how the mind of Boethius, "[a]bandoning its native light," turns toward the "steep depths below" and "purposes to go / Into the darkness of despond" (5). While the free Boethius roamed "[b]eneath the open sky" to study "heaven's domain," the imprisoned Boethius, seduced by the muses of poetry, his "mental vision dulled," "trains his downward gaze / Upon the insensate ground" (5). The muses of poetry drew his gaze downward. Lady Philosophy will strive to draw his gaze upward.

The *Consolation* variously and overtly associates Lady Philosophy with Athena. But Boethius also associates her with Wisdom. In the *Consolation,* Boethius operates almost exclusively without overt Christian or biblical imagery or allusions. However, the most direct biblical allusion Boethius makes evokes the following words from the Wisdom of Solomon: "Wisdom reacheth from one end to another mightily: and sweetly doth she order all things" (8.1). Boethius may be alluding to Wisdom 8.1 by way of the Latin Advent Antiphon sung in praise of Wisdom: "O Wisdom [Sapientia], coming forth from the mouth of the Most

High, / reaching from one end to the other mightily, / and sweetly ordering all things: / Come and teach us the way of prudence."[18] This Antiphon would have given Boethius the association of Wisdom with patient teaching, such as Lady Philosophy exhibits in working with her initially melancholic charge.

In rewriting Wisdom 8.1 perhaps by way of the Antiphon, Boethius aligns Wisdom with the highest good or *summum bonum* she and Boethius are discussing. Lady Philosophy to Boethius, echoing Wisdom 8.1 and/or the Antiphon: "So God is the highest good which governs all things powerfully, and orders them sweetly" (67). The translator here has Boethius identify the *summum bonum* or "highest good" Lady Philosophy mentions with "God," though the texts to which Boethius alludes are about Wisdom: Wisdom 8.1 is in reference to Wisdom and the Antiphon explicitly names her. In the father wisdom shows forth entirely, and in the daughter shines the very image of the father, so this substitution of father for daughter makes sense. However, the common medium or place the two inhabit in substitution emerges as anonymous and neuter. The Latin of the Vulgate Wisdom 8.1 is gender inflected female, treating of Wisdom, as is the Latin of the Antiphon. The lines of Boethius about his deity and leading up to his allusion to Wisdom 8.1 are gender inflected male, treating of the Father or "deo." The Latin in Lady Philosophy's Wisdom 8.1 allusion is gender neutral, treating of a neuter usage of the phrase *summum bonum*. Thus the anonymous 1609 English translation (signed only "I.T.") sticks close to the Latin and renders the line's opening word *est* (there is) emphasizing the neuter "it": "It is then the sovereign goodness which governeth all things strongly, and disposeth them sweetly."[19] In the anonymous, neuter *summum bonum*, the Father and Wisdom converge toward their oneness.

Boethius too would enter this oneness. The flight up toward the *summum bonum* would take Boethius ever more toward a unity ever more a perfect oneness, and this oneness orders providence, which then itself would be a mode of oneness. The apparent randomness of Fortune that Boethius laments increasingly disappears the more Boethius attains a vision of providence. To claim Boethius enacts a separation of Folly from Wisdom, of her word from hers, is tempting. In Lady Philosophy, Boethius brings forth his reimagining of Wisdom, and does not Fortune read as his reimagining of Folly? Or are the muses of poetry more Boethius's Folly? Lady Philosophy implies such: in turning away from the poetic muses and the earth and toward Lady Philosophy and the sky, Boethius turns from folly to wisdom.

In Boethius's *In Ciceronis Topica*, Boethius's treatise on Cicero's treatment of the deployment of *topoi* in rhetoric and logic, Boethius does indeed seem to argue for a separation between folly and wisdom. Cicero, Boethius explains, defined various relations between contraries. "Adverse contraries are those which are located within one genus and yet differ."[20] For example, though both belong to "one genus, namely, *color*," "white and black are very different from one another" (120). But another type of adverse contraries are those belonging to separate genera: "Those things that lie in different genera and are understood to diverge widely from one another, such as wisdom and folly, are also said to be adverse contraries, for wisdom is under the genus of *the good* and folly is under the genus of *the bad*" (120). Were Boethius to have located wisdom and folly as adverse contraries under a single genus, his thought might be more in attune with or resonant with Proverbs. But when he specifies that wisdom and folly are adverse contraries belonging to separate genera, he moves toward a separation of wisdom from folly. This separation only becomes more explicit when Boethius then ponders redefining wisdom and folly as privating contraries rather than as adverse contraries. The relation between contraries involves privation when a given contrary constitutes the privation of the other, as with "nobility and baseness": baseness is a privation of nobility (119). And thus, immediately after wondering if wisdom and folly should be thought of as adverse contraries belonging to distinct genera, Boethius then considers them as examples of privation: "for folly is the privation of wisdom, and in fact folly is nothing other than the absence of wisdom and reason" (120). With adverse contraries, Boethius can argue: "If we flee folly, we should pursue wisdom; if we long for goodness, we should flee evil" (120). But then, as with folly and wisdom, Boethius checks himself to note that the contraries evil and good may actually constitute a case of privation: "In the same way as that mentioned above [regarding folly] [...], evil can also be associated with privation" (120). Evil then would be nothing other than the absence of the good, and so evil per se would be nothing, the position Lady Philosophy takes in the *Consolation*. If wisdom aligns with the good, wisdom, like the good, could act without implicating itself in its privative contrary, folly or evil. Wisdom might operate and exist with folly wholly absent, as if a young man walking a street could encounter Wisdom without in any way encountering or risking an encounter with Folly. The young man could respond to the call with prior certainty and free of madness.

In the *Consolation*, Boethius the author has Lady Philosophy allude to Wisdom 8.1 and/or to the Antiphon in praise of *Sapientia* just before Lady Philosophy lures Boethius the character into an argument regarding the inexistence of evil. Lady Philosophy claims evil is nothing. Shortly prior to the Wisdom 8.1/Antiphon allusion, Lady Philosophy states, "God orders all things through himself alone" and then reminds Boethius of their agreement that "God [...] is the good itself" (66). Thus the Father "orders all things through the good, since we have agreed that he is the good and he governs all things through himself" (66). As the *summum bonum* who brings all into order, the Father resembles "the helm or rudder by which the frame of the universe is held steady and remains unchanged" (66). These themes of ordering, goodness, and government toward changelessness then sound and gather in Lady Philosophy's allusion to Wisdom 8.1 and/or to the Antiphon. To the character Boethius Lady Philosophy says, "It is then the sovereign goodness which governeth all things strongly, and disposeth them sweetly." Recall again the verse from the Wisdom of Solomon: "Wisdom reacheth from one end to another mightily: and sweetly doth she order all things" (8.1). The KJB translation names Wisdom, yet neither the Latin of Boethius nor the Latin of the Vulgate names either the Father or Wisdom. The Antiphon does mention Wisdom (*Sapientia*) by name, beginning: "O Sapientia."

Who sweetly orders the cosmos, the Father or the daughter? Or, in the Father, does the daughter act analogously to the all-creative and all-ordering Logos of John? The response of Boethius the character to Lady Philosophy's allusion to Wisdom 8.1 suggests the allusion encompasses *Sapientia* as a *logos* figure. In response to the allusion, the character Boethius states that Lady Philosophy's very words elicit his delight and put Folly to shame, as the anonymous translation of the *Consolation* penned in 1609 does not hesitate to emphasize. Boethius to Lady Philosophy: "'How much,' quoth I, 'doth not only the reason which thou allegest, but much more the very words which thou usest, delight me, that folly which so much vexed me may at length be ashamed of herself" (I.T., 291). Again, as with the poetic muses, the Lady shames her contrary, in this case Folly. The evocation of Folly by the character Boethius just after Lady Philosophy's allusion to Wisdom suggests the author Boethius is inventing a variation on Proverb's Wisdom/ Folly *topos*. To the character Boethius, Lady Philosophy, like Wisdom, brings delight, or her words do, and these words bring shame to Folly. The anonymous Renaissance translator renders Boethius's singular feminine noun *stultitiam* as folly and indeed as Folly. This translation conforms to the usage in the Vulgate. In the Vulgate 1 Corinthians 1.17–3.23, Paul's spiriting away of Wisdom in counterpoint to Folly proceeds by Paul discussing *sapientia* and *stultitiam* (1.21, 23). The Vulgate Proverbs uses *stultitiam* to name folly (13.16; 14.18, 29; 26.4, 5, 11) and refers to Folly or the "foolish woman" as "mulier stulta" (9.13, KJB and Vulgate). If Boethius is referring to the Antiphon, then the contrary of the Folly who undergoes shame would indeed be *Sapientia* as the Father's all-creative, cosmos-ordering word: "O Wisdom, coming forth from the mouth of the Most High, / reaching from one end to the other mightily, / and sweetly ordering all things."

Like a kind of hermeneutic Janus, the version of the Wisdom/ Folly *topos* the author Boethius articulates looks back to Lady Philosophy shaming the muses of poetry at the start of the *Consolation* and forward to the triumphant vindication of the Father (and thus of herself) Lady Philosophy will claim by the end of the *Consolation*. And yet this variation on the Wisdom/Folly *topos* plays dangerously with the slippery relation between the Father's omnipotence as the *summum bonum* and the nothingness

Lady Philosophy declares evil to be. According to the character Boethius, what exactly puts or will put Folly to shame? Folly is or will be put to shame by the words of Lady Philosophy declaring the omnipotence of the *summum bonum* in governing and ordering all, and this through *Sapientia* as the Father's word, states the Antiphon. Buckling to the shaming words and fiery glare of Lady Philosophy channeling Athena, the muses of poetry walk sadly away, their eyes diverted to the ground. Like the Folly of Proverbs, these muses, as Sirens, would lead Boethius toward dissolution and demise. Once again, Lady Philosophy to the muses: "Off with you, you Sirens! Your charms entice men to their destruction" (4). Lady Philosophy would replace these "Sirens" with her muses who, like the Wisdom of Proverbs, would lead Boethius along the path of life, albeit a life yearning to exit the sublunary into an afterlife: "Leave him to be tended and healed with the help of the Muses that attend me" (4). Lady Philosophy and her muses would heal Boethius by reorienting him to the Father, the highest good, the *summum bonum*. Omnipotent, the *summum bonum* governs and sweetly orders everything, bringing all parts into entire unity with the whole. In contrast to herself as serving the good, Lady Philosophy names the muses of poetry "harlots": are they thus servants of evil? Yet if Boethius hopes to distinguish between good and evil, between Lady Philosophy's muses and the muses of poetry, between transcendent order and apparent chaos, between being and nothingness, his bringing the Wisdom/ Folly *topos* into play poses risks of subversive resemblances and vertiginous ironies.

Consider how the ordering and the steadying of the cosmic order by the Father, the highest good, finds a privative contrary in evil, as if in relation to the steady "helm or rudder," and to the ship or "frame of the universe," evil were depths beyond the deepest and most chaotic of waters, an abyss of nothingness. Directly following Lady Philosophy's Wisdom 8.1/Antiphon allusion and the character Boethius putting the Wisdom/Folly *topos* into play, Lady Philosophy leads into her argument as to the nothingness of evil, as distinct from the Father as wholly good, by evoking the Gigantomachia, the chaotic upsurge of the giants against the Olympians. Led by Zeus, the Olympians defeated the giants, fending off chaos and establishing order. Immediately after Boethius asserts Lady Philosophy's words about the omnipotent *summum bonum* put Folly to shame, Lady Philosophy notes that Boethius is certainly familiar with the story of "the Giants who laid siege to heaven" and comments about the giants that "they too were put in their place by a kindly but firm hand" (67). Then with some zest she exclaims, "Now how about making the arguments themselves collide head on? Perhaps such a clash will cause a splendid spark of truth to fly out" (67). Of which "arguments" does Lady Philosophy speak? She has been evoking the omnipotence of the *summum bonum* in relation to *Sapientia,* and the character Boethius evokes Folly undergoing shame. Lady Philosophy's *agon* has been with the muses of poetry and the lingering effects of these muses in Boethius. When she suggests a gigantomachia of arguments, the reader will recall the conflict between her muses and poetry's.

Boethius agrees to Lady Philosophy's proposal for a gigantic clash of arguments, a collision to precipitate a "spark of truth." Lady Philosophy seeks to make omnipotence and nothingness clash. She solicits Boethius's agreement "that God has power over all things" and dances Boethius through some pirouettes with nothing:

> "Now if someone has power over all things," she added, "there is nothing that he cannot do?"
> "Nothing at all," I said.
> "But God cannot commit evil, can he?"
> "Certainly not," I replied.
> "And so evil is a nothing, for there is nothing that he cannot do, but he cannot commit evil." (68)

In this argument, the English "nothing" translates the Latin *nihil.* There is nothing God cannot do. That nothing is evil. Into the "can," this argument toys with introducing a "cannot." Into the "is," this argument plays at introducing "nothing." Into omnipotence, this argument jokes at introducing impotence. Is "nothing" difficult for logic? State: There is nothing. Or: Nothing is, as in: "evil is nothing." In this statement, does the verb "is" refer to the being of something or to the being of nothing? What kind of something could nothing be? Is the nothing the Lady names "evil" a mirage or an actuality? Though the banter between Lady Philosophy and Boethius about nothing seems light hearted, the affects of this moment of their dialog touch on an anxiety: in opening ambiguities about nothing, does the voice to which the character Boethius listens invite him to become lost forever or to find his way home, as this voice has been claiming? The voice does counsel Boethius toward his perishing, though promising an apotheosis awaits, yet what vertigo does Boethius feel, what precarious wavering, when "nothing" becomes the slippery operator of the voice's logic?

This anxiety and vertigo Boethius expresses in his response to Lady Philosophy's play with nothing. Boethius wonders if she is playing with him. He asks, "Are you making sport with me?" (68). At least for a moment, has Lady Philosophy turned sportive, letting a flash of Athena's wildness show in her? Lady Philosophy's verbal play on *nihil* seems a sportive weaving that stations Boethius in perplexity between a labyrinth and a temple:

> You are weaving a labyrinth of arguments from which I cannot find my way out. At one moment you go in where you intend to come out, and at another you come out where you intend to go in. Or are you weaving some fantastic circle of divine simplicity? (68)

For a moment Boethius dizzily confronts Lady Philosophy as indiscernibly beckoning him toward interminable wandering or eternal circling: whichever she may beckon toward, the anxiety and vertigo at the threshold feels the same, whether Boethius on heeding her voice were to enter the labyrinth or the circle. "Whoso *is* simple, let him turn in hither": in Lady Philosophy, does Folly call Boethius toward an abyssal labyrinth, or does Wisdom call Boethius toward an eternal circle? Entering the "circle of divine simplicity," the aspirer to the eternal oneness of the highest good crosses a boundary past which none of his sublunary existence may follow; he must leave behind the aspect of his soul vulnerable to the seducing mummers. Entering the realm of evil, the wanderer strays among inexistent shades, simulacra flitting about without substance. For Boethius to wander lost among the evil, for him to sink into the vast, chaotic theater of inexistent shades, for him fully to join these spectral players in their maze, would require the extinguishing within him of that "tiniest of sparks," the "spark of truth" allowing him the chance to remember and find his way back to his home with the "One Father" (17, 65). This tiny spark would be the aspect of his soul responsive to reason, to *logos*. This spark would have gone out, extinguished in the tears those stage harlots the muses of poetry solicit from Boethius, had not Lady Philosophy intervened and fanned the spark to lead Boethius toward the *anamnesis* allowing him to remember who he is and where his home is. Those theatric wantons, the muses of poetry, would lead Boethius to forget who he is and where his home is. With her fiery eyes, Lady Philosophy comports with the spark; those bringers of tears the poetic muses comport with fluid. The rudder of the highest good guides the ship through the turbulent waters. In the *Consolation*, fluidity poses a threat. The Lady's blazing eyes, the soul's spark: in the *Consolation*, fire saves.

Following hard upon Lady Philosophy's Wisdom/Antiphon allusion, the interchange about evil as nothing shows the daughter toying dangerously with the omnipotence ("omnium potens") of the father. The Wisdom/Antiphon allusion states how, as the *summum bonum*, the Father "governs [...] powerfully" and "orders [...] sweetly" "all things," somewhat like how, as Lady Philosophy explains, "a kindly but firm hand" "put [the giants] in their place." The "highest good," the Father, confronts in evil a nothingness. This nothingness escapes his omnipotence. And the reader might begin to wonder: how do Lady Philosophy, Fortune, and the muses of poetry relate to this nothingness? Lady Philosophy brings to Boethius the muse of Plato, the muse of memory, the remembrance of the highest good. The muses of poetry, in their influence on Boethius, would lead him to forget the highest good. The Father never could be so passive as to do nothing.

The Father as *summum bonum* orders a cosmos in which nothing is without cause or place within the order. As Lady Philosophy explains, "If one were to define chance as the outcome of a random movement which interlocks with no causes, I should maintain that it does not exist at all" (97). Any such random chance is "nothing substantial" because "God confines all things within due order" (97). Quite the odd phrase, "nothing substantial": chance and evil are nothing substantial. Lady Philosophy endorses the ancient saying that "nothing comes forth from nothing" (97). Any element of the "due order" loses substantiality in falling away from the place in providence the Father ordains for it. Lady Philosophy argues "wicked men" "do not exist," and they form "the majority of mankind" (75). "Whatever maintains its due order and preserves its nature, exists" (76). This existence bears the trait of unity: "every existing thing is a unity, and that unity itself is the good" (78). Only with this goodness as unity is there existence: "everything that exists is also good" (78). Those who depart from their place in the order, who depart from their unity, who depart from the good, depart from existence: "In this sense whatever departs from the good ceases to exist" (78). "[The] highest good is the aim of good and evil men alike" (74). However, while the good seek the highest good "by natural exercise of the virtues," the evil attempt "to acquire [the highest good] through desires" (74). The wicked in their desire depart from their place, their unity, their good, and so from their existence. Lady Philosophy claims such ne'er-do-wells enter inexistence: "I refuse to admit that they exist in an absolute sense" (76). Whatever "abandons its nature [...] ceases also to exist, for its existence is bound up in its nature" (76). Though "the very appearance of the human frame which they still possess shows that [the evil] were men," "by resorting to wickedness they have lost their human nature as well" (78). These former men have become "subhuman"; they have become as so many beasts: a dog, a wolf, a donkey, a "filthy sow" (78, 79). In their "desires," the "wicked," though inexistent, outstrip the omnipotent: they do nothing, they do evil, they do what the omnipotent cannot. Lady Philosophy: "nothing is more powerful than the highest good. [...] But the highest good [...] cannot achieve evil" (76). There is nothing the highest good cannot do. That nothing is evil. In evil, the beastly conduct a pantomime of human activity, and since these beastly form the "majority of mankind," what mostly goes on are theatricals the wicked play out as if they possessed human existence. When Lady Philosophy intervenes, she finds Boethius ready to abandon his nature to the passions those stage harlots the poetic muses promote.

A dramatic dialog with poetic interludes, the *Consolation* must in no way be a theatrical shadow-piece such as the muses of poetry might want to stage, similar to how the dramatic, multi-character dialogs of Plato must be distinct from the works of the theater Socrates denounces. If, in the *Republic*, Socrates declares the idea of the good beyond being, he denounces the shadowy simulacra of the stage as below being. Lady Philosophy and her muses must in no way partake in such theatrics as the poetic muses entice Boethius to indulge. When Lady Philosophy croons her poems to Boethius, they must in no way be siren songs. If finding a proper place in the divine order resembles phrases and words settling into *topoi* or commonplaces, and if falling away from the proper place resembles phrases and words as tropes swerving from *topoi,* then the *Consolation* would want to blame muses that inspire the forgetting of proper place or "home" in swerves downward toward utter chaos and to praise muses that inspire the remembrance of proper place or "home" in swerves upward toward perfect order. Recall that in the *Odyssey* the Sirens are among many women distracting Odysseus from reaching home, whereas Athena assists Odysseus in reaching his home. Swerving from the *topoi,* the swerves downward stoke the passions and dissolve order and unity like brown sugar crumble-melting into milk. The swerves upward still toward the *topoi,* toward final resting places, evermore harmonizing parts as evermore at one with the whole the *summum bonum* crowns. Evil would entail a trope departing from a *topos,* and good would entail a trope stilling into a *topos.* Should the departure of tropes from *topoi* ever become entire, an endless labyrinth of figural swerves without resting places or any home would result; should the stilling of tropes into *topoi* ever be complete, a circle circumference to all, with everything at home forever, would result. Though the dialog with Lady Philosophy projects a final return home vulnerable to turns nevermore, Boethius the prisoner ever occupies a moment between, his complete dissolution into a welter of tropes via the poetic muses undergoing a check by Lady Philosophy. Upon Lady Philosophy's play with nothing, Boethius in his imagination stands between the labyrinth and the circle, inhabiting the emptiness between, or standing as the emptiness, the nothing.

Passionate anger erupts volcanically from Lady Philosophy when she chases the muses of poetry away from Boethius, denouncing them as "harlots of the stage." Yet in this outburst the pot calls the kettle black. Lady Philosophy despises the poetic muses as flaunting theatric surfaces upon surfaces, theater masks upon wantonly painted faces. Yet Lady Philosophy herself engages in multiple maskings and even in a theatric performance. Lady Philosophy does a star turn as Fortune. Prior to the *Consolation*, the depiction of Fortune as a prostitute was well attested.[21] The wheel-spinning strumpet herself neither speaks nor appears in the *Consolation:* whenever Fortune struts across the page and declaims her sway over the happy and the hapless alike, we have Lady Philosophy treating Boethius and the reader to her theatric portrayal of the wanton. Lady Philosophy dons a persona, *persona,* character, or mask. Lady Philosophy stages her *prosopopoeia,* lends her face and voice to Fortune, only after saying: "I well know the manifold deceits of that monstrous lady, Fortune" (19). Here, "manifold" translates *multiformes* and "deceits" translates *fucos,* literally dyes or rouges—cosmetics.[22] Lady Philosophy turns mummer to mask as a woman of deceptive painted faces, Fortune, a prostitute. Fortune qualifies as a harlot, and Lady Philosophy stages her. And so Lady Philosophy risks blurring with the harlots of the stage she so vehemently dismisses as "Sirens pleasant even to destruction" (I. T., 133). Lady Philosophy must keep herself distinct from the poetic muses, though through poems she too would lead Boethius to his death, only death as transcendence toward the *summum bonum.*

Lady Philosophy's clothing complexly evokes the death Boethius awaits. As Andrea Denny-Brown so provocatively explains, from the reader's first encounter with Lady Philosophy, she associates with masks (Denny-Brown 36–37). Boethius describes the dull sootiness of her garment using in a simile the phrase *fumosas imagines*, smoky masks. The phrase refers to the masks of dead ancestors worn by mourners parading in funeral processions; between funerals, the masks would hang in the Roman dwelling's atrium and gather soot from the hearth fire. These were death masks formed in wax from the visage of the deceased. Boethius compares Lady Philosophy's robe to such a death mask. Two Greek letters, *pi* (Π) and *theta* (Θ), mark this robe: "At the lower edge of the robe was visible in embroidery the letter Π, and the neck of the garment bore the letter Θ" (4). The Greek letter *pi* stands for practical philosophy. The garment also includes "the depiction of a ladder, whose rungs allowed ascent from the lower letter to the higher letter" (4). Sixth-century Roman prison garb included a *theta* as short for *thanatos* to denote the execution awaiting prisoners held for capital offenses (Denny-Brown 36). The prison attire of Boethius the author likely bore such a *theta*.

Assume the attire of the character Boethius bears a *theta*. Upon the robe of Lady Philosophy, the *theta* stands for theoretical philosophy and hints toward the prisoner Boethius's final liberation through heeding Lady Philosophy's call to look up toward the Father. With its death-mask association and ominous *theta* suggesting the highest philosophy finds realization in state-imposed yet self-willed death (Socrates drinking the hemlock), Lady Philosophy's robe takes on some of the aura of Athena's shield bearing the head of the Gorgon. Evil may be nothing, and the poetic muses may lead toward destruction as chaotic nothingness, yet how is Boethius to know the face and voice of Lady Philosophy do not constitute yet another mask or *persona* or *prosopon* signifying nothing? About sheer random chance, which the Lady defines as a form of inexistence, she says: "[chance] is a wholly empty term denoting nothing substantial" (97). Or, in the 1609 translation: "chance is only an empty voice that hath beneath it no real signification" (I.T., 376). The word "chance" calls or signifies toward nothing. Toward the *summum bonum* Lady Philosophy calls Boethius, and her arguments lead his reason. As the dialog ends, Lady Philosophy increasingly anticipates Boethius's questions, stating them for the prisoner and responding, as if taking his reasoning being up into herself, heavenward. To the Boethius still in the prison cell, or to all readers in their prisons or bodies, she recapitulates the course of treatment she has offered Boethius, yet closes by recommending prayer: "So avoid vices, cultivate the virtues, raise your minds to righteous hopes, pour out your humble prayers to heaven" (114). In ascending toward and then past Lady Philosophy's *theta*, in heading toward the realization of his prison garment's *theta*, Boethius can only pray.

To close this chapter, a brief examination of the satanic verses incident, the supposed utterance by Mohammed of words Satan placed in his mouth, words about Allah's daughters, will suggest the vehement passions surrounding the question: does the god who called upon Abraham have any daughters? The Hebrew Scriptures (in Proverbs) and the Gnostic writings countenance their respective gods having a daughter, though for the Gnostics she is ambiguously wayward. In the New Testament, Paul spirits Hokmah away, and John excludes her. The third Abrahamic testament, the Koran, denies Allah has any daughters, and subsequent Islamic orthodoxy denies Mohammed ever slipped and suggested Allah does have daughters, even if so slipping only upon Satan's prompting. This double denial left a highly sensitive scar in the tradition of the Koran.

The daughters in question are Al-Lāt, Al-'Uzzā, and Manāt.[23] In pre-Islamic Mecca, and more broadly in the pre-Islamic Arabian Peninsula, these three were important goddesses long worshipped as the daughters of Allah. Mohammed's proclamation of Allah as the god of Abraham included the denial that Allah had any partners or helpers, much less any daughters serving such a role. The Koran declares that to associate other gods or goddesses with Allah constitutes *shirk,* that is, idolatry. For example, to say a divine daughter of Allah was with him in the beginning as an associate by his side inspiring him in his work of creation would constitute a textbook case of *shirk.*[24]

Mohammed's claim that divinity is one and that Allah is the one and only deity met with opposition from worshippers of Al-

Lāt, Al-'Uzzā, and Manāt, including members of Mohammed's own tribe, the Quraysh. Early narrative reports of the Prophet's life include an episode in which, under pressure from his opponents, Mohammed entertained a desire for reconciliation with them and for some way to end their persecution of him. The reports tell of how this desire hit the Prophet in the context of his reception from Gabriel and subsequent public recitation of Surat An-Najm, The Star, which became the fifty-third chapter of the Koran. The reports describe a recitation with both Mohammed's followers and opponents in attendance.

The Star opens with Allah insisting that Mohammed "does not err, nor does he go astray; / Nor does he speak out of desire."[25] Inspiration by desire the Koran associates with pre-Islamic poetry, especially love poetry. No, Allah insists, rather than his desire, Mohammed finds inspiration in Allah himself, who so "taught" Mohammed that he "attained completion": "And he is in the highest part of the horizon" (53.5, 6, 7). At this farthest and highest point, Mohammed gains an awe-inspiring proximity to the deity, who grants Mohammed a revelation, and still Mohammed stands unfaltering:

> Then he drew near, then he bowed,
> So he was the measure of two bows or closer still.
> And He revealed to His servant what He revealed.
> The heart was not untrue in (making him see) what he saw.
> What! do you then dispute with him as to what he saw? (53.8–12)

Given the resolve and steadfast veracity of the Prophet's "heart," any auditor should be wary of disputing Mohammed's vision. And any auditor who wants to question Mohammed's vision should know the following about the Prophet:

> And certainly he saw him in another descent,
> At the farthest lote-tree;
> Near which is the garden, the place to be resorted to.
> When that which covers covered the lote-tree;
> The eye did not turn aside, nor did it exceed the limit.

Certainly he saw some of the greatest signs of his Lord.
Have you then considered the Lat and the Uzza,
And Manat, the third, the last? (53.13–20)

In the first line of this passage, "him" translates an Arabic pronoun that can also mean "it," and the pronoun's antecedent remains unstated. Again we have Mohammed, through an ecstatic flight, attaining a remotest horizon, here one where he confronts "the lote-tree." The Sufis interpreted this "lote-tree" as marking the furthest boundary a mortal soaring the heavens may approach in seeking to confront Allah.[26] As Mohammed's "heart" showed resolve in the previously described flight toward Allah, so here the Prophet's "eye" remains steady, even though something indescribable and unapproachable enshrouds the tree, perhaps glory, the glory of Allah. The Prophet flies resolutely to the very edge a mortal may approach, there beholding the tree, and his "eye" neither "turn[s] aside" from the verge of the impossible, nor does his "eye" "exceed the limit," falsely or idolatrously taking as possible the impossible. Who but Mohammed could make such a flight and sustain such a vision? Would not most any other mortal need a high-flying intercessor to assist in such a flight or to make the flight in the mortal's stead?

In reciting The Star to an audience of both followers and opponents, having "desired within himself" for a rapprochement with his opponents, seeing his own tribe starting to turn from him, and hoping for words to bring them back, when the Prophet

> reached the verse, "Have you considered al-Lāt, al-'Uzza, and Manāt, the third, the other?," Satan cast upon his tongue because of that which he had been thinking to himself about and had been desiring to bring to his people: "Those (are the) high-flying cranes: Indeed, their intercession is to be hoped for."[27]

Or so runs the account of the satanic verses incident relayed from prior sources by the Persian scholar and interpreter of the Koran Muhammad ibn Jarir al-Tabari (224–310 AH; 838–923 CE). Though Mohammed was only to speak the words of Allah Gabriel conveyed to the Prophet, in his recitation of The Star, made vulnerable by his desire, Mohammed spoke words brought by Satan, or so the account indicates. The words Satan "cast upon Mohammed's tongue" commend Al-Lāt, Al-'Uzzā, and Manāt as high-flyers who will intercede with their father, Allah. The account describes how, when Mohammed uttered these words, the worshippers of the daughters among the Quraysh "were delighted," and the followers of Mohammed "trusted their Prophet," crediting his commendation of the daughters as high-flying interecessors and "not suspect[ing] him of an error or delusion or lapse" (Ahmed 42–43). Then, when Mohammed reached the point in the sura for the ritual prostration or *sajdah*, both the followers of Mohammed and the worshippers of the daughters performed the *sajdah* together, with the Muslims under the impression they had just learned from Mohammed that Allah does indeed have daughters and with the worshippers of the daughters under the impression Mohammed had just acknowleged their goddesses (43). Not only does the account show Mohammed as vulnerable to confusing words from Satan for the words from Allah Gabriel brings, but the account shows that vulnerablility resulting in a textbook case of *shirk*, of Mohammed promoting the belief Allah has divine companions or associates. The account's image of Muslim worshippers and worshippers of the daughters together performing the *sajdah* images distinct worships becoming indistinct, the singularity and difference of each lost in the homogenization of both. *Shirk* generally and the satanic verses incident in particular rolls back or cancels Mohammed's revelation of Allah as one and as the one and only deity, and so the utterance of the satanic verses constituted a grievous fault. The report explains how, after Mohammed let Satan's words pass through his mouth, Gabriel alerted the Prophet that those words were not from Allah, and the Prophet was appalled and grieved at his error. Allah then reassured the Prophet, telling him all prophets who feel ardent desire are vulnerable to Satan. Allah then removed Satan's words and provided words in correction. Absent the correction, the relevant verses would read as Mohammed supposedly uttered them under Satan's influence:

Have you then considered the Lat and the Uzza,
And Manat, the third, the last?
Those (are the) high-flying cranes:
Indeed, their intercession is to be hoped for.

The account of the satanic verses incident from al-Tabari specifies Allah provided corrective verses; these correspond to how the standard recieved text of The Star reads following the initial evocation of the three:

Have you then considered the Lat and the Uzza,
And Manat, the third, the last?
What! for you the males and for Him the females!
This indeed is an unjust division!
        They are naught but names which you have named, you and your fathers; Allah has not sent for them any authority. They follow naught but conjecture and the low desires which (their) souls incline to; and certainly the guidance has come to them from their Lord. (53.19–23)

Rather than commending the three, The Star scoffs at those who, wanting for themselves sons as progeny, would attribute daughters to Allah. And these daughters have no reality: they "are naught but names" and names without "any authority." Those who worship Al-Lāt, Al-'Uzzā, and Manāt do so out of "conjectures" and "low desires," ignoring the "guidance" Allah provides.

In pre-Islamic times, through the Hellenistic influences the Roman Empire spread, Al-Lāt, Al-'Uzzā, and Manāt gained association with Greek deities and notions. Worshipped in the planet Venus, Al-'Uzzā became linked with the goddess Venus (Aphrodite). A deity of fate for pre-Islamic Arabs, Manāt was associated with Nemesis. And the Semitic Palmyrenes of modern day Yemen and Syria thought of Al-Lāt in terms of Athena and of Athena in terms of Al-Lāt, so much so that their coins bore side by side the phrases "the gift of Al-Lāt" and "the gift of Athena."[28] In the city of Palmyra, statues of Al-Lāt were modeled on statues of Athena, and a statue of Athena was prominent in the temple of Al-Lāt (Christides 77, 78). Among the Palmyrenes, thinking of Al-Lāt as Athena and Athena as Al-Lāt was in evidence as early as the first century BCE and peaked in the second century CE (79). The statuary centered in the city of Palmyra, yet trade routes brought nomadic Arabs through Palmyra, possibly spreading the association of Al-Lāt with Athena (71).

An Athena and an Aphrodite converge with Fate to enter The Star just as Mohammed has evoked a moment at the limit of mortality, the fearfully beautiful, the sublime moment viewing the lote-tree. Just then Satan provokes Mohammed to describe the trio of daughters as available to intercede either in or toward such an overwhelming moment. The trio could be considered via the Greek notion of the daemonic, except that already the al-Tabari account demonizes them, aligning them with Satan while also affirming The Star's claim as to their being mere names without authority, seductive of those prey to conjecture and low desires. If to consider Al-Lāt, Al-'Uzzā, and Manāt daughters of Allah brings the charge of *shirk*, then consider thinking of them as Satan's daughters. Whoever Satan might also be, who is Satan but everything of Yahweh Christianity set aside to imagine God the Father and Islam set aside to imagine Allah? For example, among Mohammed's Allah, John's God the Father, and Proverb's Yahweh, Yahweh alone happily accepts having a daughter.

Four

The Nihilistic Muse
in Shakespeare's *Othello*

Testimony and Proof

Deceitfully staging a handkerchief's absence, Iago summons a Desdemona, a double who shadows her eponym toward oblivion. Who kills Desdemona? Othello, certainly, yet when Emilia asks the Moor's perishing wife who her murderer is, Desdemona testifies, "Nobody. I myself" (5.2.124). Does this testimony merely shift blame away from Othello, or is Desdemona implicating in her own murder someone at once inexistent and herself? To ignore Desdemona's testimony would entangle the reader in Iago's fabrication of "proof" (3.3.197). Testimony and belief are distinct from proof and knowledge. Testimony appeals to belief. Proof adheres to conventions validating knowledge. Though unknowable, nothingness remains believable: unavailable to proof yet available to testimony. Words neither provable nor disprovable may nevertheless testify.

Desdemona testifies to her fidelity, yet Othello fails to believe her, to believe in her. He accepts shadows of inexistence as proof against her. From her deathbed, Desdemona testifies, "O, falsely, falsely murdered! [...] A guiltless death I die" (5.2.117, 122). Emilia hears these words then solicits Desdemona's statement, "Nobody. I myself." Too late to save Desdemona, Emilia breaks the spell of Iago's proof by courageously testifying she, Emilia, conveyed Othello's handkerchief to Iago. Until Emilia testifies, in the contest between Iago and Desdemona for Othello's trust, proof smothers testimony and knowledge overrides belief, quite faulty knowledge, yes, but faultless knowledge ever recedes, a mirage, even if "truth is truth / To th' end of reck'ning," as Shakespeare's Isabella boldly declares while offering testimony that, replete with fictions, nevertheless speaks truly (*Measure for Measure* 5.1.45–46). Early in *Othello*, as Iago listens, Desdemona's father Brabantio, upset about his daughter's elopement, insists Othello, by using drugs and witchcraft, must have manufactured a counter-Desdemona willing to deceive her father and marry a Moor in secret (1.2.61–80). Iago takes the hint, forges a demonic yet inexistent woman, Othello's "cunning whore of Venice," and stage-manages this doppelganger to achieve Desdemona's homicide and Othello's self-apostasy (4.2.90). With the self-murder of Othello already at work in his asphyxiation of Desdemona, the play's *dénouement*, testing the limits of the bearable, approaches in difficulty for the reader Genesis's story of Yahweh commanding Abraham to sacrifice Isaac. This command Abraham keeps secret, unanswerable to any ethical norm, argues Kierkegaard, making Abraham's obedience horrifyingly murderous in socially responsible eyes however much it may appear righteously sacrificial in Yahweh's eyes. Before her asphyxiation, Desdemona testifies to her innocence, but Othello, crediting Iago's proofs, accuses her of perjury: "O perjured woman, thou dost stone my heart, / And mak'st me call what I intend to do / A murder, which I thought a sacrifice" (5.2.63–65).[1] Of these lines and the murder scene, the Shakespeare editor Samuel Johnson writes, "I am glad that I have ended my revisal of this dreadful scene. It is not to be endured."[2] Johnson's comment prompts variorum edition editor Howard Furness to note the scene's "unutterable agony" and to state: "I do not shrink from saying that I wish this Tragedy had never been written."[3] *Othello* begins with Roderigo's words: "Never tell me" (1.1.1). The wish never to have read *Othello* registers the nihilism the play confronts.

"Never tell me": Roderigo wants never to hear spoken, never to have heard spoken, words announcing what he then nonetheless knows: Desdemona has eloped with Othello. Roderigo wishes the knowledge would remain inarticulate, forever mute. In relation to Desdemona's murder, unbearable knowledge's realization awaits an articulation of what remains unspoken and perhaps unspeakable. Consider Iago's last words: "Demand me nothing. What you know, you know. / From this time forth, I never will speak word" (5.2.302–03). The apostle Paul hails Christ as the Father's Son (1 Thessalonians 1.9–10). *Othello* testifies to the ongoing abjection by which the Son's promotion would nullify Yahweh's daughter, Wisdom, casting her outward and downward. Othello to Desdemona: "Out, strumpet! [...] Down, strumpet!" (5.2.77, 79). In the playgoer's imagination, Shakespeare etches an anatomy of Wisdom's daemonic exaltation and demonic nihilation. Accomplishing Desdemona's murder, Iago gives nothing birth. Iago: "But my Muse labors, / And thus she is delivered" (2.1.126–27).

Desdemona's Wish

Desdemona and Othello's mutual wooing brings the pair into a daemonic muse scenario subject to demonization: an avatar of Wisdom taking on the traits of Athena and acting as a muse. Speaking before Venice's Duke and Brabantio's fellow Venetian senators to justify his secret marriage to Desdemona, Othello testifies how, when visiting Brabantio, he would tell the senator stories of adventure, enslavement, and war. These stories recounted the life of Othello "from [his] boyish days" to the "very moment" Othello related them to the senator and his daughter (1.3.132, 133). Othello reports how ardent Desdemona was to hear his stories: "But still the house affairs would draw her hence. / Which ever as she could with haste dispatch, / She'd come again, and with a greedy ear / Devour up my discourse" (1.3.147–50). Othello's report portrays Desdemona as hungrily participating in his stories via her imagination: he reports telling Brabantio of cannibals (the "anthropophagi" [1.3.144]) and then describes how Desdemona would "with a greedy ear / Devour" his tales. At least in Othello's testimony, Desdemona was hungry for his words. Yet her hunger's appeasement was often delayed by her requirement to perform household duties.

Othello relates how Desdemona's requirement to attend to the "house affairs" would frustrate Desdemona's fervent audition (1.3.147). In terms of the daily routines and labors of domesticity, Desdemona had taken her absent and unnamed mother's place. In

Othello, Desdemona's mother receives only two mentions. In the first, Desdemona argues to her father that, just as her mother shifted her primary duty from her father to Brabantio, she, Desdemona, may shift her primary duty from Brabantio to Othello (1.3.180–89). Before the elopement, her mother being absent, Desdemona had been for an indeterminate period both daughter and housewife to Brabantio. The imprisoning and stifling character of this existence Brabantio suggests by describing Desdemona's elopement as her "escape" and by saying, had he additional children, Desdemona's action would "teach" him to "hang clogs on them," weights warders tie to prisoners to prevent their flight (1.3.198, 199).

On one visit to Brabantio, Othello was able to solicit from Desdemona "a prayer of earnest heart," her request that he would tell her the entire story of his "pilgrimage," she having only heard snippets due to interruptions by domestic chores (1.3.152, 153). The religious diction ("prayer," "pilgrimage") resonates with quest-romance notions of love. About Desdemona's cousin Lodovico, Emilia says to Desdemona, "I know a lady in Venice [who] would have walked barefoot to Palestine for a touch of his nether lip" (4.3.38–39). At least in Emilia's account, pining for even one of Lodovico's lips, the unnamed Venetian woman imagines longing's fulfillment in terms of a religious quest. Such mixture of the amorous and the religious defines Desdemona's "prayer" to Othello requesting the story of his "pilgrimage." After receiving Desdemona's "prayer," with Brabantio presumably absent, though likely with Cassio about as a chaperon, Othello told his entire story to Desdemona. After listening to the story, reports Othello,

> [Desdemona] wished she had not heard it, yet she wished
> That heaven had made her such a man. She thanked me,
> And bade me, if I had a friend that loved her,
> I should but teach him how to tell my story,
> And that would woo her.
>
> (1.3.162–66)

To be unaware of her domesticity as imprisonment becomes untenable for Desdemona after hearing Othello's story of what he earlier calls his "unhousèd free condition" (1.2.25). Desdemona's wishes are torn. She might have remained passably content with her domestic station had "she [...] not heard" Othello's story, her wish not to have heard the story being a "never tell me" sentiment. Yet more strongly Desdemona "wished / That heaven had made her such a man." If Desdemona were "such a man" as Othello, her life could be one of roving adventure rather than domestic imprisonment. Being an Othello, she could live as a figure in a quest romance, perhaps to be enslaved but then to win freedom from slavery, or even to free another from imprisonment. In Othello, Desdemona finds the self she wishes to become.

Must she find this self in an adventurer? An adventuress might be "a cunning whore of Venice" who barters herself, trading in kisses to attain her ends. Yet what is Othello? He is a mercenary, the martial equivalent of a "whore." Perhaps this parallel contributes to Othello's acute anxiety about whoredom. Desdemona: the "whore of Venice." *Othello: The Moor of Venice.* That rhymes. That *more* than rhymes.

Brabantio describes his only child as a "maiden never bold" (1.3.95). This passive, homebound Desdemona might wish never to have heard Othello's story. Yet the bold Desdemona, or her daemon, wishes to be what Othello *was:* she wishes "heaven" had created her as the Othello of the past, the *young* Othello the Moor's tale foregrounds. This Othello fought his way from the nadir of enslavement to military renown. The Othello Desdemona meets has been languishing in peaceful disuse for nine months and has felt the need to appoint a "lieutenant," an officer who could take his place, though Othello appoints Cassio, no rival to Othello's martial prowess, as Iago might be.

Eloping with Othello, Desdemona plays out the desire for liberation her wish to have been created in Othello's younger image entails. Taking Desdemona from her father's house, Othello frees her, with Desdemona casting Othello as an alternate or wish-fulfilling version of herself. This adventurous Desdemona undertakes the perilous sea voyage from Venice to Cyprus. In braving a Mediterranean in chaotic storm and rife with enemy Turks known to sell captives into slavery, the bold Desdemona achieves a striking fulfillment of her wish for adventure.

Othello's Wish

Like Desdemona, Othello prizes liberation. The tale Desdemona intermittently heard from Othello builds toward the episode of Othello's enslavement and consequent release from bondage. Regarding the strong response of Desdemona to her more private hearing of the entire tale, Othello evokes a slave suffering the lash: "[I] often did beguile her of her tears, / When I did speak of some distressful stroke / That my youth suffered. My story being done, / She gave me for my pains a world of kisses" (1.3.156–59). Through his tale, Othello gave Desdemona his world of adventurous trials. In return, she gave him "a world of kisses"—*Othello* is a play of kisses.[4] The trade hints at Othello's exchange of his martial service for remuneration and a respectable station in polite Venetian society. The story Othello told covered almost his entire life, from his "boyish years" until the time of the story's telling during his leave from warfare. To speak of the trials that his "youth" endured as "stroke[s]" from a lash gathers all his sufferings into the category of enslavement. Iago notes, "We cannot all be masters" (1.1.41). But Othello would be free of slavery: the enslavement a prisoner of war suffers, the enslavement Othello imagines the afflictions of his life to form, and finally the enslavement of dying a thrall to death as the last master. As soon to be detailed, Othello imagines dying could enact a final liberation, but only if Desdemona takes away the sting. Othello envisions his death with her in accompaniment as a martial hero's end. Who Othello was, Desdemona wishes to be. Who was Othello? A warrior. When he elopes with Desdemona, he has not acted as a warrior for nine months. His voyage to Cyprus against the Turks will require of him no fighting, and he will last use a weapon to end his own life. Acting on her attraction to adventure, Desdemona seeks to realize her capacity for freedom. Wishes for liberation join Othello and Desdemona and result in their secret elopement. Yearnings for escape inflame their mutual enchantment, as the tale about Othello's plans Iago tells late in the play suggests: "He goes into Mauritania, and taketh away with him the fair Desdemona" (4.2.221–22). But this romance fiction Iago spins to manipulate

Roderigo barely suggests the reveries Desdemona evokes. With an aura of secrecy backlighting her flight from her father's home, Desdemona becomes the lodestar of wish fulfillment for Cassio, Iago, and Othello, each in his own way. Each praises Desdemona, and the praise discloses the place of each in the play's anatomy of Wisdom's fate. Acclaiming Desdemona in his praise, Cassio thinks of her as a daemon. Cassio's apotheosis of Desdemona through hyperbole exalts her yet leaves her selfhood unaddressed. Satirizing women in his praise, Iago sets himself on the path toward his demonization of Desdemona, which distorts her selfhood to produce her double. Aping words Cassio might use, Iago calls Desdemona a "fair lady" (4.2.118). Due to Iago's demonization, Othello eventually calls Desdemona a "fair devil" (3.3.478). Prior to Iago's gambits, when Othello thinks himself capable of sustaining her inspiration, he praises Desdemona as his "fair warrior," and that by way of a telling instance of his initial: "O my fair warrior" (2.1.177). A late-career Achilles on a sabbatical from warfare, Othello, envisioning Desdemona as his Athena, comes closest to speaking of and to Desdemona's self and desire. Cassio, Iago, and Othello praise her upon their arrival in Cyprus.

The Scene of Praise: Nothing Beckons

With Othello and Desdemona's elopement discovered and reluctantly accepted by Brabantio, the Venetian Duke and Senators send Othello in command of the Venetian fleet to Cyprus to combat the Turks, whose invading navy sails for the island. Act 2 opens in Cyprus with the governor Montano and attendant Gentlemen anxiously gazing on a Mediterranean in furious storm and bearing the Turkish enemy. Montano and the Gentlemen describe the seascape in terms of what Edmund Burke calls the sublime of terror: the spectator, though at a relatively safe remove, observes terrifying natural wonders that implicitly threaten the observer's annihilation yet uplift the observer in sublimity's transport by the observer's participation in imagination with the unbounded and uncontrollable. Foreshadowing the twentieth century's abstract-expressionist sublime (receding verges between fields of dynamic color) and hinting at an instance of the agonistic sublime Longinus cites (giants threatening to pile the mountains Pelion and Ossa on Olympus to battle Zeus[5] [in *Othello*, the tempest piles waves as mountains against ships for which Cassio implores Jove's protection]), Montano and his fellow observers describe the tempest-wracked sea's overwhelming chaotic fury—think of a seascape by J. M. W. Turner. The descriptions evoke a sublimity taken up by and transformed in Cassio's and Othello's praise of Desdemona. This Mediterranean in chaos alludes to the biblical beginning's dark and void waste of waters, where "God made heaven and earth of nothing," as the 1560 Geneva Bible's gloss of Genesis 1.1 states.

The storm disperses the Turkish fleet, as the Cypriots learn from Cassio when his vessel is the first to arrive from the perilous sea. After Cassio's ship enters the bay but before Desdemona's ship and Othello's ship arrive, as the storm rages, the coastal town on Cyprus is hauntingly vacant because the population has gathered on a promontory to search the horizon. The ship bearing Cassio arrives, and he tells of the Turkish fleet's destruction, "yet he looks sadly, / And prays the Moor be safe, for they were parted / With foul and violent tempest" (2.1.32–34). On a cliff or fortified wall abutting the raging sea, the population masses in the faint hope of witnessing Othello's ship and the rest of the Venetian fleet arrive safely through the roiling winds and waves. Their hope finds fulfillment. Exiting the town *en masse*, the citizens form a sublimely operatic chorus: "The town is empty. On the brow o' the sea / Stand ranks of people, and they cry, 'A sail!'" (2.1.53–54). Unknown to the populace, this ship is Desdemona's. Stepping beyond the town, the locale defining their everyday selves, to stand before vast waters in tempest, the citizens act out spatially the sublime transport, the standing-outside-of-themselves or *ekstasis* they are undergoing imaginatively. With intense anxiety prompting a vivid being-with-Othello in imagination, yet gathering securely on land, the citizens stand outside their quotidian rounds to view a scene of watery chaos utterly mortal to human existence. As Montano states, for a ship to "bear [...]

out" this storm seems "impossible" (2.1.19). Gathered in view of
the chaos, the citizens anticipate an invasion of Muslims. Then,
not the Islamic enemy but a Christian friend arrives, Cassio, with
news of the enemy's dispersal but anxious for Othello's safety.
Then, awaiting Othello, who is to be the island's new governor,
the townspeople descry a sail. However, Desdemona arrives in
place of the anticipated general. Finally, Othello's ship arrives.
The terror of sublime nature mixes with the fearful anticipation
of being overrun by the Turks. But who arrives triumphantly
in the wake of the Turks' destruction? Desdemona, and only
afterwards Othello, the Moor. Wondering if the saving general
will live through the storm, the Cypriots discern an approaching
ship and cry out, "A sail, a sail, a sail!": they hope to greet Othello,
as does Cassio, his response to the cry being: "My hopes do shape
him [the approaching ship] for the governor [Othello]" (2.1.51, 55).
Whose ship would lead the Venetian fleet? Othello's. But when
the heralded ship arrives, off steps Desdemona.

Before the sail of Desdemona's ship appears, the Burkean
sublime of terror corresponds with a failure or breakdown of
cognition, a balking of sight. The current governor of Cyprus
Montano asks a Gentleman, "What from the cape can you
discern at sea?" (2.1.1). Speaking for the citizens gazing seaward,
Montano's anonymous interlocutor replies, "Nothing at all. It is a
high-wrought flood. / I cannot, 'twixt the heaven and the main, /
Descry a sail" (2.1.2–4). "Nothing at all": From this nothingness,
stepping ashore from the chaos where the enemy found defeat,
Desdemona emerges. In *Othello*, the word "nothing" echoes,
sounding the collapse of sense, purpose, and coherence. Absent a
metonymy of human purposiveness, "a sail" to orient perception,
"the heaven and the main" chaotically mix as the gaze strains
to the horizon. After Cassio's ship appears and safely makes
port, Montano can acknowledge this breakdown of the sea–sky
boundary, but only as if his encounter with this blurring were a
matter of his own volition:

Let's to the seaside, ho!
As well to see the vessel that's come in

As to throw out our eyes for brave Othello,
Even till we make the main and the aerial blue
An indistinct regard.

(2.1.36–40)

Countering the anonymous Gentleman, who helplessly sees "Nothing" between "the heaven and the main" and so confronts the possible defeat of the organizing gaze, Montano suggests a recuperation of nothingness, a recentering of cognition in an I/ eye active and in charge of its own destiny, as appropriate for a governor. So Montano says that he and his compatriots will "make the main and the aerial blue / An indistinct regard," staring into the chaos of sea and sky until the boundary between the two blurs. The very disruption of cognition the anonymous Gentleman cannot but let happen, Montano claims to "make" happen.

Montano exclaims that the tempest threatens the town's fortifications and any naval vessel or sea-going extension of land-based military structures:

Methinks the wind hath spoke aloud at land,
A fuller blast ne'er shook our battlements.
If it hath ruffianed so upon the sea,
What ribs of oak, when mountains melt on them,
Can hold the mortise?

(2.1.5–9)

Threatening the "battlements," the wind may have "ruffianed so upon the sea" as to bring up waves like "mountains" that, in crashing onto any ship, may shake it apart. To survive such waves, says Montano, should be "impossible."

Cassio's Praise

The impossible happens: Desdemona's ship survives the storm. Or, rather, in Cassio's praise of her, Desdemona triumphs over the storm. Cassio's ship arrives at Cyprus safely, having skirted the full brunt of the tempest. But will the rest of the Venetian fleet pass intact through the chaos? Anxiously waiting for ships to arrive, Cassio responds with exalting rhetoric to Montano's question, "is your general wived?" (2.1.60):

> Most fortunately. He hath achieved a maid
> That paragons description and wild fame,
> One that excels the quirks of blazoning pens,
> And in th' essential vesture of creation
> Does tire the ingeniver.
>
> (2.1.61–65)

Seeking to praise Desdemona adequately, Cassio exalts her as defying the limits of praise. She "paragons," both defines and surpasses, the outermost edge of "description and wild fame." She exceeds any phenomena by which her votary Cassio could describe her, so any tropes pens scribble fall short of her. By exalting Desdemona as in excess of any aspect of the created world, Cassio situates her in the place of Wisdom, there, at the beginning, standing with her father prior to the creation. As a muse, Wisdom inspires her father to engineer the creation, to accomplish the "essential vesture of creation," to fashion from the watery chaos an orderly "creation," an effort tiring the deity ("tire the ingeniver"), necessitating a day of rest, the seventh, Cassio reasonably associating the deity of Proverbs 8 with the deity of Genesis 1.

Cassio's hyperbolic praise of the "divine Desdemona" situates her at the sublime's furthest verge and hails her as a divinity whose beauty subdues the chaos of waters, transforming the sublimity of terror to a sublime beauty or glory (2.1.73). Desdemona lands at Cyprus as if she were no part of nature but an uncreated spark, a Gnostic daemon (Des-*demon*-a, Des-daemon-a^6) who, Cassio exalts, may inspire Othello to "[g]ive renewed fire to our extincted spirits" (2.1.81). As if gloriously in triumphant procession through a creation she exceeds, Desdemona sails through the storm unharmed. Again, Cassio:

> Tempests themselves, high seas, and howling winds,
> The guttered rocks, and congregated sands,

Traitors ensteeped to clog the guiltless keel,
As having sense of beauty, do omit
Their mortal natures, letting go safely by
The divine Desdemona.

(2.1.68–73)

After her sea-birth, Aphrodite (Venus) was blown to Cyprus's
shore, an allusion implicit in Cassio's praise of Desdemona's
"beauty." In Cassio's rhetoric, Desdemona becomes "divine," first
as Wisdom and then as Venus, yet she is still subject to death, as
her safety depends on the "seas," "rocks," and so on setting aside
their "mortal natures." The "congregated sands" are potential
"Traitors" to Desdemona, as are the rocks, waves, and winds.
As Brabantio imagines placing clogs on offspring as if they were
criminals who seek to escape imprisonment, so the rocks and
sands would "clog the guiltless keel" to prevent the ship from
escaping the storm. Cassio's use of "clog" figures elements of
nature as wardens, as if the creation were a prison. But this ship's
"keel" is no criminal: it is "guiltless."

Or, by metonymy, the "keel" as "guiltless" figures Desdemona
as free of guilt and so of sin, as if she were exempt from Eve's
transgression and from the entirety of fallen existence. Desdemona
will persuasively testify she dies a guiltless death. Paul declares
all deaths guilty, the results of sin. If Eve's sin brought death into
the world, Desdemona in her innocence reverses the fall. This
innocence of Desdemona translates as a glorious beauty. Cassio
personifies the sea, wind, rocks, and sands as "having sense of
beauty." This "sense" leads them to "omit / their mortal natures,"
their participation in the fallen universe death pervades. Given
their "sense of beauty," Desdemona enchants them, so they forgo
their "mortal natures," which would otherwise sink her ship
and drown her—smother her breath. The glory of the "divine
Desdemona" disarms them, as Milton will have the unfallen Eve's
beauty momentarily abstract Satan from his evil.

Cassio continues with his praise when, having disembarked
from her ship, Desdemona comes before Montano and the
Gentlemen:

> O, behold,
> The riches of the ship is come on shore.
> Ye men of Cyprus, let her have your knees.
> Hail to thee, lady, and the grace of heaven,
> Before, behind thee, and on every hand
> Enwheel thee round!
>
> (2.1.82–87)

In ancient and medieval Christian paintings, often a nimbus of light circles the head of Jesus, Mary, or a saint, a halo signaling glory, but when a painting depicts the manifestation of glory as a sphere of light encircling the entire figure, the manifestation is an aureola. Commanding Montano and his attendant Cypriot Gentlemen to kneel before Desdemona, Cassio implores the "grace of heaven" to form an aureola around Desdemona. Cassio imagines Desdemona as the divine's intermediary: glorious in grace's aureola, free of sin. Iago will cast Desdemona as sin.

With the safe arrival of the ship bearing Iago and Desdemona, Cassio addresses his exalted rhetoric toward Othello in anticipation of the Moor's arrival. In Cassio's praise of Desdemona, her beauty pacifies deadly nature. In Cassio's words hailing Othello, what counters the chaos of the storm is Jove's breath in the ship's sail, the wind becoming like the wind, breath, or spirit that swept over the waters in their chaos (Genesis 1.2):

> [...] Great Jove, Othello guard,
> And swell his sail with thine own powerful breath,
> That he may bless this bay with his tall ship,
> Make love's quick pants in Desdemona's arms,
> Give renewed fire to our extincted spirits,
> And bring all Cyprus comfort!
>
> (2.1.77–82)

By filling the "sail" of Othello's ship, the breath of Jove overcomes the chaos of water and sky, which bears the enemy Turk. The "breath" of "Jove" will allow Othello to "bless" the "bay," consummate his marriage with Desdemona, and bring to life again his comrades' "extincted spirits." Cassio's linkage of breath, life, and spirit in imagining Othello and Desdemona's consummation of their union becomes ironic when Othello asphyxiates Desdemona on their marriage bed.

Iago's Praise

After Cassio, Iago praises Desdemona. Cassio's praise takes from Proverbs an exalted vision of Wisdom, with Cassio reading Wisdom in terms of Platonic traits. These traits attach to Wisdom only by fading into the background her ambiguous standing on the public way where the young man of Proverbs may always find Folly, the prostitute, the "whore," to use a word important to Othello and to *Othello*. A symptom of how Cassio's vision of Desdemona rehearses the Platonization of Wisdom emerges in Cassio's callousness toward his mistress Bianca, the prostitute Cassio would never think of confusing with Desdemona, though Iago, in one of his gambits to ensnare Othello, plays out such confusion, having Cassio talk of Bianca while arranging for Othello to think Cassio is talking of Desdemona. Iago's praise of Desdemona works to bring into *Othello* Proverbs' Wisdom/ Folly ambiguity, the ambiguity Cassio's praise must deny, hence Cassio's abasing treatment of Bianca. Iago's praise of Desdemona reworks the Wisdom/Folly ambiguity of Proverbs, yet in doing so Iago precludes the vision of Desdemona as a warrior. There is the "divine" Desdemona. There is the "whore" Desdemona. But there also is the "warrior" Desdemona.

To distract from the anxiety of waiting to see if Othello will survive the storm and reach Cyprus safely, Desdemona asks Iago how he would praise her: "What wouldst thou write of me, if thou shouldst praise me?" (2.1.116–17). She repeats her request: "Come, how wouldst thou praise me?" (2.1.123). Relenting, Iago offers praise as to anonymous women he speaks of in the third person, decorum preventing his satirical observations from referring directly to Desdemona. To tag Iago as a fine soldier yet an amateur scholar, Cassio notes how Iago's observations are such as a "scholar" would make, underscoring how Iago's Wisdom/

Folly *topos* stems from biblical and learned tradition, as do the *topoi* of Cassio's praise (2.1.163).

Taking up the terms for assessing women Proverbs juggles, Iago's satiric praise treats of women in terms of their "folly" and "wisdom," addressing particular cases, the first of which Iago proposes: the "fair and wise" woman (2.1.135, 151, 128). Desdemona and Emilia propose alternate cases: Desdemona asks about the "black and witty" woman, Emilia about the "fair and foolish," and finally Desdemona about the "foul and foolish" (2.1.130, 133, 138). Iago's praise of these types works to erode the distinction between wisdom and folly. Concerning the woman "fair and wise," Iago's praise morphs her wisdom into "wit," which her "fairness" "useth," presumably in amorous pursuits, as when Desdemona drops her "hint" to Othello that any friend of his telling her his story would win her (2.1.28–29). The "black and witty" woman uses her "wit" to acquire a lover (2.1.130, 131–32). In the first two cases, wisdom as wit helps the woman to secure a man. With the third case, that of the "fair and foolish" woman, Iago gives folly the mate-securing role the first two cases reserve for wisdom: "She never yet was foolish that was fair, / For even her folly helped her to an heir" (2.1.134–35). The distinction between the "fair and wise" woman and the "fair and foolish" woman wavers: no "fair" woman ever finally "was foolish" precisely because her "folly" or strategic sexual availability attains for her what wisdom does for the "fair and wise" woman: a husband due to inherit wealth. The erosion or blurring of the wisdom/folly distinction becomes complete in Iago's praise of the "foul and foolish" woman: "There's none so foul and foolish thereunto, / But does foul pranks which fair and wise ones do" (2.1.139–40). Desdemona notes the confusion of kinds: "Thou praisest the worst best" (2.1.141). She then asks Iago how he would praise "a deserving woman," a woman who would exceed the terms of the game so far, especially with wisdom's equation with wit: "One that, in the authority of her merit, did justly put on the vouch of very malice itself?" (2.1.143–44). This woman Iago praises extensively as deploying her merits with modesty, discretion, and self-control and as being "in wisdom never [...] so frail / To change the cod's head for the salmon's tail" (2.1.151–52). Yet Iago concludes this woman's destiny is to "suckle fools and chronicle small beer" (2.1.157). Iago's conclusion does parry Desdemona's calling his mocking praises of the various cases of women "old fond paradoxes to make fools laugh i' the alehouse," but his conclusion also casts the woman of "merit" as destined to a dreary life of childrearing and household chores, just the contrary to the life Desdemona envisions for herself and has begun to enjoy with Othello (2.1.136–37).

Cassio paints Desdemona in the colors of his bookish, Platonizing rhetoric.[7] For Cassio, Desdemona arrives in Cyprus in triumph as "our great captain's captain" (2.1.74). In the context of his Platonist praise of Desdemona, Cassio's phrase implies Desdemona manifests the ideal or Platonic idea "captain" Othello would then seek to embody. The phrase "our great captain's captain" skews the relationship toward Othello trying to exemplify the model Desdemona embodies in submission to her. Consider: Cassio implores Montano to give Desdemona his knee. To praise Desdemona, Iago mock-praises women as cunning operators seeking their own wills. In accordance with this mock-praise, Iago satirically posits Desdemona as ruling over Othello: "Our general's wife is now the general" (2.3.294–95). Iago also imagines a relation of submission. Neither Cassio nor Iago allow for reciprocity between Othello and Desdemona: either she is the ideal Othello follows (Cassio) or she holds the superior rank in the relationship (Iago). Must Desdemona seeing herself in Othello and Othello himself in her result in a form of subordination, or might the energizing inspiration between the two continue, escaping the domestications Cassio and Iago imply? Does Othello's praise of Desdemona offer a different vision?

Othello's Praise

Both Desdemona and Othello confront the tempest. The storm's overwhelming of the Turks gives the Venetian navy victory. In this triumph Desdemona participates no less than Othello.

The trial by storm separates victors from losers, and Desdemona undergoes this adventure as fully as does Othello. In the process, Desdemona realizes her wish to have been created such a man as Othello. She even precedes Othello in her triumphant arrival at Cyprus. When Othello arrives, his praising salutation to Desdemona acknowledges her attainment of her wish: "O my fair warrior!" (2.1.177).[8]

Cassio praises Desdemona to the Cypriots in her absence and then in her presence but addressing Montano and the Gentlemen, in his praise talking of her, not to her. In response to Desdemona's request for praise, Iago addresses his praise to instances of the generality of women, speaking to Desdemona but (ostensibly) not of her. Safely reaching Cyprus, speaking to Desdemona and of her, Othello exclaims, "O my fair warrior!" and then elaborates on the praising import of his salutation:

> It gives me wonder great as my content
> To see you here before me. O my soul's joy.
> If after every tempest come such calms,
> May the winds blow till they have wakened death,
> And let the laboring bark climb hills of seas
> Olympus-high, and duck again as low
> As hell's from heaven. If it were now to die,
> 'Twere now to be most happy, for I fear
> My soul hath her content so absolute
> That not another comfort like to this
> Succeeds in unknown fate.
>
> (2.1.178–88)

As Cassio notes, Iago's ship, the ship carrying Desdemona, a ship most likely toward the rear of the Venetian fleet, arrives at Cyprus a week earlier than expected, somehow in the chaos of the storm outrunning Othello's ship, the ship properly heading the fleet (2.1.76–77). Besides her being alive, her ship's almost miraculous precedence of arrival contributes to Othello's deep "wonder" on finding Desdemona there "before" him.[9] This "wonder" matches his "content." Othello does recapitulate the movement from the terrible storm to the serene arrival of Desdemona that Cassio's praise emphasizes. In Cassio's praise, Desdemona's beauty, a glory of grace, overcomes what gives death insofar as it may give death, so only life follows in Desdemona's wake. A Venus in Cassio's praise of her beauty, Desdemona becomes a Minerva in Othello's praise.[10] The relations between life and death Cassio evokes take a Homeric turn in Othello's praise. Achilles, by accepting his fate, accepts his death. After greeting Desdemona as his "fair warrior," Othello welcomes demise. Desdemona, in Othello's imagination, heralds a "content" so "absolute" that it threatens to cross into the death Othello would welcome as its only adequate or appropriate sequel. In Cassio's imaginings, Desdemona becomes a goddess or daemon mortality cannot touch. In Othello's praise, Desdemona becomes the fateful woman who induces Othello to contemplate and welcome his own perishing, more a daemon like Athena, Achilles's daemon. As a triumphant warrior, Othello should always bestow and never receive death. Desdemona becomes the only warrior from whom he could welcome death, as from Athena alone does Achilles welcome his imminent demise as central to the fate she heralds. By welcoming his fate from Athena, Achilles rejects suicide. The welcome to perishing Desdemona inspires in Othello should preclude his suicide.

In Othello's praise, the "here" where he "see[s]" Desdemona with "wonder great as [his] content" becomes the very verge of perishing, the moment when a tempest yields to calm, the moment when life yields to death: "If after every tempest come such calms, / May the winds blow till they have wakened death." In Cassio's praise, death goes dormant or slumbers; in Othello's praise, death awakens. The naturalistic effect of wind on water, the production of waves, and the naturalistic aftermath of wind's cessation, "calms," come to figure the apocalyptic and the extra-natural with the waking of "death": "And let the laboring bark climb hills of seas / Olympus-high, and duck again as low / As hell's from heaven." The wave crests and troughs, natural phenomena, come to figure the extranatural distance of hell from heaven. The ship confronting the storm becomes a *barco del alma,* a ship of the soul, but this soul orients itself via a mixture of classical (Olympus, fate) and Christian (hell, heaven) allusions. Cassio speaks of Jove's breath, then Othello's, to evoke "spirits" as receptive to reanimation, to becoming again alive. Othello speaks of his "soul" as attaining a "content so absolute" death becomes the only and a welcome sequel. Othello, his soul, beholding Desdemona, contemplates death's verge. Unlike Cassio's praise of Desdemona, Othello's rhetoric exalting her brings the winds and waves to no omitting of their mortal natures. Quite to the contrary, precisely with the natural elements bringing "death" awake, precisely at the verge where life gives way to death, does the sight of Desdemona become the "joy" of Othello's soul. Cassio imagines Othello and Desdemona bringing life to "extincted spirits." Othello imagines her being his joyous wonder and content at the farthest edge of his perishing. And the "content" of his "soul" in his vision of her before him is "so absolute" as to disallow any possibility of "another comfort like to this" to come about in "unknown fate." The positioning of the moment of contentment with Desdemona between life and death, between anything of life and anything of any sequel, suggests the Christian heaven becomes superfluous, offering no greater contentment, and the Christian hell a speculation, fate being rigorously "unknown."

Dying Now

Othello's praise of Desdemona evokes the punctuality of a now: Othello's last moment, the general entering an irreversible encounter with the moment. A trumpet heralds Othello's arrival at Cyprus. Iago and Cassio know their commander is about to join them when they recognize the trumpet. Even in this recognition Iago and Cassio are rivals. Iago: "The Moor. I know his trumpet" (2.1.174). Cassio: "'Tis truly so" (2.1.174). Othello also hears the trumpet announcing his entrance, and then, in his praise of Desdemona, he takes the winds to be apocalyptic trumpets, last trumpets precipitating and announcing death's arrival: "May the winds blow till they have wakened death." The trumpet heralding Othello sounds a "now" in which converge his vision of his "fair warrior," his sense of his soul's "absolute" "content," and his dying.

How does Othello's sense of the "now" of his dying compare to Hamlet's? Being a nobleman, a dead king's son, Hamlet takes almost his entire play to assimilate his mother's advice that he cease to "[s]eek for [his] noble father in the dust" and accept death as "common" (1.2.71, 72). This acceptance only arrives when the colloquy with the gravedigger leads to Hamlet's contemplation of how even Alexander the Great and Julius Caesar returned to dust (5.1.196–217). Accepting the common demise of all, however noble, allows Hamlet to parse his "now" in relation to his dying: "If it be now, 'tis not to come; if it be not to come, it will be now; if it be not now, yet it will come—the readiness is all" (5.2.220–22). This moment of dying Hamlet defines as an entirely punctual moment: this "now" will come, yet its arrival precludes any further "to come" whatsoever.

Othello sets a condition to his "readiness" for his "now": Othello imagines dying but with Desdemona rendezvousing with him in his "now," being there before him (preceding him, facing him) at the farthest verge of dying. The "wonder" of her arriving "before" him at Cyprus, preceding him, and his "content" at his vision of her "before" him, in front of him, fuse in his praise with his dying so that, in his imagination, she, his "fair warrior," will be there "before" him in the "now" of his dying, as if of his last moment he could say what he says of his current moment: "If it were now to die, / 'Twere now to be most happy." Othello imagines Desdemona giving him his last moment as a moment of ecstatic happiness. Amply ready, Hamlet perishes in tune with his statements about the "now" of his dying. Othello fails his vision of his dying "now," acting out first that vision's cruel inversion in murdering Desdemona and then its dismally ironic parody in killing himself.

What is happiness for Othello? Release from slavery. Othello tells Desdemona of his enslavement, she pities this, and she as a warrior would allow Othello to embrace death, which he must otherwise combat, locked in the bondage of master and slave, the bondage to which Iago's machinations return Othello. In her bringing Othello to an exaltation open to perishing, Desdemona is the Athena-like muse of his deliverance from the deadlock of slave and master, a deadlock evoked at the play's end by Cassio's endless will to torture Iago into speech and Iago's endless will to persist in silence. In his praise, Othello imagines Desdemona allowing him to accept his dying, liberating him from any enslavement to death, from the self being subject to death as master or driven to seek mastery over dying in a fruitless duel of I and not-I. His praise imagines his dying now as a moment never for an I and a not-I but always for an I and a thou, himself and Desdemona. When Iago's manipulations thwart this vision of Desdemona as bearing Othello the gift of death, Othello returns to relating to his dying as a duel of I and not-I. The self-murderer hallucinates mastery over the self's dying now. Through the impasse of Othello attempting to be master over his dying, to give himself death, he suffers a return to dying as occurring in, yet futilely refused by, the master/slave, I/not-I deadlock.

Quite sensibly, in reply to the doom-eager pathos of Othello's praise, Desdemona says, "The heavens forbid / But that our loves and comforts should increase / Even as our days do grow" (2.1.188–90). Of war, Othello's experience is unmatched. What amorous experience does Othello possess before meeting Desdemona? Perhaps little, even no more than Desdemona possesses, yet, about their love, she can meet his hyperbolic rhetoric with pragmatic sense. Othello's praise correlates his relation to Desdemona with the sequence: life→death, so that the sequence the absence of Desdemona→the presence of Desdemona comes to suggest a sequence of a life in chaos (the "tempest," "wind," and "Olympus-high" waves) followed by an another life of beatitude (the "calm" and the "content so absolute") with his "fair warrior," an unsurpassable repose only aberrantly confusable with death. To lose Desdemona would be to regress in the sequence—or, worse, to move forward toward death without her. With Iago's plot working on his trust in Desdemona, Othello feels the possibility of returning to the chaotic tumult of waters: "Perdition catch my soul, / But I do love thee. And when I love thee not, / Chaos is come again" (3.3.91–93).

Gazing into the chaotic sea, the Gentleman sees "[n]othing"; eventually, from this nothing, Cassio envisions Desdemona arriving as exemplary of a divine no-thing-ness incomparable with any thing: Cassio sets Desdemona up as the embodiment of nothing. Does nothingness bring a sublimely terrifying chaos or a beautifully sublime repose? The answer, for Othello, depends on his love for Desdemona, which in turn depends on her fidelity. But why must Othello predicate love on fidelity? As a warrior Othello greets Desdemona: "O my fair warrior!" To Othello Desdemona images back his being, his warriorhood. But if she were to be nothing embodied, what would Othello be? Nothing. Her nihilation in Othello's mind rebounds on Othello, disclosing him as or as harboring within himself a vertiginous abyss. To tip Othello into this void is Iago's purpose.

Nothing Virtual

To destroy Othello with nothing, Iago choreographs Cassio's and Desdemona's behaviors to refer, for Othello, to nonoccurring actions taken by inexistent entities: amorous dalliances between a lustful, devious wife and a treacherous betrayer of an officer. So much do Iago's plots and insinuating comments work on Othello that the general orders Iago to murder Cassio and resolves to himself murder Desdemona. Othello's fateful decisions and subsequent actions result from his ensnarement in a virtual scenario Iago sculpts into the actual, a fictive *mise en scène* that invades and subsumes Othello's relationship to Desdemona.

After falling into the snare Iago sets, Othello ponders a shift in phenomena:

> What sense had I of her stolen hours of lust?
> I saw't not, thought it not, it harmed not me.
> I slept the next night well, was free and merry.
> I found not Cassio's kisses on her lips.
>
> (3.3.338–41)

Iago's manipulations work on Othello a virtualization of the inexistent John Donne attributes to poetry: "How weak a thing is poetry! (and yet Poetry is a counterfeit Creation, and makes things that are not, as though they were)."[11] Rather than referring to things in their absence, words for Othello come to refer to an absence amidst things. The phenomena there for Othello begin to manifest phenomena that never will have been there. Othello turns from the kisses there on the lips of Desdemona (his kisses with her) toward kisses that never will have been there (her kisses with Cassio). These inexistent kisses become so many impingements of nothingness. Are not kisses purely relational events, in no way things? Yet, for Othello, kisses that have taken place yield to kisses that never will have taken place. What exists undergoes negation by what exists not, the type of negation Paul articulates in 1 Corinthians. What Othello supposes he saw not, which unbeknownst to him indeed was not, comes to define what he does see. The world of kisses there for Othello undergoes a voiding. Othello begins to wish he had never known what he supposes he is beginning to know: "He that is robbed, not wanting what is stolen, / Let him not know't, and he's not robbed at all" (3.3.342–43). A counterfeit X would have allowed Othello to be robbed of X yet want not what was stolen had X been stolen, but nothing has been stolen. The dramatic irony allows the reader to realize that Othello is "not robbed at all." Only nothingness has been stolen by Iago for his purposes, including the nothingness of kisses. Othello reaches a "Never tell me" moment: "I had been happy if the general camp,/ Pioneers and all, had tasted her sweet body, / So I had nothing known" (3.3.345–47). Othello insists to Iago, "I'll see before I doubt," but soon after, having witnessed nothing, Othello blurts out, "Now I do see 'tis true" (3.3.191, 444). Or rather, Othello has only witnessed the costumed nothing Iago stages for Othello's undoing. When, feigning to urge patience, Iago says, "Yet we see nothing done," he declares what Othello will ever witness done between Desdemona and Cassio (3.3.432). So indeed, after Iago's stagings, Othello has "nothing known," has "witnessed nothing."

Othello involves something more than and distinct from metatheater, the action hinging on a play Iago stages within

Shakespeare's play. Does Othello's relation to Desdemona ever exclude the virtual? Certainly not: Othello for Desdemona and Desdemona for Othello serve as the virtual embodiment of each other's desired existence, with the dissymmetry that what Othello was, an Achilles of a warrior, defines the referent on which both Othello and Desdemona model the virtual image of what they hope yet to be. Even before Iago's manipulation, the Othello/Desdemona relation dances around a mirage fueling the inspiration the two find in each other.

Emilia discloses another example of how the virtual is an irreducible aspect of Desdemona's relation to Othello and of Othello's relation to Desdemona: Desdemona "so loves the token [the handkerchief] / [...] That she reserves it evermore about her / To kiss and talk to" (3.3.293–96). Again, the play highlights kissing. The handkerchief emblematizes the role of the virtual or "counterfeit" in *Othello* (the word "counterfeit" appears at 2.1.236, 3.3.356, and 5.1.43). Shakespeare repeatedly calls the reader's attention to the fact that anyone with the skill could make a copy of the handkerchief. When Othello carelessly allows the handkerchief to drop to the floor, Emilia picks it up and says to herself, "I'll have the work taken out, / And give't Iago" (3.3.296–97). To "have the work taken out" is to have the handkerchief's embroidery pattern copied on another, blank, handkerchief, like taking a blank sheet of paper and writing "whore" or "wife" upon it. Seemingly, Emilia plans to make a copy of the handkerchief, give the copy to Iago, and surreptitiously return the "original" to Desdemona. Emilia knows how important the handkerchief is to Desdemona: "This was her first remembrance from the Moor. / My wayward husband hath a hundred times / Wooed me to steal it" (3.3.291–93). But, just when Emilia finds and picks up the handkerchief, Iago enters, and Emilia fatally gives it to him, shelving her intent to secure a copy of it. Iago arranges for Cassio to find the handkerchief in his rooms, and Cassio takes it to his mistress Bianca, commanding her, "Take me this work out," that is, make a copy (3.4.179). Bianca immediately becomes jealous, suspecting the handkerchief to be "some token from a newer friend" (3.4.180). Bianca: "Why, whose is it?" (3.4.186). Cassio:

> I know not [...]. I found it in my chamber,
> I like the work well. Ere it be demanded,
> As like enough it will, I'd have it copied.
> Take it, and do't, and leave me for this time.
>
> (3.4.187–90)

Given the handkerchief's promiscuous susceptibility to being copied, who could vouch with certainty that the handkerchief Othello gave Desdemona was the "original" and not a copy, a counterfeit? What would the term "original" signify in reference to such an item? The handkerchief emblematizes the counterfeit, the virtual, the inexistent acts and entities that nevertheless lead one character to posit knowledge of another. Othello claims to know that Desdemona is a "whore" on the basis of the handkerchief. Brandishing this supposed knowledge, Othello demonizes Desdemona.

Demons

First Desdemona's father Brabantio and then Othello attribute Desdemona's actions to demonic influence. In both cases, Iago's manipulative rhetoric linking sexuality, animality, and the satanic prompts the accusation of demonic possession. Absent Iago's intervention, when and how did Othello and Desdemona plan to reveal their marriage? Iago forces this secret's disclosure. At the start of the play, with Roderigo standing unhidden, Iago stands hidden below Brabantio's window and raises the alarm:

> Even now, now, very now, an old black ram
> Is tupping your white ewe. Arise, arise,
> Awake the snorting citizens with the bell,
> Or else the devil will make a grandsire of you.
> Arise, I say.
>
> (1.1.86–90)

Othello replicates this rhetoric of the sexually outlandish demonic animal in denouncing Desdemona:

> Damn her, lewd minx! O, damn her! damn her!

Come, go with me apart, I will withdraw
To furnish me with some swift means of death
For the fair devil.

(3.3.475–78)

Iago would have Brabantio fear that his daughter betrays him with a Moor, a man of non-Christian origins and therefore damned. Brabantio to Othello: "Damned as thou art, thou hast enchanted her" (1.2.62). (To damn—a speech act Desdemona never pronounces.) Iago's "snorting citizens" verge on being a lynch mob. When this torch-brandishing mob arrives due to Iago's direction or stage management, Iago says to Othello, "Those are the raisèd father and his friends. / You were best go in" (1.2.28–29). Othello too plans the gruesome death of his devilish enemies, Desdemona and Cassio.

In this play whose characters are so concerned with hell, the reader cannot help but notice the letters h-e-l-l in the general's name; from the drama's first scene to the last, Iago, Othello, and Emilia refer to others as the Devil or as a devil. Desdemona never calls another character the Devil or a devil, though her own name bears the word demon within it. With this aphasia, Desdemona shows demonization to be a behavior alien to her. Yet Iago precisely achieves her demonization in Othello's eyes. Iago seeks to demonize the very character resonant with Wisdom and Athena. The daemon Cassio imagines, the Athena-like "fair warrior" Othello claims to love, the bearer of the fruitfulness of the creation, precisely she Iago destroys by her demonization. Displacing Othello's trust from Desdemona to himself, Iago carries on the work of replacing Yahweh's daughter Hokmah with a son. This work involves Iago bringing out the hell in Othello.

Lies, Hell, and Fate

As much as the threshold of death, the gateway to Hades, Achilles hates the man who lies, who says one thing yet within harbors another. If Shakespeare read the *Iliad*, it was likely in Chapman's translation. In this translation, speaking to Ulysses, Achilles declares, "like hell mouth I loathe [he] / Who holds not in his words and thoughts one indistinguish'd troth."[12] In Chapman's translation of the *Odyssey*, Ulysses, appropriating Achilles's words, declares, "No less I hate him than the gates of hell, / That poorness can force an untruth to tell" (14.231–32). Achilles and Othello respond to liars with rage. An Achilles who has long squandered his heroism in mercenary work, Othello draws as an antagonist Iago, whose discrepancy between outer demeanor and inner disposition feigns so completely Iago can say, "I am not what I am" (1.1.63). The father of myriad lies, Iago repeats about himself an epithet, "honest," Desdemona might in all reasonableness claim for herself in her relations with Othello. The artist of deception, Iago, declares himself honest and brings Othello to see Desdemona as a sophisticate at the spinning of falsehoods. Iago's words to Othello recounting Cassio's supposed words about Desdemona, Cassio admitting that he did, says Iago, "Lie [...] With her, on her, what you will," bring to Othello a pun, "lie" as falsehood and "lie" as sexual act (4.1.33–34). Registering this pun, Othello raves: "Lie with her? Lie on her? We say lie on her, when they belie her" (4.1.35–36). And just before falling into a fit, Othello says of these words, "It is not words that shake me thus," yet words alone bring Othello to collapse raging (4.1.40–41). Just prior to murdering Desdemona, when she denies giving Cassio the handkerchief, Othello says to her, "Sweet soul, take heed, / Take heed of perjury; thou art on thy death-bed" (5.2.50–51). Just after murdering Desdemona, who, slowly dying, replies, "Nobody. I myself" to Emilia's query ("O who hath done the deed?"), Othello again singles out Desdemona as a liar:

SHE DIES

Othello	Why, how should she be murdered?
Emilia	Alas, who knows?
Othello	You heard her say herself it was not I.
Emilia	She said so. I must needs report the truth.
Othello	She's like a liar gone to burning hell. 'Twas I that killed her.

(5.2.126–30)

Othello rejects Desdemona's testimony, calling her a "liar." On her "death-bed," Desdemona must avoid "perjury," Othello insists, and he also insists she commits perjury in testifying, "Nobody, I myself." Achilles associates the liar with Hades's gate, death's threshold. For Othello, Desdemona is a "perjured woman" who, as a "liar," goes to "hell" (5.2.63). But in calling Desdemona a liar, Othello enters the coils of the I/not-I impasse he will then travail in until his death, the impasse between "it was not I" and "'Twas I." When Othello verges on his own lie, saying to Emilia, "You heard her say herself it was not I," he moves toward the I/not-I impasse. What exactly did Desdemona "say"? "Nobody, I myself": by calling "not I" the "Nobody, I myself," Othello defines the self Desdemona's word "myself" designates, Desdemona's self, as not Othello, erasing Desdemona as a distinct "you" he could address and positing her as the negation of his own self, as his "not I." Othello had envisioned his exalted sense of self in Desdemona, his "fair warrior"; Iago triumphs over Othello by steering Othello away from discovering in Desdemona the image of the fullness of his self and toward finding Desdemona to embody the negation of his self.

Is there a Desdemona who acts as Othello's negation? One candidate would be the "Nobody," the Desdemona Iago invents, Othello's "cunning whore of Venice," due to whom, Othello exclaims, "Othello's occupation's gone." Another candidate would be Othello's "fair warrior" from whom he had envisioned receiving the now of his dying as a moment of supreme happiness in which no contradiction would pertain between his being a warrior and his perishing. But Othello's "fair warrior" can only bring the Moor his dying now as the most beneficent of gifts insofar as she remains with him as a "you" in that now. Should she morph into his "not I," then, rather than being with him at the very gate of death, she becomes as the gate of death, she becomes a liar such as Achilles hates, a "fair devil."

From whose head is the devil Desdemona born? Iago's scheming brain certainly brings about the conditions for her birth. But Othello, Zeus-like, is the one who suffers a headache. Iago knows Desdemona to be innocent; only from Othello's thoughts of Desdemona come the doubts and fears that give birth to her phantom double. Iago can only be a midwife to this birth. Preparing to interrogate Desdemona, but casting Emilia as a "bawd" keeping watch and Desdemona as a "whore," and with choleric sarcasm pretending he would have privacy with Desdemona for sexual relations, Othello says to Emilia: "Leave procreants alone and shut the door. / Cough, or cry hem, if anybody come" (4.2.20, 21, 28–29). The irony of "procreants" is sharp: Iago has taught Othello to despise the burgeoning fruitfulness of the creation and the procreation the deity commands. Rather than any procreation, behind the closed doors ensues Othello's painful questioning and berating of Desdemona, for example: "Heaven truly knows that thou art false as hell" (4.2.39). The interrogation session done, Othello calls Emilia back, saying Emilia "keeps the gate of hell," the doorway to the room where the mock tryst of the "procreants" took place, though recall here "hell" is Renaissance slang for vagina (4.2.93). Emilia reenters, Othello exits, and Emilia asks Desdemona, "Alas, what does this gentleman conceive?" (4.2.96). Othello has conceived no child with Desdemona; he has only further gestated the "conception" with which he "groan[s]," his conviction of Desdemona's affair with Cassio (5.2.55, 56).

At the peak of Othello's delight in Desdemona, Othello claims he can graciously accept death as he happily moves toward his "unknown fate." Joy in Desdemona allows his soul unsurpassable contentment and wonder as his soul approaches death's verge with fate unknown and heaven and hell suspended as significant destinies. With Iago's mirage of a lying adulteress pressing on his mind's eye, Othello reverses his stance toward fate. Voicing a palinode to his previous thoughts on "unknown fate," Othello bemoans his supposed cuckoldry in terms of a Homeric notion of fate: "'Tis destiny unshunnable, like death. / Even then this forkèd plague is fated to us / When we do quicken" (3.3.275–77). The cuckold's horns became Othello's fate at birth, and the destiny of being a cuckold resembles death, both being "unshunnable." Now fate becomes unbearably known and, "like death," something Othello would shun if only he could. Othello equates his death with his betrayal by his deceptive wife, so Othello recapitulates the Achilles who says: "I hate that man like the very Gates of Death / who says one thing but hides another in his heart" (9.378–79). Though Othello's fate is set, still he seeks to prevent the same fate from overtaking others: "Yet she must die, else she'll betray more men" (5.2.6). And in her killing, the destinations of heaven or hell become of the utmost significance to Othello, who pleads with Desdemona to pray for forgiveness for any "crime / Unreconciled as yet to heaven and grace," to "confess" her "sin" because he would not "kill [her] unprepared spirit": "I would not kill thy soul" (5.2.26–27, 53, 31, 32). Desdemona bewilderedly testifies she has committed no such sin requiring repentance or confession, so, in her death, says Othello, "She's like a liar gone to burning hell" (5.2.129).

The traits of Desdemona Othello found praiseworthy Iago manages to revalue in Othello's mind. During their final colloquy, Othello commands Desdemona, "Peace, and be still" (5.2.46). Then, having asphyxiated her, Othello sarcastically queries the dying Desdemona: "Ha, no more moving? / Still as the grave" (5.2.93–94). Othello accuses her very ability to move, say, out of her father's house and toward freedom. Whereas before Iago's manipulations Othello imagined Desdemona as rendering moot for him any question of heaven or hell, Iago's ruinous effects continue after Othello's murder of Desdemona, for though to her very end she never renounces her love for him, Othello cannot but now imagine her as determining his soul's destination. In declaring Desdemona his "fair warrior," Othello spoke of himself as a ship caught in wave crests and troughs as far from each other as heaven and hell, and he welcomed his "unknown fate." With the scheming of Iago partly revealed and his own manipulation into murder known, Othello asks, "Who can control his fate?" and compares himself to a ship reaching its "journey's end" (5.2.264, 266). Viewing Desdemona's corpse on the marriage bed, Othello exclaims, "When we shall meet at compt, / This look of thine will hurl my soul from heaven, / And fiends will snatch at it" (5.2.272–74). With the reinstatement of heaven and hell as significant coordinates for Othello's thought, Othello's hard-fought overcoming of being a slave unravels, as the general berates himself as a "cursèd, cursèd slave," and now the wind and waves he would have had waken death to seal the finality of his joy in Desdemona he thinks of as among the eternal torments that will separate him ever more finally from her, and the slave-master's lash returns: "Whip me ye devils, / From the possession of this heavenly sight! / Blow me about in winds, roast me in sulphur, / Wash me in steep-down gulfs of liquid fire!" (5.2.275, 276–79).

Names and Faces

Torn by the doubts Iago induces, Othello exclaims, "My name, that was as fresh / As Dian's visage, is now begrimed and black / As mine own face" (3.3.386–88). Goddess of the moon, huntress, in ancient Rome a favorite of slaves for whom her temples were places of refuge, whose day of celebration was a holiday for slaves: Diana is the goddess in whose face Othello can see his name as "fresh," as new and vital again, as free.[13] As mirrored in this face, the name "Othello" finds refuge from association with slavery. This freshness of his name Othello finds in Desdemona's face, just as his marriage to her would signal and seal his final overcoming of slave status. But when, entertaining the doubts Iago insinuates, Othello cries out, "I'll have some proof" (3.3.386), his belief in Desdemona wavers, and his name falls toward inescapably mirroring his "own face" as "begrimed and black." Such is the face Brabantio imagines when, in Othello's presence, he declares if Othello's marriage to Desdemona stands, "Bond slaves and pagans shall our statesmen be" (1.2.98). Knowing Othello once was a slave and was born to non-Christians, Brabantio throws these facts in Othello's face, as if any children the senator's daughter might bear by Othello will carry these traits as stigmas despite any achievement of Othello, any status he may attain among the Venetian ruling elite, any service he might do the Venetian state. Later, before the Duke and with Othello present, Brabantio compares Othello taking Desdemona to the Turks taking Cyprus, implying Othello will always carry the stigma of having been an outsider, someone always thinkable as among the enemy (1.3.211). In defending Othello and declaring her love for him before the

Duke and her father, Desdemona avows, "I saw Othello's visage in his mind" (1.3.253). Desdemona saw Othello's face in his mind, or she saw his face as he sees it in his own mind, as he wishes to see it: as he wishes to see his name, "as fresh / As Dian's visage." The testimony of Desdemona counters her father's accusation that Othello must have used magic or drugs, for otherwise Desdemona, a "maiden never bold, / Of spirit so still and quiet that her motion / Blushed at herself," could never have "fall[en] in love with what she feared to look on," Othello, his face (1.3.95–97, 99). Looking into Desdemona's face, Othello sees a "fair warrior." In her face Othello sees his wished-for image, his name as fresh as Dian's visage. But with the shattering of that mirror by the doubts Iago cultivates, Othello's name reverts to being "begrimed and black" as his "own face."

Othello Encaved

As Iago's stratagems return Othello to the abjection of a slave, at least in his own self-judgment, these stratagems also bring forth a void within Othello or Othello's self as an inner emptiness. In telling Brabantio and Desdemona of his adventures and hardships, Othello speaks of caves, "antres vast" (1.3.140). Like many of the items Othello's fantastic tales mention, caverns become a motif in the play. Asking Othello to hide himself to observe Cassio supposedly speaking of his trysts with Desdemona, Iago says to the general, "Do but encave yourself" (4.1.81). Given the frequently ironic cuts Iago's words perform on the unwitting Othello, Iago's request that Othello "encave" himself should give the reader pause. To name the most intolerable condition he would choose to endure rather than accept other men's sexual access to Desdemona, Othello imagines being a "toad" confined to a "dungeon" (3.3.270, 71). Existence in such confinement associates with the enslavement Othello lists to Brabantio and Desdemona as among the sufferings of his youth. Realizing Desdemona's innocence and his own heinousness for having killed her, Othello describes himself as a "cursèd, cursèd slave." In the process of his fall into Iago's hologram of infidelity, Othello again suffers the conditions of his youth from which his martial career and rise to the Venetian generalship had freed him. Or at least Othello reverts to the imagery and diction descriptive of those sufferings to speak of his state in the throes and aftermath of Iago's manipulation. So, if in his youthful wanderings he endured "[r]ough quarries, rocks," under the pressure of Iago leading him to consider Desdemona engaged in infidelity, Othello imagines a stony "dungeon." If the perils of his youth included "vast" caverns, when the perplexed Desdemona asks Othello, "Alas, what ignorant sin have I committed?," Othello replies that her sin is so notorious that even the "bawdy wind, that kisses all it meets, / Is hushed within the hollow mine of earth / And will not hear of it" (4.2.70, 78–80). "Never tell me": the wind would refuse to hear of Desdemona's vagaries. But from such a "hollow" where the wind flees to avoid hearing of Desdemona's "sin," Othello calls forth vengeance as a personified blackness. Beginning to believe Iago's charges against Desdemona, Othello commands, "Arise, black vengeance, from thy hollow hell!" (3.3.447). Here the cave, the hollowness, takes on the name of hell, the hell of Othello, or the emptiness opening within him with his ensnarement in Iago's plot.

Between Worlds

Crying out an invocation ("Divinity of hell!" [2.3.326]), Iago conjures within Othello a "hollow hell," Iago himself having undergone an inner voiding. Othello's passing Iago over for promotion devastates him. From the devastation of his world, Iago directs his pawns into free-floating type-scenes of adultery, jealousy, and revenge. Shifting among worlds, Iago inhabits a significance-free interzone out of which he spins significations. Othello and Desdemona also traverse such an asemantic passageway allowing for worlds yet being of nary a world whatsoever. Moving from her father's house in Venice to Othello's citadel in Cyprus, Desdemona traverses the chaotic waters where the Christian and Muslim worlds graze each other amidst the worldless sea. Desdemona and Othello each think of the other as in excess of a world and so as putting worlds into play. Othello reports how he told Desdemona the entire account of his "pilgrimage": "My story being done, / She gave me for my pains a world of kisses." Othello recounts a world of distress, enslavement, and suffering, and receives another in exchange, a "world of kisses." This initial exchange, with the sensation of lips on lips offered in the swap, echoes through the play. Reeling at Othello having named her a "whore," Desdemona declares to Iago, "I cannot say whore. / It does abhor me now I speak the word. / To do the act that might the addition earn / Not the world's mass of vanity could make me" (4.2.161–64). A "whore" exchanges caresses for a price. Desdemona imagines the "world" as a fee, with the client conveying and the "whore" receiving as payment the "world's" entirety—the encounter between the parties puts in play the world and so happens in excess of the world. Desdemona had offered Othello a world of kisses, and in doing so took a step beyond her world, the house of her father, toward Othello's world, the world he offered her. Iago keeps promising to procure Desdemona for Roderigo if only the gull will give Iago enough cash to convey the proper inducements of jewelry. In a polite counterpart to Iago's ersatz pimping, Brabantio had paraded before Desdemona the "wealthy curlèd darlings" of Venice as marriage prospects (1.2.67). A woman as traversing from one world to another and as the aworldly medium for the exchange of worlds: the term "whore" may name a disposition of Desdemona at stake in any such exchange, whether prostitution, a brokered marriage, or the most demure offer of a world of kisses

Desdemona asks Emilia if she thinks there are any wives who grant men distinct from their husbands sexual favors in exchange for gifts. Emilia says, "There be some such, no question," prompting Desdemona to ask her: "Wouldst thou do such a deed for all the world?" (4.3.64, 65). Emilia returns the question to Desdemona, and after Emilia's humorous quibble about doing such a deed not "by this heavenly light" but in "the dark," the insistent Desdemona poses her question again, her wording's exact repetition being a tell suggesting her stake in the issue (4.3.68, 69). Recall that Desdemona took over for her absent mother in her father's household and ask: did she not "betray" her father by offering Othello herself in exchange for the world Othello could give her? Again, Desdemona to Emilia: "Wouldst thou do such a deed for all the world?" (4.3.70). Declaring the world "a great price for a small vice," Emilia wonders "who would not make her husband a cuckold to make him a monarch," prompting Desdemona again to deny she would "do such a wrong for the whole world" (4.3.72, 78–79, 80–81). Emilia's next reply requires some comment: "Why, the wrong is but a wrong i' the world. And having the world for your labor, 'tis a wrong in your own world, and you might quickly make it right" (4.3.82–84). The aworldly "labor" facilitating the exchange of a world only is "a wrong" in the "world," yet exceeding the world and precipitating the world's exchange, this very "labor" the world's new owner may deem "right." Note how the "labor" thus becomes the semantically neutral bearer of meanings ("wrong," "right") wholly relative to the worlds the said "labor" displaces into processes of exchange. Desdemona bathed in such neutrality in her exchange of worlds, her father's for Othello's, the world of Venice for the world of Cyprus. In this neutrality, the question of whether Desdemona is "false" or "true," "whore" or "wife," becomes inarticulate and moot. Or rather: the terms "false" and "whore" attempt to domesticate the fluid, semantic neutrality that allows for those terms and for the terms "true" and "wife" yet is thinkable via neither pair of terms.

Water

A worldless element of semantic neutrality, water, open to any form yet without form, favors Desdemona, as her sea adventure suggests. Consider the face in the water Desdemona evokes. Desdemona perceives herself in her mother's maid, who sang a song of a woman weeping near a willow over the loss of her beloved. The maid perceived herself in the woman of the willow song. The woman of the song hears and arguably sees herself in a stream by which the weeping willow grows. Desdemona singing the song: "Her hand on her bosom, her head on her knee, / Sing willow, willow, willow. / The fresh streams ran by her, and murmured her moans" (4.3.42–44). With fluidity, the boundaries separating contraries waver, say the boundary between soft and hard. The willow song describes how the falling "salt tears" of the woman "softened the stones" (4.3.46). Though in Cassio's praise the beauty of Desdemona causes stones to omit their mortal nature, and Othello worries that her beauty will dissuade his murderous purpose, Othello's "heart is turned to stone," and Desdemona's testimony of innocence only further "stone[s]" his "heart" (4.1.175, 5.2.63). After Iago's manipulations, Othello's heart refuses softening. Othello admits his preference for "hardness" (1.3.234). Desdemona's element, water, Othello learns to abhor. Debating over the corpse of Desdemona as to her nature, Othello exclaims to Emilia, "She was false as water" (5.2.134). Johnson glosses Othello's simile: "As water that will support no weight, nor keep any impression."[14] Yet the Iago-harried Othello would capture water in the distinction between false and true.

After murdering Desdemona, Othello tells Emilia Iago knew of Desdemona's affair with Cassio. In reply, Emilia asks incredulously: Iago knew that Desdemona "was false to wedlock?" (5.2.140). Othello:

> Ay, with Cassio. Nay, had she been true,
> If heaven would make me such another world
> Of one entire and perfect chrysolite,
> I'd not have sold her for it.
>
> (5.2.141–44)

In his praise of Desdemona, Othello imagined arriving with her at the verge of death as a matter of water in flux from storm to calm. Lost in Iago's demonization of Desdemona, to imagine a utopia, Othello envisions a "chrysolite" world that precludes fluidity. False or true, "Ay" or "Nay": Othello imagines a world as a static, fixed gemstone and Desdemona as never entering into exchange, fused with one semantic pole in an opposition of the type Emilia treats with skepticism. If for Othello fluidity eventually defines the false, then the true for Othello becomes the contrary of fluid, as Othello suggests when he says to Emilia that, if Desdemona "had been true," he would refuse to exchange her for a heaven-built world made of "one entire and perfect chrysolite," the rigid form of the gem-world being outdone in trueness or nonfluidity only by a true Desdemona.

Iago's Will, Will's Iago

In contrast to fluidity is Iago's vision of the will. A will to dominate drives Iago. Iago inspires his dupes to adopt this will. Inspiration toward such a will operates in Iago's relationship to Roderigo. Being told by Iago of the elopement, Roderigo despairs of ever attaining Desdemona and proposes suicide: "I will incontinently drown myself" (1.3.306). Note the phrase: "I will." As a potential suicide, Roderigo imagines the will ending the self. Suicide pictures a mirage of mastery: the self as disembodied will disposing of the self as embodied life. A will to power over life attracts Roderigo toward suicide precisely because his will appears lacking. Roderigo follows his suicide statement with a confession: he is unable to "amend" his being desperately "fond" of Desdemona, lacking the "virtue" to master his emotions (1.3.318). The "vir" in "virtue" comes from the Latin for man, manliness, or hero. To counter his lack of virtue, of the volition to "amend" his fondness for Desdemona, Roderigo wishfully envisions his volition as wholly untrammeled and irreversibly final: his will standing above his life and ending it.

Far from refuting suicide in his advice to Roderigo, Iago reinforces his gull's vision of the will as the supra-corporeal arbiter (and sometime abattoir) of the corporeal. To the suicidal Roderigo, Iago explains, "Our bodies are gardens, to the which our wills are gardeners" (1.3.320–21). Iago extols free will, volition untrammeled, the will choosing through a reasoning process. Whichever bodily passions we may "plant," "sow," or "weed up," Iago insists "the power and corrigible authority of this lies in our wills" (1.3.321, 322, 324–25). The relationship of the will to the self Roderigo's suicidal wish implies Iago embraces and repackages as self-control defined as sovereignty over the body as plant or animal. So Iago tells Roderigo that what Roderigo calls his "love" for Desdemona belongs among the "unbitten lusts": what Roderigo feels toward Desdemona "is merely a lust of the blood and a permission of the will" (1.3.331, 330, 333–34). Iago's advice reinforces a suicidal vision of the will. Or as Nietzsche might ask: where else but through suicide, through the suicidal logic of Christianity, does the modern will, the "free" will, arrive? Iago personifies a will to self-negation: "I am not what I am." Or such a will manifests on stage as an uncanny personage: Iago. Infected by Iago with this will, Othello first exercises free will over Desdemona by killing her, and Othello thinks of his act as a killing of her body but a freeing of her soul. Then he exercises will over himself in committing suicide.

Iago imagines the will as a god of volition walking amidst a garden and tending the plants. Precisely in the Cyprus citadel's garden does this Iago bring Othello to the decision to murder Desdemona (or so two among the prompt books indicate[15]). This Iago Emilia unknowingly equates with Eden's serpent. Unaware who fed Othello the rumor of Desdemona's infidelity, Emilia declares to the jealous Othello, "If any wretch have put this in your head, / Let heaven requite it with the serpent's curse!" (4.2.15–16).

As *Hamlet* ends, having become able to be unable, Hamlet says, "Let be" and restfully enters silence: "The rest is silence" (5.2.358). This will-relenting release into silence Iago parodies. As *Othello* ends, Iago wills his own silence, an unrelenting will to unrelenting silence. The final victim of Iago, of his will, is his own voice, particularly the yes, promise, or prayer each act of speaking implies, or so Lodovico hints (5.2.304). Iago's will to negation will ever sound as Iago's silence: "From this time forth, I never will speak word" (5.2.303).

I, Not I

In his willing negation, Iago emerges as a parody of Paul. Among the apostles who saw Christ, belated Paul claims to be the last. Of his vision of Christ Paul writes: "And last of all he was seen also of me as of one, born out of due time" (1 Corinthians 15.8, Geneva 1560). About his calling to apostleship and his being a follower of Christ, Paul states, "But by the grace of God, I am that I am," and Paul credits the overflowing abundance of his apostolic labor not to himself but to grace: "not I, but the grace of God which is with me" (1 Corinthians 15.10, Geneva 1560). Grace both gives Paul his "I am" yet entails the negation of Paul's "I," as if Paul ultimately could be an "am" without being an "I." Paul's "I" undergoes nihilation, while grace, Paul states, "is in me" (1 Corinthians 15.10, Geneva 1560). Void of "I," Paul's "me" contains grace. For Paul's "me" to become a vessel of grace Paul's "I" must become "not I": the apostle's only "I" becomes the evacuation or voiding of his "I." As the fullness of grace within Paul's "me" nears, the most complete emptying out or kenosis of Paul's "I" approaches. The 1587 Geneva Bible's marginal gloss tags as "divine inspiration" the state of belated Paul in his self-humbling.

Taking up such voiding of the "I" as his inspiration toward action, Iago is both wickedly and insightfully Pauline when he refracts Paul's "I am that I am" into: "I am not what I am" (1.1.63).[16] Iago states his formula of self-negation ("I am not what I am") to sum up how his "outward action" can in no way be taken as the "complement extern" of the "native act and figure of [his] heart" (1.1.59,61, 60). Here too Iago argues in a Pauline mode: his "outward action," his literal act, may be the opposite of or simply uncorrelated with the "native act" in his heart, his figural ("figure") "heart." Paul distinguishes external, literal circumcision of the "flesh" from internal, figural circumcision, the "spiritual" circumcision of the heart. Iago works with Paul's distinction between the literal and the figural to persuade Roderigo that he, Iago, only appears to be Othello's loyal follower but is actually disloyal. In carrying Othello's flag into battle as the general's "ancient" (ensign, standard bearer), Iago fearlessly bore amidst the enemy the sign of his worshipful loyalty toward and love for the general. Wounded to the quick by Othello's rejection of him for the lieutenancy, Iago learns to be more circumspect with his emotions. Recasting enemy soldiers trying to desecrate Othello's flag as crows, Iago declares his refusal ever again to "wear [his] heart upon [his] sleeve / For daws to peck at" (1.1.62–63). To Roderigo Iago explains his dissimulation of loyalty and its formula ("I am not what I am") in the course of arguing that he, Iago, in no way "love[s] the Moor," words prompting Roderigo to say to Iago, "I would not follow him, then" (1.1.38).

In response, Iago claims that in remaining in Othello's service, he only adopts the "forms and visages of duty" while pursuing his own interests (1.1.48). The complex self-negation Iago's argument entails specifies the import and logic of Iago's "I am not what I am":

> For, sir, it is as sure as you are Roderigo,
> Were I the Moor, I would not be Iago.
> In following him, I follow but myself.
> Heaven is my judge, not I for love and duty,
> But seeming so for my peculiar end.
>
> (1.1.54–58)

Iago's abyssal yet precise logic gives a nihilistic resonance to a phrase echoing through the play: "not I." Iago's first premise ("it is as sure as you are Roderigo") entails an "I am that I am" in the sense of Roderigo being Roderigo. Iago's hypothetical statement "Were I the Moor, I would not be Iago" posits Othello as the not-Iago. Via hypothetically being the Moor, the "I" (Iago) becomes "not I" (not Iago). How can this logic then lead to Iago saying of Othello, "In following him, I follow but myself"? Othello, as Iago's self, is Iago-in-negation, so Iago, in following Othello, follows but himself, only negated.

Paul could say, "In following Christ, I follow but myself, only negated." Yet how is Shakespeare thinking of Paul in having Iago's logic of self-negation closely resemble the belated Apostle's? Nietzsche could be describing Iago when, in *The Antichrist*, Nietzsche writes of Paul as a "hate-inspired counterfeiter": "On the heels of [Jesus's] 'glad tidings' came the *very worst*: those of Paul. In Paul was embodied the opposite type to that of the 'bringer of glad tidings': the genius in hatred, in the vision of hatred, in the inexorable logic of hatred! *How much* this dysangelist sacrificed to hatred! Above all, the Redeemer: he nailed him to *his own* cross."[17] Nietzsche suggests Paul, from his self-hatred, brings forth a vision and message implying hatred of the self, negation of self. Roderigo's "Never tell me" casts Iago as a dysangelist. What Nietzsche's Paul may have done to Jesus, Shakespeare's Iago certainly does to Desdemona: he nails her to *his* cross.

Saying, "I am not what I am," Iago states a condition inseparable from the voiding of his self by Othello's passing over Iago for the lieutenancy in favor of Cassio. Immediately after Iago says, "I am not what I am," Roderigo says of Othello: "What a full fortune does the thick lips owe" (1.1.64). Being of fullness, Othello makes of Iago emptiness. A similar logic, a reactive one of *ressentiment*, operates when Iago says of Cassio, "He hath a daily beauty in his life / That makes me ugly" (5.1.19–20). If Cassio walks in beauty, Iago does not. If Cassio is Othello's lieutenant, Iago is not. If Desdemona is Othello's "fair warrior," Iago is not.[18]

Iago Replaces Desdemona

Iago enters into rivalry with Desdemona over Othello. Othello's attribution of warriorhood to Desdemona again slights and demotes Iago, who, having been on the same ship as Desdemona, would also be a candidate for being the warrior who braves chaos with Othello to defeat the Turks. With Iago standing near, along with Iago's wife Emilia and Iago's nemesis Cassio, with the greatest triumph over the Turks inadvertently achieved via the storm, Othello praises Desdemona: "O my fair warrior!" Othello imagines her as a warrior and the tempest she and he have just survived as a titanic battle. How does Othello's praise of Desdemona work on Iago, already madly resentful of Cassio's promotion, the Cassio with no military experience to speak of? Othello then asks Iago to see to Othello's luggage and to bring by the captain of Iago's ship so Othello might pay his respects: the reader might well think *Iago's* occupation's gone, the courageous and experienced flag officer reduced to a bellhop (2.1.202–06).

Iago overtly states his resentment of Cassio, but his resentment of Desdemona also is evident. Iago duels over Othello with Desdemona more than with Cassio. Through Iago's machinations, the epithet Iago most deserves, the epithet provoking Othello's utmost enmity, "liar," becomes descriptive of Desdemona, while the epithet most appropriate to her, "honest," becomes

Othello's refrain to describe Iago, following the lead of Iago's self-descriptions. And due to Iago's "honesty," the love, trust, and intimacy in self-disclosure Othello owes to Desdemona he bequeaths to Iago.

As a force of negation toward chaos, Iago acts as Desdemona's contrary. On landing at Cyprus and deploying lavish rhetoric, Cassio extols the consummation of Othello and Desdemona's marriage Cassio anticipates will take place during the couple's first night on the island. This consummation of the marriage Iago's machinations will thwart; Iago excitedly implores Othello, "Do it not with poison, strangle her in her bed, even the bed she hath contaminated" (4.1.199–200). Thus the bed where Othello and Desdemona would have consummated their marriage becomes the bed where Othello will murder her.

Iago has a muse, and his muse becomes pregnant with an improvisation, an unfolding scheme forever thwarting Desdemona from becoming pregnant. Against Desdemona's fruitfulness, Iago wills his own nihilistic fruitfulness to bring multiple deaths into the world. Iago thinks of his own will to power over others in terms of pregnancy and birth. Assuring Roderigo of eventual access to Desdemona, Iago says, "There are many events in the womb of time which will be delivered" (1.3.366–67). Othello has not been at war for "nine moons," the term of a pregnancy (1.3.85). Alone on stage, musing over how to wrest the lieutenancy from Cassio, Iago conceives of the scheme to insinuate to Othello that Cassio is having an affair with Desdemona, and declares to himself in triumph, "I have't. It is engendered. Hell and night / Must bring this monstrous birth to the world's light" (1.3.396–97). To Roderigo Iago calls "most pregnant" the supposition that, tiring of Othello, Desdemona will seek a new love interest and find one in Cassio (2.1.229). Anxiously waiting for Othello's ship safely to reach Cyprus, Desdemona distracts herself from her worry by asking Iago how he would praise her. After some deliberation, Iago introduces his praise as follows: "But my Muse labors, / And thus she is delivered" (2.1.126–27). Iago attributes Desdemona's honesty to himself. Iago also attributes fertility, pregnancy, and birth to himself, or to his Muse, qualities the new bride Desdemona should be able to claim as her own.

These qualities converge as "fruitfulness." Iago gets Cassio drunk, sets Roderigo on the lieutenant to start a brawl, and the resulting uproar delays the consummation of Othello and Desdemona's marriage. The outraged Othello strips Cassio of his lieutenancy. Iago advises the disgraced Cassio to petition Desdemona to plead with Othello for Cassio's reinstatement. Pondering in soliloquy this advice, Iago declares Desdemona to be "framed as fruitful / As the free elements" and so likely to be easily won over by Cassio to press his suit with Othello (2.3.318–19). This very fruitfulness Iago will morph into a detriment. He vows to transform this "virtue" into "pitch" (2.3.337). Approaching Desdemona to beg her assistance, Cassio hails her as "[b]ounteous madam" (3.3.7). As a Wisdom figure, Desdemona participates bountifully in the fruitfulness of the creation. For Iago to win Othello over to her destruction requires Othello to despise in Desdemona what he might more reasonably love. As Emilia reports to Cassio, even before Cassio has had a chance to request to Desdemona that she speak for him to Othello, she has already been doing so. Emilia tells Cassio that Othello has said to Desdemona that although "wholesome wisdom" suggests he not reinstate Cassio, his love for Cassio will persuade Othello to reinstate Cassio as soon as is politic (3.1.46). Othello would listen to "wholesome wisdom," but who can discern Wisdom from Folly, the turn to one from the turn to the other? Othello believes he can. To Emilia, to justify his murder of Desdemona, Othello says of her, "She turned to folly. And she was a whore" (5.2.32).

The more Desdemona pleads for Cassio, the more Iago's insinuations work on Othello, to the point where he can only think to chastise her fruitfulness. Taking her hand, Othello finds it to be "moist," and he says to Desdemona:

> This argues fruitfulness and liberal heart.
> Hot, hot, and moist. This hand of yours requires
> A sequester from liberty, fasting, and prayer,
> Much castigation, exercise devout,

For here's a young and sweating devil, here,
That commonly rebels.

(3.4.34, 36–41)

"Be fruitful, and multiply" (Genesis 1.28, Geneva, 1587): the fruitfulness the first biblical commandment celebrates and welcomes, the fruitfulness of the animals and the humans that carries forward the deity's fruitful work of creation—Othello casts that fruitfulness as devilish, as something demonic requiring exorcism via strict ascetic discipline. Othello speaks his admonition to Desdemona with a veneer of frivolity, but he is in deadly earnest. Given the fruitfulness of Desdemona, under Iago's tutelage Othello feels compelled to ask: is Desdemona a whore or not? The question implies another: on the street corner, will the young man encounter Wisdom or Folly? Demonizing what Genesis praises as the bounteousness active there in the beginning, Othello can only think of Desdemona's fruitfulness as licentiousness. Proverbs stages bounteous Wisdom and licentious Folly as enigmatically indistinguishable in their calls. To distinguish them becomes precarious, a decision bordering on madness. Othello insists in Desdemona he knows he encounters Folly. In the impromptu quasi-marriage ceremony ending with Iago exclaiming to Othello, "I am your own for ever," Iago offers to relinquish his will over his own "wit, hands, [and] heart" so that they may enter into the "wronged Othello's service" (3.3.479, 466, 67). To Iago's offer, Othello replies, "I greet thy love / Not with vain thanks, but with acceptance bounteous" (3.3.469–70). From Iago Othello accepts hands and love in bounteousness, again a privilege Desdemona should be able to claim. But her hand and fruitfulness Othello demonizes.

Othello's repugnance toward Desdemona's fruitfulness reaches a hysteric crescendo in relation to toads. Bemoaning his inability to control Desdemona's "appetites" even though, as her husband, she is his own, Othello declares, "I had rather be a toad, / And live upon the vapor of a dungeon, / Than keep a corner in the thing I love / For others' uses" (3.3.270–73). To be this toad is the alternative to willing that Desdemona be sexually available to others, and Othello's verb for this willingness is "keep." In his rage of jealousy, in his hysteric attribution to others of the sexual congress with Desdemona he hesitates to attempt, Othello brings back this verb "keep" to consider Desdemona a "fountain" from which his existence as water either flows or "dries up," a "fountain" about which he agonizes whether to "keep [...] as a cistern for foul toads / To knot and gender in" (4.2.59, 60, 61–62). The "dungeon"-solitary and celibate "toad" Othello would be rather than "keep" Desdemona for "others' uses" morphs into the "foul toads" rampantly in orgy within the "cistern." Othello enters a jealous rage over imagining other toads enjoying the pleasure he denies himself or refrains from as a toad. So the initial alternative (be a toad or others enjoy Desdemona) can be translated as: I would rather be a toad celibate and solitary than a toad in orgy. The jealousy is over what he refrains from doing; he is jealous finally of what he denies in himself, or the violence toward Cassio comes down to a displaced acting out of his violence toward himself, which he soon enough acts out. In the incoherence or bad faith of his jealousy, Othello clings to fabricated proof to justify his rage.

Proof Smothering Testimony

Iago works to simulate what Othello demands: "ocular proof" of Desdemona's affair with Cassio (3.3.360). To Othello, Desdemona, in her last moments, testifies to her innocence of any such affair. Iago attempts to stage proof's triumph over testimony, though his manipulations of proof eventually collapse before Emilia's testimony. Iago's murder of Emilia even becomes an allegory of an impotent rage of proof before impassioned testimony. How do proof and testimony cross paths? Consider the adulterer surprised in the act who claims innocence, expostulating to the on-looking and aggrieved spouse, "Who are you going to believe? Me or your lying eyes?" These sentences dexterously confuse yet appeal to the distinction between proof and testimony. The eyes that would see proof are accused of the lying anyone offering testimony may or may not do. The "me" that would offer testimony then implicitly stands as proof anyone can verify. Thus the sentences blur the falsifiability of proof with the believability of testimony, so, by a slight of hand, the testifying "me" dons proof's mantle of certainty while implying ocular proof is a kind of testimony always open to disbelief.

Proof encompasses falsifiable knowledge, while testimony must be taken on faith. Reason can evaluate proof; testimony commands or fails to command belief. Testimony can come only from a singular witness whose words may always be false yet, as testimony, escape from the logic of falsifiability. To believe a witness is no less a leap of faith than to disbelieve a witness. Iago seeks to so manipulate proof as to render Desdemona's testimony unbelievable. Yet no amount or quality of proof can of its own override the believability of testimony. Never by proof alone can Iago necessitate Othello's loss of belief in Desdemona. Such belief may certainly come to seem unreasonable given such and such a proof, but an ineradicable distinction separates falsifiable knowledge from testamentary belief. The judgment between proof and testimony can finally be neither a matter of proof nor of testimony. A fiction or narrative intervenes to allow for judgment. Othello lets Iago's proofs abnegate his belief in Desdemona by way of a kind of bad faith, Othello's unthinking acceptance of a likely story. To span the chasm between proof and testimony and solicit Othello's adherence to proof and dismissal of testimony, Iago manipulates the verisimilitude of a narrative. Speaking ill of the dead, Othello says of Desdemona, "She's like a liar gone to burning hell." The simile announces the likely story or verisimilar narrative necessary to Othello's judgment of her testimony as perjury.

Addressing the audience, Iago asks, "And what's he, then, that says I play the villain?" (2.3.313). To rebut the accusation of villainy, Iago, in two separate soliloquies, confronts the playgoer or reader with the probable verisimilitude of the imaginary scenarios he weaves. He calls his advice to Cassio to implore Desdemona to intervene with Othello "[p]robal to thinking, and indeed the course / To win the Moor again" (2.3.315–16). Of the heart of the story he foists on Othello, the love of Desdemona for Cassio, Iago says, "That Cassio loves her, I do well believe't. / That she loves him, 'tis apt, and of great credit" (2.1.275–76). Thus twice does Iago suggest to the audience that he merely offers Othello hints toward a verisimilar narrative and that what Othello makes of that narrative is entirely Othello's responsibility. Before Othello, Montano, and Gratiano, Emilia pleads with Iago to refute Othello's claim that Iago had told Othello Desdemona was "false," and by this refutation prove that he, Iago, is "not such a villain" (5.2.171, 72). In reply, Iago again pleads verisimilitude: "I told [Othello] what I thought, and told no more / Than what he found himself was apt and true" (5.2.174–75).

A proof may be a counterfeit, like a handkerchief's copy standing in for the handkerchief. Emilia and Cassio both want a copy of the incriminating handkerchief made, and, like an admonishing neon sign, the word "counterfeit" flashes through the play. Iago's proofs are counterfeits a likely story supports.

Othello Fails His Muse

In sonnet 116, Shakespeare argues that love "looks on tempests and is never shaken" and "is the star to every wand'ring bark" (6, 7). Unhesitant, even when facing the sea in however great a storm, love is the guide for any "bark" lost at sea. In no way "Time's fool," resolute to the very last moment, "Love alters not with his brief hours and weeks, / But bears it out even to the edge of doom" (9, 11–12). Praising Desdemona, comparing himself to a "bark" braving a tempest, Othello declares his love, Desdemona, would buoy him "even to the edge of [his] doom," making of his dying now a moment of ecstatic happiness. This sublime vision Othello fails, as he fails his muse, his "fair warrior." Through Iago's demonization of her fruitfulness, Desdemona undergoes a metamorphosis for Othello from a "fair warrior" to a "fair devil." In *Paradise Lost*, Milton's God, looking into Christ's face, sees his glory there imaged. Milton's Satan, looking into Sin's face, sees his glory there imaged. Prior to Iago effecting a revaluation, in the Desdemona who withstood the chaotic storm Othello sees his "fair warrior": she images as "fair" the honor Othello in his career has striven to attain: being a warrior. The Venetian state acknowledges Othello as a warrior. As does Achilles in Briseis, Othello in Desdemona finds his glory made manifest. And, as with Achilles on the loss of Briseis, when Othello assumes Desdemona to be lost to Cassio, he imagines his warriorhood vacated: "O farewell, / Farewell [...] all quality, / Pride, pomp, and circumstance of glorious war! / [...] Othello's occupation's gone" (3.3.350–57). As his "fair warrior," Desdemona images for Othello his self at the zenith of his pride and glory, the "noble Moor" Venice's "full senate" could proclaim "all in all sufficient" (4.1.257, 58). This fullness Desdemona's supposed loss voids. As Othello's "fair devil," Desdemona takes on a force of negation. Talking with Emilia and Desdemona, feigning surprise at Othello's anger, Iago speaks of Othello as usually unshakable, even by the most trying circumstances of battle. Iago describes Othello as having faced cannon that "like the devil from his very arm / Puffed his own brother" (3.4.134–35). The devil's (cannon's) obliteration of Othello's comrade or "brother": this negation or voiding Desdemona as adulteress brings to Othello, and so she forthwith becomes in his mind a devil. Consider how, raving about Desdemona lying about, with, or under Cassio, just before the fit overtakes his coherence altogether, the last syllables Othello manages to utter are: "O devil!" (4.1.42). Othello's decision to murder Desdemona and his first calling her a devil coincide: "O, damn her! damn her! / [...] I will withdraw / To furnish me with some swift means of death / For the fair devil" (3.3.475–77).

Having survived the storm, Othello declares Desdemona his "fair warrior" and states his willingness to die: "If it were now to die, / 'Twere now to be most happy." As his "fair warrior," Desdemona relieves Othello of the master/slave dilemma, so his dying he can accept freely. But Othello fails his vision of Desdemona, and his declared happiness to die undergoes an ironic reversal at the play's end. The manipulations partially exposed, Othello attempts to kill Iago, but only wounds him. Attempting to reply to Iago's taunt ("I bleed, sir—but not killed"), Othello says, "I'd have thee live. / For in my sense, 'tis happiness to die": at this point, his equation of dying with happiness is a bitterly ironic echo of his previous declaration (5.2.287, 288–89). Roderigo wishes to hear nothing. At the play's end, Iago insists on saying nothing: "From this time forth, I never will speak word"(5.2.303). Hearing Iago's vow of silence, Othello comments, "Well, thou dost best" (5.2.305). From Iago, Othello took the idea of stopping Desdemona's voice. Following the example of Iago's vow of silence, Othello considers stopping his own voice. He will do so by taking his own life.

Consigning himself to silence, Othello commits the suicide by throat slashing that Achilles forgoes. Rather than cutting his throat, Achilles cries out to give voice to himself as embracing the fate his daemon Athena brings. Playing out a combination of the violence to the throat Achilles refuses and Achilles's hatred of lies, Othello strangles Desdemona because from her throat lies emanate. Othello follows Iago into silence emphasizing the throat:

> And say besides, that in Aleppo once,
> Where a malignant and a turbaned Turk
> Beat a Venetian and traduced the state,
> I took by th'throat the circumcisèd dog
> And smote him thus.
>
> (5.2.351–55)

Finishing these words, Othello wounds himself mortally with a dagger. In beating the Venetian, the Turk produced from his throat slanderous words that "traduced the state." Othello seized this throat to kill and so silence the Turk. How are readers to imagine Othello's suicide by dagger? Othello's lines about the Turk suggest a resolute slash to the throat. The self-murder by throat slitting Achilles refuses Othello acts out. Not only does Iago go silent: so do Desdemona, Othello, and Emilia. Only Cassio, whose praise daemonized Desdemona, remains willing and able to speak at the play's end.

Othello gives Desdemona death, having claimed he could happily welcome his demise from her. The being-with-her- on-death's-verge Othello called a "now" becomes the "now" of Othello's rush to strangle Desdemona without leaving her time for a last prayer:

Othello   Out, strumpet! Weep'st thou for [Cassio] to my face?
Desdemona O, banish me, my lord, but kill me not!

Othello	Down, strumpet!
Desdemona	Kill me tomorrow, let me live tonight!
Othello	Nay, if you strive—
Desdemona	But half an hour!
Othello	Being done, there is no pause.
Desdemona	But while I say one prayer!
Othello	It is too late.

(5.2.77–83)

The time frame narrows as Othello forces Desdemona downward and outward into the now of her dying. Like a hapless Abraham futilely negotiating with a Yahweh bent on killing, Desdemona begs for the rest of her life, then for a night, then for a half hour, and finally for seconds of prayer. But Othello would bring her to the "now" of dying, of "[b]eing done," the "now" void of any time to come, the "now" where "there is no pause." In such a "now" Othello had hoped to die with the face of Desdemona before him. Instead, presuming to be the agent of the "now" of her dying, Othello gazes on her face as he kills her. Othello's silencing of prayer Iago too embraces.

The "calm" Othello thought would characterize his death with Desdemona she manifests in her dying while Othello rages. Othello had exclaimed the "now" of his death would be "happy": Desdemona's murder defines unhappiness. Othello kisses then kills Desdemona after having claimed, given his sojourn in her world of kisses, he would die willingly. In effect, Othello had imagined receiving a last kiss from Desdemona in the now of his dying. At the play's end, throwing himself on her corpse, dying from his self-inflicted wound, Othello exclaims to Desdemona, "I kissed thee ere I killed thee. No way but this, / Killing myself, to die upon a kiss" (5.2.357–58). Words Iago would criticize as over theatrical, the "to-die-upon-a-kiss" flourish of Othello voices his belated recommitment to his resolution to die with Desdemona before him. Yet the suicide would refuse to let his dying be, to receive death as a gift a "you" facilitates. The suicide would have his "I" master his dying, with the "I" attempting to negate itself, with the "I" seeking to achieve "not-I" all the while refusing the passivity in dying Maurice Blanchot associates with "the space of literature."[19] The Othello who could welcome death as a gift from his muse could enter the space of literature. The Othello who acts out suicide has failed his muse and can only stage a gruesome parody of following her into literature's space.

To Nihilate Breath, to Nihilate Light

Be thou assur'd, if words be made of breath,
And breath of life [...]
—Shakespeare, Hamlet (3.4.197–98)

We have no categories at all that permit us to distinguish a "world in itself" from a "world of appearance." All our categories of reason are of sensual origin: derived from the empirical world. "The soul," "the ego"—the history of these concepts shows that here, too, the oldest distinction ("breath," "life")—
—Nietzsche, The Will to Power[20]

A linguist explaining the relations of consonant and vowel sounds to modulations of breath could agree with Gertrude's first premise ("if words be made of breath"), but, critical of "soul" as a hypostasis of "breath," Nietzsche would be wary of Gertrude's second premise, that "breath" is made of "life," since this premise easily calls up another, that human "life" gains animation from the "soul," such that, when the "soul" departs the "body," the "body" dies, even if the "soul" may persist in an afterlife. Querying such "logical-metaphysical postulates" (*Will*, 270), *Othello* dramatizes the perspectives of Cassio and Iago as antagonistic yet collaborative in drawing the Moor into the nihilation of breath and light.

In the course of praising the "divine Desdemona," Cassio deploys a logic uniting breath, life, and spirit. Cassio entreats "Great Jove" to use his "powerful breath" to "swell" the "sail" of Othello's ship so that ship may "bless this bay." The breath becomes "love's quick pants" and, as words made of breath, Othello's martial rhetoric, Cassio hopes, will "[g]ive renewed fire to our extincted spirits." Cassio aligns the deity's "breath" with "spirit" as life. Cassio implicitly accepts the logical-metaphysical postulate that in breath, life as spirit inheres. When Desdemona sails through the storm, she brings a glorious beauty evaporating the mortal nature of rocks and sands, as if these became immaterial or otherworldly. The "grace of heaven" Cassio implores to encircle Desdemona would spirit away natural light into a light or nimbus not of this world. Shakespeare discovers to the reader how, following Iago's prompts, Othello snuffs out light and breath in the name of light and breath. Invoking Desdemona's soul and spirit, Othello suffocates Desdemona.

Soon to murder Desdemona, Othello ponders how he can, at will, extinguish or rekindle a candle yet can only extinguish, not rekindle, Desdemona. In the following words Othello speaks, the word "light" appears for the last time in the play:

> Put out the light, and then put out the light.
> If I quench thee, thou flaming minister,
> I can again thy former light restore,
> Should I repent me. But once put out thy light,
> Thou cunning'st pattern of excelling nature,
> I know not where is that Promethean heat
> That can thy light relume.
>
> (5.2.7–13)

Othello wonders from where the fire would come to "relume" Desdemona should he kill her. The Shakespeare of the sonnets urges the young man, in view of his mortality, to deliver his natural pattern to the future by fathering a child. Upon Othello and Desdemona's arrival in Cyprus, invoking the "Promethean" element, fire, Cassio associates the couple's consummation of their marriage on the island with Othello giving "renewed fire to our extincted spirits." But Iago manages to delay that consummation, to conjure the "cunning whore of Venice," and to deliver Othello to his marriage bed with only a will to murder.

On this bed, rather than impregnate Desdemona, Othello himself would give birth. When on her soon-to-be deathbed

Desdemona denies giving Cassio the handkerchief, Othello tells
her to "confess" her "sin": "For to deny each article with oath /
Cannot remove nor choke the strong conception / That I do groan
withal. Thou art to die" (5.2.54–56). Desdemona's protestations of
innocence can neither abort ("remove") nor, with its birth, "choke"
the "conception" which Othello in labor "groan[s]" to give birth:
"Thou art to die." Desdemona's testimony cannot prevent Othello
from giving birth to the thought that Desdemona is to die. Othello
usurps the role of Desdemona's confessor ("confess thee freely of
thy sins"). He commands that she admit her "sins" so in killing
her he will not kill her "unprepared spirit" ("I would not kill thy
soul"). By murdering Desdemona, Othello would translate her
from her body of sin to her eternal redemption, with his own
birthing-"groan" hinting at a wicked parody of Paul. In Romans,
Paul aligns the cosmos and the individual Christian through
the metaphor of birth to describe the apocalyptic deliverance of
the "creature" "from the bondage of corruption into the glorious
liberty of the sons of God" (8.21, Geneva 1560). In describing
how the "whole creation groaneth" in the pangs of birth, as "we
ourselves groan," Paul figures as a birth the redemption of the
fallen creation and the body of sin (8.22, 23, Geneva 1587). Othello
would deliver Desdemona from her sin by killing her. He groans
with the conception.

Painfully ironic allusions to the consummation of marriage
operate when, prior to awakening her to command her confession
and kill her, Othello speaks to the sleeping Desdemona: "When
I have plucked the rose, / I cannot give it vital growth again, / It
must needs wither. I'll smell it on the tree" (5.2.13–15). Rather than
of deflowering Desdemona, Othello here speaks of murdering
her. The rose he stoops to smell and kiss is her mouth (Othello
earlier speaks of "rose-lipp'ed cherubin" [4.2.63]):

> O balmy breath, that dost almost persuade
> Justice to break her sword. One more, one more.
> Be thus when thou art dead, and I will kill thee,
> And love thee after. One more, and that's the last.
> So sweet was ne'er so fatal. I must weep,

But they are cruel tears. This sorrow's heavenly,
It strikes where it doth love.—She wakes.

(5.2.16–22)

Othello would love Desdemona's "balmy breath," and the attendant world of kisses, yet, with Iago's persuasions working on him and against the persuasions of Desdemona's breath, Othello imagines doing so "after," after her death, as if what Othello loves of her will live, will breathe after asphyxiation: a metaphysical breath, a soul. Othello's "tears" are "cruel" yet his "sorrow's heavenly" because it "strikes where it doth love." Shakespeare has Othello, for self-justification, consider the duality of his weeping through Paul's distinction between godly and worldly sorrow: "For godly sorrow worketh repentance to salvation not to be repented of: but the sorrow of the world worketh death" (2 Corinthians 7.10, Geneva 1587). The Geneva gloss of 7.10 explains Paul as stating worldly sorrow balks at the punishment the Christian god would meet out, while "godly sorrow" expresses regret at "having offended God." This "godly sorrow" or, as Othello calls it, "heavenly sorrow," moves toward "repentance" and the correction of, as the gloss of 2 Corinthians

7.9 states, "obscene behaviour and sins." The "godly sorrow" motivates "yea, what a zeal: yea, what revenge" (7.11), or as the 1560 Geneva has it, "yea, what punishment" (7.11). In exercising this zealous revenge or punishment with "godly sorrow," believers show themselves to be "pure" (7.11, Geneva 1587). So Othello does weep tears, and shedding them will bring death to Desdemona, but his tears also express the "heavenly sorrow" out of which Othello would "strike" what he or "it," the "heavenly sorrow," loves, Desdemona's breath, and so enact Desdemona's salvation from sin. The stop Othello brings to her "breath" will release her breath, her soul, should she repent. Othello would still Desdemona's breath, but he would not kill Desdemona's soul. What is Iago's most nihilistic triumph? Othello's suicide? Hardly. To arrange for Othello, invoking Desdemona's "soul," to asphyxiate Desdemona: thus does Iago the gardener bring nihilism to flower.

Shakespeare has Desdemona foreshadow her murder. In the second of the only two mentions of Desdemona's mother in *Othello,* Desdemona tells Emilia of an episode of a lost love:

> My mother had a maid called Barbary,
> She was in love. And he she loved proved mad,
> And did forsake her. She had a song of "willow,"
> An old thing 'twas. But it expressed her fortune,
> And she died singing it. That song tonight
> Will not go from my mind. I have much to do
> But to go hang my head all at one side
> And sing it like poor Barbary. Prythee dispatch.
>
> (4.3.25–32)

How did Barbary die? The episode of her abandonment took place while Barbary was in the service of Desdemona's mother. Desdemona reports the maid died while singing the willow song. To die while singing: is that impossible? Did Desdemona witness this death? Consider the willow in *Hamlet*, accessory to the singing Ophelia's death by drowning, perhaps a suicide. Consider the posture Desdemona describes she would mimic if she were to imitate Barbary singing the song Barbary sang dying: "hang my head all at one side." Does Desdemona describe a suicide by hanging? To Iago, Othello says of Desdemona, "Hang her" (4.1.180).

Othello begins with Roderigo's pained exclamation to Iago: "Never tell me." Pining for Desdemona, Iago's dupe wishes not to hear of Desdemona's clandestine marriage to Othello. Iago, in his last words, embraces Roderigo's play-opening injunction of silence: "Demand me nothing. What you know, you know. / From this time forth, I never will speak word." Iago refuses to testify. Bereft entirely of address to any other whomsoever, Iago's silence deserts the prayerful altogether, as Lodovico notes about the villain's determination "never" again to "speak word": "What? Not to pray?" (5.2.304). Iago would keep his doings and motives secret, so he will say "nothing." Yet Iago's soliloquies and ruses testify precisely to nothing's conjuration and nihilistic yet poetic conjugation.

The play ends with Lodovico giving Cassio the duty to torture Iago, to force testimony from a forger of proof vowed to silence. Having praised Desdemona as a daemon, Cassio is to use any cruelty to coerce speech from Iago, whose machinations brought to Othello the hallucination of Desdemona as a demon. Finishing with this tableau of an endless standoff between Cassio and Iago, between daemonization and demonization, *Othello* leaves on stage no one to speak either for Othello's vision of his "fair warrior" or for Desdemona's yearning to attain the freedom in worldliness the unfallen Moor embodied for her.

Five

Milton's *Paradise Lost*:
Sin's Ambition, Eve's Flight

In *Othello,* the couple Othello–Iago undoes the couple Othello–Desdemona. A couple resembling a father and a son achieves the destruction of a couple resembling a father and a daughter. The nihilistic logic of the father-son couple demonizes the fruitfulness Desdemona manifests in her welcome to more life. The ironically Pauline Iago bears fruit for death in the very process of "spiritualizing" Othello's stance toward Desdemona. The play ends with Emilia exposing the inexistence of the "cunning whore of Venice" and with Othello's apostrophes to the dead Desdemona (4.2.90). The Moor speaks to her corpse of meeting her in heaven at the last judgment when the "look" now on her corpse's face "will hurl [his] soul from heaven" (5.2.273). And then come Othello's last words: "I kissed thee ere I killed thee: no way but this, / Killing myself, to die upon a kiss" (5.2.357–58).

In John Milton's *Paradise Lost,* Desdemona undergoes several afterlives. The bold and adventurous Desdemona contributes to Milton's Eve. The Desdemona of "soul" and "spirit" resonates with Milton's Wisdom. But the inexistent "cunning whore of Venice" manifests in Milton's Sin. Milton's epic tells of the struggle between two couples: a father and a son and a father and a daughter. God the Father and Christ the Son contend with Satan and his daughter Sin. These two couples contend over the fate of a third: Adam and Eve. A fourth couple tells the tale: Milton and his muse, Urania. Among each couple and amidst all four, the energies of demonization and daemonization course and cross paths. Milton captures demonization in the mirror of daemonization and daemonization in the mirror of demonization. Vowels differentiate the Son and Sin, the Son's kenotic "o" and Sin's assertive "i." Despite God and his Son's victories over Satan and Sin, Sin partially attains her ambition and with her dream of flight, the bold Eve acts as *Paradise Lost*'s barely covert heroine. Before discussing Sin's ambition and Eve's dream of flight, an exploration of Milton's attitudes toward muses as they manifest in "On the Morning of Christ's Nativity" and "Lycidas" would be useful.

The Fiery Muse in "On the Morning of Christ's Nativity"

Long before his blindness, long before undertaking *Paradise Lost* with the aid of his "Heavenly Muse," Milton had invoked her, describing her as bringing a reassuring and inspirational fire to save a newborn from becoming lost in utter darkness. This invocation takes place in the prologue of "On the Morning of Christ's Nativity." This muse's task to bring fire to the infant Christ of the prologue emerges as crucial to the mission of the militant Christ of the poem's main part, the "Hymn."

The prologue's first stanza evokes the "happy morn" on which was "born" "the son of Heav'ns eternal King," who, "from above," brought a "great redemption" to earthbound humanity, our "release" from our "deadly forfeit" and into the "perpetual peace" he "with his Father" will "work us" (1–7). However, Christ can only accomplish this redemption by abandoning "Heav'ns high council-table" (10). In heaven, Christ sits between the Father and the Holy Ghost at this table. There, amidst the "Trinal Unity," Christ shines, his "glorious Form" effusing a "Light unsufferable" and a "far-beaming blaze of Majesty" (11, 8–9). This glorious "Form," "Light," and "blaze" Christ "laid aside; and here with us to be, / Forsook the courts of everlasting day, / And chose with us a darksome house of mortal clay" (12–14). Like a Socratic figure who, having bathed in sunlight, turns from the sun to enter the cave and redeem the dwellers in darkness, Christ volunteers to give up light and descend to the "darksome house." Void of heaven's light, this darkness glowers where mortality entirely wants for immortality and kenosis completely empties divine fullness. Altogether vulnerable, a human baby, at birth, drops from entire darkness into a place of light. A day-born baby's eyes, at birth, undergo suffusion with light. Born to Mary in the predawn night, and born from heaven's overwhelming, all-pervasive, shadow-free light into the fallen creation's abyssal darkness, Milton's infant Christ in effect undergoes a traumatic blinding. At birth, Christ goes from a place of "everlasting day" to a place of mortal darkness. As Plato's cave escapee returning to the cave undergoes a disorienting blindness, so does Christ in being born into our "darksome house of mortal clay."

Milton imagines his "Heav'nly Muse" delivering his poem, specifically the "Hymn," to the infant Christ as a gift mitigating the blindness Christ traumatically undergoes in being born (15). Milton implores his muse to reach the infant Christ before the sun dawns and while the stars still "keep watch in squadrons bright" (21). Milton's "Heav'nly Muse" must arrive first so Milton's poem will bring to the infant Christ a saving spark from Heaven: "Have thou the honour first, thy Lord to greet, / And join thy voice unto the angel quire, / From out his secret altar toucht with hallow'd fire" (26–28). The Father, and so the Son, even the infant Christ ("his"), has a "secret altar" where coals burn, seraphim praise the Father's glory (and so the Son's, even the infant Christ's), and where one seraph touches a coal to the prophet's lips so he may prophesize (Isaiah 6.1–9). The seraphim call out to each other, "Holy, holy, holy, *is* the Lord of hosts: the whole earth *is* full of his glory" (6.3). They sing of the Lord's glory encompassing the entire earth, as does Milton's "Hymn," which sings of the infant Christ overcoming all other gods, chasing them away, so that his glory encompasses the entire earth. In the night of kenosis, "toucht with hallow'd fire," Milton's muse sings Milton's "Hymn" to Christ, and so the poem brings to Christ a heavenly spark. In the utter darkness the infant Christ will synaesthetically hear yet see the "hallow'd fire," giving him, even in his limitless kenosis, a reminder of the realm from which he came, a narrative of his glorious triumph over all other deities, and so inspiration toward his mission.

Only if the "Heav'nly Muse" heeds Milton's injunction to speed to Christ and deliver the poem "Now" will the infant Christ have a chance to encounter the "hallow'd fire": "Hast thou no verse, no hymn, or solemn strain, / To welcome him to this his new abode; / Now while the Heav'n by the sun's team untrod, / Hath took no print of the approaching light [?]" (17–20). Horses pull the sun god's chariot across the sky, and their hooves will mark the sky with tracks, "print[s]." These marks make of light a kind of writing, with light an inscription of letters rather than an expression of voice. The muse must sing expressing the fire from the "secret altar" before the hoofs write. Prior to the writing of the Greco-Roman sun god and his horses, there must be a Biblical, that is, a Miltonic expression pure of inscription, a "verse," a "hymn," a "strain": note how this list moves ever more toward voice. This *agon* for priority between the Biblical prophetic voice and the Greco-Roman letter returns in the "Hymn" as Christ driving out the Greek, Roman, and other gods.

The Milton of "On the Morning" imagines Christ as a Platonic spelunker, leaving a realm of unremitting and overawing light for a realm of darkness, the fallen creation as a cave of shadows. In Plato's *Republic,* the *logos*-figure suffers temporary blindness in transitioning from the light of the intelligible realm to the darkness of the sensible realm, from the abode of the sun (the Good) to the cavern of shadowy appearances. Yet, even in the darkest corner of the cave, even in the most flitting and contradictory of shadows, some minimal particle of intelligibility's light must inhere for the cave dweller to apprehend, say, a circular shadow as a circular shadow. The sublunary realm features mingling, wavering sensations. The celestial realm features perfect, eternal circles. Through and in her Satan-given dream of flight, Eve becomes a sublunary muse. Milton never overtly invokes a sublunary muse, only a "Heav'nly Muse," the muse Milton in *Paradise Lost* will call Urania, the Greek muse of astronomy. In the "Nativity" ode, Milton's "Heav'nly Muse" delivers to the infant Christ a particle of burning light, a spark from the realm above. The "Heav'nly Muse" thus becomes a bringer of *logos* down into the shadowy flux and so, paradoxically, brings the *logos* to the infant Christ. As an utterly kenotic death, the birth of Christ empties him entirely, yet the spark the Heavenly Muse brings offers a resurrection.

This resurrection allows for the transition from the prologue's vulnerable baby shorn of all glory to the all-powerful infant of the "Hymn." The invulnerable strength of the infant Christ of the "Hymn" manifests as light. The "Hymn" ends with the star of Bethlehem (guide of the gift-bearing wizards) and the sun, the lights Milton asks the Heavenly Muse to preempt, both becoming figurations of the light of Christ. Christ's light penetrates to and blinds the Egyptian god of the underworld and of the dead, Osiris: "Naught but profoundest Hell can be his shroud" (218). Though shrouded in the most profound darkness of hell, Osiris "feels from Juda's land / The dreaded Infant's hand, / The rays of Bethlehem blind his dusky eyn" (221–23). The darkness-ensconced Osiris being blinded by the divine light reverses what the deliverance of the spark prevents: the trauma of the infant Christ undergoing blindness in moving from divine light to the darkness of the mortal realm. In Egyptian belief, Osiris died yet rose from the dead, and believers in him hope through his name to wake from death into eternity. Osiris's parallels to Christ make Osiris's blinding by Christ, specifically by the "rays of Bethlehem," an all the more a striking inversion of Christ's transition from the light of Heaven to the "darksome house of mortal clay." In this deployment of light to blind, the infant Christ evidences the full reversal of the kenosis of his birth: "Our Babe, to show his Godhead true, / Can in his swaddling bands control the damned crew" (227–28). These lines become the opening of a simile comparing Christ to the sun and all the gods Christ routs to shadows: "So when the sun in bed, / Curtain'd with cloudy red, / Pillows his chin upon an orient wave; / The flocking shadows pale / Troop to th' infernal jail" (229–33).

In the last stanza of "On the Morning of Christ's Nativity," the infant Christ in the manger, the "Prince of light," after his birth, attains his first sleep, and the Heavenly Muse is to end Milton's song to avoid disturbing that rest: "But see the Virgin blest, / Hath laid her Babe to rest. / Time is our tedious song should here have ending" (62, 237–39). Between the birth of Christ and his first sleep, that song has narrated to him in preview his role as the redeemer of fallen nature, as the sufferer on the cross who redeems human kind, and as the triumphant warder of all previous deities. This entire career arc the Heavenly Muse reveals to Christ in the song the muse gifts to the newborn, the song bearing the spark.

"On the Morning of Christ's Nativity" dramatizes the Heavenly Muse as crucial to Christ's redemptive overcoming of mortality. From his kenotic birth, his dying to his divinity, Christ undergoes a rebirth to "Godhead," a resurrection to triumphant glory (227). The Christ of the "Hymn" who drives away all other gods anticipates the Christ of *Paradise Lost* who drives Satan and his "damned crew" from heaven (228). The Christ of the "Nativity" ode, in his birth, receives crucial assistance from a muse capable of singing Christ toward his rebirth to glory and away from being born to death only. In the "Nativity" ode, Milton trusts the entire burden of his resounding of Christ's triumph to his "Heav'nly Muse." In "Lycidas," this trust in a muse undergoes a crisis. Something of this crisis sounds in Milton's *The Reason of Church Government* (1642), in which Milton asks his readers to await patiently the great poetic work Milton promises to deliver. This work, however, is not to "be rays'd from the heat of youth, or the vapours of wine, like that which flows at wast from the pen of some vulgar Amorist, or the trencher fury of a riming parasite, nor to be obtain'd by the invocation of Dame Memory and her Siren daughters."[1] Mnemosyne, "Dame Memory," gives birth to the muses, but Boethius's Lady Philosophy claims poetic muses are treacherous sirens whose song leads sailors to their deaths. These muses might entice the sexually passionate or the wine inebriated, a "vulgar Amorist" or a "riming parasite." Milton associates these sirens with the pleasures and passions of the flesh, with the sin yielding only death. Milton envisions himself becoming a poet who rejects the classical muses in favor of "devout prayer" to the "eternal Spirit who can enrich with all utterance and knowledge, and sends out his Seraphim with the hallow'd fire of his Altar to touch and purify the lips of whom he pleases" (924). In "On the Morning of Christ's Nativity," Milton is willing to call the bringer of the divine spark a muse, the "Heav'nly Muse."

Milton's "Lycidas" shows Milton rejecting Dame Memory's siren daughters. They can only sing a poet toward mortality.

The Refusal of Mortality in "Lycidas":
Muses, Fluid, and Glory

In the *Iliad*, Achilles undergoes full and daemonizing inspiration by Athena at the cost of his acceptance of and final movement toward his own mortality. Rather than salvation, Athena brings Achilles exaltation. The *ekstasis* of the hero blends into his irreversible rush to his demise. No wonder Athena becomes, in *Paradise Lost*, the model for Sin, whose son is Death. Milton would forbid death final triumph, and this refusal bears on the poetic matter of Milton's stance toward muses. In "Lycidas," the refusal of mortality threatens to shut down the speaker's opening to any muse. Rather than with a divine fire, in "Lycidas" muses associate with a perilous, mortal fluidity, evoking in the speaker an anxiety of waters. This anxiety yields ambivalence toward muses and precipitates a demeaning of the classical muses.

As Laertes says of his drowned sister Ophelia, Lycidas has had too much of water, and in "Lycidas" Milton finally would forbid his tears from flowing, yet Milton's elegy also strives mightily yet ambiguously both to overcome and to redeem fluidity and so to assuage the speaker's anxiety of waters. After the poem's opening lines lamenting the untimely earliness of Lycidas's death, the speaker aligns the elegiac verses he will take on the duty to write with fluid, with tears:

> Who would not sing for Lycidas? he knew
> Himself to sing, and build the lofty rhyme.
> He must not float upon his wat'ry bier
> Unwept, and welter to the parching wind,
> Without the meed of some melodious tear.

> (10–14)

Coleridge takes up the parching situation of Lycidas in "The Rime of the Ancient Mariner." To appropriate Coleridge's words, Lycidas floats with "[w]ater, water every where" yet without a single "drop to drink."[2] The drowned Lycidas thirsts only for life; amidst the death-bringing seawater, he is parched for the waters of life. His thirst intensified by the "parching wind," Lycidas requires desperately some "meed." In early usage, the word "meed" refers to a wage and, by Milton's time, a gift, recompense, or reward. Meed shares aspects of its etymology and the same pronunciation with "mead," an alcoholic beverage made from fermenting a mixture of honey and water. The goal of alleviating Lycidas's thirst and singing of a "recompense" calls forth the meed/mead pun (184). Yet what fluid would slake this thirst? Rather than the meed of more salty fluid, "of some melodious tear," would not the parched Lycidas prefer some honey-sweet mead? The expert Latinist Milton would hear in the word "melodious" the Latin *mel*, honey, and very likely would be aware that, by this association, the Latin *melodia* fostered the commonplace of song being sweet.[3]

Lycidas "well knew / Himself to sing, and build the lofty rhyme": the word "well" puns on a water source that does contrast to the tower of "lofty rhyme" Lycidas "knew" to "build." But from what well, urn, or jug will the speaker draw the meed/mead he hopes to offer Lycidas? Who will provide the meed, and how will this mead avoid contributing to Lycidas's fate of drowning and rather give Lycidas life?

Besides ambivalence toward fluid, "Lycidas" shows the speaker wrestling with ambivalence toward muses. To begin speaking about the Greek pastoral youth he spent with Lycidas, the speaker of the poem invokes the Greek muses: "Begin then, sisters of the sacred well" (15). The "well" of the muses recalls the adverbial "well" of Lycidas's knowing to sing. With no indication he invoked or credited the Muses, Lycidas "well knew / Himself to sing." The speaker moves further toward accepting the drowning of Lycidas when he calls on the Greek muses: "Begin, and somewhat loudly sweep the string" (17). Gathering about their "sacred well," the muses become a chorus of mourners. The writing of an elegy implicitly demands the acceptance of mortality. The speaker of "Lycidas" invokes the muses' aid to overcome his reluctance to begin, as to begin requires him to relinquish his "denial vain" of Lycidas's death and to forgo any "coy excuse" to avoid his elegiac duty (18). "Who would not sing for Lycidas?" The speaker initially would not, because to sing elegiacally for Lycidas requires the acceptance of the death of Lycidas. The overcoming of his reluctance to sing brings the speaker to his invocation of the muses. The speaker then links a future poet's acceptance and singing of the speaker's death with the future poet being a muse.

The music of the mourning muses gathered about the well becomes in the speaker's imagination the mournful memorial words a future poet will sing to mark the passing of the speaker. As he now elegizes Lycidas, the speaker hopes this future poet will elegize him, apostrophizing his funereal urn. Having called on the muses to inspire his elegiac words, the speaker imagines the future poet as a muse. The muses gather around their well, their music mourning Lycidas, who knew how to build in song a tower. But with the loss of Lycidas comes the loss of his voice building the "lofty rhyme," the poem as tower. With this voicing of verticality lost, Lycidas is left to float silently on the vast horizontality of his "wat'ry bier." Life is erect, death, prone.

In the future scene of mourning the speaker imagines, again the loss of a poet leaves a muse to mourn by a kind of well. The muses' "sacred well" becomes a funereal urn. A receptacle for water, the urn as a mode of interment becomes a receptacle for ashes, what Sir Thomas Browne studies in his essay on water-jar burial, *Hydriotaphia: Urn Burial, or a Discourse of the Sepulchral Urns lately found in Norfolk.*[4] At this point in "Lycidas," the speaker identifies with the muses-in-mourning, implicitly imagining himself as such a muse or poet mourning for Lycidas in hopes that a future poet will contribute words commemorating him upon his corpse's interment. To take up the writing of the elegy requires the speaker of "Lycidas" to imagine his own demise, which imagination awakens his hope to receive elegiac or memorial verses after his own passing: "So may some gentle Muse / With lucky words favor my destin'd urn; / And as he passes turn, / And bid fair peace be to my sable shroud" (19–22). Note the rhyme: "urn," "turn." As a "Muse," a future poet may write in memory of the speaker. The speaker imagines his own being-dead as the unavoidable fixity of his "destin'd urn." Like an open mantle, the "sable shroud" drapes over the urn, allowing the passerby to read the memorial inscription. In the *Iliad*, after burning Patroclus's body, the Achaeans gather the bones, place them in an urn, and drape the urn with a shroud (23.278–92). Adopting a similar funereal practice, the Romans would burn the body, place the ashes in an urn, and then drape the urn with a shroud. Milton has the speaker of "Lycidas" imagine a shroud mantling his urn.

The future poet will write verses for inscription on the urn, yet, "as he passes," as he passes away, as he travels toward his own death, he may still "turn" and speak to "bid fair peace" to the "sable shroud" mantling the "urn." The letters on the urn, and the shroud, partake of the dying toward fixity the speaker anticipates, while the future poet's "turn" and voice remain momentarily with life, even as the future poet "passes." As a "Muse," the future poet lives on toward mortality and may help to memorialize the past poet. Yet the future poet cannot save the past poet from the death the future poet also approaches. Walking toward his own destiny, the future poet "turn[s]" to speak to the prior poet who has undergone his fate. The future poet's "turn" becomes an apotropaic act to ward off fate only by addressing the prior poet's fate. In turning to the dead poet's urn, the future poet will turn away from his own "destined urn," the fate of urning that ends all turning. By imagining the future poet as a muse who turns, the speaker of the poem struggles to gain a perspective on his own situation as a poet who, to confront Lycidas's mortality, must confront his own. A future poet as muse will sing an elegy for a prior poet, who, as a muse, had sung in elegy for a prior poet. Prior to drowning, before entering the repetitions of urning and turning, Lycidas sang *himself,* or so the line easily reads: "He well knew / Himself to sing, and build the lofty rhyme." A poet singing himself and building a tower, his voice neither referring to another, a dead other, nor requiring the inspiration of another, a muse: this scenario implicitly images life unmarred by death. Lycidas "well knew / Himself," sang himself, with the adverb "well" bringing a source of meed/mead within his self-knowing self-singing. Unlike this Lycidas, the speaker is caught up in urning and turning. The poet calls on the muses, by their "sacred well," to aid his singing of the dead Lycidas.

What shall the poet consider sacred, a well or a head, the muses' "sacred well" or Lycidas's "sacred head" (15, 102)? In "Lycidas," the image of dying is of a head sinking beneath waters, as when the speaker chastises "nymphs" for failing to aid the drowning Lycidas: "Where were ye, Nymphs, when the remorseless deep / Clos'd o'er the head of your lov'd Lycidas?" (50–51). And again, later in the poem, when the speaker relays the words of the "herald of the sea," who would clear Neptune and the ocean of blame, the sinking of Lycidas's head images dying: "It was that fatal and perfidious bark, / Built in th' eclipse, and rigg'd with curses dark, / That sunk so low that sacred head of thine" (89, 100–02). By this point in the poem, rather than the well ("sacred well"), the "head" is "sacred." What precise figuration occurs here with Lycidas's head? The head serves as a synecdoche of the sinking body but also as a metonymy of the self as alive. The loss of the head becomes the loss of life. But then what definition of life does the head (synecdoche of the body, metonymy of life) imply? In "Lycidas," life is erect or vertical, like a tower, so the dying head is a "drooping head," as the speaker describes the setting sun as a simile for the sinking Lycidas (169).

Lycidas will never turn again, will never return: "But O the heavy change, now thou art gone, / Now thou art gone, and never must return!" (37–38). The shepherd Lycidas of the poem's first pastoral interlude has passed away, and the speaker recalls Lycidas as an Orpheus whose songs were able to move the trees: "The willows, and the hazel copses green, / Shall now no more be seen, / Fanning their joyous leaves to thy soft lays" (42–44). This attribution of Orphic power to Lycidas prepares for the speaker denouncing the muse Calliope for failing to save her son Orpheus from his fate. First the speaker accuses the "nymphs" or muses of being elsewhere than with the drowning Lycidas and so of not saving him (50–55). But then the speaker states that to believe the muses could have saved Lycidas is a mere dream: "Ay me, I fondly dream! / Had ye been there . . . for what could that have done? / What could the Muse herself that Orpheus bore, / The Muse

herself," what could she have done to save "her enchanting son"
Orpheus from the "rout" of crazed women who tore him asunder
and "sent" "His gory visage down the stream […] / Down the
swift Hebrus to the Lesbian shore [?]" (56–59, 61, 62–63). The
speaker's denunciation of the muses reaches back in the poem to
suggest the ultimate futility of the future poet or "Muse" writing
for and turning toward the speaker's "destined urn." The future
poet may memorialize yet not save the prior poet. The future
poet's effort, or Milton's effort in "Lycidas," would be futile from
the perspective of a hope for salvation as distinct from an urn, a
turn, an urn, a turn, the endless end of each poet anticipating yet
turning from the poet's own death, a kind of world of urns and
turns without end. This entropic process operates in the pastoral
elegy for Bion attributed to Moschus. Invoking the "Sicilian muse"
and calling Bion the "Dorian Orpheus," the poet describes the
gifts of the muses to Bion as dying with the poet, as the Sicilian
muse's gift of song to him will perish when he dies.[5] In "Lycidas,"
Milton abjects the muses as unable to save, as unable to inspire
a poem that would be not merely memorial but also salvational.

And so the speaker of the poem considers abandoning his
dedication to the muses: "Alas! what boots it with incessant care
/ To tend the homely slighted shepherd's trade, / And strictly
meditate the thankless Muse?" (64–66). Why not rather "sport
with Amaryllis in the shade, / Or with the tangles of Neaera's
hair?" (68–69). The promise of fame offers a type of salvation from
mortality. However, though a poet may "turn" or trope against
death, the Fate Atropos ("without turn") the speaker calls a Fury
may intervene just as the poet would utter the poem he hopes
will win fame. Just then "[c]omes the blind Fury with th' abhorred
shears / And slits the thin-spun life" (75–76).

The speaker associates inspiration by the muses with mortality.
When the speaker toward the end of the poem proclaims the
resurrection of Lycidas and his ascension to an eternal pastoral
scene in heaven, "Lycidas" becomes what Wordsworth would call
an ode intimating immortality. In Wordsworth's "Ode: Intimations
of Immortality from Recollections of Early Childhood," the
poet, unobservant of the messiness of human births, imagines

the newborn coming into the world "trailing clouds of glory."[6] Milton specifies that Calliope "bore" Orpheus, and perhaps her only way to have saved him were to have never given him birth, Milton's phrase "gory visage" perhaps evoking the newborn's face Wordsworth overlooks; does Atropos cut the umbilical cord? In 1637, before the composition of "Lycidas," Milton's mother died, leaving the poet bereftly born in the world. In idealizing birth, Wordsworth's "Ode: Intimations of Immortality" turns away from "Lycidas," a poem haunted by birth as a fall into mortality.

If this intuition of birth as an issue in "Lycidas" holds merit, the complex imagery of the fluid in the poem needs consideration. And consider the parallels between the helpless panic of drowning and the helpless panic of birthing. In "On the Morning of Christ's Nativity," Milton implores his "Heavenly Muse" to bring some comfort to the newborn Jesus, some intimation of the immortality he left in being born into the "darksome house of mortal clay." The panic and disorientation of that birth experience must be allayed, and the muse with her singing voice is to do the comforting. In "Lycidas," muses only sing toward mortality, and are unable to offer salvation from the panic and disorientation of being born toward dying, much less from dying.

In "Lycidas," after the speaker envisions the "abhorred shears" of Atropos cutting off his life, the god of the sun and of poetry, "Phoebus" Apollo, attempts to rejuvenate the poet's commitment to poetry, and so to the muses, by saying, however arbitrarily life may be cut off, seeming to defeat the effort of the poet, the "praise" of the poem will live on eternally, Jove stepping in as a critic doling out "fame" (77, 76, 84). Orpheus undergoes the muse Calliope's failure to save him. As a muse or late-comer poet charged with the duty of elegiac memorialization, the speaker would fail the Orphic Lycidas, would fail to save Lycidas, if he were merely to write memorial verses and commit a turn in turn destined for an urn. To begin his elegiac words about Lycidas, the speaker imagines his future memorializing muse or passing poet performing a turn toward the urn and its sable shroud. Rather than such turning oriented only toward urning, a turn intimating salvation must be had. Ending his elegiac words and before

uttering consoling words, the speaker asks St. Michael to turn
his gaze toward home: "Look homeward Angel, now, and melt
with ruth: / And, O ye dolphins, waft the hapless youth" (163–64).
Standing atop a mountain near Land's End, the angel is to turn
his gaze upon Lycidas. Rather than toward a fixed and dead urn
holding ashes problematic for the resurrection of the body, the
angel is to turn to see an intact body born up by dolphins. This
turn prepares for the poet's immediately subsequent vision of
consolation.

In this vision, Apollo suffers a going-under as the sun to
become a figure of Lycidas in his salvation by Christ:

> Weep no more, woeful shepherds, weep no more;
> For Lycidas your sorrow is not dead,
> Sunk though he be beneath the watry floor;
> So sinks the day-star in the ocean bed;
> And yet anon repairs his drooping head,
> And tricks his beams, and with new-spangled ore
> Flames in the forehead of the morning sky:
> So Lycidas sunk low, but mounted high,
> Through the dear might of him that walk'd the waves[.]
>
> (165–73)

Here, the speaker denies Lycidas's death, but this would be
no "denial vain" such as the poet had to dismiss to begin his
elegiac words. The speaker does "burst out into sudden blaze,"
yet he sings now another turn to his tropes without fearing the
"abhorred shears" of the "blind Fury" or Fate Atropos. The oddly
formed Homeric simile becomes the vehicle for a Christian tenor
keeping both vanity and fate at bay. Calliope could not save
Orpheus; Milton imagines Christ saving Lycidas. Paul says the
resurrection of the dead will take place in a "moment," in the
"twinkling of an eye" (1 Corinthians 15.52). The transition from
dying down into water and rising up into life ("So Lycidas sunk
low, but mounted high") makes of death the briefest of intervals,
a moment between a comma and a conjunction, a Pauline blink of
an eye strikingly parallel to the foreshortening of Christ's sojourn
in death in *Paradise Lost*, which again is the interval between a

comma and a conjunction: "so he dies, / But soon revives; Death over him no power / Shall long usurp" (12.419–21).

The sun "sinks" down seaward, as Lycidas sank, yet the sun soon rises and "[f]lames" with glory, "with new spangled ore." This sun "tricks his beams," his streaming, glorious hair. The poem "Lycidas" treats the reader to "the tangles of Neaera's hair," mentions the "mantle hairy" of Camus, and has St. Peter shake "his mitr'd locks" (69, 104, 112). In a poem so decked with hair, in which so many of the personages enjoy a hair close-up, Milton neglects to mention the muses' hair, even neglecting Calliope's hair. Milton is a poet for whom hair matters. Known in his student days at Christ College as the "Lady of Christ," Milton wore his hair long. In *Samson Agonistes*, Milton expends his last imaginings on a hero whose hair bore his strength. In *Paradise Lost*, Milton specifies that, for his manifestation in the dream he gives Eve, Satan scents his hair with ambrosia the more to seduce her. Milton revels in describing Adam's hair and Eve's. The hair of Sampson embodies his strength. The ambrosia Satan treats his hair with connotes the Tree of Life's ambrosial fruit. Eve's hair and Adam's token their respective beauties. Strength, life, and beauty: these together may define glory. In "Lycidas," the hair of the resurrected sun manifests glory. Recovering in the realm above from drowning in the realm below, the resurrected Lycidas "[w]ith nectar pure his oozy locks he laves" (175). So where in "Lycidas" is the hair of the muses?

An examination of Milton's revisions to his initial version of "Lycidas" shows Milton eliding the name and hair of Calliope. In the initial draft of the poem, the speaker hails this highest of muses as "the golden hayrd Calliope."[7] These words Milton cancelled from the poem, to replace them with: "the muse herself" (58). In the first draft, by name and with golden hair, standing high upon Helicon, Calliope beholds the head of her son Orpheus adrift along the shore of Thrace: "she beheld (the gods farre sighted bee) / his goarie scalpe rowle downe the Thracian lee" (60–61). These lines Milton excised, denying Calliope her height upon the mountain and her divine acuity of vision, qualities Milton reserves in the final draft for the archangel

Michael. Though a Greek muse is more a daemon than a god or Olympian, still the muses are divine. To emphasize Calliope as divine might bring into question whether or not she could have helped Orpheus had she been, not high on the mount, but by Orpheus's side when the "rout" sought his *sparagmos*. However, more significantly, by retracting the word "gods" as descriptive of Calliope, Milton retracts from her the divinized status he grants the Lycidas whom he compares to a risen sun with streaming hair, dazzlingly golden: "And tricks his beams, and with new-spangled ore / Flames in the forehead of the morning sky" (170–71). The vision of a divine, farseeing, golden-haired Calliope high on the mountain too much resembles this arisen sun and so must be withdrawn from the poem.

In revising the poem, Milton takes the magnificent golden hair of the muse Calliope and grants it to the sun metaphoric of the risen Lycidas. He also shifts the divinity of Orpheus's head toward Lycidas's. From first to final drafts, Calliope loses her name, yet Orpheus gains his. The description of the head of Orpheus evolves through three versions. First, the golden-haired and name-bearing Calliope looks on from afar to see "his goarie scalpe rowle downe the Thracian shore." Yet a "scalpe" implies hair. Then, with Calliope's name, hair, vision, and divinity elided, nature steps in as mournful observer, joined by personified heaven and hell. What could the muse herself have done for her son, "whome universal nature might lament / and heaven and hel deplore / when his divine head downe / the streame was sent / downe the swift Hebrus to the Lesbian shore [?]" (59–63). Yes, in the elegy Orpheus shares with Lycidas the fate of his head being abandoned to waters. Yet only the head of Lycidas may merit a sobriquet like "divine." And, though Olympus and Tartarus may be the implication here, the Christian-associated co-ordinates of "heaven and hel" must not deplore the fate of Orpheus. And a "head" implies hair.

In the third and final version, after again thinking better of "divine" ("divine visage" becomes "gory visage"), Milton ends up with the following evocation of Orpheus's fate, with the name Orpheus appearing:

Where were ye, Nymphs, when the remorseless deep
Clos'd o'er the head of your lov'd Lycidas?
[...]
Ay me, I fondly dream!
Had ye been there . . . for what could that have done?
What could the Muse herself that Orpheus bore,
The Muse herself, for her enchanting son
Whom universal Nature did lament;
When by the rout that made the hideous roar,
His gory visage down the stream was sent,
Down the swift Hebrus to the Lesbian shore?

(50–51, 56–63)

For the hope the muse Calliope may have saved Lycidas to be exposed as futile and unsubstantial, as a "dream," the divine qualities of Calliope must be withdrawn. Rather than among the "gods" and "farre sighted," Calliope becomes merely the one who "bore" Orpheus. Her giving birth to Orpheus the final draft emphasizes. Without mentioning his name, the initial draft calls Orpheus the son of Calliope without the emphasis on her having given birth to him. Rather than being able to save Orpheus, all she could do is give him birth, and this gift brings him to his mortality. Milton's mother died in April 1637; Edward King drowned in August 1637. Bloom finds in the lines about Calliope in the final draft "a movement of psychic regression," one "all but universal in men whose mother, in dying, on some level of consciousness reminds them that in giving birth, she also gave mortality."[8]

As the poet elides the hair of the muses and of Calliope, so he does their heads. Or rather: the muses become in "Lycidas" somewhat acephalic agents who may birth a poet into song yet who in this birthing abandon the poet to fluidity, to the sinking of the poet's head into waters, to drowning, to death. The "sacred sisters" sport near a well; Milton would be quite aware of the type-scenes of betrothal in the Hebrew Bible in which women attend uteral wells. The muses may inspire the poet to begin his song, but this performance will only be such as the poet hopes a future poet will offer him once he dies and his ashes reside in his "destined urn": the muses only birth the poet to a song hailing death, and that associated with a water container turned funereal urn. From their well, the muses bring the poet to his urn. Calliope gives birth to Orpheus, gives him birth into song, only to abandon him to his decapitation and the helpless floating of his singing head "[d]own the swift Hebrus to the Lesbian shore" (63). The muses inspire to song, but in "Lycidas" the din of the Thracian women drown out this song as the ocean waters drown Lycidas.

Through the "might" of Christ, the speaker claims to step beyond the interminable approach to death, the interminability of dying the urn/turn/urn sequence implies (173). The speaker imagines the future poet as muse, in turning to view the speaker's urn, strangely addressing the shroud: "So may some gentle Muse / With lucky words favor my destin'd urn; / And as he passes turn, / And bid fair peace be to my sable shroud." After the cremation, the speaker's ashes are "destined" for the "urn," around which will be draped the shroud. Having provided "lucky words" for inscription on the urn, the "gentle muse" is to "turn" and address, not the deceased poet, but the "shroud." The shroud mantels the urn. Does the reader, in looking back at "Lycidas," spy a well-wrought urn? The words of consolation, and the final pastoral scene in Heaven, would preclude "Lycidas" from the fate of being a "sable shroud," however well woven, and a "destined urn," however well wrought.

Rather than toward a "destined urn," the speaker of "Lycidas" walks toward "pastures new," wearing, rather than a "sable shroud," a "mantle blue," as the final speaker of the poem tells the reader in the surprise ending revealing the speaker of the majority of the poem to have been an "uncouth swain":

> Thus sang the uncouth swain to th' oaks and rills,
> While the still morn went out with sandals gray;
> He touch'd the tender stops of various quills,
> With eager thought warbling his Doric lay:
> And now the sun had stretch'd out all the hills,
> And now was dropt into the western bay;

At last he rose, and twitch'd his mantle blue:
Tomorrow to fresh woods, and pastures new.

(186–93)

Something of a residual anxiety toward a "sable shroud" inheres in the way the "swain" "twitch[es]" his "mantle blue" about his shoulders. Rather than a shroud draping an urn, the last speaker of "Lycidas" looks back to see a living "swain" in a "mantle blue" walking toward "fresh woods, and pastures new." The "swain" rises for his walk after twilight, after the low sun stretches out the hills in long shadows presaging nightfall. The setting sun emblematic of Lycidas's death here becomes a sun setting with finality: "And now the sun [...] was dropt into the western bay." This sun drops never to rise again in the poem; rather, the poet rises in the night ("At last he rose") and dons a sky, the "mantle blue," and walks toward a "[t]omorrow" whose arrival the poem puts in abeyance. Through the night the swain will walk clothed in his "mantle blue": in the sable shroud of night, does the mantle in its blueness evoke the sky of Heaven where the poet imagines Lycidas residing eternally or the waters where Lycidas drowned? When the reader looks back on "Lycidas," rather than a shrouded urn to which every poet is destined, the reader glimpses the swain, mantled in blue, crossing the night toward newness.

Calling on the muses, the speaker forgoes his "denial vain" of Lycidas's death. With the arrival of Christ in the poem, the poet cries out, "Weep no more, woeful shepherds, weep no more; / For Lycidas your sorrow is not dead" (165–66). The final movement of the poem would announce the complete overcoming of the urn and shroud. The muses mourning the drowned Lycidas give way to the chorus of saints singing to the forever-risen Lycidas. The Greek pastoral scene Lycidas enjoyed, with its "fountain, shade, and rill," gives way to an eternal Christian pastoral scene (24): "Where other groves and other streams along, / With nectar pure his oozy locks he laves" (174–75). The meed/mead the Lycidas parching in the wind so desperately needed arrives as this "nectar pure." The Greek muses were to inspire the poet to offer the dead

Lycidas "the meed of some melodious tear." The singing saints "wipe the tears for ever from his eyes" (181).

Most significantly, the Christ who can save displaces the Calliope who could not. The maternal Calliope, chief among the sisters of the sacred well, who failed her son, gives way to a Son whose Father cannot fail and whose mother makes nary an appearance in "Lycidas." The speaker who calls on the muses imagines being one in a series of mourning poets mourning prior poets. The Lycidas whom Christ saves himself becomes a savior, the local deity, "the genius of the shore" who "shalt be good / To all that wander in that perilous flood" (183–85). Having sung Lycidas into eternity, the speaker never looks back but strides toward "pastures new."

Visiting Cambridge's Trinity College, Charles Lamb viewed the manuscript of "Lycidas," and he was appalled to find Milton's cross-outs and revisions. The manuscript becomes for Lamb a forbidden fruit giving him knowledge he wishes he had never acquired:

> I had thought of the Lycidas as of a full-grown beauty—as springing up with all its parts absolute—till, in an evil hour, I was shown the original copy of it, together with the other minor poems of its author, in the library of Trinity, kept like some treasure, to be proud of. I wish they had thrown them in the Cam, or sent them after the latter cantos of Spenser, into the Irish Channel. How it staggered me to see the fine things in their ore! interlined, corrected! as if their words were mortal, alterable, displaceable at pleasure! as if they might have been otherwise, just as good! as if inspiration were made up of parts, and these fluctuating, successive, indifferent![9]

The ocean waves Lycidas drowns in are "fluctuating, successive, indifferent!" Prior to seeing the manuscript, Lamb had thought of "Lycidas" as an Athena, born from Milton's head "a full-grown beauty." To know otherwise is to fall, to become Milton's Eve, whose "rash hand in evil hour" reaches for the fruit (9.780). "[I]n an evil hour," Lamb encounters the manuscript.

Rather than an Athena in whose beautiful wholeness each part has its place immutably, Lamb finds a fluid procession of "parts," these flowing like ocean waves: "fluctuating, successive, indifferent!" Lamb registers the poem's anxiety of fluid. Lamb would rather the manuscript had been drowned, consigned to the "Cam" or to the "Irish Channel," to sink in Irish waters like Edward King. Lamb wishes never to have known the flux of the manuscript, and paradoxically would drown this fluidity in fluid. Lamb's note on the "Lycidas" manuscript appeared with the first publication of "Oxford in the Vacation" in the *London Magazine*, yet when Lamb gathered the essay for publication in *The Essays of Elia* (1823), he suppressed the note, acting out a version of his wish to drown his knowledge. This wish repeats the wish of the poem, to leave behind the *sparagmos* of Orpheus and achieve the full and eternal unity of Lycidas in his resurrection. Yet Lamb has eaten the fruit, so his wish remains only a wish: to drown his knowledge of the poem's aura of immutable unity drowning in the flux of the manuscript. Lamb calls the finished poems "fine things" but the manuscript "ore." Precisely the removal of Calliope's "golden hair" allows Milton to stage the resurrection of Lycidas as the sun rising with hair of "new-spangled ore." Milton shows the resurrected Lycidas washing "his oozy locks" using "nectar pure." While cleansing his hair, Lycidas "hears the unexpressive nuptial song" the "saints" "sing," who "singing in their glory move, / And wipe the tears for ever from his eyes" (176, 178, 180–81). At the start of the poem, the poet hopes to offer Lycidas a "melodious tear," and so invokes the muses: "Begin then, sisters of the sacred well." But, inspiring such a tear, the muses only bring the poet into the mortality of urns and turns. Even the "muse herself," Calliope, only births Orpheus towards his rending by "the rout that made the hideous roar," a sound the far contrary of the "unexpressive nuptial song" as is the ooze from the "nectar pure."

From Lamb to Woolf, from a lamb wishing to drown knowledge of the flux to a wolf curious to know it: in *A Room of One's Own*, Virginia Woolf evokes Lamb's trip to Cambridge, collapsed by Woolf with Oxford to form "Oxbridge":

Lamb then came to Oxbridge perhaps a hundred years ago. Certainly he wrote an essay—the name escapes me—about the manuscript of one of Milton's poems which he saw here. It was Lycidas perhaps, and Lamb wrote how it shocked him to think it possible that any word in Lycidas could have been different from what it is. To think of Milton changing the words in that poem seemed to him a sort of sacrilege. This led me to remember what I could of Lycidas and to amuse myself with guessing which word it could have been that Milton had altered, and why.[10]

Her musings lead Woolf, or her persona Mary, to wish to see that very manuscript of "Lycidas," she recalling the library at Oxbridge houses it: "one could follow Lamb's footsteps across the quadrangle to that famous library where the treasure is kept" (7). Mary sets off following Lamb's steps only to be denied entrance to the library as no woman may enter unless "accompanied by a Fellow of the College or furnished with a letter of introduction" (8). Author of *The Waves*, Woolf would know the flux Lamb would forget, yet she writes Mary as blocked from this knowledge by a male authority. Woolf would be very interested to find the words Milton "altered" concern a repressive flight from the fluid, from finitude, from the muses.

Milton's Muse in Paradise Lost

The concern with Orpheus's fate and the connection of this fate to Calliope, the muse of epic poetry, persists from "Lycidas" into *Paradise Lost*. Nightly, Milton's muse Urania visits him, whispering into his ear the visions of the poem, *Paradise Lost*. Through Urania's inspiration, Milton flies to heaven to view how the unfallen angels live. Urania takes Milton to heaven and is herself heavenly, unlike Calliope in her failure to protect Orpheus. In the following words of Milton the narrator, "thou" refers to Urania, "she" to Calliope: "For thou art Heav'nly, she an empty dream" (7.39). How does Milton contrast the heavens and dreams? The two must remain distinct. The dream Satan gives Eve involves her in a confusion of waking, sleeping, and dreaming. When Urania visits, does Milton wake or sleep? He must not merely dream, or so his rejection of Calliope as an "empty dream" implies. The anxiety about keeping his heavenly muse distinct from an "empty dream" manifests in the episode of the belated peasant. Approaching a "forest side" or a "fountain," the "belated peasant" "sees" a dancing band of "faery elves" amidst their "midnight revels" (1.781–83). "Or dreams he sees": this vision, whether a waking vision or a dream landscape, comes to the peasant as "overhead the moon / Sits arbitress, and nearer to the earth / Wheels her pale course" (1.784–86). The moon's orbit around the earth is elliptical, and, when that orbit's perigee corresponds with a full moon, the moon, closer to the earth, appears noticeably bigger and brighter in the sky. Under the influence of a moon "nearer to the earth," the "belated peasant" becomes particularly vulnerable to confusing seeing and dreaming. Yet Milton evokes the peasant envisioning the elves as an analogy to the situation of the reader envisioning Satan's numberless crew of rebel angels gathering within the council room of Pandemonium, the palace they build as the capital of hell: "Behold a wonder! they but now who seem'd / In bigness to surpass Earth's giant sons / Now less than smallest dwarfs, in narrow room / Throng numberless" (1.777–80). In beholding this wonder, the reader becomes as the peasant, whose response to the vision is divided: "At once with joy and fear his heart rebounds" (1.788). This joy and fear are Milton's also in his encounters with Urania. Anxious fears of abandonment haunt Milton's invocations of his muse Urania in *Paradise Lost*. Yet the first invocation makes a bold claim: "on the secret top / Of Oreb, or of Sinai," a muse, the "Heavenly Muse," inspired Moses to compose the Genesis account of the creation (1.6–7). Mediating between Heaven above and earth below, the "secret" mountain peak hosts a muse whose sister is Wisdom.

In Proverbs, Wisdom describes her birth from her father and her being with him: "When there were no depths, was I begotten, when there were no fountains abounding with water. Before the mountains were settled: and before the hills, was I begotten [...] Then I was with him *as* a nourisher, and I was daily his delight, rejoicing always before him" (8.24–25, 30, Geneva 1560). Rewriting these verses that describe Wisdom being with God prior to the creation, Milton states that his muse, the Heavenly Muse, was there with God too. Milton's muse was Wisdom's twin sister. With her sister Wisdom Milton's muse did talk and cavort prior to the creation and to the delight of the deity. Milton addressing his muse: "Before the hills appear'd, or fountains flow'd, / Thou with eternal Wisdom didst converse, / Wisdom thy sister, and with her didst play / In presence of th' Almighty Father, pleas'd / With thy celestial song" (7.8–12). Rather than sublunary, the song of the Heavenly Muse is "celestial." She sang this song in the beginning, before the creation, when Wisdom her sister, as a master builder, inspired the deity, their father-mother, to form the cosmos. Much less any Heavenly Muse, Proverbs 8.22–31 mentions no third party, as if, before the creation, when God was with Wisdom, only the first- and second-person pronouns were operative, I and You, with an "I" only being with a "You," speaking ever to each other, never speaking of each other except in speaking to each other. In this colloquy, neither would God ever be a "he" for Wisdom nor would Wisdom ever be a "she" for God. God was utterly alone with Wisdom, each an I alone with a thou. To what innovation does Milton aspire by introducing a third into the God-Wisdom colloquy?

In the full primordiality of the time before time, in the space before space, three shared delight and song: God, Wisdom, and the Heavenly Muse. Before the creation, there were three. The marginal gloss to Proverbs 8.22 (Wisdom: "The Lord hath possessed me in the beginning of his way: *I was* before his works of old") in the 1560 Geneva Bible is insistent: "He declareth hereby the divinity and eternity of this wisdom, which he magnifieth and praiseth through this book: meaning thereby the eternal son of God Jesus Christ our Saviour, whom S. John calls the word that was in the beginning, John 1.1." The Geneva marginal gloss to Proverbs 8.30 (Wisdom: "Then I was by him *as* a nourisher, and I was daily *his* delight, rejoicing always before him") explains that, for the words "I was by him *as* a nourisher," "Some read a chief worker: signifying that this Wisdom, even Christ Jesus, was equal with God his Father, and created, preserved and still worketh with him, as John 5.17." Following John 1.1, into Proverbs 8.22–31 the Geneva translators introduce Christ, reading Wisdom as Christ and Christ as "equal with God his father." Into Proverbs 8.22–31, Milton introduces his Heavenly Muse. If, in the beginning, Christ as the Word was with God and was God, and if this word was Wisdom, and if Wisdom had a sister, who was this sister? Consider the Heavenly Muse as a manifestation of the Holy Spirit.[11]

Pleading for a companion his equal with whom he can talk, Adam asks God, "In solitude / What happiness?" (8.364–65). To Adam, God poses this conundrum: "What think'st thou then of me, and this my state? / Seem I to thee sufficiently possest / Of happiness, or not? who am alone / From all eternity, for none I know / Second to me or like, equal much less" (8.403–07). Is God always alone, having no one his equal with whom to converse, or, prior to and in the act of creating the creation, was another or were others with God? Milton's Eve faces a dilemma: insofar as she is rational, she is potentially yet not actually Adam's equal. The potential equality inheres in her bearing rationality or *logos*; her actual inequality inheres in her being female. Implicit here is a developmental *telos* for Eve in which, the closer she comes to being Adam's equal, the closer she would come to her womanhood being the same as manhood. Something like this endpoint manifests with Wisdom in the Geneva gloss: Wisdom is Christ, who is God's equal. A female, prefiguring the Logos, becomes equivalent to a male and the equal to another male. So anchored in an androcentric allegorization, Wisdom never may undergo rich confusion with Folly. Milton's archangel Raphael is very confident he can distinguish Wisdom from Folly. The reading of Wisdom as Christ shuts down or spirits away the abyssal yet wonderful ambiguity Proverbs sets up, with Wisdom only approachable by way of the irreducible risk of confusing Folly for Wisdom or Wisdom for Folly.

To claim Wisdom as his muse would be direct blasphemy on Milton's part by implying Milton's equal status as a creator with "the Almighty Father." For Milton to claim Wisdom as his muse would bring the poet close to Satan who, inspired by Sin, seeks to displace the Father. In Ibsen's *The Master Builder*, the architect Solness, in taking Hilda Wangel as his muse, implicitly takes Wisdom the architect as a muse, and so ends the play in her exalted vision grappling with the divine only to fall to his death. No, Milton does not call upon Wisdom as his muse, but upon Wisdom's twin sister, the Heavenly Muse whom he gives the name Urania. This same muse inspired Moses, not to build the creation, but to sing of its building, to instruct "the chosen seed, / In the beginning how the Heav'ns and earth / Rose out of Chaos" (1.8–10). This muse Milton claims as his own, speaking of her and to her. Othello speaks less to Desdemona of Desdemona than to Iago about her.

With Moses, the Heavenly Muse stood atop Sinai in secret. Milton invokes the Heavenly Muse, and he only speaks to her of her. The reader may overhear him address words to his muse, and some of these words may be about her, yet Milton never addresses words to the reader about her. The relation remains one of an "I" addressing a "You." Implicit in this mode of address is a fiction of secrecy. Reading the book one and the book seven invocations, the reader listens to words Milton utters as if no one but Milton's muse were there to hear them, as if he spoke to her entirely in secret.

Folly and Wisdom Crossing in Sin

Milton scatters through *Paradise Lost* the *topos* of Wisdom and Folly's mutual crossing. Caught by the angels Ithuriel and Zephon whispering into Eve's ear, and brought by them to the guardian of Eden's gate, the archangel Gabriel, Satan asserts the wisdom of his fleeing hell because hell is pain, and who would embrace pain? Satan to Gabriel: "Lives there who loves his pain? / Who would not, finding way, break loose from Hell, / Though thither doom'd?" (4.888–90). Satan tells Gabriel he would do the same, were he bound in hell. Satan asks his question in response to Gabriel's question as to why Satan has broke free from hell and into Eden, potentially to disturb Adam and Eve's "bliss" (4.884). Gabriel's very question makes Satan "doubt" whether Gabriel is "wise," as was his reputation in heaven (4.888, 886). Ready to trade insults as to who is or is not wise, Gabriel replies by speaking of Satan but at first not to him, with Ithuriel and Zephon as audience:

> O loss of one in Heav'n to judge of wise,
> Since Satan fell, whom folly overthrew,
> And now returns him from his prison scap't,
> Gravely in doubt whether to hold them wise
> Or not, who ask what boldness brought him hither
> Unlicenc't from his bounds in Hell prescrib'd.
>
> (4.904–09)

Gabriel accuses Satan of being unlicensed. With passionate eloquence, in the *Areopagitica* Milton makes the case for "the Liberty of unlicenc'd Printing," the freedom to publish without attaining a license from a government censor who claims the authority to judge the wisdom or folly of a text's appearing before the reading public.[12] In the pamphlet, Milton deploys the Wisdom/Folly *topos,* arguing for the pernicious futility of licensing, since from any book the wise will glean wisdom while the foolish will glean folly: "there is no reason that we should deprive a wise man of any advantage to his wisdome, while we seek to restrain from a fool, that which being restrain'd will be no hindrance to his folly. [...] a wise man will make better use of an idle pamphlet, then a fool will do of sacred Scripture" (1008). Further, the "prescription" licensing constitutes would keep readers in a perpetual "childhood," yet readers are post-Adamic, and know evil, and good only by evil, the two contraries being intermixed almost past sorting out (1008, 1010). Yet our virtue only merits the name because of our trial to sort out good from evil, being fully exposed to both:

> I cannot praise a fugitive and cloister'd vertue, unexercis'd & unbreath'd, that never sallies out and sees her adversary, but slinks out of the race, where that immortal garland is to be run for, not without dust and heat. Assuredly we bring not innocence into the world, we bring impurity much rather: that which purifies us is triall, and triall is by what

is contrary. That vertue therefore which is but a youngling
in the contemplation of evill, and knows not the utmost that
vice promises to her followers, and rejects it, is but a blank
vertue, not a pure; her whiteness is but an excrementall
whitenesse. (1006)

In their dispute over wisdom, Satan taunts Gabriel as unable
to grasp the argument as to the wisdom of escaping pain and
seeking pleasure because he, Gabriel, is innocent of, untried by,
evil: "To thee no reason; who know'st only good, / But evil hast
not tri'd" (4.895–96). Gabriel would have Satan never cross the
bounds "prescrib'd" for him, Gabriel's initial question to Satan
being: "Why hast thou, Satan, broke the bounds prescrib'd / To
thy transgressions[?]" (4.878–79). In saying "folly overthrew"
Satan in heaven, Gabriel implicitly equates Sin with folly, Sin the
unlicensed publication emanating from Satan's head. In the same
speech, speaking of Satan and then to him, as if at a Cambridge
debate exercise, Gabriel mocks Satan's claim to wisdom by
ironically using the term to refer to Satan's folly:

> So wise he judges it to fly from pain
> However, and to scape his punishment.
> So judge thou still, presumptuous; till the wrath,
> Which thou incurr'st by flying, meet thy flight
> Sevenfold, and scourge that wisdom back to Hell,
> Which taught thee yet no better, than no pain
> Can equal anger infinite provok't.
>
> (4.910–16)

Is Sin Satan's folly or Satan's wisdom? She certainly is his love.
In imagining God's "wrath" will "scourge that wisdom back to
Hell," Gabriel imagines Satan's folly driven back within Satan, if,
as Satan states, he carries hell within himself. Satan, Gabriel states,
"incurr'st" "wrath" "by flying," by flying pain and so flying past
the "bounds" to which he has been "prescribed." Satan will tempt
Eve in a dream with a dream of flight promising in that flight she
will cross the limit of the sublunary and enter into the celestial,
there to know and join the life of the immortals. At the epic's start,

Milton calls on his "Heavenly Muse" to inspire him to a poetic flight past the bounds of all previous literary achievement and beyond the high abode of the Greek muses (1.6, 12–16). Milton claims his muse is the sister of Wisdom and in no way Folly, yet his association of his muse with Wisdom inevitably invites Urania being caught up in the Wisdom/Folly ambiguity. The clarification Gabriel attempts in Satan's case seeks to use irony: Gabriel says "wisdom" when he means "folly," but that irony remains subject to the reversal of intending to and saying "folly" and yet referring to "wisdom." And so on, the ironic involutions also operating in Satan's claim to be wise in fleeing pain. When Gabriel mockingly bemoans Heaven's loss of Satan as a judge of wisdom ("O loss of one in Heav'n to judge of wise"), Gabriel does touch on the question: who can judge whether the voice calling is Wisdom's or Folly's? But in his denunciations of Satan, Gabriel would set himself up as a "judge of wise." At the end of their dispute, Gabriel threatens to return Satan to Hell by force should Satan again trespass into Eden. Refusing to bow to this threat, Satan prepares to fight Gabriel and his compeers. Rather than see Eden and the broader new creation possibly ruined by this fight, God, as though he were Zeus, sets his "golden scales" in the sky; in one pan, God places a weight for "parting" and in the other one for "fight" (4.997, 1003). The weight for parting outweighs the one for fighting. Seeing the scale tip, Gabriel believes this indicates his strength is greater than Satan's, but to "boast" of strength, as Satan does, is, Gabriel says, a form of "folly," as all strength, his or Satan's, is what "Heav'n permits" (4.1007–09).

Folly and Wisdom Crossing in Eve

The wisdom/folly *topos* complexly guides Adam's interchange with Raphael in which Adam relates his origin and Eve's and his first meeting with Eve. Raphael takes up the wisdom/folly *topos* in the advice he gives Adam about Eve. Adam shows himself subject to mistaking wisdom for folly and folly for wisdom. The account Adam gives of his first encounter with Eve shows Adam misreading Eve's turn away from him, which Eve recounts to Adam prior to his conversation with Raphael. In her account to Adam of this meeting, Eve tells him how she first came to awareness by a pool in which she saw a beautiful and beguiling reflection. A divine voice explained to her the reflection was of her self. This voice then asked Eve to leave the image and follow toward her fit locus of desire, Adam. However, Eve explains to Adam, on her first seeing him, he compared poorly with the image in the pool. The voice led her to walk on:

> Till I espi'd thee, fair indeed and tall,
> Under a platan, yet methought less fair,
> Less winning soft, less amiably mild,
> Than that smooth watery image; back I turned[.]
>
> (4.477–80)

Her account seems plain and direct: she turned from Adam because, though fair and tall he was, he could not compete with the "smooth watery image." And yet Adam, in later relating this same encounter to Raphael, tells the angel that Eve, innocent yet seeking to be "woo'd, and not unsought be won" and to make herself "more desirable," therefore turned from him to spark his pursuit: "seeing me, she turn'd" (8.503, 505, 507). The two accounts of Eve's turn back to the image in the pool flatly contradict each other. And in the tale he tells Raphael, Adam ignores the account Eve had given Adam of her own desire: Eve specified to Adam that she turned away from him due to her desire for the image in the water, yet to Raphael Adam claims she turned away from him to augment his desire for her. This boosting of desire may have been the effect on Adam of her turning away, but this effect was in no way Eve's purpose, if the reader credits her testimony. Adam's misrepresentation of Eve's turn casts into an ironic shade Adam's claim to be Eve's superior in mental acumen. Adam makes this claim in the course of relating to Raphael Eve's turn and its aftermath. After Eve turned, Adam says, he "followed her": "she what was honor knew, / And with obsequious majesty approv'd / My pleaded reason" (8.508–10). In his account, Adam claims his "pleaded reason" won Eve to him. In her account, Eve does recite the reasoning Adam offered, his claiming Eve as his "flesh, his bone" and "[p]art of [his] soul" (4.483, 487). Eve is the part, Adam the whole. Yet Eve also recalls how, immediately after offering his reasons, and giving Eve no opportunity to reply, Adam seized her hand: "With that thy gentle hand / Seiz'd mine, I yielded, and from that time see / How beauty is excell'd by manly grace, / And wisdom, which alone is truly fair" (4.88–91). Eve learns to devalue her "beauty" and her own desire as implicitly folly, as she learns to value Adam's "manly grace" and "wisdom."

Adam leaves out of his account the force Eve implies prompted her to yield her desire to his, to relent in her effort to return to her own image or "beauty," and to acknowledge "manly grace" as excelling that beauty. And the effect of this force is to coach Eve to associate "wisdom" with Adam and to disassociate "wisdom" in its being "truly fair" from "beauty" and so from her own "watery image," this image then implicitly a folly. This lesson the voice and Adam compel Eve to learn and that she articulates to Adam is lost on Adam. Adam again shows himself deaf to Eve, because, in his discourse with Raphael, Adam explains how for him Eve's triumphant beauty takes the place of wisdom and puts wisdom in the place of folly.

The section of Adam's musings on Eve in which Adam invokes the wisdom/folly *topos* merits quoting in full. The lines involve a dense set of tropes complexly lining up with what Adam calls the "inward" and the "outward." Adam speaking to Raphael of Eve:

> For well I understand in the prime end
> Of Nature her th' inferior, in the mind
> And inward faculties, which most excel;
> In outward also her resembling less
> His image who made both, and less expressing
> The character of that dominion giv'n
> O'er other creatures; yet when I approach
> Her loveliness, so absolute she seems
> And in herself complete, so well to know
> Her own, that what she wills to do or say
> Seems wisest, virtuousest, discreetest, best;
> All higher knowledge in her presence falls

Degraded; Wisdom in discourse with her
Loses discount'nanc't, and like Folly shows.
Authority and Reason on her wait,
As one intended first, not after made
Occasionally, and, to consummate all,
Greatness of mind and Nobleness their seat
Build in her loveliest, and create an awe
About her, as a guard Angelic plac't.

(8.540–59)

These impassioned words Adam utters having told Raphael that, after seeing Eve in the "trance" God placed him under to remove the rib, Adam then saw Eve when he awoke, yet she appeared as she did in his trance-state "dream" (8.462, 482). The sights, sounds, and smells of Eden are "delight[s] indeed," yet Eve altogether excels them: "but here / Far otherwise, transported I behold, / Transported touch" (8.524, 528–30). With his sense of touch having been torched, Adam reports to Raphael how, though he "well […] understand[s]" that Eve is his "inferior" in terms of "mind," that she "resembl[es] less" God's "image," and that she in her person "less express[es]" the "character" of the "dominion" God has given humanity over the animals, yet in the presence of her "loveliness" all these hierarchies setting him over her seem overturned. Far from "inferior" in "mind," Eve appears to be the "seat [of] / Greatness of mind" and "nobleness." Far from Eve being less expressive of "dominion," "Authority and Reason" "wait" upon her. Rather than condescension, Eve solicits "awe."

These reversals partake of the reversal of wisdom into folly or, better, Wisdom into Folly. Here if anywhere retaining the capitalization of Wisdom in the first and second editions of *Paradise Lost* makes sense: Adam is speaking of Wisdom, and though neither the 1667 nor the 1674 *Paradise Lost* capitalizes the "folly" in Adam's speech, the edition used here rightly emends "f" to "F": "Wisdom in discourse with [Eve] / Loses discount'nanc't, and like Folly shows." In debate with Eve, Wisdom loses her composure, loses face, and just plain loses, and so "like Folly shows." Wisdom seems Folly, and, with nobility and greatness of mind, Eve appears as Wisdom exalted, though, Raphael will claim, this appearance instances Adam's folly. Eve's appearance of completeness and self-knowledge precipitates Adam's vision of Eve as triumphing over yet embodying Wisdom. In her "loveliness," Eve seems "absolute," "in herself complete," and fully able "to know / Her own." This is the Eve who can find her image her desire, the Eve who would have stayed forever gazing into the pool.

Raphael feels he must with all urgency argue Adam down from his vision of Eve. Raphael borders on casting Eve as Folly. Adam wonders if, in his vulnerability to Eve, "[n]ature failed" him, leaving him "weak" when confronting "the charm of beauty's powerful glance" (8.534, 532, 533). Raphael counters, telling Adam, "Accuse not Nature" (8.561): "she hath done her part; Do thou but thine, and be not diffident / Of Wisdom, she deserts thee not, if thou / Dismiss not her, when most thou need'st her nigh" (8.561–64). Adam most needs Wisdom nearby when Eve's "outside" "transports" him, says Raphael (8.568, 567). Adam should honor, cherish, and love Eve in her beauty, but in no way should Adam allow her beauty to bring about his "subjection" (8.569–70). Raphael says to Adam, "[Eve] sees when thou art seen least wise" (8.578). Like Eve, Adam is naked, so his arousal by her beauty is visually evident to her. Rather than allow himself to suffer "subjection" to Eve-as-Folly, Adam must practice "self-esteem": "of that skill the more thou know'st / The more she will acknowledge thee her head, / And to realities yield all her shows" (8.572, 573–74). Raphael's "head" metaphor for a woman's subjection to a man comes from Paul: "But I would have you know, that the head of every man is Christ; and the head of the woman *is* the man; and the head of Christ *is* God" (1 Corinthians 11.3). In this strange hierarchy, only one head, as a head, exists truly: God's. God has a head but owes it to no one. A man has a head, but only insofar as Christ does, and Christ has a head, but only insofar as God does. And, unlike the man and Christ, the woman does not in turn exercise a head: her head is man, but she is the head of no one. In Paul's metaphor, woman as woman remains anencephalic, a body without a head, or, Raphael implies, mostly a body ungoverned by reason and somewhat beastly.

Raphael reminds Adam that, among the beasts, he found no mate. Raphael notes to Adam that what in his folly "transports [him] so," Eve's "fair" "outside," moves "the sense of touch," as Adam's phrase "[t]ransported touch" had indicated (8.567, 568, 579, 530). Given Adam's "[t]ransported touch," Raphael asks Adam to take the cold mental bath of remembering he shares such touch in common with all the beasts: "But if the sense of touch, whereby mankind / Is propagated seem such dear delight / Beyond all other, think the same voutsaf't / To cattle and each beast" (8.579–82). If Adam enjoys such touching in "common" with the beasts, there must not be "aught / Therein enjoy'd [...] worthy to subdue / The soul of Man, or passion in him move" (8.583–85). Rather than the beastly, Adam is to love in Eve what is "higher": "What higher in her society thou find'st / Attractive, human, rational, love still" (8.586–87). This love "hath his seat / In reason" (8.590–91): this is love from and of the head, that is, a love proceeding from the sovereign head, a love of Eve insofar as she may have a head, though she may eventually have a head only through Adam and in becoming the androcentric equal of Adam. The love based in reason is proper to Adam insofar as he has a head. Such "true love," says Raphael to Adam, "is the scale / By which to Heav'nly love thou may'st ascend, / Not sunk in carnal pleasure" (8.589, 591–94). Anencephalic despite their apparent heads, their touch of propagation disoriented from reason, the beasts too enjoy carnal pleasure, yet the beastly as such will never find a ladder by which to climb toward "Heav'nly love." Raphael to Adam: "for which cause / Among the beasts no mate for thee was found" (8.593–94).

Paul's metaphor of the head carries with it Paul's spirit/ flesh distinction. Raphael's invocation and elaboration of Paul's metaphor puts Eve in an awkward position. Only insofar as Eve has a head may she serve as Adam's proper mate. Yet Adam claims Eve to be his inferior in reason, in sovereignty over the beasts, and in resemblance to the ultimate head, God. Never quite Adam's equal yet also capable of reason, Eve hovers between the beasts and the "human." Insofar as Eve's "outside" tempts Adam to overvalue "touch" and place himself among the beasts, argues Raphael, Eve threatens to subject Adam. Because Eve is Adam's sub-version, Adam must not be subject to Eve, yet Adam claims he wants an equal as his mate. In this perilous situation, Adam must both guard against Eve's Circe-like ability to make men beasts, or rather to make the man, Adam, a beast, while also engaging and so cultivating Eve's reason, her humanity, her resemblance to God. Raphael would divide Eve between her "outside" and her inside. Yet is Eve a divided being? Rather, in his approach to Eve, Adam suffers a division between love and passion. Or at least the Pauline Raphael insists that Adam accept this division: "In loving thou dost well, in passion not, / Wherein true love consists not" (8.588–89). In reference to women, or to the woman, Eve, Adam confuses her for Wisdom and Wisdom for Folly. Raphael implicitly claims to be able to distinguish Wisdom from Folly.

Eve's Desire

To Adam Eve speaks of her desire. First, before Satan's temptation of her, yet with Satan nearby to overhear the tale, Eve tells Adam of her first awakening into existence and finding a lake. Looking down onto the surface, she views an image beckoning to her from the water the divine voice says is a mirror. She falls in love with this image. Satan strategizes to seduce Eve by using what he learns of her desire. While "all ear," listening to Eve and Adam speak, Satan begins to craft a dream, which he then whispers into Eve's ear. *Othello* plays on lips and kisses. *Paradise Lost* favors the ear. Eve wakes and tells Adam of her dream culminating in flight. In the dream, Satan promises Eve she may fly to heaven. The waters in which Eve sees the image are "a liquid plane," serenely still or "unmoved" and "[p]ure as th' expanse of Heav'n" (4.455, 456). Eve explains, "the clear / Smooth lake [...] to me seem'd another sky" (4.458–59). In this sky resides the beautiful image Eve desires. In the dream, Satan promises Eve she may reside in Heaven. All she need do is eat the fruit. What is the relationship between the fulfillments of desire the woman in the lake and Satan offer Eve? Satan forms the dream to flatter Eve's desire. Neither God nor Adam speaks to Eve's desire; Satan does. Neither God nor Adam affirms Eve's desire; Satan does.

Consider the following irony: Eve tells her story of her awakening to her desire for her own image just after Adam speaks to her a gushing paean to God. To Eve, Adam praises God for allowing the first couple "[f]ree leave" to partake in "all things" the garden has to offer (4.434). With the exception of the forbidden fruit, God allows the two "choice / Unlimited of manifold delights" (4.434–35). The story Eve tells Adam in response to his paean recounts the limitation the divine voice wants Eve to place on her delight, qualifying her "[f]ree leave." Left to her own choice, Eve tells Adam, she would have remained ever by the lake gazing at the image, what God or the divine voice Eve hears calls her own image. Eve recounts to Adam how God's disembodied voice dissuades her from exercising her choice.

A sound other than God's voice had led Eve to the lake. Upon her awakening, she finds herself "reposed / Under a shade on flow'rs," there "much wondring" as to "where" and "what" she is and "how" she came to be (4.450–52). A murmur calls Eve from her bed of flowers and toward the lake:

> Not distant far from thence a murmuring sound
> Of waters issu'd from a cave, and spread
> Into a liquid plain, then stood unmov'd,
> Pure as th' expanse of Heav'n. I thither went
> With unexperienc't thought, and laid me down
> On the green bank, to look into the clear
> Smooth lake, that to me seem'd another sky.
>
> (4.453–59)

Fluidity speaks to Eve. Eve narrates how she heard the waters' murmur as calling her to the lake. Eve listened to this voice with "unexperienc't thought." She took the lake, reflecting the sky, to be "another sky." A lesson Plato's Socrates would teach is to distinguish reflections from realities. The newly created Eve's thought, lacking experience, had yet to make this distinction. In retrospect, with her thought more experienced, the Eve recounting her origin to Adam knows the lake was a lake, but at the time she took it for "another sky." The simile Eve uses describing the lake as "[p]ure as th' expanse of Heav'n" also indicates the narrating

Eve's relative experience. The narrated Eve taking the lake to be "another sky" implies her innocence. In this innocence, Eve gazed into the lake:

> As I bent down to look, just opposite
> A shape within the watry gleam appear'd,
> Bending to look on me. I started back,
> It started back, but pleas'd I soon return'd,
> Pleas'd it returned as soon, with answering looks
> Of sympathy and love[.]
>
> (4.460–65)

At this point in Eve's tale of her origins, the narrated Eve's falling in love with her own image takes place innocent of itself, unknowingly. Eve responds to her own responsiveness, unaware she is peopling her own solitude. In the process, Eve undergoes something parallel to yet contrasting with Adam's search for a companion among the beasts. Upon God's request, Adam names all the beasts. But Adam finds none among them suitable, Adam complaining that, since they are not his equals, they leave him still in solitude, though he is in their company. Adam rejects and even defies God's apparent wish that Adam find companionship among the beasts. When Adam refuses to give way on his desire for a fit companion, God praises him as knowing himself well and, God says, as "[e]xpressing well the spirit within thee free, / My image, not imparted to the brute" (8.440–41).

In contrast to God's acceptance and approval of Adam's desire, when Eve settled down on the grassy bank by the lake for a long and longing gaze at the woman she saw looking back at her, God intervened, as Eve recounts:

> [T]here I had fixed
> Mine eyes till now, and pin'd with vain desire,
> Had not a voice thus warn'd me: "What thou seest,
> What there thou seest, fair creature, is thyself,
> With thee it came and goes: but follow me,
> And I will bring thee where no shadow stays
> Thy coming, and thy soft embraces; he

Whose image thou art, him thou shalt enjoy
Inseparably thine, to him shalt bear
Multitudes like thyself, and thence be call'd
Mother of human race[.]"

(4.465–75)

Notice the insistence of the lesson with the rising admonitory
tone in the repetition: "What thou seest, / What there thou seest."
God warns the Eve reclining by the lake as he teaches her. In her
desire, she wants to admire the image, but God would direct her
toward marriage and motherhood. The Adam who freely asserts
his desire God praises as expressive of God's "image." As Adam
is God's image, so Eve is Adam's image ("he / Whose image thou
art"), but Eve is Adam's image only insofar as she gives way on her
desire for the image in the lake. Between Adam's desire and Adam's
exercise of free will God places no impediments. But, in seeking to
direct Eve's desire toward Adam, God sets aside Eve's will.

Had she her choice, Eve would have remained with her image,
she tells Adam in retrospect. Only in retrospect does she call her
desire "vain." The narrated Eve rejects Adam in favor of her image
even after learning from God's voice that the woman who beckons
is her "shadow" or insubstantial simulacrum, God using the word
"shadow" in a Platonic sense. Despite God telling Eve that what
she sees in the water is herself, or more precisely the non-gender
differentiated "thyself," Eve commits an act of rebellion, even if at
first the voice guiding her to Adam seems to her one she has no
choice but to obey:

[W]hat could I do,
But follow straight, invisibly thus led?
Till I espi'd thee, fair indeed and tall,
Under a platan, yet methought less fair,
Less winning soft, less amiably mild,
Than that smooth watry image; back I turned[.]

(4.475–80)

When Eve arrived at the lake, she was unexperienced in
"thought." The voice of God tries to teach her the Platonic lesson

of distinguishing a "shadow" from a reality and to shift her desire from shadows to realities. When God's voice leads Eve to the sight of Adam, Eve does exercise thought ("methought"). But, rather than seeking to distinguish a shadow from a reality, and to reject her shadow and cleave toward the reality of Adam, Eve assesses the relative degrees of aesthetic pleasure her shadow and Adam provide her eye. "[T]hough fair indeed and tall," Adam is to Eve's thought "less fair, / Less winning soft, less amiably mild, / Than that smooth wat'ry image." In *The Republic,* Plato has Socrates distinguish two parts of the soul, a inferior part seducible by shadows, deceptive images, and a superior part responsive to realities, especially the realities numbers denote. The part of the soul that longs for shadows Socrates calls "beastly," a "many-colored, many-headed beast" in which "all the desires, pains, and pleasures" throng and which must be "held down by force" and "ruled" (571c, 588c, 606d, 606a, 606d). This part of the soul loves poetry, specifically Homer's, and Socrates pictures the soul's inferior, vulnerable-to-loving-Homer part as feminine (605e). This part of the soul would remain forever in or return to the cave of Plato's allegory, there to enjoy shadows. Eve follows the murmurs of waters emanating from a cave, comes to the lake, finds her reflection, and would remain there gazing and longing. This vulnerability to pleasing appearances aligns Eve with the part of the soul Socrates calls feminine and diagnoses as in need of being ruled by the part responsive to realities, the male part of the soul. This part of the soul Adam claims to be, but with Milton assimilating Plato to the Pauline chain of command (God—Christ—Man—Woman) in which the head, though part of the body, rules the body, with the head figuring the man, Adam, and the body figuring the woman, Eve.

Milton has Adam persist in misreading Eve's desire, and this misreading Adam conjoins to his claims to be Eve's superior who should rule her. After Eve explicitly tells Adam that she turned from him to return to her image, in conversation with Raphael Adam claims Eve turned from him to inflame his desire for her, to render herself the "more desirable" (8.505). This is the Adam who says of Eve to Raphael: "For well I understand in the prime end

/ Of Nature her th' inferior, in the mind / And inward faculties, which most excel" (8.540–42). But does Adam "understand," much less "well"? He shows himself to misunderstand Eve's desire. And while Eve emphasizes the force with which Adam's "hand / Seiz'd" her hand, and so prevented her turn back to her own image, Adam claims she yielded to his "pleaded reason" (4.488–89, 8.509). Plato does have Socrates indicate the feminine part of the soul must be ruled by force, yet cave dwellers should be brought from the shadows to the sun by rational dialogue.

How committed is *Paradise Lost* to a Platonic-Pauline reformation of Eve from her desire? The narrator Milton offers a description of Eve as subject to Adam and yet, in this subjection, as being "coy" to provoke desire. This description depicts Adam and Eve as Satan first views them soon before he will first hear them speak and hear Eve speak of her desire. Though in both Adam and Eve the "image of their glorious Maker shone," the two remain unequal:

> Not equal, as their sex not equal seem'd;
> For contemplation he, and valor, form'd,
> For softness she and sweet attractive grace;
> He for God only, she for God in him.
> His fair large front and eye sublime declar'd
> Absolute rule; and hyacinthine locks
> Round from his parted forelock manly hung
> Clustring, but not beneath his shoulders broad:
> She as a veil down to the slender waist
> Her unadorned golden tresses wore
> Dishevell'd, but in wanton ringlets wav'd
> As the vine curls her tendrils, which impli'd
> Subjection, but requir'd with gentle sway.
> And by her yielded, by him best receiv'd,
> Yielded with coy submission, modest pride,
> And sweet, reluctant, amorous delay.
>
> (4.292, 294–311)

As will Adam in conversation with Raphael, here the narrator Milton associates Eve's Pauline subjection to Adam ("He for God only, she for God in him.") with her yielding to Adam only in turning away from him, her being "coy" and exercising a "sweet, reluctant, amorous delay." Before Eve's creation, Adam asks God for a companion who would be his equal, for, as he queries God, "Among unequals what society / Can sort, what harmony, or true delight?" (8.383–84). In perplexity, Adam criticizes the only companions God has offered, the beasts. Adam hopes for a companion "fit to participate / All rational delight, wherein the brute / Cannot be human consort" (8.390–92). Adam asks God, "Hast thou not made me here thy substitute, / And these inferior far beneath me set?" (8.381–82). Incapable of reason yet sharing with Adam a desire for sexual intercourse, the beasts offer no fit companion for him. Eve shares reason with Adam, but an inferior degree of reason, and, in contradiction to Eve's account, the narrator and Adam agree Eve most provokes his desire in coyly turning from him yet then yielding to him in submission. Thus, while not to be found among the beasts, Eve remains beastly: moving toward equal discourse with Adam yet, in her coyness, drawing Adam toward what the two share with the beasts. Eve praises Adam as her ideal: "O sole in whom my thoughts find all repose, / My glory, my perfection" (5.28–29). She is to become him: her limited reason is to become his more fully realized reason. But insofar as she is a woman, she is distinct from Adam, and Adam and the narrating Milton define this distinction as inferiority to Adam in reason. Insofar as she manifests her desire she manifests her difference from Adam and so her inferiority. The equality Adam wants with Eve would require her to abandon her distinctness from Adam.

Among the Shadows

Milton calls Death Sin's "shadow." Milton combines the act of "man" ("distrust," "breach," "revolt," in sum, "disobedience") with the act of "Heaven" ("distance," "distaste," "Anger," "rebuke," in sum, "judgment") as together having "brought into this world a world of woe, / Sin and her shadow Death" (9.6–12). The "world" of "Sin and her shadow Death" itself shadows "this world" to form a realm doubling the creation with its fallen version, and the installation of this shadow world forwards Sin's ambition, giving her a realm appropriate for her throne. There is "this world," the creation, and then there is the "world of woe" Sin and Death bring. Like an invasive hologram, the world of Sin and Death mocks up vain shadows. Like fleeting "aërial vapours," "all things transitory and vain" constitute Sin's realm: after the fall, "sin / With vanity [...] filled the works of men" (3.445–47). In *Othello*, this realm Desdemona names "the world's mass of vanity" she would not take in trade for sexual favors (4.2.164). The vain doubles in *Paradise Lost* partake of false worship or idolatry. Doubling the chariot of the deity Ezekiel describes and Christ will mount to enter the war in Heaven, Satan arrives to the field of battle: "[E]xalted as a god, / Th' Apostate in his sun-bright chariot sate, / Idol of majesty divine, enclos'd / With flaming cherubim, and golden shields" (6.99–102). Sir Francis Bacon took up the equation of Plato's cave shadows with idols implicit in Paul's Middle-Platonic revision of the Hebrew Scriptures' discourse on idolatry. In his *Novum Organum* (1620) Bacon names as "Idols of the Cave" those shadows flitting through the mind.[13] Bacon describes this mind as a cavern. The waters Eve sees her shadow in emanate from a cavern. When Sin gives birth, she flees her offspring, crying out a name for her son: "I fled, and cried out DEATH; / Hell trembl'd at the hideous name, and sigh'd / From all her caves, and back resounded DEATH" (2.787–89). The echoing of Death's name suggests what Milton imagines death to be: an echo, specifically an echo of the self, the self reflecting back to itself, as at a pool that mirrors. For Eve to see and fall in love with her image reflected in water, for Satan to see and fall in love with his own self-in-glory mirrored in his daughter Sin, is for Eve and Satan already to partake of death and to begin to enter death's realm. Self-idolatry inheres in idolatry, Milton suggests, the false worship Percy Bysshe Shelley calls in *The Revolt of Islam* "the dark idolatry of self."[14] Shelley locates this idolatry as at work in regret and exhorts his readers to leave off the hell of remorse for lost paradises: "O vacant expiation! be at rest—/ The past is Death's, the future is thine own" (3394–95). Having revised Milton's Death as "Hate—that shapeless fiendly thing / [...] / Whom self-contempt arms with mortal sting," Shelley claims "love and joy can make the foulest breast / A paradise of flowers" (3379–81, 3395–96). Yet Shelley's advice against "the dark idolatry of self" repackages Satan's claim to be able to make of the hell within him a heaven.

Satan tells Sin and Death that, once he pioneers their way to the new creation, "[T]here ye shall be fed and fill'd / Immeasurably, all things shall be your prey" (2.843–44). Smiling, Death takes glee at the prospect. *All* things will be his. Every aspect of the creation will be subject to death, will only exist in the anticipation of death, will fall under death's shadow and so become a shadow and find a place in the world Death and Sin bring to the world. Consider the narrator Milton's phrase "[a] universe of death" (2.622). In hell, after Satan sets off for Earth, some fallen angels begin to explore their realm. They reach "the river of oblivion," "Lethe," one drop of which would allow them to forget their "former state and being" and all "joy and grief, pleasure and pain" (2.583–86). Like all the damned, the fallen angels might wish to drink from Lethe, and "with one small drop to lose / In sweet forgetfulness all pain and woe," yet "Medusa with Gorgonian terror" guards the stream, blocking any from tasting (2.607–11). Unable to forget, the fallen angels wander aghast in the icy and fiery realm beyond Lethe: "A universe of death, which God by curse / Created evil, for evil only good, / Where all life dies, death lives, and Nature breeds, / Perverse" (2.622–25). When Death arrives in the new creation, Death will assimilate it to the "universe of death" where death presses constantly on the mind, unforgettable. The more the logic of death colonizes the new creation, the more hellish it becomes. Death becomes the operator of memory, but with memories flattened out, spare of affect, a dry procession of loss and regret and anxiety, something like the holographic London of T. S. Eliot's "The Wasteland": "Unreal City, / Under the brown fog of a winter dawn, / A crowd flowed over London Bridge, so many, / I had not thought death had undone so many."[15]

Eve's Dream of Flight

The realm of shadows arrives from Satan's seduction of Eve. Satan gives Eve a dream of flight he designs to answer her desire. In the lake, Eve sees her image, with the "[s]mooth lake" seeming to Eve "another sky" (4.459). Eve's reflection seems to exist in that sky, and Eve contemplates in her image her desire. As God rests on the seventh day, a chorus sings his praise and describes "this new-made world," the creation, as "another Heav'n" (7.617). Eve imagines another sky; God lets be another heaven. Both realms arise from waters, Eve's "[s]mooth lake" and Genesis's void waste of waters, the "face of the deep" (4.459, Genesis 1.2). The beckoning image in the lake seems the goddess of the realm of "sky" Eve imagines: the realm of her shadow would be a mere reflection absent Eve's eye, Eve's "I," Eve's self-as-imagination. Thus Eve, her thought, creates the realm of "another sky," parallel to how God, his voice or word, his thought, creates "another Heav'n" after, Genesis could imply, looking into the waters, the "face of the deep." In the lake, Eve envisions her heaven, her realm of desire's realization, seeing there a face. There she wishes to be, and by the pond she would remain in contemplation of her image's "answering looks," except God's voice calls her away, to Adam and his voice (4.464).

If the dream Satan brings to Eve troubles her with the thought of disobedience, the dream only does so by troubling her with her own desire. Credit for a moment the ardent reader of *Paradise Lost* Sigmund Freud when he claims a dream images the fulfillment of a wish. Satan provides Eve a dream imaging a fulfillment of her wish, and, whispering the dream into Eve's ear, Satan speaks the language of her desire. If God's voice and then Adam's sought to educate her desire away from her image, Satan's voice enacts in Eve a counter-education. From the lake, God's voice draws Eve to Adam, to Adam's voice. As Eve's recounting to Adam of the dream indicates, Satan draws Eve from Adam first by imitating Adam's voice but then by leading Eve to stray from that voice.

On the morning following the night of the dream, Adam observes the "unwak'nd Eve" (5.9). Seeking to awaken Eve, Adam whispers to her, Milton neglecting to specify if he whispers toward her or more directly into her ear, and if so, into which one: the same or the opposite ear into which Satan whispered the dream? Milton does associate Adam's whisperings with the west, since Adam whispers "with voice / Mild, as when Zephyrus on Flora breaths," Zephyrus being the west wind and Flora the goddess of flowers (5.15–16). (In *The Tree of No, Flor*ian will have her protagonist's desire awakened by "words no western man can wet" [1]). Significantly, Milton writes, not that Adam's whispers awaken Eve, but that: "Such whispering wak'd her, but with startl'd eye / On Adam" (5.26–27). Eve awakes to Adam in confusion, her "eye" or "I" in the dream having already dreamt of awaking to his whispering voice. The dream (which features a nightingale) closes with Eve, in the dream and asleep, thinking she falls asleep, only she then wakes to Adam, to his whispering. Eve could ask with the Keats of "Ode to a Nightingale": "Was it a vision, or a waking dream? / Fled is that music—Do I wake or sleep?"[16] This confusion of sleeping, dreaming, and waking places Eve in what Florian in *The Tree of No* calls "the awkward position of waking" (1), but Eve recovers her poise, embraces Adam, and begins to recount to him her dream.

Eve's initial words to Adam form an artful example of the trope protherapeia, praising Adam to reassure him and to dampen the shock to come of Eve telling him someone other than he encountered her in the dream:

> O sole in whom my thoughts find all repose,
> My glory, my perfection, glad I see
> Thy face, and morn returned, for I this night,
> Such night till this I never pass'd, have dream'd,
> If dream'd, not, as I oft am wont, of thee,
> Works of day past, or morrow's next design,
> But of offence and trouble, which my mind
> Knew never till this irksome night.
>
> (5.28–35)

The dream ends with Eve, her thoughts, finding sleep or repose and this through someone other than Adam, this someone, unbeknownst to Eve, being Satan. So when Eve says to Adam that he is the "sole in whom [her] thoughts find all repose," she is preemptively attempting to deny to Adam the end of the dream she will shortly relate, in which she, specifically her thoughts, find repose via another, an angelic other. She usually dreams about Adam and their past or future labor; the dream she reports departs from this usual routine. She dreamt of "offence and trouble," yet the night she passed in this dream was unlike any she has passed dreaming of Adam.

At the lake, God's voice attempted to teach Eve, her inexperienced "thought," to discern shadows as shadows and to leave shadows behind. About her Satan-induced dream, Eve wonders if it was a dream or not ("If dream'd"), a shadow or not. Eve recounts her dream as a matter of her thought: "Methought / Close at mine ear one call'd me forth to walk / With gentle voice, I thought it thine" (5.35–37). "*Me*thought," "*I* thought": Eve, her thought, meets Satan's whisperings at least halfway. However roused by Satan, the dream is *Eve*'s dream. The desire the dream solicits exists in potential within Eve. The guardian angels find Satan in the form of a toad whispering into Eve's ear. These whispers conjure from within Eve a dream, a phantasmal scene of sights and sounds desire pervades altogether. In his whisperings to Eve, Satan uses his "devilish art to reach / The organs of her fancy, and with them forge / Illusions as he list, phantasms and dreams" (4.801–03). As at the lake Eve's imagination partakes in creating the shadow she sees gazing back at her, so in her dream "her fancy" allows Satan to forge shadows: "Illusions, [...] phantasms, dreams." Because he can "reach" the "organs" of Eve's fancy, Satan can "forge" the shadowy, hallucinatory, moonlit *mise en scène* of Eve's dream. Reflecting the sun's light, the moon shines while Satan whispers, the Lucifer (Light Bearer) whose glory was a reflection of God, who is light (4.798). And the whisperings, by Satan's venomous breath, "taint" the "animal spirits that from [Eve's] pure blood arise" and so "raise" in her "distemper'd, discontented thoughts, / Vain hopes, vain aims, inordinate desires, / Blown up with high conceits ingend'ring pride" (4.804–09). From Eve's beastliness ("animal spirits")

Satan conjures in Eve discontent "thoughts" symptomatic of an imbalance of the humors and so "distemper'd." Insofar as Eve is beastly, Satan can inflame in her "inordinate desires." Milton's God stations Eve below the exemplary human Adam and above the beasts. Raphael tells Adam to love and cultivate in Eve what is human. Satan energizes within her what is beastly.

Or, the desire in Eve God would shift from her image and edify toward being a desire for Adam Satan would render "inordinate" by being "[b]lown up" through the "pride" "high conceits" or sublime thoughts engender. "Blown up": this phrasing Milton borrows from Paul: "Knowledge puffeth up, but charity edifieth" (1 Corinthians 8.1, Geneva 1587). As the Geneva marginal gloss explains, knowledge "[g]ives occasion of vanity and pride." The gloss explains how, when not "tempered" by charity, knowledge becomes "the mistress of pride." Some Corinthian Christians claim to "know that an idol is nothing in the world," or, as the gloss states, "a vain imagination" or "a vain dream" (8.4). Puffed up in their pride of knowledge, these Christians believe they may eat of food offered to an idol because, the idol being nothing, eating the food entails no false or idolatrous worship. However, argues Paul, former believers in the idol unaware of its nothingness, on seeing the knowers eat, may also eat, yet in belief in the idol, and so commit false worship, turn from God, from God as Christ, and so "perish" (8.11). Equivocating in regard to the idols' nothingness in speaking to the Christians in his audience born Jews, Paul argues the "Gentiles" who make food offerings to idols "sacrifice to devils" (10.20). Thus the gloss claims any Christian, whether born Jewish or Gentile, who eats food offered to an idol risks falling to the "wiles of Satan." These unwary eaters resemble the Israelites who, worshipping the golden calf, conduct an orgy of food, drink, and fornication: "The people sate downe to eat and drinke, and rose up to play" (Paul plausibly reads "play" as orgiastic "fornication") (10.7–8). The golden calf worshipers exemplify those who "lust after evil things" (10.6). The gloss describes Paul's example of the golden calf worshipers as "[a]n amplifying of the example against those who are carried away with their lusts beyond the bounds which God has measured out. For this is the beginning of all evil, as of idolatry (which has gluttony as a companion), fornication, rebelling against Christ, murmuring, and such like."

Milton dramatizes Eve in her paradoxical relation to Adam through Paul, both in Eve's subordination (Adam as her "head") but also in her insubordination. This insubordination plays out in terms of the elements the 1587 Geneva 1 Corinthians outlines: "desire" (Milton) or "lust" (Paul) that is "inordinate" (Milton) or "beyond the bounds [...] God has measured out" (Geneva gloss), a temptation to eat taboo food tied to a claim to knowledge and to the demonic (Milton and Paul), a prideful one inducing an innocent one to eat and so fall away from God/Christ and so be subject to death (Milton and Paul), the eating to be followed by "fornication" (Milton on Eve's post-fall sex with Adam and Paul on the golden-calf orgy). The complex interferences between knowing, pride in knowledge, and not knowing or misguided belief at work in 1 Corinthians 8 also are at work when Satan offers Eve the fruit, first in the dream and then later in the Garden. In *Paradise Lost,* the censorious Milton tends to be a Pauline Milton. When Milton wants to disparage the symposium of thought the rebel angels conduct in Hell, he calls their proceedings "[v]ain wisdom all, and false philosophy" (2.565). These words echo in combination Paul's denunciation of the "wisdom of this world" as "foolish" and Paul's warning against "philosophy" as "vain deceit" (1 Corinthians 1.20; Colossians 2.8, Geneva 1587).

In the dream Satan provokes in Eve, the "high conceits ingend'ring pride" begin with Satan miming Adam's voice. In her partner's voice, Satan whispers to Eve praise of her beauty:

> Methought
> Close at mine ear one call'd me forth to walk
> With gentle voice, I thought it thine; it said,
> "Why sleep'st thou, Eve? now is the pleasant time,
> The cool, the silent, save where silence yields
> To the night-warbling bird, that now awake
> Tunes sweetest his love-labour'd song; now reigns
> Full-orb'd the moon, and with more pleasing light
> Shadowy sets off the face of things; in vain,

If none regard: Heav'n wakes with all his eyes;
Whom to behold but thee, Nature's desire?
In whose sight all things joy, with ravishment
Attracted by thy beauty still to gaze."

(5.35–47)

Again Milton emphasizes Eve's thought: "Methought." God called Eve away from the image of her beauty and toward Adam; after Adam speaks to her and seizes her hand, Eve learns to "see / How beauty is excell'd by manly grace / And wisdom, which alone is truly fair" (4.489–91). Yet in the dream what Eve takes to be Adam's "gentle voice" praises her "beauty." God's voice then Adam's had taught Eve to reject her "smooth watery image," to reject shadowy beauty for true beauty. Satan mimes Adam's voice to exalt precisely a beauty amidst shadows: Eve's beauty the "more pleasing light" of the moon "[s]hadowy sets off." In this dream reigns no Platonic sun emanating "male" light but a moon providing "female light" (8.150). The lake reflected light back to Eve's eye: reflected light and therefore female. This view of her own beauty in the lake Eve finds on her first awaking into her existence. The dream Satan orchestrates restages this awakening of Eve to her beauty. The morning Adam calls Eve awake from her dream, he first gazes on her, on her beauty. He "beheld / Beauty, which whether waking or asleep, / Shot forth peculiar graces" (5.13–15). For Adam, or so Milton narrates, Eve's beauty remains uncorrelated with Eve's consciousness, her being asleep or her being awake. In the dream, in Adam's voice, Satan whispers for Eve to awake to the universal praise of her beauty. Bathed in and revealed by the light of the moon, this beauty would exist "[i]n vain, / If none regard," but Eve is to awake to how "Heav'n wakes with all his eyes [...] to behold" Eve, her beauty. God's voice by the lake insures Eve's awakening there finally becomes an awakening, not to her own beautiful image but to Adam, the lake's reflected so female light yielding its hold on Eve to the voice of the male all light, God. In the dream, all the stars, providers of male light, yield to the sovereign moon and gaze adoringly on Eve: "Heav'n wakes with all his eyes, / Whom to behold but thee, Nature's desire?"

God's face shines in Christ's, and Christ's in Adam's, and the Eve of the lake is to turn to Adam's face and leave off adoring her own femalely reflected face, male light overcoming female. The Satan-ventriloquized voice of Adam in the dream exalts female light. By saying "all things" are "with ravishment / Attracted by [Eve's] beauty still to gaze," that is, to persist in gazing, Adam's voice endorses what was Eve's desire at the lake: to continue gazing at her own beauty. In the dream, the desire for Eve, for her shadowy, beauteous image, Adam's voice calls "Nature's desire." How could nature's desire be among the "inordinate desires" Satan's whisperings are to provoke in Eve? An answer to this question will arrive soon with Satan's solicitation in the dream of Eve's desire to cross in flight the boundary between the sublunary and the celestial realms.

To examine this solicitation, we must first follow Eve in her walk to find the Adam she thinks whispers her awake:

> I rose as at thy call, but found thee not;
> To find thee I directed then my walk;
> And on, methought, alone I pass'd through ways
> That brought me on a sudden to the tree
> Of interdicted Knowledge: fair it seem'd,
> Much fairer to my fancy than by day:
> And as I wondering lookt, beside it stood
> One shap'd and wing'd like one of those from Heav'n,
> By us oft seen; his dewy locks distill'd
> Ambrosia[.]
>
> (5.48–57)

What seems Adam's "call" authorizes Eve to awake, arise, and walk. Her arrival "on a sudden" at the forbidden tree suggests the "surprise" by which Sin operates. The moonlight makes the tree seem "fairer" to Eve's "fancy" than the tree seems in sunlight. And a reassuring figure of authority stands by the tree, the angel's being next to the tree already working to lend the tree legitimacy. Awake in Eden, Eve never talks directly to an angel; only Adam does and relates the angel's lessons to Eve. In the dream, Eve enjoys the Adamic privilege of direct colloquy with an angel. This angel's luxurious hair exudes the odor of ambrosia. To further Eve's seduction in the dream, Satan laves his hair with ambrosia, the aroma of life, heaven, and God. At the center of Eden stands "the tree of Life," "blooming ambrosial fruit" (4.218–19). This fruit links the earthly paradise with the heavenly, as "in Heav'n the trees / of life ambrosial fruitage bear" (5.426–27). In heaven, when God speaks, "ambrosial fragrance" fills the air (3.135). God's "altar breathes / Ambrosial odours and ambrosial flowers" (2.244–45). With his hair's ambrosial odor and his form's angelic authority, Satan works on Eve's thought and "fancy" to associate the tree of life, God's blessing of life, with the "forbidden tree, whose mortal taste" will bring "Death into the world" (1.2–3).

The angel models to Eve the courage to taste without hesitation:

> [O]n that tree he also gaz'd;
> And "O fair plant," said he, "with fruit surcharg'd,
> Deigns none to ease thy load, and taste thy sweet,
> Nor God, nor Man? is knowledge so despis'd?
> Or envy, or what reserve forbids to taste?
> Forbid who will, none shall from me withhold
> Longer thy offer'd good; why else set here?"
> This said, he paus'd not, but with venturous arm
> He pluckt, he tasted; me damp horror chill'd
> At such bold words voucht with a deed so bold[.]
>
> (5.57–66)

The angel desires to eat of the fruit and refuses to give way on his desire. At the lake, Eve gave way on her desire and entered into domesticity with Adam. The domestic prisoner Desdemona who falls in love with Othello would appreciate the angel's boldness toward adventure ("venturous arm"). Indeed, hearing the angel's "bold" words and viewing his "bold" act, Eve goes "damp." This response Eve perceives as caused by "horror," yet for "chill'd" read "thrilled." The desire she disavowed at the lake returns as "horror." However, if Adam intersperses with kisses the lessons of the angels he relates to Eve, what amorous acts would he have inadvertently suggested Eve should expect in learning directly from an angel?

Satan takes a cue from Sin in shaping his pitch to Eve to eat the fruit. Prior to Eve, the only woman Satan has encountered is his daughter Sin. When at the gates of hell Satan meets Sin, she complains bitterly of her being "confin'd" there by God, who has imposed on her the "hateful office" of minding the gate (2.859). Somewhat petulantly, Sin concludes God "hates" her, she being an "[i]nhabitant of Heav'n and heav'nly-born" yet by God "thrust [...] down / Into this gloom of Tartarus" (2.857, 860, 857–58). She tells Satan she will happily open the gate because, reversing God's punishment, Satan, providing her access to earth, will give her back the heavenly lifestyle she is used to: "thou wilt bring me soon / To that new world of light and bliss, among / The gods who live at ease" (2.866–68). Thinking of Eden and the creation as a new heaven, Sin is ambitious again to "live at ease" as a goddess among "gods." Satan assumes Eve hankers for such a life. Having tasted the fruit, Satan as the unknown angel offers Eve further arguments to justify her eating:

> "O fruit divine!
> Sweet of thyself, but much more sweet thus cropt,
> Forbidd'n here, it seems, as only fit
> For gods, yet able to make gods of men:
> And why not gods of men, since good, the more
> Communicated, more abundant grows,
> The author not impair'd, but honour'd more?
> Here, happy creature, fair angelic Eve,
> Partake thou also; happy though thou art,
> Happier thou may'st be, worthier canst not be:
> Taste this, and be henceforth among the gods
> Thyself a goddess, not to Earth confin'd,
> But sometimes in the air, as we, sometimes
> Ascend to Heav'n, by merit thine, and see
> What life the gods live there, and such live thou."
>
> (5.67–81)

Moments before entering the serpent, Satan voices Sin's opinion that Eden resembles heaven: "O Earth! how like to Heav'n [...]!" (9.99). Before his serpent episode, in the dream Satan must concede to Eve that, in Eden, she is happy, but he urges her to consider becoming herself a "goddess" through eating the fruit. Then, by her own "merit," Eve may fly to heaven, observe the heavenly life, and then join that life. Again Satan picks up an aspect of Eve's sojourn by the lake, where her image seemed to reside in "another sky," a kind of heaven. Sin felt "confin'd" in hell; Satan tells Eve she will, by eating the fruit, no longer be "to earth confined." Eden is a heaven, but if thought can make a hell of a heaven, Satan would seduce Eve into thinking Eden a confining hell. Sin's ambition to gain earth as a heaven, Eve's dream of flight to leave earth for Heaven: Satan recasts the desire Eve felt by the lake into an "inordinate desire" for the heavenly life, a desire making life in Eden seem inadequate. Seem? Is Edenic life with Adam adequate for Eve, given the renunciation of her desire that life assumes? Eve's desire only became ordinate through its disavowal in favor of Eve becoming Adam's. If God and Adam discipline Eve's desire, Satan undisciplines it. After Eve recounts the dream, the archangel Raphael visits, eating the food Eve gathers. With Eve perhaps within earshot, Raphael argues to Adam that he and Eve, if they "be found obedient," may eventually partake of the food angels eat in heaven and their "bodies may at last turn all to spirit," so that, "wing'd," they may "ascend / Ethereal" and dwell at will in Eden "or in Heav'nly Paradise," Raphael too agreeing Eden is an alternate heaven (5.501, 497–500). But, emphasizes Raphael, the eventual promotion to wingedness and the opportunity to fly to and dwell in heaven depends on Adam and Eve continuing to "retain / Unalterably firm his love entire" (5.501–02). So, in the meantime, the two should be content with Eden and Edenic "happiness," being at present "incapable of more," of more happiness, Raphael inadvertently seconding to Eve the dream-angel's statement that she could be happier than she is (5.504, 505). Raphael counsels patience, yet Satan seeks to persuade Eve she need not wait to eat divine food and to fly to heaven. The Eve who eats the fruit Kafka accuses of impatience: "[P]erhaps there is only one major sin: impatience. Because of impatience they were expelled, because of impatience they do not return."[17]

Before eating the fruit awake, the sleeping Eve eats the fruit in her dream. The angel proposes to Eve that she eat and fly to heaven:

> So saying, he drew nigh, and to me held,
> Even to my mouth of that same fruit held part
> Which he had pluckt; the pleasant savory smell
> So quick'nd appetite, that I, methought,
> Could not but taste. Forthwith up to the clouds
> With him I flew, and underneath beheld
> The Earth outstretcht immense, a prospect wide
> And various: wondering at my flight and change
> To this high exaltation; suddenly
> My guide was gone, and I, methought, sunk down,
> And fell asleep: but O how glad I wak'd
> To find this but a dream!
>
> (5.82–93)

Eve does fly, yet her flight ceases when she and the angel touch the boundary separating the sublunary from the celestial. Milton urges his own muse, Urania, to take him on a flight beyond the sublunary and into heaven so there Milton may observe the life of the divine beings, as Satan promises Eve she will. Eve falls asleep in Eden, hears a voice, and then meets a being offering her an ecstatic flight. Upon waking, Eve reports her dream of flight to Adam. The blind Milton falls asleep, Urania gives him a poetic vision, and then, upon awakening, Milton reports the vision to whichever amanuensis may be at hand. The Lady of Christ's College, John Milton, upon awakening from a muse visitation, would complain, if the amanuensis was late, that he needed to be "milked," thus comparing himself to a female in need of having her breasts relieved. As Urania is to Milton, Satan is to Eve. Satan is Eve's daemonic muse, and, in Eve's inspiration toward flight, Milton imagines an *ekstasis* dangerously close to his own. Eve wakes to say she is relieved her flight was but a dream. The muse Calliope failed to save Orpheus; Milton cries out to his muse Urania, "So fail not thou, who thee implores: / For thou art Heav'nly, she but an empty dream" (7.38–39). Should

Urania fail Milton, his vision of heaven would turn shadowy, flitting, a fading derivative of lost earthly sight; like Eve, Milton would bathetically sink at the sublunary's border, earthbound and empty of the true.

Achilles and Athena, Satan and Sin

Promoting his muse entails Milton demeaning Athena. Even in Chapman's translation, the *Iliad* outraged Shakespeare. From the Shakespeare of *Troilus and Cressida*, Milton learned the demeaning of Homeric personages. Milton demeans Achilles and Athena to invent Satan and Sin. Homer's Athena checks Achilles's rage so the warrior will not kill Agamemnon and become a version of Agamemnon but will live out his heroic fate of battling Hector and then dying. In the battle with Hector, rather than checking Achilles, Athena acts through him, her hand joining his in throwing his spear. Achilles avoids his other possible fate, leaving the battle at Troy for home and living out his remaining years comfortably, something like retiring to Stratford-upon-Avon. The fight with Hector, who wears Achilles's armor, stages an uncanny confrontation, with Achilles becoming fully daemonized in facing off with an embodiment of his own inertia or resistance to daemonization. This daemonization comes at the price of realizing Achilles's death. Toward and through the fight with Hector, Achilles defines the agonistic sublime, or so Longinus suggests. The fight Athena prevents would have leveled Achilles with Agamemnon.

In Satan's confrontation with his son Death, Milton replays Athena's checking of Achilles's rage. Milton has Sin check Satan's rage so the fallen angel will not battle Death, a grand confrontation that would have been resonant with Achilles's fight with Hector. By preventing this battle, Sin ushers Satan to his fate: to precipitate the fall of Adam and Eve's fall. Rather than throw his spear at Death, that is, throw his spear in the act of confronting death, as does Achilles inspired by Athena, Satan will say one thing to Eve while having another in his heart, the definition of the contemptible according to Achilles. Athena's shield bears the image of the snake-haired head of the gorgon Medusa. In heaven, Sin emerges from Satan's head "shining heav'nly fair, a goddess arm'd" (2.757). An Athena in heaven, Sin undergoes a demeaning metamorphosis in her fall. The Sin Satan finds at the gate of hell "seem'd woman to the waist, and fair, / But ended foul in many a scaly fold, / Voluminous and vast, a serpent arm'd / with mortal sting" (2.650–52). The echo of the words "fair" and "arm'd" between the two descriptions serves to underline the contrast between the Athena Sin was in Heaven and the scaly and mortal Medusa she has become.

The realization of his fate Achilles undergoes no one may share with him, his fate being the idiom of his daemonization and demise. The *Iliad* allows the auditor or reader to imagine being Achilles and undergoing Achilles's fate, to imagine sharing in an ultimately unsharable and secret moment, that of Athena interfusing with Achilles in the throwing of his spear to kill Hector yet also to give birth to his own death. Milton has Sin check Satan's throwing of his spear at Death, and Milton reworks the secret moment of Achilles's interfusion with Athena as the incest Satan commits with Sin in secret to engender Death. Milton demeans Achilles and Athena through Satan and Sin: in Satan's potential fight with Death that Sin checks Milton overlaps Achilles's potential fight with Agamemnon Athena checks and the death-confrontative killing of Hector by Achilles, which Athena inspires.

In the *Iliad*, fiery Athena inspires Achilles. However much Milton demeans Athena in Sin, Athena's daemonic fire bursts into the cosmos of *Paradise Lost* with Sin's birth, as Sin recounts to Satan during their encounter at hell's gate. Satan in heaven stood amidst the angles leagued with him in "bold conspiracy against Heav'ns King" (2.751). Then, says Sin to Satan,

All on a sudden miserable pain
Surpris'd thee, dim thine eyes, and dizzy swam
In darkness, while thy head flames thick and fast
Threw forth; till on the left side op'ning wide,
Likest to thee in shape and count'nance bright,

Then shining heav'nly fair, a goddess arm'd,
Out of thy head I sprung[.]   (2.752–58)

In Sin Satan views his "perfect image," becomes "enamour'd," and so, as Sin explains to Satan, "such joy thou took'st / With me in secret, that my womb conceiv'd / A growing burden" (2.764–67). Athena's fire within Achilles becomes Sin's fire within Satan. With Sin and Satan's fall from heaven, this fire conflagrates as hell. Milton's Heavenly Muse Urania associates with the Father and Son's serene "holy Light," but Satan's muse Sin brings to Milton's epic Athena's dynamic fire (3.1).

Is Sin Nothing?

If Milton can call the muse Calliope an "empty dream," to what genre of inexistence does Milton cue the reader to assign Sin, Satan's muse (7.39)? Ecclesiastes insists nothing new exists under the sun, every element of the creation whatsoever being the deity's gift; for a created being to claim to add something to the creation would be the sheer self-idolatry of claiming the deity's creative power as one's own, like a poet invoking Wisdom as a muse, the Wisdom who inspired Yahweh toward creation. In such idolatry, to claim credit for anything in creation is to hypostasize that thing into an inexistent mirage reflecting the self-idolater's inexistent capacity to contribute anything new to the creation. As Yahweh creates or births Wisdom, so Satan creates or births Sin, yet however new and surprising she may be, is she not nothing? In her, Satan views, as in a mirror, his perfect image, his glory, yet this glory he owes entirely to God, the light Lucifer bore being from God altogether. In claiming this glory as his own, the self-idolizing Satan renders his glory a mirage. As Othello's "ancient," Othello's standard bearer, Iago bore Othello's flag into battle; the glory Iago finds in being Othello's favorite he loses to Cassio. This wounds Iago's pride. In heaven, Lucifer bore God's glory, God's light. The glory Lucifer finds in bearing God's light he loses to Christ, who becomes the highest bearer of that light, wounding Lucifer's pride. The fallen Lucifer, Satan, would uphold his glory in Sin, the idolatrous image of his self. The muse of Satan's self-glorification, Sin exists only in a mode of inexistence. In Sin, nothing of the Word would be, and her name, Sin, would reference nothing. If all that was created came into being only through the Word, Sin is nothing of the creation, and so nothing of the providential, and so a fully radical surprise, an epiphenomenon of Satan's free will. Out of his free will, Satan chooses Sin and engenders Death. Out of his free will, Christ chooses his kenosis and accedes to his death. Out of her free will, Eve chooses to eat the fruit and so welcomes "Death into the world" (1.3). Sure, Milton introduces Satan's grand/son Death to the reader at line 666 of book two, but the association of death's arrival with acts of free will hints at a satanic element more broadly distributed among the epic's characters than just in Satan.

Nothing is secret from God. This sentence leaves open one opportunity for a secret from God: nothing. Sin claims to have had amorous relations with Satan in heaven in "secret" (2.766). After Satan brings about Eve's fall, and through Eve Adam's, Sin, though far separated from Satan, claims to sense his victory and so hers:

> Methinks I feel new strength within me rise,
> Wings growing, and dominion giv'n me large
> Beyond this Deep; whatever draws me on,
> Or sympathy, or some connatural force
> Powerful at greatest distance to unite
> With secret amity, things of like kind
> By secretest conveyance. (10.243–49)

When Satan arrives to tell her and Death of his triumph, she explains how her "heart divin'd" his success: "My heart, which by a secret harmony / Still moves with thine, join'd in connexion sweet" (10.357, 358–59). Is Sin mistaken, or do she and Satan share a connection indeed secret? With an omniscient deity about, is a secret possible or impossible? If impossible, does the impossible happen between Sin and Satan? With an omnipotent deity about, nothing may be impossible in the sense that the omnipotent deity may bring any imaginable thing into the realm of the possible.

Yet what about the impossible happening as impossible? With Sin, does the impossible happen?

Like Sin, Eve wonders if her transgression may be a secret. After eating the knowledge-tree's fruit, Eve praises the tree: "[T]hou op'nst Wisdom's way, / And giv'st access, though secret she retire. / And I perhaps am secret; Heav'n is high, / High and remote to see from thence distinct / Each thing on Earth" (9.809–13). Though Wisdom may "retire" to some "secret" place, the fruit opens the path to her. Wisdom is most secret from the creatures in her being with the creator. By eating the fruit and so being able to follow Wisdom into her secret retirement, Eve wonders if she, Eve herself, may have become secret. Milton tells us that, in eating the fruit, Eve entertained "expectation high / of knowledge, nor was Godhead from her thought" (9.789–90). For Eve to reach Wisdom in her place of secrecy and "perhaps" herself be "secret" would imply Eve attaining to "Godhead." In her hopeful speculation as to her secrecy, certainly Eve is mistaken? Two witness her as she soliloquizes as to her being secret and as she subsequently gives Adam the fruit to eat. After Satan as the serpent persuades her to eat, "[b]ack to the thicket" he returns: "He, after Eve seduc't, unminded slunk / Into the wood fast by [...], changing shape / To observe the sequel," and he does so: he sees the fallen Eve and then sees her bring Adam to eat just as he had brought her to eat (9.784, 10.332–34). He "saw his guileful act / By Eve, though all unweeting, seconded / Upon her husband" (10.334–36). She acts unknowing of his witness. Eve's second witness, God, also sees her seduced by Satan: "how / He in the serpent, had perverted Eve, / Her husband she, to taste the fatal fruit, / Was known in Heav'n; for what can 'scape the eye / Of God all-seeing, or deceive His heart / Omniscient?" (10.2–7). Satan and God see Eve eat the fruit and offer the fruit to Adam. Do Satan and God hear Eve soliloquize in speculation as to her secrecy? The speech of Adam, when first heard by Satan, "[t]urn'd him all ear to hear new utterance flow" (4.410). To the music of the spheres "God's own ear / Listens delighted" (5.626–27). Yet does either ear hear Eve when she utters words hoping for secrecy?

If the cosmos of *Paradise Lost* exists under the purview of a deity at once omnipotent and omniscient, then must not any creature attempting to keep a secret inevitably fail? No creature can keep a secret from the omniscient God. This God would have a complete monopoly on secret keeping: this God alone, and none of his creatures, can have a secret. God can keep secrets from the creatures, yet the creatures are never able to keep a secret from him. Any creature hoping to keep a secret desires the impossible. Yet when dealing with secrets, Milton's God himself may touch on the impossible.

In relation to secrets, the omnipotence and omniscience of Milton's God may enter contradiction. What if Sin or Eve were to pose the following question to God: can you keep a secret from yourself? If God fully is omnipotent, the answer should be yes. To keep a secret from himself would be an act on God's part, and an omnipotent being is capable of all acts whatsoever. All acts fall within God's potency; keeping a secret from himself would be an act on God's part; so keeping a secret from himself falls within God's potency. Yet if God fully is omniscient, the answer should be no. A secret known no longer is a secret kept, and an omniscient being knows everything whatsoever. An omniscient being knows all things; any secret is a thing; so an omniscient being knows any secret. When dealing with secrets, God may be either omnipotent or omniscient but not both at once.

Is there a way out of this dilemma making the omnipotence and the omniscience of Milton's God incompatible? Maybe if, rather than a thing, a secret were nothing, God could be both omnipotent and omniscient. Recall how Boethius's Lady Philosophy plays on nothing (there is nothing God cannot do, God cannot do evil, evil is a nothing God cannot do), and consider: there is nothing an omnipotent being cannot do, and there is nothing an omniscient being cannot know. What if a given secret were just such a nothing? Then could God both do and know it, do and know this nothing, this secret? And if a secret were nothing, might this allow a creature to keep it? A creature's secret, as nothing, would slip away from God's doing and knowing.

An omniscient and omnipotent being should be totally immune from surprises. Knowing everything whatsoever, whether of the past, or the present, or the future, an omniscient being should never be surprised. And omnipotence precludes the balking of potency a surprise entails. Milton's God should never even surprise himself. Yet what if Sin or Eve were to ask God: *can* you surprise yourself? A similar dehiscence between God's omnipotence and God's omniscience as occurs with the question of his being able to keep a secret from himself occurs with the question of his ability to surprise himself.

Sin claims for herself both secrecy and surprise. She thus becomes the radical fissure in the cosmos of *Paradise Lost*. Her surprising genesis from the head of Satan shows his head not quite sovereign over itself and so not quite a head in the sense that Adam is supposed to be the head of Eve. The secrecy of her affair and sympathy of heart with Satan further would fully separate Satan from God, if that secrecy indeed remains secret. If God may neither keep a secret from himself nor surprise himself without contradicting himself, Sin precisely would be radically foreign to God, to God's coherence, and Milton would place God at the very pinnacle of reason.

Perhaps God's eye never overlooks a secret and never encounters surprise, but what about God's ear? Giving a speech to the rebel angels arguing they war with God for freedom, Satan "with calumnious art / Of counterfeited truth [...] held their ears" (5.770–71). Standing among the rebel angels listening to Satan's speech, "the seraphim / Abdiel" speaks out in zealous reproach: "O argument blasphemous, false, and proud! / Words which no ear to hear in Heav'n / Expected" (5.804–05, 809–11). Yes, Abdiel speaks a hyperbole, yet his statement does include God's ears among those that would be surprised to hear Satan's speech. The ear is subject to odd states of counter-factual perception, or at least Adam's ear is when Raphael ceases to speak: "The angel ended, and in Adam's ear / So charming left his voice, that he a while / Thought him still speaking, still stood fixt to hear" (8.1–3). The fallen Adam blames specifically Eve for her loose deployment of her ear: "O Eve, in evil hour thou didst give ear / To that false worm, of whomsoever taught / To counterfet man's voice" (9.1067–69). Adam unknowingly agrees with Milton the narrator: Satan "counterfeited truth," and he teaches the serpent to "counterfet man's voice," the voice therefore of Adam, the only man, and, as the man, the voice of truth for Eve. In the dream Satan brings to Eve, Satan at first counterfeit's Adam's voice. If, as Adam says, the serpent spoke to Eve with "man's voice," this could only be modeled on Adam's voice.

When God the Father's ear hears the voices of the fallen Adam and Eve, the divine ear becomes an eye. In perhaps Milton's most startling revision of Genesis, Milton reads the Genesis 3.8–17 description of God walking the garden and not finding Adam and Eve (who hide having realized their nakedness) as Christ the Son walking the garden having been sent from heaven by the Father to judge the fallen pair. Though Christ proceeds to judge them with benignity rather than wrath, the judgment leads to Eve proposing to Adam that the two commit suicide to spare future generations from punishment. Or if suicide does not appeal to Adam, Eve proposes the two at least to forbear having children to spare future generations. After Adam rejects Eve's proposal of suicide, Adam tells Eve the two should pray because God's "pitying while he judg'd" suggests his openness to prayer: "How much more, if we pray him, will his ear / Be open, and his heart to pity incline" (10.1059, 1060–61). To Eve Adam suggests they should pray "with [their] sighs the air / Frequenting, sent from hearts contrite, in sign / Of sorrow unfeign'd and humiliation meek" (10.1090–92). Milton the narrator specifies that they do so pray, repeating exactly Adam's words. Milton reports that Adam and Eve pray "with their sighs the air / Frequenting, sent from hearts contrite, in sign / Of sorrow unfeign'd, and humiliation meek" (10.1102–04). Milton then describes how "their prayers" fly up to heaven, where they enter "[d]imensionless through Heav'nly doors" (11.14, 17). The prayers are "then clad / With incense" by Christ acting as "their great Intercessor" (11.17–19, 19). So "clad," the prayers "came in sight / Before the Father's throne" (11.19–20). Through Christ's mediation, the prayers become holograms of Adam and Eve. In Eden, before the fallen pair pray, "grace [...] had remov'd / The stony from their hearts, and made new flesh / Regenerate grow instead," so the two "sighs now breath'd / Unutterable, which the Spirit of prayer / Inspir'd, and winged for Heav'n with speedier flight / Than loudest oratory" (11.3–8). These prayers or "sighs," though paradoxically "[u]nutterable" and so silent, outspeak the "loudest oratory." The sighs as silent, incense-clad prayers Christ asks the Father to see, and though the prayers/sighs are from both Adam and Eve, in seeing them, the Father will see only the "first-fruits" of "Man": "See, Father, what first-fruits on earth are sprung / From Thy implanted grace in Man" (11.22–23). Eve achieves a kind of equality with Adam, the two equally fallen yet equally recipient of grace and so, Paul would say, equally in Christ, one in Christ (Galatians 3.28). Yet, with Adam and Eve becoming one in Christ, sexual difference drops out androcentrically, and the voice and words of Eve as woman disappear into the prayers of "Man." The Father will hear the prayer of "Man." Christ asks God's ear, become a kind of eye, to hear, that is to see, these silent suppliants, the prayers of "Man" kneeling before the Father: "Now therefore bend thine ear / To supplication, hear his sighs, though mute" (11.30–31). The muteness of these prayers, a symptom of their being the fruit of grace, also sounds the silence, the silencing, of Eve. If, in *Paradise Lost*, Satan's is the voice of "loudest oratory," his muting too obliquely resonates in this silence. As the Father contemplates the prayers kneeling before him, the Son interprets, makes articulate in speech, the mute sighs of "Man": "Unskillful with what words to pray, let me / Interpret for him" (11.32–33). In the translation from the fallen creation to heaven, from the state of sin to the state of grace, in the flight of sighs from Eden to heaven, Adam and Eve praying in Eden, "they" ("they, in lowliest plight, repentant stood / Praying" [11.1–2]) become "him," "Man." This sublime flight of the sighs, "which the Spirit of prayer / Inspired," parallels Milton's poetic flight to heaven inspired by the Heavenly Muse.

Does Milton's God ever hear Eve's words? Yes, but only as her prayer, through grace, becomes morphed into the silent sigh of "Man." Simone Weil calls the influx of grace the decreation of the "I," whereas Weil, following Paul, finds the voice articulating the "I" to be sin's: "The sin in me says 'I.'"[18] A reader could certainly say of Milton's Satan, Sin in him does voice his proud "I" and its "loudest oratory." A glory of *Paradise Lost*, Satan's vaunting speech, Milton self-punishingly designates the "loudest oratory" as distinct from the mute sigh of "Man."

But what is the fate of Eve's speech? *Paradise Lost* ends with Adam again seeking to awaken Eve, as he had done when she had reported the dream Satan had given her. But this time he finds Eve already awake, and she reports a dream not from Satan but from God (via the archangel Michael, unless in her dream Eve mistakes Michael for God). Eve tells Adam, "Whence thou return'st, and wither went'st, I know; / For God is also in sleep, and dreams advise, / Which he hath sent propitious" (12.610–12). Except for the narrator Milton, Eve speaks the last words of *Paradise Lost*, words indicating to Adam her consolation that, though Eden was lost to her and Adam by her act, "By [her] the promis'd Seed shall all restore" (12.623). As Michael explains to Adam, and as Eve knows from her God-given or Michael-brought dream, from the royal line of King David "shall rise / A son, the Woman's Seed to thee foretold," Christ the redeeming and eternally reigning king (12.326–27). However, Adam also learns from Michael that Eve will again be submissive: the Eve who has the last word is a newly domesticated Eve. Besides giving Eve knowledge of the Son, the God-given dream acts as a counter-narcotic to Eve's dream of flight, the dream Satan provided. As Michael bested Satan in the first day of battle in Heaven, so the dream from Michael expunges from Eve any remaining effects of the dream from Satan. The dream Michael delivers relieves Eve of her excess desire. The archangel Michael explains to Adam, "[G]o, waken Eve; / Her also I with gentle dreams have calm'd, / Portending good, and all her spirits compos'd / To meek submission" (12.594–97). The dream Satan gave Eve discomposed her spirits, and Adam, waking her, woke her toward her self-assertion and the forbidden tree. Countering Satan's dream, the dream Michael provides composes Eve's spirits and gives Adam another chance to awaken Eve, this time toward her "meek submission," yet she has awoken already. In *Paradise Lost*, the voice of Eve, the beastly temptress of Adam, disappears into silence.

When Christ the Son translates Adam and Eve's holographic prayers for God the Father, Christ acts as the "great Intercessor" or

"Mediator" between the human couple and the deity (11.19, 10.60). Christ is the mediator because, after the idolatry of the golden calf, God will never directly show his face again: "to God is no access / Without mediator," and Moses, as mediator, prefigures ("in figure bears") Christ (12.239–40, 241). Milton relies on Platonic-Pauline allegory, on Christ as the Word or the Logos, to bring the words of Adam and Eve from earth to Heaven. Only insofar as their words pass into the Word does God hear them. This translation of words through the Word and into God's presence parallels the final gathering of believers through Christ into eternal oneness with God. To the Father the Son states his eager anticipation of everlasting unity: "in the end / Thou shalt be All in All, and I in thee / For ever, and in me all whom thou lov'st" (6.731–33). This statement comes a few lines after Milton describes how the Father "on His Son with rays direct / Shon full, he all his Father full exprest / Ineffably into his face receiv'd" (6.719–21). These "rays direct" achieve expression yet undergo nothing of reflection. The expression of the uncreated light from the Father and into the Son involves only fullness, never the desire Eve feels for the image of her own face reflected in the lake, or the desire Satan feels for Sin as the mirror of his glory. The Father/Son couple enjoys a mutual investment of light and glory (Narcissus) without anything of Echo or desire. The Father expresses his glory into the face of the Son, and this glory the Son expresses back to the Father without anything of reflection occurring. In heaven, when God declares to the assembled loyal angels and the Son that Adam and Eve will fall yet "find grace," the Son manifests the Father: "Beyond compare, the Son of God was seen / Most glorious, in him all His Father shon, Substantially express'd, and in his face / Divine compassion visibly appear'd, / Love without end, and without measure grace" (3.131, 138–42). The mirroring of Eve's face in the lake or of Satan's in Sin involves the echoing of an image. Whenever the Father manifests in the Son, expression occurs. The Son expresses the Father without echoing him whatsoever. In *Paradise Lost*, desire and echo entangle with death, that is, with the son of Sin, Death, whose name echoes. Prayers uttered in grace become mute sighs. After giving birth to her son, Sin flees him, crying out his name, precipitating sighs, the sighs of the caves echoing Death: "I fled, and cri'd out DEATH; / Hell trembl'd at the hideous name, and sigh'd / From all her caves, and back resounded death" (2.787–89). Hell is female ("her"), replete with womb-like caves. By tasting the prohibited fruit, Eve gives Death his second birth. Milton's phrasing underscores the birth-like quality of this event: the fruit's "mortal taste / Brought Death into the world" (1.2–3). Eve's birthing Death into the world will undergo reversal when Mary births Christ into the world. Sin's birthing of Death and his second birth into the world via Eve initiate the turnings of birth and death, each birth, tainted by sin, being another turn toward death and so toward elegiac words and funereal urns. Only one birth, Christ's, will occur without initiating another turn toward death. Only after Christ's birth could the mother cry out, "Life!" Yes, Christ too is born to death, but his is the death to end all deaths, to end all echoing, mirroring, turning, and desire. None of these will abide when the Father, in the end, becomes "All in All." Nothing of the adventurous Eve who eats the fruit, none of her echoing, mirroring, turning, or desire, none of her words, will enter through the Word, Christ, into the eternal oneness with the Father.

Six

Melville's *Moby-Dick*:
Sin Finds Her Throne

The Muse as Point

Herman Melville's *Moby-Dick* opens with an allusion to *Othello* and closes with an allusion to *Paradise Lost*. The *Othello* allusion would table suicide; the *Paradise Lost* allusion would give death a voice. Between these allusions, Melville struggles to envision anew the nihilistic muse Shakespeare bequeaths him by way of Milton. In Melville's novel, this muse manifests as the daemon Ahab calls his "queenly personality," a point of void at his center inspiring his quest of ever-widening circumference.[1] The trope for deity Emerson in his essay "Circles" attributes to Augustine ("St. Augustine described the nature of God as a circle whose center was everywhere and its circumference nowhere"[2]) echoes through *Moby-Dick,* only with the center a vacancy, Melville perhaps also knowing the trope as attributed to Empedocles, thinker of Love, Strife, and apotheosis by volcanic immolation. Desdemona's murder should baffle attempts to justify the ways of Paul's god. *Othello* performs this god's death. Thus Bloom can write, "Iago shines equally as nihilistic death-of-God theologue and as advanced dramatic poet."[3] Iago births from Othello an inexistent Desdemona whom Milton revises as the Satan-born Sin, a sensible nothing who brings surprise to the cosmos Milton's god oversees, bringing the omniscience of Milton's god into contradiction with his omnipotence. Sin articulates to Satan her dream of his enthroning her in the "new world": "I shall reign / At thy right hand voluptuous, as beseems / Thy daughter and thy darling, without end" (2.867, 868–70). In *Moby-Dick*, Sin attains her throne as the "queenly personality" Ahab exalts. As Sin mirrors the glory Satan takes for his own, so Ahab's "queenly personality" manifests the indomitable selfhood Ahab champions past return. As with Achilles's fateful Athena, Ahab's "queenly personality" mounts to her epiphany only when her captain embraces a moment pregnant with his demise. Consider Athena, with her helmet of death, and Sin, with her son Death, and realize: Ahab finds his "queenly personality" to die for. Ahab reprises Milton's Satan and so Homer's Achilles; Ahab's "queenly personality" reprises Milton's Sin and so Homer's Athena. Ultimately, Milton seeks to demean Satan and Sin, and thus Achilles and Athena. Melville would exalt Ahab, and celebrates through Ahab's last act the daemonization Athena brings to Achilles. Yet Melville would no less celebrate the bible-soaked Ishmael. In *Moby-Dick*, through Ishmael's narration of Ahab's quest, the Hebraic sublime of life burgeoning in the proliferate creation and the Homeric sublime of the death-bound *agon* for the foremost place counter-magnetize each other, energizing the narrative and disclosing the ocean realm as both a "wonder-world" and a "waste" (7, xxiv). Aligning himself placidly with the wisdom of Ecclesiastes (all striving amounts to vanity), Ishmael advocates the light of the creation. Struggling agonistically with the uncreated fire he previously worshiped, Ahab affirms the turn away from light his muse inspires. The distinction between Ishmael and Ahab inheres in their contrasting stances toward the moment, their divergent yet complementary longings for epiphany. Ishmael quests to recover the moment as a first moment, the moment of the beginning, while Ahab drives toward the moment's flowering as his last moment, the moment in which he enacts his fate.

Ishmael through Roderigo to Desdemona

In *Othello*'s first scene, learning of Desdemona's elopement and concluding Desdemona will remain forever inaccessible despite Iago's promises, Roderigo declares, "I will incontinently drown myself" (1.3.306). Hoping to take more coin from Roderigo on the pretext of securing him access to Desdemona, Iago pretends to offer friendly advice: "Drown thyself? [...] Put money in thy purse [...]. It cannot be that Desdemona should long continue her love to the Moor" (1.3.334–41). Roderigo's funds are as low as his hopes, but Iago duplicitously raises both. Iago: "No more of drowning, do you hear?" (1.3.374). Roderigo: "I am changed. I'll go sell all my land" (1.3.375). After Iago suggests Roderigo load his "purse with money," instead of drowning himself Roderigo liquidates his real estate and disguises himself with a "usurped beard" so he can join the party boarding the Venetian ship carrying Desdemona and Iago toward a possible naval battle with the Turks and onward to Cyprus (1.3.344–45, 339). In *Othello*, this voyage takes place offstage in the interval between acts one and two, with a storm dispersing the Turks. In *Moby-Dick*, this voyage extends to epic length and the *Pequod* engages Turks frequently, fatefully, and fatally: in the *Pequod*'s war on whales, Ishmael refers to the leviathanic foes as Turks (392).

The reader of *Moby-Dick* first encounters Ishmael by way of an allusion to Roderigo's empty purse (Iago: "put money in thy purse" [1.3.339–40]), suicidal mood, and decision to voyage. Ishmael begins his story: "Call me Ishmael. Some years ago—never mind how long precisely—having little or no money in my purse, and nothing particular to interest me on shore, I thought I would sail about a little and see the watery part of the world" (3). As Ishmael explains, whenever he begins to feel "a damp, drizzly November in [his] soul," whenever he begins to consider suicide, he goes to sea: "This is my substitute for pistol and ball. With a philosophical flourish Cato throws himself upon his sword; I quietly take to the ship" (3). Committing suicide, taking to a ship: as for Roderigo, so for Ishmael the latter action becomes a "substitute" for the former. And to say a sea voyage offers fit replacement for suicide makes sense when the voyage in question is the *Pequod*'s, as the narrating Ishmael well knows.

Melville's refraction of the prevoyage Ishmael through Roderigo begins Ishmael's narrative. Oblique and overt allusions to *Othello* pepper *Moby-Dick*. Melville evokes yet swerves away from Shakespeare's play. Pushing away what makes *Othello* almost unbearable, Melville embraces what in the play makes for romance and sublimity. In *Moby-Dick*, a Desdemona attains love and adventure without then suffering murder through deceit and mistaken jealousy, and an Othello displays heroism to the last without falling into disgrace and self-murder.

Moby-Dick gets underway with the narrating Ishmael dramatizing his prevoyage self through an allusion to *Othello's* most bathetic character, Desdemona's least likely suitor. Yet the suicidal Ishmael stands in for everyman. After saying for himself an ocean voyage substitutes for suicide, Ishmael claims, and this is the last sentence of the novel's first paragraph: "If they but knew it, almost all men in their degree, some time or other, cherish very nearly the same feelings towards the ocean with me" (3). The next few paragraphs attempt to explicate these feelings. In a suicidal mood, Ishmael "find[s] [him]self involuntarily pausing before coffin warehouses" (3). His feelings toward the ocean draw Ishmael away from the coffin warehouses, though the novel implies any warehouse resembles a coffin warehouse, storing in lifeless fixity what once participated in the creation's vital, fluid burgeoning. The generality of men in Manhattan act out Ishmael's move from coffin warehouse to water. Rather than loiter "under the shady lee of yonder warehouses," these myriads of water-gazers "must get just as nigh the water as they possibly can without falling in" (4). Where lower Manhattan meets water, as close to the water as they can get "without falling in," "stand thousands upon thousands of mortal men fixed in ocean reveries" (4). Falling into reverie, falling into water: set to walking, "the most absent-minded of men [...] plunged in his deepest reveries [...] will infallibly lead you to water" (4). The exemplary "absent-minded" individual would be "a metaphysical professor. Yes, as every one knows, meditation and water are wedded for ever" (4). The "artist" and the "poet" also feel the "magic" attraction of water (4, 5). Ishmael offers an interpretive "key" to this attraction:

> And still deeper the meaning of that story of Narcissus, who because he could not grasp the tormenting, mild image he saw in the fountain, plunged into it and was drowned. But

that same image, we ourselves see in all rivers and oceans. It is the image of the ungraspable phantom of life; and this is the key to it all. (5)

At the start of *Othello*, Desdemona remains the "tormenting, mild image" Roderigo has been unable to "grasp," motivating his wish to drown. And she images forth life, the abundant "fruitfulness" Iago attributes to her. *Othello* maps out the narcissistic identification informing the characters' attraction to Desdemona, including Roderigo's. Milton's Eve momentarily enjoys desire for a watery image before a divine voice insists she know the image as her own. Roderigo thinks he can buy Desdemona's favor and favors, but none can purchase or "grasp" either. Ishmael can evoke an "unfallen, western world," where, as an "archangelic apparition," the nobly galloping "White Steed of the Prairies [...] to the eyes of the old trappers and hunters revived the glories of those primeval times when Adam walked majestic as a god, bluff-bowed and fearless as this mighty steed" (191). But Roderigo bears little if any resemblance to this Miltonic Adam. Rather than to an "unfallen" wilderness, Roderigo belongs to what Ishmael calls the "the all-grasping western world" (380). Having been accused and humiliated by Othello, in her own pondering of a suicidal mood, Desdemona evokes and identifies with her departed mother's maid Barbary, who sang of a maid who died singing as she gazed into a stream. Through his words about Narcissus, with their allusion to Milton's Eve and thus to Desdemona, Ishmael transitions from an allusive relation to Roderigo to an allusive relation to Desdemona. Yet this Desdemona will never undergo the cruelty and murderousness of the Iago-duped Othello. The Desdemona who names himself Ishmael will find only adventurous companionship with Queequeg, whom Ishmael discovers in New Bedford.

Ishmael's mood stays largely in the Roderigan-melancholic as, in a freezing December, Ishmael makes his way north from Manhattan to New Bedford, arriving there late on a "dismal night, bitingly cold and cheerless" (9). Ishmael walks as among the dead: "Such dreary streets! blocks of blackness, not houses, on either hand, and here and there a candle, like a candle moving about in a tomb" (9). In his most suicidal mood, Ishmael tells the reader, "I find myself involuntarily pausing before coffin warehouses, and bringing up the rear of every funeral I meet" (3). This is the mood of Ishmael's land journey, and of Ishmael's December night wandering New Bedford in search of lodging. Eventually, Ishmael finds "The Spouter-Inn," proprietor "Peter Coffin," where Ishmael first encounters Queequeg (10). Coffins bookend Ishmael's relationship to Queequeg. After "pausing before coffin warehouses," Ishmael first meets Queequeg through the auspices of Peter Coffin, and after Queequeg sinks with the Pequod and drowns, Ishmael survives by clinging to Queequeg's coffin-turned-lifebuoy. From coffins, to Queequeg, to a coffin: the narrating Ishmael tells of his voyage with Queequeg, the time of his vital and adventurous existence, the time before and after being of coffins. What Othello promises yet fails to become for Desdemona, Queequeg becomes and remains to the end for Ishmael: a muse-companion for a life of adventure.

At the Spouter Inn's bar, Ishmael finds "a little withered old man, who, for their money, dearly sells the sailors deliriums and death" (14). The pages describing Ishmael's nighttime walk through New Bedford include mirth and irony, and these continue as the landlord of the Spouter Inn informs Ishmael the only room left Ishmael would have to share with a harpooner. The landlord has great fun telling Ishmael said harpooner will not arrive until very late since he is out selling his head, which turns out to be not the harpooner's head itself but one of several shrunken heads. The paragraphs are comical that narrate the nervous Ishmael in the bed first catching sight of this harpooner who, on entering the room, getting into bed, and discovering Ishmael, threatens murder: "Who-e debel you? [...] you no speak-e, dam-me, I kill-e" (23). This threat of murder abed comes from a harpooner who reincarnates Desdemona's Moor.

After Ishmael shouts for help, Queequeg again threatens murder: "Speak-e! tell-ee me who-ee be, or dam-me, I kill-e!" (23). The landlord arrives, reassures Ishmael Queequeg will not harm him, and tells Queequeg Ishmael is to be his roommate. Ishmael quickly reconciles to the situation: "I turned in, and never slept better in my life" (24). The "next morning" Ishmael awakes to find "Queequeg's arm thrown over [him] in the most loving and affectionate manner" (25). Ishmael states, "You had almost thought I had been his wife" (25). No Iago arranges to disrupt or to turn tragic Ishmael and Queequeg's honeymoon. Rather than the jealous, murderous Othello, Queequeg turns out to be the Othello Desdemona fell for: exotic, noble, and adventurous.

After an adventure at sea, Desdemona goes to her murder in the bed where she should have consummated her marriage. After the comic scene of the murder Queequeg threatens in what becomes his and Ishmael's honeymoon bed, Ishmael goes to an adventure at sea. As with Ishmael's words about Narcissus, this comic avoidance of domestic murder further transitions Ishmael from his opening allusive link with Roderigo to his allusive link with Desdemona. Ishmael approaches the *Pequod* and the ship's voyage along Roderigo's path, yet in the transition from land to water, this path becomes Desdemona's, except reversed. In *Othello*, after the voyage to Cyprus, Desdemona makes her way to the marriage bed where Othello asphyxiates her. From the episode most realizing her wish for adventure, the voyage, Desdemona descends toward her murder abed. Ishmael moves from his comic near murder abed by Queequeg to a voyage with Queequeg.

That Melville reincarnates Desdemona's bold yet kind converted Moor in Queequeg becomes clear after Ishmael's first encounter with the harpooner. Thinking of Queequeg's worship as Islamic, Ishmael calls Queequeg's fast a "Ramadan," and worshiping Queequeg's god, Ishmael "salamed before [Yojo] twice or thrice" (84, 52). A harpooner responsible for using a "boarding-sword" to sever the massive blubber strips hoists rip from whale corpses, Queequeg, like Othello, is an "accomplished swordsman" (304; see *Othello* 1.2.59). Queequeg tells Ishmael stories of cannibals. Seducing Desdemona with exotic tales, Othello tells her of "the cannibals that each other eat—/ The anthropophagi" (1.3.143–44). Before Iago's manipulations, the Venetian senate and Desdemona find Othello "all in all sufficient," at one with himself, unmarred by civilized sophistication or sophistry (4.1.258). Describing Queequeg in just such terms, Ishmael relates how Queequeg, like other "savages," exhibits a "calm self-collectedness of simplicity [that] seems a Socratic wisdom" (50). Apparently, Queequeg has "no desire to enlarge the circle of his acquaintances" (50). Maintaining "the utmost serenity," Queequeg seems "content with his own companionship; always equal to himself" (50). Ishmael finds in this calm self-containment "a touch of fine philosophy" and feels that in Queequeg's deportment "there was something almost sublime" (50). As Othello's being "all in all sufficient" and exotic knowledge entrance Desdemona, so Queequeg's being "always equal to himself," "Socratic wisdom," and cannibal tales enthrall Ishmael. As Desdemona is to Othello, Ishmael is to Queequeg.

Desdemona prepares for her tragic bed thinking of a suicide, the maid Barbary. Ishmael makes his way to his comic bed in a suicidal mood. Switching allusive associations from Roderigo to Desdemona, Ishmael transforms the suicidal mood of his New Bedford sojourn. Rather than drown himself, Roderigo goes seaward. Rather than commit suicide, Ishmael goes seaward, imagining he will enter a world of wonders through a whaling voyage, such a world as Desdemona hopes to enter by her voyage. The opening to wonder happens for Ishmael by way of Queequeg. In chapter one, before he narrates his trip to New Bedford and his meeting with Queequeg, the narrating Ishmael describes in retrospect his motives to go whaling, beyond the avoidance of suicide:

> Chief among these motives was the overwhelming idea of the great whale himself. [...] Then the wild and distant seas where he rolled his island bulk; the undeliverable, nameless perils of the whale; these, with all the attending marvels of a thousand Patagonian sights and sounds, helped to sway me to my wish. [...] I love to sail forbidden seas, and land on barbarous coasts. Not ignoring what is good, I am quick to perceive a horror, and could still be social with it—would they let me—since it is but well to be on friendly terms with all the inmates of the place one lodges in. (7)

This last sentence foreshadows Ishmael's becoming friends with Queequeg in the place Ishmael lodges, the Spouter Inn. Ishmael offers his willingness "to be on friendly terms" with his fellow lodgers as explanatory of his "itch for things remote," the "Patagonian sights and sounds" sailors encounter in "wild and distant seas" while in pursuit of whales and the white whale. The willingness of Ishmael, nay, his desire to befriend his fellow "inmates," however strange or wild, signals his ability to "perceive a horror" yet "still be social with it." Perhaps a wonder himself, such an inmate or friend becomes a guide leading the way to wonders. As her relation to Othello grants Desdemona *entrée* to her sea voyage, so Ishmael's relationship with Queequeg grants Ishmael *entrée* to the voyage on the *Pequod* (Ishmael jokingly concludes Yojo destined Queequeg and Ishmael to sign on to the *Pequod* [16]). Becoming with Queequeg "bosom friends," enjoying in bed with Queequeg their "hearts' honeymoon," Ishmael already begins his journey amongst ocean wonders. So Ishmael's relationship with Queequeg is implicit in the sentence immediately following Ishmael's declaration of his resolution "to be on friendly terms":

> By reason of these things, then, the whaling voyage was welcome; the great flood-gates of the wonder-world swung open, and in the wild conceits that swayed me to my purpose, two and two there floated into my inmost soul, endless processions of the whale, and, midmost of them all, one grand hooded phantom, like a snow hill in the air. (7)

In and through his relationship with Queequeg, for Ishmael "the great flood-gates of the wonder-world swung open," just as these gates swing back shut when Queequeg sinks with the Pequod, leaving the bereft Ishmael clinging to the coffin-lifebuoy.

Moby-Dick turns away from the shore, from the familial, from domesticity, from erotic impasse, from suicide. These all come back lugubriously in the novel Melville penned immediately after *Moby-Dick*, the novel *Pierre, or The Ambiguities*, which ends with the mock-Shakespearean suicides of the incestuous half-siblings Pierre and Isabel. The narrator of *Pierre* considers how, in an intense friendship between male youths, "The sight of another lad too much consorting with the boy's beloved object, shall fill him with emotions akin to those of Othello's."[4] Jealousy never mars the relationship between Ishmael and Queequeg. The two flee land for ocean. Turning away from suicide as an overt act, in *Moby-Dick* the Desdemona named Ishmael and the Othello named Queequeg live out their fates as the exalted adventure Desdemona dreamt of and Othello promised, as if Shakespeare's fated pair, aboard the same ship, were never to step ashore at Cyprus but rather cruise the seas for Turks, with Othello dying the ardent and courageous lover of Desdemona and she living on to write his praise.

Ishmael begins as a Roderigo with no money in his purse and bent on drowning himself. Ishmael walks toward the ocean as his substitute for suicide, yet the voyage of the *Pequod* becomes an extended sojourn toward the drowning of all her crew except Ishmael. Ishmael becomes a Desdemona to Queequeg as a version of the unfallen Othello, the Othello Desdemona envisions: vital, adventurous, and kind. The vengeful Othello who strangles Desdemona undergoes some redemption in the vengeful Ahab who dies by strangulation. This Ahab, an active nihilist, resolutely pursues his fate to the very doom, attaining the exaltation of his "fair warrior" or "queenly personality," an exaltation Othello promises himself and Desdemona yet only realizes in the most ironic travesty. In *Moby-Dick*, Ishmael can say, "My Queequeg" without ever having to pronounce Desdemona's words: "Nobody, I myself." Or rather: Ishmael, a passive nihilist, yearns to say, "Nobody, I myself" without contradiction between "nobody" and "myself."

Does Ishmael Say Nothing?

Moby-Dick's narrator asks the reader to call him Ishmael. The reader never learns if Ishmael is the name another gave the narrator or what his given name might actually be. At the novel's end, Ishmael calls himself an orphan, maybe one bereft of parental naming. Though each bears the name Ishmael, chasms yawn between the prevoyage Ishmael and the voyaging Ishmael and between the voyaging Ishmael and the postvoyage Ishmael. Among these three distinct sensibilities, only the last Ishmael, the postvoyage Ishmael, narrates *Moby-Dick*. Melville's novel distributes voice and silence, name and namelessness, among these Ishmaels. The postvoyage Ishmael tells his story as a complex first-person narrator. This narrator reports the speech of the prevoyage Ishmael. Yet the narrating Ishmael silences the voice of the voyaging Ishmael, the novice whaler *in situ* aboard the *Pequod*. Neither does the narrating Ishmael allow anyone to address his autobiographical character Ishmael by that or any other name during the voyage. What are the stakes of this silencing of voice and withdrawal of name?

The novel's land-based chapters report words the prevoyage Ishmael utters: "'Broke,' said I—'*broke*, do you mean?'" (18). This voice, Ishmael's voice, is absent from the postvoyage Ishmael's narration of the voyage. With only two exceptions, and those reinforce the silence under consideration, nowhere in the voyage chapters does the narrating Ishmael report the voyaging Ishmael's speech. Missing from these chapters is any instance of the tone or emphasis of the *in situ* Ishmael's voice in speaking aloud of anything or to anyone. Once the voyage begins, Ishmael never reports himself as an "I" speaking to a "you" about a he, a she, or an it, again with the only two exceptions making his general anonymous silence as an *in situ* whaler more evident. Nor does the narrating Ishmael ever grant the voyaging Ishmael a soliloquy, a report of what he said aloud to himself.

One seeming exception when Ishmael reports his speech to others, the chapter titled "The Town Ho's Story," is no exception at all. Ishmael takes care to ask the reader to indulge his telling the story as he told it once *after* the *Pequod*'s voyage and *on land*: "For my humor's sake, I shall preserve the style in which I once narrated it at Lima, to a lounging circle of my Spanish friends, one saint's eve, smoking upon the thick-gilt tiled piazza of the Golden Inn" (243). This device allows Ishmael to report his speech to others yet to do so without breaking the injunction he follows (with just one exception): never to report speech he uttered on the Pequod during the voyage. And still, in reporting his conversation with his friends in Lima, Ishmael never once allows himself to say to the reader: "I said." Among the very rare times Ishmael uses this phrase in the novel, he reports his saying of nothing: "I said nothing" (75); "I said nothing" (93); "I said nothing" (97).

The narrating Ishmael underlines the silencing of the voyaging Ishmael. This silencing occurs immediately upon the voyage's commencement. The narrating Ishmael dramatizes how, during the voyage's initial moments, just as the *Pequod* begins to ship anchor, a nullification of the voyaging Ishmael's name and speech occurs by way of Captain Peleg, the only character in the novel besides Ishmael ever to utter aloud the name "Ishmael," and then only before the voyage.[5] At some point in the process of Ishmael signing on to be a crewmember of the *Pequod* and negotiating his remuneration or "lay," Ishmael mentions his name to Peleg, as the reader only knows from Peleg's statement to Ishmael: "Now then, my young man, Ishmael's thy name, didn't ye say? Well then, down ye go here, Ishmael, for the three hundredth lay" (78). The postvoyage Ishmael refrains from narrating the prevoyage Ishmael stating his name to Peleg, yet Peleg's statement indicates Ishmael did so. The only character besides Ishmael to speak Ishmael's name, Peleg becomes instrumental to the eventual silencing of Ishmael's voice and name in the postvoyage Ishmael's narrative of the *Pequod*'s journey. During the entire voyage, no one ever pronounces the name "Ishmael" aloud. The possibility that the narrating Ishmael only puts the name "Ishmael" in Peleg's mouth, that captain having heard from Ishmael another name, the actual name of the novel's narrator or another alias, only serves to emphasize the concern of the narrator to silence his name, at least the name he gives himself, "Ishmael." Or because the voyage plunges Ishmael so intensely into anonymity, does his bearing a name become altogether problematic? Ishmael will emerge from the *Pequod*'s sinking as an anonymous "one."

The narrated Ishmael's bustling into silence occurs just as the *Pequod* transitions from anchorage to voyage. After Ishmael and Queequeg sign on for the voyage, and upon their "Going Aboard" the ship at anchorage, a crewmember tells Ishmael, "The Captain came aboard last night" (100). Ishmael's question in reply is virtually the last speech of Ishmael's the narrator reports: "What Captain?—Ahab?" (100). Virtually the last word the reader hears the sailor aboard the *Pequod* named Ishmael speak is "Ahab." After having asked, "What Captain?—Ahab?," the voice of Ishmael the character goes silent in the whaling saga Ishmael the narrator recounts (with the non-exception of "The Town Ho's Story" and one other non-exception to be considered shortly). Worrying about not having met Ahab before the voyage's start, Ishmael states that a man already sensing a problem may try to hide "his suspicions even from himself": "And much this way it was with me. I said nothing, and tried to think nothing" (97).

Having asked his question ("What Captain?—Ahab?"), and having received the response, "Who but him indeed?," Ishmael joins the rest of the crew in the final preparations to sail (100). The actual departure takes place in the chapter "Merry Christmas," the chapter immediately following "Going Aboard." Peleg and Bildad supervise the crew in the last preparations before these two captains, having acted as harbor pilots, leave the ship via a small sailboat. Initiating the voyage, Peleg orders some crewmen to raise the anchor. They do so by using handspikes to turn a windlass that reels in the anchor chain. Ishmael and Queequeg are among the crewmen hauling in the anchor. Observing how "Captain Peleg ripped and swore astern in the most frightful manner," Ishmael begins to worry that Peleg "would sink the ship before the anchor could go up" (103). Due to this worry, Ishmael, without thinking, *speaks* to Queequeg an order contradicting Peleg's order to raise the anchor and thus start the voyage, though the narrating Ishmael mentions but does not reproduce the shipboard Ishmael's speaking of this counter-order: "[I]nvoluntarily I paused on my handspike, and told Queequeg to do the same" (103). Ishmael then receives a kick from Peleg: "I felt a sudden sharp poke in my rear, and turning round, was horrified at the apparition of Captain Peleg in the act of withdrawing his leg from my immediate vicinity. That was my first kick" (103). With this kick, the voyaging Ishmael goes silent.

Ishmael seeing Peleg withdraw "his leg from [Ishmael's] immediate vicinity" enjoys prevoyage foreshadowing. During Ishmael's interview with Peleg about signing on to the *Pequod*, Ishmael mentions his experience as a sailor on merchant ships. This statement angers Peleg, merchant and whaling voyages being so distinct. The first time Ishmael speaks of his merchant service, Peleg interrupts Ishmael into silence and threatens to kick him: "Marchant service be damned. Talk not that lingo to me. Dost see that leg?—I'll take that leg away from thy stern, if ever thou talkest of the marchant service to me again. Marchant service indeed!" (71). Peleg imagines his threatened kick would surprise Ishmael, the sensation of the kick being followed by the sight of Peleg's leg: without eyes in the back of his head, Ishmael would only be able to infer that the leg he would see going "away from [his] stern" had just kicked him. During the interview, the second time Ishmael mentions his merchant experience, again Peleg interrupts and silences Ishmael's voice: "Hard down out of that! Mind what I said about the marchant service—don't aggravate me—I won't have it" (72).

The sight Peleg threatens Ishmael with for speaking of the merchant service, the sight of Pe*leg* "withdrawing his leg" from Ishmael, Ishmael does indeed see upon contradicting Peleg's order to raise the anchor. After delivering the kick, Peleg brings Ishmael into anonymity and silence:

> "Is that the way they heave in the marchant service?" [Peleg] roared. "Spring, thou sheep-head; spring, and break thy backbone! Why don't ye spring, I say, all of ye—spring! Quohog! spring, thou chap with the red whiskers; spring there, Scotch-cap; spring, thou green pants. Spring, I say, all of ye, and spring your eyes out!" (104)

On signing Ishmael up for the voyage, Peleg had pronounced and acknowledged Ishmael's name. At the very start of the voyage, having kicked Ishmael, Peleg pointedly omits pronouncing Ishmael's name. Resuming his prevoyage tiff with Ishmael when he had threatened to kick Ishmael for mentioning the merchant service, Peleg, in his first words after kicking Ishmael, pronounces a question that assimilates Ishmael to an anonymous "they": merchant sailors in their possibly typical characteristics: "Is that the way they heave in the marchant service?" Peleg speaks about Ishmael, asking if he exemplifies a "they": merchant sailors as anonymous, substitutable entities. Prevoyage, during the interview, Peleg had forbidden Ishmael to speak of the merchant service, both injunctions stopping Ishmael's speech, as the dashes ending Ishmael's sentences indicate: "I've been several voyages in the merchant service, and I think that—"; "'Sir,' said I, 'I thought I told you that I had been four voyages in the merchant—'" (71, 72). Prior to the voyage, Peleg insists Ishmael not speak of the merchant service to him, or he will kick Ishmael. Just as the voyage begins, Peleg kicks Ishmael for ceasing to perform and countermanding Peleg's order and then asks Ishmael a question that would require Ishmael to speak of the merchant service—such speech would countermand Peleg's prevoyage order that Ishmael never speak to Peleg of the merchant service (or be kicked). The voyage begins with the prevoyage Ishmael becoming the voyaging Ishmael by way of a question placing him in a double bind: Peleg asks Ishmael to speak about what Peleg had forbidden Ishmael to speak about. In posing this question, Peleg implicitly challenges Ishmael either to revolt by replying with speech about the merchant service or silently to follow Peleg's prior order not to speak about the merchant service and to carry out Peleg's current order to raise the anchor. Ishmael chooses silence and continues to raise the anchor.

And in choosing this silence, Ishmael implicitly accepts the anonymity to which Peleg's sentences consign him. The Scottish sailor at the windlass receives the epithet "sheep-head." The etiology of this food-tropes-ethnicity epithet Sir Walter Scott suggests in his *Tales of a Grandfather*: "Sir Patrick Hume was fond of sheep's head, [...] being a good Scotsman in all respects."[6] As Peleg roars his epithets, "he moved along the windlass, here and there using his leg very freely" (104). Via a misnomer ("Quohog" names a type of clam), Peleg addresses Queequeg, and Peleg addresses another Scottish sailor also via an ethnic moniker ("Scotch-cap"). Among the sailors Peleg addresses, he only refrains from addressing Ishmael by a name, even if an ethnic epithet, a misnomer, or an ethnic nickname.

On first introducing Peleg and Bildad, the narrating Ishmael notes how, like many Nantucketers, both are Quakers who grew up "imbibing the stately dramatic thee and thou of the Quaker idiom" (73). This idiom maintains the distinction in English between singular (thou, thee, thine) and plural (ye, you, your) second-person pronouns. Peleg addresses various sailors at the windlass with the singular second-person pronoun "thou," for example one Scottish sailor: "thou sheep-head." Unnamed Ishmael Peleg assimilates to the plural second-person pronoun "ye": "Why don't ye spring, I say, all of ye—spring!"

Ishmael listens to Peleg roar more orders and watches him kick other sailors. The narrating Ishmael then reports something the voyaging Ishmael *thought to himself but did not say aloud:* "Thinks I, Captain Peleg must have been drinking something to-day" (104). From Ishmael's query "What Captain?—Ahab?" and the episode of the kick to the last page of the narrative, the narrating Ishmael, as an "I," reports to the reader, a "you," what the voyaging Ishmael heard, saw, felt, smelt, tasted, and thought, and what others said to themselves and to others, yet the narrating Ishmael virtually never reproduces anything the voyaging Ishmael said aloud to himself or to others. Nor does the narrating Ishmael reproduce any instance in which any sailor, harpooner, or officer on the *Pequod* addresses Ishmael by that or any other name. The voyage narrative plunges Ishmael into anonymous silence.

In the novel's first paragraph, Ishmael makes the distinction between suicide and voyaging a contrast between speech and silence: "With a philosophical flourish Cato throws himself upon his sword; I quietly take to the ship" (3). Rather than live under Julius Caesar's tyranny, Marcus Porcius Cato Uticensis (95 BCE–46 BCE) committed suicide, reading Plato's *Phaedo* as preparation, the dialog in which Socrates willingly dies by drinking the hemlock the state offers. George Washington's favorite play, which Washington had staged at Valley Forge to inspire the troops, Addison's highly popular *Cato, A Tragedy* (1712) dramatizes the republican Cato prepping for suicide by paraphrasing Plato's *Phaedo* to the effect that whatever happens to the body, the soul is immortal.[7] In contrast to the Ishmael who turns from suicide by "quietly" turning to the voyage, the prevoyage Ishmael indulges in just such a "philosophical flourish" as Cato's. In the "Whaleman's Chapel," viewing the plaques memorializing whalers lost at sea, and realizing "there is death in this business of whaling—a speechlessly quick chaotic bundling of a man into Eternity," the prevoyage Ishmael waxes Platonic and boasts: "In fact take my body who will, take it I say, it is not me. And therefore three cheers for Nantucket; and come a stove boat and stove body when they will, for stave my soul, Jove himself cannot" (37). However, just as the voyage begins with the raising of the anchor, fearing a perhaps drunk Peleg will sink the ship, Ishmael stops raising the anchor and orders Queequeg to do the same: upon the merest instant of voyaging, the anchor just lifting off the harbor floor, Ishmael gives over his boast he would welcome death at sea in a sinking whale ship. In the chapel, Ishmael, in his boast, would make of his death an event he suicidally welcomes yet an event touching only his body, never his soul. This Platonic disregard for the body, or for the bodily, *in situ* self, Ishmael abandons immediately upon the raising of the anchor, when Ishmael realizes his fate resides with the captain's errant will and the contingencies of the voyage. To accept silence and anonymity also entails accepting the voyage as a watery path toward oblivion. At the whaleman's chapel, the prevoyage Ishmael noisily asserts the immunity of the soul from transience. Through undergoing the voyage, the narrating Ishmael has learned the utter transience of all, including any soul, and affirms the wisdom of Ecclesiastes regarding this all-pervading finitude: "Ecclesiastes is the fine hammered steel of woe. 'All is vanity.' ALL" (424).

Besides the "Town-Ho's Story," the second exception to the ban on Ishmael's voice in the voyage chapters shows Ishmael lightheartedly accepting the voyage as a wandering journey toward extinction. In the "The First Lowering," the chapter describing the first hunt, Ishmael rows in the whaleboat Starbuck commands, with Queequeg the harpooner. Despite an oncoming squall, Starbuck urges his rowers to pursue a whale. When the boat rides up on the whale, Queequeg casts his harpoon, but the merely grazed whale upheaves the boat, tossing all aboard into the squall-stoked ocean. Ishmael and the rest are able to regain their positions in the swamped boat: "The wind increased to a howl; the waves dashed their bucklers together; the whole squall roared, forked, and crackled around us like a white fire upon the prairie, in which, unconsumed, we were burning; immortal in these jaws of death!" (225). Night comes on, and the boat's crew despairs of being found by the *Pequod.* The following dawn, in thick mist, the *Pequod* accidentally runs over the boat, forcing Starbuck and his crew to dive into the water; they are then taken aboard: "The ship had given us up, but was still cruising, if haply it might light upon some token of our perishing,—an oar or a lance pole" (225).

Immediately after "The First Lowering," in the chapter titled "The Hyena," Ishmael explains how his first whale hunt and first ocean stranding prompt him to a mood of jovial nihilism, indeed to the uncanny laughing mood of a hyena. In this mood, "a man takes this whole universe for a vast practical joke, though the wit thereof he but dimly discerns, and more than suspects that the joke is at nobody's expense but his own. However, nothing dispirits, and nothing seems worth while disputing" (226). In this "wayward mood," what to a man

> just before might have seemed to him a thing most momentous, now seems but a part of the general joke. There is nothing like the perils of whaling to breed this free and easy sort of genial, desperado philosophy; and with it I now regarded this whole voyage of the Pequod, and the great White Whale its object. (226)

This mood contrasts diametrically to the prevoyage Ishmael's Platonic boast welcoming his body's destruction in the name of an indestructible soul. In Ishmael's Cato-like Platonic boasting, the assumption of an indestructible soul allows for a point of stable presence to stand before and despite the memorial plaques in the Whaleman's Chapel, with their "bitter blanks" and the "despair" of their "immovable inscriptions," the "deadly voids and unbidden infidelities in the lines that seem to gnaw upon all Faith, and refuse resurrections to the beings who have placelessly perished without a grave" (36). In "The Hyena," Ishmael lets go of the reassurance of such a soul in favor of a strange living on as a ghost.

Ishmael confirms his mates share his hyena-mood when, being "the last man" "dragged" soaking from the water and back onto the *Pequod,* he enquires as to whether such courting of fatality is routine in whaling (226). In the single exception to the ban on the voyaging Ishmael's speaking and having speech addressed to him, Ishmael asks Queequeg, Stubb, and Flask in turn versions of this question and receives suitably cavalier replies: "'Queequeg,' said I [...] 'Mr. Stubb,' said I [...] 'Mr. Flask,' said I" (226–27). Given this trio's affirmations of the routine nature of plunging toward oblivion in whaling, Ishmael decides to "make a rough draft of [his] will": "'Queequeg,' said I, 'come along, you shall be my lawyer, executor, and legatee'" (227). The voyaging Ishmael assumes Queequeg will survive him, yet the reverse occurs: Ishmael survives Queequeg. Ironically, Ishmael inherits all that will remain of Queequeg after the Pequod sinks, the coffin-become-lifebuoy.

The completion of the draft will leaves Ishmael in the state of having resurrected prior to his anticipated death. Ishmael thinks of himself as a kind of Lazarus. Before the voyage, in icy, late-night New Bedford, before entering the Spouter Inn, Ishmael observes a homeless man lying at the curb and slowly freezing. The prevoyage Ishmael thinks of this man as the starving beggar Lazarus the Gospel of Luke describes lying at the gate of a rich gourmand's abode. The beggar hopes "to be fed with the crumbs which fell from the rich man's table," but the beggar dies, presumably from starvation, "and was carried by the angels into Abraham's bosom" (Luke 16.21, 22). The rich man then dies and, in hell, looks up to see the beggar with Abraham. "[B]eing in torments," the rich man begs Abraham's "mercy": "send Lazarus, that he may dip the tip of his finger in water, and cool my tongue; for I am tormented in this flame" (16.23, 24). This request Abraham refuses, noting the reversal of fortune between the beggar and the rich man but also explaining: "between us and you there is a great gulf fixed: so that they which would pass from hence to you cannot; neither can

they pass to us, that *would come* from thence" (16.26). Melville has
Ishmael ironically exploit this barrier "gulf." Traditionally named
"Dives," from the Latin for wealthy, Luke's rich man suffers the
flames of hell. Ishmael imagines his homeless Lazarus in contrast
to a Dives snug before a blazing hearth. Fireside, this Dives
praises the "frosty night" and "northern lights" and dismisses
his acquaintances who travel to escape the New England winter:
"Let them talk of their oriental summer climes of everlasting
conservatories; give me the privilege of making my own summer
with my own coals" (10–11). Though Ishmael says of this Dives
"in his red silk wrapper" that "he had a redder one afterwards"
(10), Ishmael leaves his Dives warm and content, enjoying flames
and in need of no cooling drop. Rather than a potential bringer of
lower temperatures, Ishmael's freezing Lazarus would very much
prefer to travel to warmer climes:

> But what thinks Lazarus? Can he warm his blue hands by
> holding them up to the grand northern lights? Would not
> Lazarus rather be in Sumatra than here? Would he not far
> rather lay him down lengthwise along the line of the equator;
> yea, ye gods! go down to the fiery pit itself, in order to keep
> out this frost? (11)

In Luke, a "gulf" divinity "fixed" separates cool, comfortable
heaven from fiery, torturous hell and prevents the residents of
one region from traveling to the other (16.26). Ishmael's Lazarus
cannot travel to warm equatorial climes only because he does not
have the funds of Dives's friends. This homeless Lazarus, Ishmael
suggests, would venture to "the fiery pit" for warmth. While
nature's laws keep icebergs from appearing in the tropics, what
keeps Lazarus in the cold? Ishmael: "Now, that Lazarus should
lie stranded there on the curbstone before the door of Dives, this
is more wonderful than that an iceberg should be moored to
one of the Moluccas" (11). The prevoyage Ishmael focuses on the
presence or absence of money in the purse. This merchant sailor,
thinking of the sea, thinks of economic exchange: "There now is
your insular city of the Manhattoes, belted round by wharves as
Indian isles by coral reefs—commerce surrounds it with her surf"

(3). The Lazarus story in Luke this Ishmael ponders maps this world and the next in terms of monetary privation or abundance, and the prevoyage Ishmael's ironic twists on that story retain its theme of wealth and poverty so that, in this Ishmael's version, Ishmael conceives the relation to phenomena, to pleasure and to pain, in terms of the economic determinant. Roderigo believes he can buy access to Desdemona.

The narrating Ishmael believes "there is an aesthetics in all things" (278). The capture of the prevoyage Ishmael's thoughts about Lazarus by an economic matrix undergoes suspension in the voyaging Ishmael's identification with Lazarus subsequent to his first whale encounter and his redrafting of his will. The voyaging Ishmael who writes his will after his first whale hunt conceives of his transformation by the experience of the hunt in terms of Jesus's resurrection and the Lazarus Jesus resurrects. Brother to Martha and Mary of Bethany, this Lazarus has been four days dead in the cave-crypt ("It was a cave, and a stone lay upon it") before Jesus arrives, and, when Jesus asks, "Take ye away the stone," Martha worries only a stench will emanate: "Lord, by this time he stinketh" (John 11.38, 39). Jesus insists not stench but glory will emanate: "Jesus saith unto her, Said I not unto thee, that, if thou wouldest believe, thou shouldest see the glory of God?" (11.40). Jesus wins this point: "Then they took away the stone *from the place* where the dead was laid [...] And he that was dead came forth" (11.41, 44). Ishmael alludes first to the "stone" an angel "rolled back [...] from the door" of Jesus's tomb and then to the Lazarus who emerges from the cave once the stone is removed (Matt. 28.2). After drafting his will, Ishmael states:

> I felt all the easier; a stone was rolled away from my heart. Besides, all the days I should now live would be as good as the days that Lazarus lived after his resurrection; a supplementary clean gain of so many months or weeks as the case might be. (227–28)

Ishmael feels like Lazarus resurrected yet underscores and embraces the awkward point that the Lazarus Jesus raised from the dead will eventually die. However, notes Ishmael, "the days" of the Lazarus Jesus resurrected were "good." Paul says, "The wages of sin *is* death" (Romans 6.23). Born in sin, our lives are beholden to sin; even if life lasts but a moment, to sin we owe a death. But, by dying, Lazarus had already paid that debt before his being brought from the cave. However much life he may afterwards enjoy, those years or months or weeks or days or hours or moments are his as "clean gain," "clean" of any sin-related debt. He may live them as "supplementary," as free from any calculation of credit and debt. Such days the voyaging Ishmael claims for himself as a silent ("quiet") post-death entity "clean" of any burden of sin: "I looked round me tranquilly and contentedly, like a quiet ghost with a clean conscience sitting inside the bars of a snug family vault" (228).

When the prevoyage Ishmael looks without and within, all seems dismal winter, and he frequents coffin warehouses and funerals, and the accidental visit to the "negro church," "The Trap," brings about an anxiety of punishment in hell or "Tophet": "[T]he preacher's text was about the blackness of darkness, and the weeping and wailing and teeth-gnashing there" (10, 9, 10). Before the voyage, the Nantucket hotel Ishmael and Queequeg stay at features as signage two wooden replica try-pots hanging "from the cross-trees of an old top-mast" that remind Ishmael of a gallows (66). He worries to himself: "A Coffin my Innkeeper upon landing in my first whaling port; tombstones staring at me in the whalemen's chapel; and here a gallows! and a pair of prodigious black pots too! Are these last throwing out oblique hints touching Tophet?" (66). This Ishmael all too eagerly would pay his debt, the death he owes, a problematic payment by suicide. The voyaging Ishmael, after his first whale hunt, and his shift toward a hyena mood, has a change of heart. The crypt of Ishmael's heart has its stone rolled away. The melancholy of the prevoyage Ishmael finally leaves him, and this sea change seems a kind of resurrection. This feeling leads Ishmael to contemplate himself as the Lazarus Jesus called out of a cave and back from death. The swerve from the biblical resurrections Ishmael evokes is his contention that his resurrection leaves him free to voyage toward dying. Or a version of himself dies and another lives on: having completed his will, a final financial dealing, the merchant sailor or commerce-oriented prevoyage Ishmael goes by the wayside and the voyaging Ishmael enters a wonder world of beauties and sublimities.

Exactly which of his selves does the voyaging Ishmael survive? This would be the self who bore a debt of sin payable by death: "I survived myself; my death and burial were locked up in my chest" (228). The prevoyage Ishmael makes a suicidal boast: "[C]ome a stove boat and stove body when they will, for stave my soul, Jove himself cannot" (37). This boast assumes an immortal soul. The Ishmael who, after the whale hunt, makes his will and survives himself makes a statement similar to yet crucially different than his prevoyage boast: "Now then, thought I, unconsciously rolling up the sleeves of my frock, here goes a cool, collected dive at death and destruction, and the devil fetch the hindmost" (228). This statement assumes only the supplementary, debt-free days to which Ishmael resurrects. Resurrects from what to what? From his suicidal mood asserting an eternal soul to his affirmative mood open to his going under into anonymity.

As soon as the voyage begins, Ishmael begins to go under in an almost Nietzschean manner of *untergehen*, Ishmael's name and voice going silent. This silencing requires and encompasses the narrating Ishmael's avoidance of mentioning the voyaging Ishmael as the recipient of speech. This avoidance entails avoiding the name Ishmael. This name the narrator mentions on a postvoyage occasion, his novel-opening request to the reader. The character Ishmael evidently mentioned his name aloud on a prevoyage occasion, his registration with Peleg as a crewmember. In a few rare instances, the narrator Ishmael speaks to the reader or to himself of the voyager Ishmael by name. Spinning his yarn about Ahab's ritual oath, "Death to Moby Dick!," the narrating Ishmael says, "I, Ishmael, was one of that crew; my shouts had gone up with the rest; my oath had been welded with theirs" (166, 179). The narrating Ishmael will address the voyaging Ishmael by name: "But how now, Ishmael? How is it, that you, a mere oarsman in the fishery, pretend to know aught about the subterranean parts of the whale?" (448). But the narrating Ishmael sidesteps mentioning the voyaging Ishmael as the recipient or as the producer of speech, as engaging or as being engaged in conversation. In the chapters narrating the voyage, the Ishmael *in situ* facing the drudgeries, frustrations, excitements, and perils of whaling remains voiceless and anonymous. The narrator asks the reader: "Call me Ishmael," yet, in the entire narrative of the voyage, this narrator never reports anyone ever calling Ishmael by that name or by any name.

During the voyage, this astonishing silence in anonymity persists with a rigor worthy of Maurice Blanchot's theorizations of "the space of literature." This silent anonymity remains in force even in episodes touching Ishmael intimately. Ishmael loves Queequeg. When describing how, during the voyage, Queequeg saves Tashtego from drowning, to the reader the narrating Ishmael adoringly exclaims, "a loud splash announced that my brave Queequeg had dived to the rescue" (343). Yet even in an episode where the voyaging Ishmael may lose his beloved Queequeg, the narrator elides reference to the voyaging Ishmael as a person to whom another person speaks. This elision occurs in Ishmael's narration of Queequeg's nearly fatal illness. Introducing this episode, Ishmael underscores his loving possessiveness: "Now, at this time it was that my poor pagan companion, and fast bosom-friend, Queequeg, was seized with a fever, which brought him nigh to his endless end" (476). After Queequeg recovers by (so he claims) willing himself to live, Ishmael underscores his own personal stake in the harpooner's recovery: "So, in good time my Queequeg gained strength" (480). Yet, in the midst of the episode, when Queequeg seems nearest death and willing to die, the narrating Ishmael suppresses reference to his voyaging self at the very moment Queequeg asks the voyaging Ishmael for what seems a last favor. Telling how Queequeg tests out his coffin and asks for his god-statuette Yojo to be brought to him, the narrating Ishmael refers to a certain anonymous "one": "Queequeg now entreated to be lifted into his final bed, that he might make trial of its comforts, if any it had. He lay without moving for a few minutes, then told one to go to his bag and bring out his little god, Yojo" (479). This "one" is Ishmael: why does the narrating Ishmael not say, "Queequeg [...] then told [me]"? To do so would call attention to speech being directed to the voyaging Ishmael. Such attention the narrating Ishmael prefers to avoid. Voiceless, nameless: in this odd state of sailing aboard the *Pequod* as if he were assimilated to the anonymous, voiceless ocean backdrop, the voyaging Ishmael must remain.

Another example of Ishmael referring to himself as "one," this time the enumerative "one" rather than the pronoun, occurs in the chapter titled "The Mast-Head." Ishmael admits that he "kept but sorry guard" while on mast-head duty by ignoring "all whale-ships' standing orders, 'Keep your weather eye open, and sing out every time'" (158). Not in articulated speech but in his own thoughts, Ishmael warns the "ship-owners of Nantucket" that "sunken-eyed young Platonist[s] will tow you ten wakes round the world, and never make you one pint of sperm the richer" (158). Such a Platonist boards a whaling ship with "the Phaedon instead of Bowditch in his head," that is, having memorized Plato's dialog of Socrates's suicide by state-mandated hemlock, the *Phaedo*, instead of any work on navigation by the American mathematician and astronomer Nathaniel Bowditch (1773–1838) (158). Whaling captains, Ishmael reports, frequently "take those absent-minded young philosophers to task, upbraiding them with not feeling sufficient 'interest' in the voyage" (159). The narrating Ishmael then reports a dialog between a harpooner and such a Platonist: "'Why, thou monkey,' said a harpooneer to one of these lads, 'we've been cruising now hard upon three years, and thou hast not raised a whale yet. Whales are scarce as hen's teeth whenever thou art up here'" (159). Using the anonymous "one," the narrating Ishmael avoids reporting the voyaging Ishmael as the recipient of speech.

What the narrating Ishmael says of the Platonist masthead stander suggests the state in which the voyaging Ishmael's identity undergoes suspension. The melancholy prevoyage Ishmael makes his Platonic boast while visiting a chapel with stone plaques memorializing whalers lost at sea and presumed drowned. The inscriptions on the plaques, when read by widows, move them to new grief. Yet in response to these plaques the prevoyage Ishmael waxes Platonic: "we have hugely mistaken this matter of Life and

Death" (37). Plato's *Phaedrus* describes the soul as "fettered" to the "body" "like an oyster to its shell."[8] In the *Phaedo*, Socrates claims that, afflicted with bodies, we resemble people who, though inhabiting the ocean floor, believe they reside on the earth's surface. Viewing the sun, they mistake the sea they gaze through for the sky.[9] Also in the *Phaedo*, Socrates lauds his execution as allowing him to poison his body and so to medicate his soul into eternity without violating the suicide taboo.[10] Alluding to these dialogues, the prevoyage Ishmael compares humans to "oysters" that, dimly "observing the sun," confuse "thick water" for the "thinnest of air" (37).[11] Recognizing as "true substance" the "soul" the many ("they") designate a "shadow," the prevoyage Ishmael welcomes the destruction of his "body," "the lees of [his] better being" (37). Exalting the soul as eternal, the prevoyage Ishmael suicidally proclaims, "[C]ome a stove boat and stove body when they will, for stave my soul, Jove himself cannot" (37).

So the prevoyage Ishmael signs on to the *Pequod* precisely with "the Phaedon instead of Bowditch in his head." During the voyage, atop the masthead, the youthful yet "sunken-eyed" Platonist, an "absent-minded youth," becomes "lulled into such an opium-like listlessness of vacant, unconscious reverie [...] by the blending cadence of waves with thoughts, that at last he loses his identity" (37, 159). In the narrating Ishmael's account of the voyage, the shipboard Ishmael's "identity" goes missing. This is the Ishmael who in his mortal, bodily existence engages in whaling. The voice of this situated selfhood goes silent in the narrating Ishmael's account. The story of the Platonic masthead stander also tells of the silencing of voice. The Platonic masthead stander blends into his reverie Emerson's all-pervading "Over-soul." This masthead stander reads the "mystic ocean" as "the visible image" of the Emersonian-Platonic "soul" "pervading mankind and nature" and reads each creature in the ocean as an "undiscernible form," "the embodiment of those elusive thoughts that only people the soul by continually flitting through it" (159). This masthead stander would want to agree with the Platonizing Ishmael of the chapel visit about the indestructibility of his "soul."

The "almost omniscient look-outs at the mast-heads" allegorize an all-knowing narrator's "stand-point" (460, 504). Recalling the "absent-minded" "metaphysical professor" who, though "plunged in his deepest reveries," when he walks "will infallibly lead you to water," and whose plunging into reverie suggests Narcissus's plunging into water and drowning, the Platonist, also "absent-minded," ascends the masthead (4). Contemplating "the problem of the universe" while on masthead duty, Ishmael "kept but sorry guard," raising nary a whale so exemplifying the "sunken-eyed young Platonist" against whom Ishmael warns "ship-owners" (158). Gaining the masthead's "thought-engendering altitude," such "young Platonists" allow the "blending cadence of waves with thoughts" to entrance them into "an opium-like listlessness of vacant, unconscious reverie" in which the Platonist "loses his identity" at the moment he "takes the mystic ocean at his feet for the visible image of that deep, blue, bottomless soul, pervading mankind and nature" (158, 159). Were the lookout to persist in this loss of self, he would have "no life in" him but "that rocking life imparted by a gently rolling ship; by her, borrowed from the sea; by the sea, from the inscrutable tides of God" (159). The "Platonist" would gaze like noon's "all-seeing sun" (281). But when the lookout approaches in his "reverie" melding with Platonic godhead, "vortices" swirl open below:

> But while this sleep, this dream is on ye, move your foot or hand an inch, slip your hold at all; and your identity comes back in horror. Over Descartian vortices you hover. And perhaps, at mid-day, in the fairest weather, with one half-throttled shriek you drop through that transparent air into the summer sea, no more to rise for ever. (159)

Attaining the masthead of omniscience, the soul floats, buoyed by the ship resting on deity's benign ocean. Any "absent-minded" bodily movement causing the "Platonist" lookout to "slip" dispels this "dream": "[W]ith one half-throttled shriek," he plunges into silence as the ocean morphs into "vortices" spinning opposites into blank centers. Such a vortex submerges all at the novel's end, drowning any perspective betokening omniscience. Drowning in an ocean vortex precludes resurrection into immortality: "no more to rise for ever." One can only rise on a coffin lifebuoy.

The anonymous "one" by which the narrating Ishmael refers to his voyaging self returns in the novel's "Epilogue." The "Epilogue" explains how the story of the *Pequod* can be told despite the ship having sunk, Ahab being gone, and the harpooners and crewmen drowned, all but *one*: "*The drama's done. Why then here does any one step forth?—Because one did survive the wreck*" (573). The "Epilogue" then elaborates how *"one" "did survive"*: "*It so chanced, that after the Parsee's disappearance, I was he whom the Fates ordained to take the place of Ahab's bowsman, when that bowsman assumed the vacant post; the same, who, when on the last day the three men were tossed from out the rocking boat, was dropped astern*" (573). On the second day of the final battle with Moby Dick, the Parsee Fedallah is lost. In Ahab's whaleboat, on the third and last day of the encounter, the bowsman takes the Parsee's place, and Ishmael takes the bowsman's. Of this *"one,"* the narrating Ishmael says, *"I was he"*: the first person was the third person, as the narrating Ishmael states in his account of this *"one's"* being tossed from Ahab's whaleboat in the final confrontation. When, the whale swimming so near Ahab is veiled by the mist of the whale's spout, Ahab throws "his fierce iron," and the writhing whale knocks hard against Ahab's whaleboat: "three of the oarsmen [...] were flung out; but [...] in an instant two of them clutched the gunwale again, and rising to its level on a combing wave, hurled themselves bodily inboard again; the third man helplessly dropping astern, but still afloat and swimming" (569). This "third man" is the *"one"* who survives, Ishmael, or, again as the narrating Ishmael says of this *"one," "I was he,"* the "third man," but also the grammatical third person, the "I" entering into, being lost in, an anonymous "he" or *"one."* Tossed out of Ahab's whaleboat and *"dropped astern,"* this *"one,"* the "I" as *"he,"* is left *"floating on the margin of the ensuing scene, and in full sight of it"* (573). Thus this *"one"* may narrate Ahab's being snatched out from his boat and down into the ocean by Moby Dick, the *Pequod*'s sinking, and the drowning of all the crew in the spinning vortex. This *"floating on the margin"* of the anonymous, voiceless *"one"*: from the moment the voyage begins,

Ishmael transforms into this silent, nameless, and as if inexistent observer who later becomes the narrator. This narrator associates with a neutral, floating passivity on the vast horizontality of the ocean, rather than with the vertical height of any near-omniscient masthead.

About Queequeg's seemingly last thoughts while apparently dying of a fever, Ishmael says:

> An awe that cannot be named would steal over you as you sat by the side of this waning savage, and saw as strange things in his face, as any beheld who were bystanders when Zoroaster died. For whatever is truly wondrous and fearful in man, never yet was put into words or books. And the drawing near of Death, which alike levels all, alike impresses all with a last revelation, which only an author from the dead could adequately tell. (477)

Floating on the margin of the voyage's final catastrophe, rather than an omniscient narrator, does Ishmael more resemble "an author from the dead"? This would be an author who could narrate a last moment, such as the various last moments occurring for Ahab, for the ship, and for the crew at the end of the third day of the chase. Having written his will, the narrating Ishmael has the voyaging Ishmael claim to have survived himself, like a ghost. Yet this voyaging self still undergoes the final catastrophe, like a prisoner against a wall observing others being shot, for all he knows being next to be shot, yet then to receive in what seems the very final instant a reprieve. After the *Pequod* sinks, for the Ishmael being *"slowly" "drawn towards the closing vortex,"* the reprieve arrives in the form of the *"coffin life-buoy"* (573). The *Rachel* picks up a passively floating Ishmael, *"one"* irreversibly bathed in anonymity.

Blanchot compares an author's entrance into the space of literature to the suicidal person's shift from (A) the I he or she would assert even, or perhaps especially, in the act of self-murder, a mirage of the "I can" defining death as *my* death, to (B) the person's relinquishing of the "I," the "I can," in the actual anonymity of dying, with the "I" becoming as a "he," a neutral, anonymous third-person narrator (*Space*, 26–31, 96–107). Blanchot learned to describe the space of literature in part by reading *Moby-Dick*.[12] Though a first-person narrator, the narrating Ishmael reports the events of the voyage with the voyaging Ishmael becoming more and more a neutral, voiceless, nameless third before whom a conversation between an "I" and a "you" may take place or before whom a scene may unfold. So the virtual disappearance of Ishmael's distinct narrative voice in the three-day finale, rather than in contradiction to his being the narrator, plays out his entrance into what Blanchot calls the space of literature, a drift of the "I" toward becoming an anonymous "he" or "one." Beset with suicidal melancholy, the prevoyage Ishmael substitutes the voyage for suicide. Iago says to Roderigo: rather than drown yourself, take to the ship carrying Desdemona. Wanting complete sovereignty over itself and over death, the self hoping to kill itself would keep at bay the very death it would give itself, as dying voids sovereignty.

Only the nameless calls for naming. *Moby-Dick* begins with a request for and an enactment of a name: "Call me Ishmael." At the end of the novel, with Ahab's disappearance and the *Pequod*'s sinking, the sailor Ishmael fully enters anonymity. In the course of the novel, the narrator's name, voice, and personality go quiet aboard the *Pequod*. Ishmael addresses his every word to the reader, a "you." Until the start of the voyage, Ishmael reports what he, as an "I," says to various characters. Once the voyage begins, the narrating Ishmael will refer to himself as "I" but will never (with one exception supporting the rule) allow voice to the "I" of the *in situ* voyaging Ishmael.

What motivates the device of the narrating Ishmael never reporting the voyaging Ishmael as the producer of speech or as the recipient of speech? One motivation is this: this device keeps the narrator from ever reporting an occasion of Ishmael speaking to or being spoken to by Ahab. Ishmael never addresses Ahab, so Ahab never becomes a "you" from the perspective (Ishmael's) mediating Ahab for the reader. Ahab says "I" and addresses the crew and the harpooners, but never the reader as a voyager aboard via Ishmael's imagination. Ishmael can imagine addressing the sailor Bulkington who, early in the narrative, seems a candidate for being the novel's protagonist though he disappears after his eponymous chapter. Ishmael on the death Bulkington will encounter voyaging on the *Pequod:* "Terrors of the terrible! is all this agony so vain? Take heart, take heart, O Bulkington! Bear thee grimly, demigod! Up from the spray of thy ocean-perishing—straight up, leaps thy apotheosis!" (107). Ishmael describes Bulkington as a favorite of his fellow sailors and compares him, at the ship's helm, to a ship that is like a soul striving for the independence of the open ocean. Though Ahab too has a soul, with the haughty pride of his daemon, his "queenly personality," Ahab remains aloof from and not easily approached by the crew. The fate Ahab's "queenly personality" drives toward in no way enacts an "apotheosis," a raising up to divine status. Yes, Ahab is a "a grand, ungodly, god-like man," yet his final moment involves his instant removal outward and downward from his whaleboat and, as he predicts for his boat, his own likely shredding tangled in the line: "[L]et me then tow to pieces, while still chasing thee, though tied to thee, thou damned whale! *Thus,* I give up the spear!" (79, 572). To maintain his place on the margin and his nameless, voiceless neutrality, Ishmael must never, at least as narrated, speak to or be spoken to by Ahab.

Does Ahab Believe Nothing?

To conclude Iago believes nothing comes almost too easily. Milton's Lucifer believes in the supreme deity of *Paradise Lost,* at least insofar as Lucifer perceives the value he grants himself to depend on that god's favor, on having no rival for that god's esteem. The promotion of Christ as the prime light-bearer shatters Lucifer's belief. Melville finds *Paradise Lost* to harbor in Satan a suspension of belief. Consider Melville's annotation of the argument for eating the forbidden fruit Satan, in serpent form, makes to Eve. Satan questions why God would keep Adam and Eve from knowledge. Melville marked Satan's questions: "Why then was this forbid? Why but to awe, / Why but to keep ye low and ignorant, / His worshippers" (9.703–05). About these and the adjacent lines Melville writes: "This is one of the many profound atheistical hints of Milton. A greater than Lucretius, since he always teaches under a masque, and makes the Devil himself a Teacher & Messiah."[13] Melville wants to believe about Milton that, in writing Lucifer's translation into Satan, Milton hinted at atheism or an evasion of belief, and Melville has Ahab baptize the harpoon he intends for the white whale not in the name of the Father, but in the name of the Devil: "'Ego non baptizo te in nomine patris, sed in nomine diaboli!' deliriously howled Ahab, as the malignant iron scorchingly devoured the baptismal blood" (489). In a letter to Hawthorn Melville states of *Moby-Dick*: "This is the book's motto (the secret one),—Ego non baptizo te in nomine—but make out the rest yourself."[14] About Melville himself, Hawthorne reports, "He can neither believe, nor be comfortable in his unbelief."[15] A hive of quandaries regarding belief buzzes in Ahab. Like a fish inquiring about air, Ahab can mockingly ask, "Faith? What's that?" (528). Yet Ahab embraces as his own "a prouder, if a darker faith," a faith Athena or Sin could praise, a faith in his queen (497).

As an Iago, Ahab manipulates his crewmen and harpooners for his own purposes and toward their deaths, though unlike Iago, Ahab expresses qualms and finally attempts to shield Starbuck, the *Pequod*, and much of her crew from catastrophe. Toward the start of the voyage, through manipulation of whatever stage props are at hand, Ahab draws the crew into beliefs he himself treats with irony. In suborning the crew to these beliefs, Ahab, like Satan, exercises a vehement eloquence. But Ahab also suspects nothing warrants these beliefs. Ahab persuades the crew to believe, and speaks authentically of himself while conducting the persuasion, yet Ahab's most authentic self acts in defiance of any object of belief and disdains the restriction of the self any belief entails. Ahab would believe in nothing; Ahab's drive to evade belief becomes indistinguishable from Ahab's insistence on believing in the void or nothing his personality is.

Ahab's staging of the oath committing the crew to hunt Moby Dick evidences Ahab's ambivalence toward belief. When Ahab gathers the crew and harpooners to join in the oath, he stages a show worthy of the most remorseless of confidence men. Utilizing his intimidating demeanor, the authority of his command, the automaticity of the sailors' obedience, the aura of whaling lore, the promise of a windfall (the doubloon), and a round of grog, Ahab persuades the crew and harpooners to swear their allegiance to his quest. Ahab stages the oath as a religious ritual and invokes a deity at the climax: "Drink, ye harpooneers! drink and swear, ye men that man the deathful whaleboat's bow—Death to Moby Dick! God hunt us all, if we do not hunt Moby Dick to his death!" (166).

The inducements to belief Ahab stages he himself discounts. To think Ahab credits these proceedings would be like thinking Iago credits the scenarios he stages to manipulate Othello. For Iago to fall for such manipulations would embarrass him utterly. When Iago goads Othello into kneeling to make a "sacred vow" not to waver until "a capable and wide revenge / Swallow" Desdemona and Cassio, and when Iago too kneels to swear by the "ever burning lights" his allegiance to Othello's purpose, Iago suitably plays out his role in the dark charade he stages (3.3.461, 459–60, 463). However, in the midst of this charade, the proceedings cut Iago to the quick when Othello declares, "Now art thou my lieutenant," to which Iago chillingly replies: "I am your own for ever" (3.3.478–79). In staging the oath with Othello, Iago gains the lieutenancy he had lost to Cassio. Amidst and at a climax of Iago's plotting, as Othello swears an oath of revenge (Death to Cassio and Desdemona!), a revenge that will sink the general, Iago confronts the wound to his self (Othello's passing him over for the lieutenancy) that set Iago's plots in motion. Staging belief while disdaining belief, Iago confronts the wound that precipitated his loss of belief in Othello and his entrance into his belief in nothing.

The standard for unbelieving manipulation Iago sets Ahab approaches. But amidst the showy props of rounds of grog, and crossed harpoons, and a fearful oath, like Iago, Ahab too confronts the never-evadable dynamic of belief within himself of which the oath-ritual can seem the public travesty. After gathering the crew and harpooners, Ahab engages in a call-and-response routine to exhort them into pledging themselves to the hunt for Moby Dick. He gains their assent: "'What say ye, men, will ye splice hands on it, now? I think ye do look brave.' 'Aye, aye!' shouted the

harpooners and seamen" (163). Ahab then orders up the grog for
the ritual oath, but at this point notices Starbuck's discontent with
the scene. All aboard but Starbuck take the oath. Though in the
rest of the crew Ahab induces belief in the hunt for Moby Dick,
to Starbuck Ahab attempts to explain his own belief. Thus Ahab's
disquisition on pasteboard masks takes place as an extended
aside to Starbuck midway through the process of Ahab achieving
his persuasion of the crew and harpooners. To answer Starbuck's
objection to Ahab's revenge being a concern of the voyage, Ahab
says, "But come closer, Starbuck; thou requirest a little lower layer"
(163). As the singular "thou" suggests, Ahab speaks confidentially
to Starbuck while the rest of the crew are distracted by grog or
at a distance. Stubb sees Ahab talk with Starbuck, and Stubb
sees Ahab striking his own chest for emphasis, yet Stubb does
not hear the words Ahab pronounces to Starbuck: "'He smites his
chest,' whispered Stubb, 'what's that for? methinks it rings most
vast, but hollow'" (163). Think of the stage convention whereby
the audience understands an actor in actuality within earshot of
a conversation to observe the interlocutors without hearing their
words. The oath chapter, "The Quarter-Deck," is one of several
Ishmael relates as a scene in a drama, as the stage direction below
the title indicates: *Enter Ahab: Then, all*" (160).

Ahab's words to Starbuck pose ambiguities and impasses
regarding belief in the hunt for Moby Dick. Ahab confides these
ambiguities and impasses to Starbuck but refrains from articulating
them to the generality of crewmen, officers, and harpooners. Such
articulation could only weaken if not defeat Ahab's persuasion.
Not partaking in belief in the hunt for Moby Dick, Starbuck can be
an audience for thoughts that, while in no way simply opposing
belief in the hunt, complicate that belief and even suggest the belief
to be the belief in a fiction. Ahab subjects the crew to persuasive
strategies he himself does not credit, yet the pathos enlivening his
persuasion remains authentically his. To Starbuck Ahab elaborates
the dynamics of that pathos, an elaboration Ahab's persuasion of
the crew and harpooners must leave silent.

When Starbuck insists that he is "game for [Moby Dick's]
crooked jaw, and for the jaws of Death too," but only to "hunt

whales" for profit, "not [for his] commander's vengeance," Ahab says to Starbuck that Starbuck requires "a little lower layer," a supplemental explanation, to understand Ahab's motives (163). To Starbuck's question as to the value of Ahab's revenge in the "Nantucket market," Ahab, fist thumping his chest, exclaims, "my vengeance will fetch a great premium *here!*" (163). This claim to Starbuck suggesting monetary remuneration is not the only measure seems fairly straightforward. But Starbuck's next objection to Ahab brings a much more elaborate response. Starbuck: "To be enraged with a dumb thing, Captain Ahab, seems blasphemous" (164). Again, Ahab says Starbuck needs "the little lower layer," but now, with the charge of blasphemy challenging Ahab to justify his belief, the captain gives Starbuck an impassioned and intricate response (164):

> All visible objects, man, are but as pasteboard masks. But in each event—in the living act, the undoubted deed— there, some unknown but still reasoning thing puts forth the mouldings of its features from behind the unreasoning mask. If man will strike, strike through the mask! How can the prisoner reach outside except by thrusting through the wall? To me, the white whale is that wall, shoved near to me. Sometimes I think there's naught beyond. But 'tis enough. He tasks me; he heaps me; I see in him outrageous strength, with an inscrutable malice sinewing it. That inscrutable thing is chiefly what I hate; and be the white whale agent, or be the white whale principal, I will wreak that hate upon him. Talk not to me of blasphemy, man; I'd strike the sun if it insulted me. For could the sun do that, then could I do the other; since there is ever a sort of fair play herein, jealousy presiding over all creations. But not my master, man, is even that fair play. Who's over me? Truth hath no confines. (164)

If the crew were told they are to risk their lives and livelihoods in support of their captain's hatred of the "inscrutable," they would be unlikely to assent. The persuasion to the crew states their target is Moby Dick, a well-known, malicious whale, not an ambiguous and "unknown" "reasoning thing" that may or may not stand behind the prison "wall" Moby Dick is to Ahab. This ambiguity in withdrawal from the phenomenal may even be nothing: "Sometimes I think there's naught beyond." Naught, not, knot: perhaps all that will drag Ahab to his death will be a contingent twist in the rope of his fate, a random knot of hemp. Not that what the crew or Ishmael might call a "meaning" necessarily inhabits this "naught." Yes, after Moby Dick sinks the *Pequod*, Ishmael is able to cling to Queequeg's coffin-made-lifebuoy because, when the *Pequod*'s carpenter reworked the coffin into a lifebuoy, he made sure to attach sections of rope each with a knot at the end that resembles a turban; these are "Turk's-headed life-lines" (526). Yes, as "voicelessly as Turkish mutes bowstring their victim," Ahab dies by the line the "turbaned Turk" Moby Dick pulls (572, 184). Ishmael suggests that Ahab would find a meaning in such apparently random coincidences as rope letting Ishmael live yet bringing Ahab toward his death. And Ishmael defines such meaning-finding as pathological. Ishmael says that to Ahab, as "to any monomaniac man, the veriest trifles capriciously carry meanings" (237). But the reader must remember: Ishmael is telling the story in retrospect. The carpenter gives the coffin-lifebuoy "Turk's-headed life-lines." But the narrating Ishmael calls Moby Dick a "turbaned Turk." When Fedallah prophesizes to Ahab, "Hemp only can kill thee," Ahab takes this to imply a knot: a noose, the gallows (499). But the narrating Ishmael, in retrospect, calls whale lines, such as the line that strangles Ahab, "hangman's nooses" (280). Melville the writer has Ishmael the narrator lard the narration with opportunities for the novel's readers, by finding various "trifles [to] capriciously carry meanings," to themselves warrant the label "monomaniac." Fedallah's "pledges" regarding the necessary conditions for Ahab to die seem to find fulfillment (499). Ahab will die with hemp around his neck. As Ahab's quest ends, Fedallah's mysterious prophecy, "Hemp only can kill thee," seems to become an unambiguous denotative statement. Case closed.

Yet how does this monomaniac mode of reading relate to Ahab's quest? In Ahab's reply to Fedallah's hemp-prophecy, notice the captain's laughter: "'The gallows, ye mean.—I am immortal then, on land and on sea,' cried Ahab, with a laugh of derision;—

'Immortal on land and on sea!'" (499). What or whom exactly does Ahab's laughter deride? Ahab assumes Fedallah's prophecy implies a hangman's noose, and since Ahab cannot imagine himself ever facing capital punishment, he assumes the prophecy implies his immorality. Ahab's previous encounter with Moby Dick gave the captain strong indications of his mortality. After that encounter, to harbor a wish for immortality could only be laughable. Besides Fedallah as prophet, Ahab's derisive laughter mocks the captain's own impossible ambition.

Ahab intimates this ambition when, during his aside about pasteboard masks, he exclaims to Starbuck, "Who's over me? Truth hath no confines." This last statement closely echoes one Ishmael makes in his paean to Bulkington. Ishmael admires Bulkington for his valiant drive to join another whaling voyage so soon after having completed a previous one. Seeing Bulkington at the helm as the Pequod first sets out, Ishmael says, "The land seemed scorching to his feet. Wonderfullest things are ever the unmentionable" (106). About Bulkington, Ishmael tries to express the inexpressible by drawing an analogy between Bulkington at the helm and a ship a pilot struggles in a storm to steer away from the "leeward land" (106). The ship must strive seaward, for "one touch of land, though it but graze the keel, would make her shudder through and through" (106). As with the ship, so with Bulkington: though also the place of home and safety, in a storm, the land toward the lee figures fatality. The struggle to keep the ship from "The Lee Shore" requires the ship ("her") to plunge toward "landlessness" and find "refuge[]" only in "peril," "her only friend her bitterest foe!" (106). By convention, ships are female, as is the soul. From Bulkington, to the ship, and then to the soul: in the next twist to the analogy, the land's fatality threatens the soul: "Glimpses do ye seem to see of that mortally intolerable truth; that all deep, earnest thinking is but the intrepid effort of the soul to keep the open independence of her sea; while the wildest winds of heaven and earth conspire to cast her on the treacherous, slavish shore?" (107). As the soul's struggle toward the sea, "thinking" orients toward a free openness rather than any determinate thought or truth. This definition of "thinking" remains the most difficult "truth" to accept, as its acceptance and dying, or the acceptance of dying, overlap. To steer a ship toward the open waters for which the soul thirsts steers the soul toward the actuality of dying. Or so the next lines suggest: "But as in landlessness alone resides the highest truth, shoreless, indefinite as God—so, better is it to perish in that howling infinite, than be ingloriously dashed upon the lee, even if that were safety!" (107). These words obliquely echo Satan's: "Better to reign in Hell, than serve in Heav'n" (1.263). Sin brings Satan to this pass of embracing independence though in hell and spurning servitude though in heaven. Bulkington's "soul" moves the whaler to scorn the "slavish shore," "the lee," though it offers "safety," and to embrace the "howling infinite" as a place of "open independence." The sailor confronts two fates: to steer homeward to the shore, toward the soul's enslavement, or to steer seaward, toward the sailor's perishing. These fate options parallel those of Achilles. The soul inspires the sailor to steer toward ocean and perishing. The soul in her desire for freedom becomes an Athena for Bulkington, as his adherence to her wish leads both to his demise and to his fame: "Bear thee grimly, demigod! Up from the spray of thy ocean-perishing—straight up, leaps thy apotheosis!" (107). Ashore, at the port, can be found "all that's kind to our mortalities" (106). Yet, during a storm, "the port, the land" is the "ship's direst jeopardy" (106). Bulkington would not be Bulkington were he to favor the shore. What would harbor Bulkington from death, the shore, would sink the ship. To keep the ship from shore exposes Bulkington to mortality yet frees the ship from the danger of crashing ashore. For Bulkington to "perish" in the "howling infinite" saves his "soul" from being "ingloriously dashed upon the lee." If such an eventuality would be inglorious, for Bulkington the glorification of his soul and his dying become one event: "Up from the spray of thy ocean-perishing—straight up, leaps thy apotheosis!"

A Platonic-Christian soul may move up to heaven, but a Homeric shade moves down to Hades. Ahab's "queenly personality" resembles a Homeric shade more than a Christian soul, and Ishmael distinguishes Ahab's daemon, his monomaniac drive for revenge, from Ahab's soul. In their association with truth as boundless, Bulkington and Ahab do seem to parallel.

Yet reconsider Bulkington at the *Pequod*'s helm being analogous to a ship analogous to the soul: these "linked analogies" imply an imperishable ship of the soul distinct from the sinkable ship that perishes, as in Whitman's 1867 redo of Melville's Bulkington chapter, "Aboard at a Ship's Helm," in which a bell warns a ship away from the shore and so from ruin: "But O the ship, the immortal ship! O ship aboard the ship! / Ship of the body, ship of the soul, voyaging, voyaging, voyaging."[16] There is a ship, but then there is a "ship aboard the ship," the "immortal ship" or soul aboard the body. Whitman captures the body-soul distinction operative in Ishmael's Bulkington-ship-soul analogies. Or consider the final lines of the poem "Invictus" written in 1875 by William Ernest Henley in defiance of the amputation of one of his legs: "I am the master of my fate: / I am the captain of my soul."[17] Here again, whatever happens to the body, the ship of the soul remains intact. Ishmael apostrophizes Bulkington and speaks of his perishing. In relation to Bulkington, Ishmael is willing to imply Bulkington's "apotheosis" overcomes or redeems vanity ("[I]s all this agony so vain?") and is a glory, in contrast to being "ingloriously dashed upon the lee" (107). Yet Ishmael later declares all "vanity" and rejects titanic striving of Ahab's type in favor of modest, land-based "attainable felicit[ies]" (416). Ishmael's personality withdraws into anonymous silence, and Ahab's personality steps forward.

Ahab's Personality

Ashore, Ahab has a "young girl-wife [he] wedded past fifty" and who has borne him a son (544, 532). But "more a demon than a man," Ahab abandons his wife and son to pursue whales and finally to hunt Moby Dick (544). Ahab abandons his wife and son only to embrace she who achieves his daemonization, yet in doing so Ahab consigns himself and the entire crew (save Ishmael) to "the jaws of Death" (163). The Satan named Ahab, consorting with his daemonic muse, exalts her yet fathers only death. Opening the gates of hell to send her Satan on his mission to sink the new creation, Sin anticipates taking her throne in the fallen realm Satan will prepare for her: "I shall reign / At thy right hand voluptuous, as beseems / Thy daughter and thy darling, without end" (2.868–70). An actual nothingness who images Satan's personality, Sin, by opening the gates of hell, allows Satan to deliver humanity to her and to her son Death's all-devouring "maw" (2.847).

Ahab exalts his Sin in the midst of a storm threatening to sink the *Pequod*. Apostrophizing the lightning that flames atop the *Pequod's* masts during the storm, Ahab speaks defiantly of his muse to the "the white flame [that] but lights the way to the White Whale," even as he indirectly speaks to the crew gathered in terror (507):

> Oh! thou clear spirit of clear fire, whom on these seas I as Persian once did worship, till in the sacramental act so burned by thee, that to this hour I bear the scar; I now know thee, thou clear spirit, and I now know that thy right worship is defiance. To neither love nor reverence wilt thou be kind; and e'en for hate thou canst but kill; and all are killed. No fearless fool now fronts thee. I own thy speechless, placeless power; but to the last gasp of my earthquake life will dispute its unconditional, unintegral mastery in me. In the midst of the personified impersonal, a personality stands here. Though but a point at best; whencesoe'er I came; wheresoe'er I go; yet while I earthly live, the queenly personality lives in me, and feels her royal rights. (507)

Heaven-born, Sin insists on her royal right to a throne. Satan's would-be queen returns in *Moby-Dick* as Ahab's "queenly personality." Sin inspires Satan to undertake his ruinous and hopeless quest to challenge God. Ahab's "queenly personality" inspires Ahab's doomed voyage in pursuit of vengeance on Moby Dick. In acknowledging yet refusing to bow to the "power" of the fire, Ahab follows Satan. Speaking to Beelzebub about God, the fallen Satan refuses to "bow and sue for grace / With suppliant knee, and deify his power" (1.111–12). These lines Melville marked in his copy of *Paradise Lost*. Satan acknowledges God's "power," yet Satan will not "deify" this "power." For Satan to bend his "knee" before God would involve the idolatry of confusing God's "power" for God, making Satan a worshiper of God's "power" rather than of God. In this idolatry, God would become an idol unresponsive to reason. God has encouraged just such idolatry by forsaking reason for force, or so Satan argues, claiming in "reason [he, Satan,] hath equall'd [God], [whom only] force hath made supreme / Above his equals" (1.248–49). As Ahab would explain, Satan's "defiance" entails, ironically, adherence to "right worship."

In his apostrophe to the "white flame," Ahab announces his "defiance" of the "flame" as the "personified impersonal." Iago once worshipped Othello. Satan once worshiped God. Ahab "once did worship" the "clear spirit of fire" but, having been burned and scarred by it, he "now know[s] it." He acknowledges the fire's "speechless, placeless power," but rather than idolize that power, he would "dispute its unconditional, unintegral mastery in [him]." The fire's "power" in him being "unconditional" would preclude his "defiance" or "right worship." Such "mastery" could only be "unintegral" or incoherent, as, being total, it would deny Ahab's existence as the mastered. A master requires a subject, but the very existence of the subject implies a limit to mastery. This impasse relates to the impasses of apostrophe and belief at work when Ahab declares, "In the midst of the personified impersonal, a personality stands here." Ahab's "Oh! thou" personifies the lightning, and the limit to anthropomorphizing the "impersonal" becomes the negation of Ahab's "personality." That "personality" asserts itself in an act of "defiance," yet to defy the fire personifies the fire, treats as personal the impersonal. *Moby-Dick* is a book sensitive to dilemmas between "who" and "what." Exasperated by Peter Coffin's obscure talk about Ishmael's possible bedmate, Ishmael exclaims, "I now demand of you to speak out and tell me who and what this harpooneer is" (18). In "The Town-Ho's Story," Don Pedro asks Ishmael about canallers: "Pardon: who and what are they?" (248). Is Moby Dick a "who" or a "what"? Ahab, his "personality," stands amidst the impersonal, the what, yet distinct from any what. However, his "personality" also remains distinct from any "who" insofar as a "who" comes down to the personification of a what: to ask, "who is John?" and to answer, "John is a _____ " asks and answers after John insofar as John may be thought to personify _____ , whatever _____ may be. Ahab's "personality" evades being the personification of any what, of any thing, of whatever example of the impersonal. Any such thing Ahab personified would be above Ahab as an idol or model imposing upon Ahab a foolish consistency: if Ahab where to personify X, he would have to conform always to the predicates of X. But Ahab insists, "Who's over me? Truth hath no confines." Before the voyage, Ishmael persistently asks after Ahab. Straining to answer, Peleg says to Ishmael, "*he's Ahab,* boy" (79). At the close of the second day of the final chase after Moby Dick, to Starbuck Ahab says, "Ahab is for ever Ahab, man" (561). Ahab, his personality, evades impersonalizing or personifying predication, being reducible to nothing empirical.

A Kantian idea of space acts as the nondimensional condition for the cognition of dimension. If a thing implies dimension, a point is no thing. His "personality" Ahab calls "but a point": like a Kantian idea, his personality withdraws from any empirical determination. Ahab's sentence suggests this withdrawal: he is Ahab, yet his "personality" exists deep within: "Though but a point at best; whencesoe'er I came; wheresoe'er I go; yet while I earthly live, the queenly personality lives in me." Ahab: my "personality lives in me." His "personality," his "I," "lives" within the deepest interior of his "me," and, given how this "personality" revises Milton's Sin, would Ahab concur with Simone Weil's statement about the self: "The sin in me says 'I'" (76)? Starbuck might call sinful the principle or dynamic articulating Ahab's "I," the "I" willing to risk Ahab's life and the lives of the crew for a proud whim of revenge. But at least to Captain Peleg, Ahab seems "a grand, ungodly, god-like man" (79). However much Ahab may reject the godly, he himself can seem "god-like," and so despite Ahab's attempts to untangle himself from belief, Ahab himself, especially Ahab in the throes of his ambition, may solicit belief, including his own. Belief becomes for Ahab an impasse because he believes in himself, he affirms his earthbound self, his "personality." Ahab believes in nothing out of belief in the point of nothingness his "queenly personality" is. To believe in any thing would deny his personality through its reification in subordination to a personified impersonal.

An incident during the first day of the climactic confrontation with Moby Dick emphasizes how the "point" of Ahab's self becomes both a grand circle's center and a locus concentrating nothingness. Having smashed Ahab's whaleboat in half, sending Ahab indecorously into the water, Moby Dick keeps Ahab's Parsee rowers from helping their captain, "so revolvingly appalling was the White Whale's aspect, and so planetarily swift the ever-contracting circles he made" (551). These swift circles eddy around Ahab. To avoid goading the whale into destroying Ahab and his crew, the crews of the other whaleboats "dared not pull into the eddy to strike" (551): "With straining eyes then, they remained on the outer edge of the direful zone, whose centre had now become the old man's head" (551). As the Pequod approaches, Ahab manages to gasp out, "Sail on the whale!—Drive him off!" (551). The Pequod does so, "breaking up the charmed circle" (551).

With the whale circumferencing and Ahab centering an ocean *mêlée* of chaotic dynamism and sublime terror, the geometry of this circle becomes in the narration's next few sentences the informing seascape analogy of a diagnosis of Ahab's astonishingly rapid recovery. "Dragged into Stubb's boat," Ahab lies in ruins, "like one trodden under foot of herds of elephants":

> But this intensity of his physical prostration did but so much the more abbreviate it. In an instant's compass, great hearts sometimes condense to one deep pang, the sum total of those shallow pains kindly diffused through feebler men's whole lives. And so, such hearts, though summary in each one suffering; still, if the gods decree it, in their life-time aggregate a whole age of woe, wholly made up of instantaneous intensities; for even in their pointless centres, those noble natures contain the entire circumferences of inferior souls. (551–52)

These sentences describe Ahab's life as achieving in extremity what Walter Pater recommends: maximally epiphanic moments, though Ahab's intensities are of "woe." Notice the language of a concentration toward an instant in time without empirical duration and a locus in space without empirical dimension. A number of "shallow pains" are "diffused through feebler men's whole lives." The "sum total" of this series "great hearts," within "an instant's compass," "condense to one deep pang."✳ The epiphanic moment takes the analogy of a limitlessly small circle: "an instant's compass." To reach this circle's center would be an infinite journey, as within any circle can be drawn another. The very pointless point of the center is nothing, nothing temporal. Yet, just so, compressing to "instantaneous intensities," vast times, a "whole age of woe," may condense there. This "pointless center" is nothing, nothing spatial. Yet, just so, it may contain the "entire circumferences of inferior souls."

In *Paradise Lost,* after hearing Raphael describe the process of the creation, Adam calls the earth a "punctual spot," "a spot, a grain, / An atom, with the firmament compar'd / And all her number'd stars" (8.23, 17–19). The earth Adam calls a "punctual spot" Ahab defines as the provenance of the *punctum* his "queenly personality" is: "Though but a point at best; whencesoe'er I came; wheresoe'er I go; yet while I earthly live, the queenly personality lives in me, and feels her royal rights." Whatever Ahab's beginning and whatever Ahab's end, whether he comes from a beginning prior to the Hebraic creation (or the Pauline cosmos) or whether he heads toward an end in the Hebraic Sheol (or New Testament hell), whatever blank eternity preceded or will follow the ephemeral moment of his existence, his personality belongs to his "earthly" life and so "lives in" him wholly of the earth. Ahab's transport is earthbound. If *Moby-Dick* were a Sufi poem, Ahab's "queenly personality" would be Ahab's angel of the earth or Fatima. Ahab's assertion of and about his earthbound personality's nobility, of and about his personality's life in him, counters such statements of Paul as: "I am crucified with Christ: nevertheless I live; yet not I, but Christ liveth in me" (Galatians 2.20). Ahab asserts his earthbound self, his personality, lives in him only insofar as he Ahab is earthly, of the earth, Adamic. Ahab takes upon himself the Adamic, "a whole age of woe": all the time since the beginning bears down on Ahab: "I feel [...] as though I were Adam, staggering beneath the piled centuries since Paradise" (544). This Adam Paul calls the old Adam, by whom "sin entered into the world, and death by sin; and so death passed upon all men" (Romans 5.12). The sin piles up over the centuries, a growing burden, so "death reigned from Adam to Moses," yet the old Adam is a "figure" presaging Christ, whose crucifixion destroys the old Adam: "[O]ur old man is crucified with *him*, that the body of sin might be destroyed" (5.14, 6.6). Only via this expiating death will Christ, and the believer in imitation of Christ, rise *"in the likeness* of *his* resurrection" (6.5). Ahab feels himself to be the old Adam staggering under the centuries, yet rather than from a Pauline kenosis unto death of the I, Ahab's redemption comes from an exaltation of his I, who reincarnates the Sin of *Paradise Lost*, aligning Ahab with (Milton's) Satan as anti-Christ, if we let Paul define Christ. If Ahab can seem an anti-Christ, he may still seem a Christ, insofar as Ahab claims in and through him the entire temporal span of fallen humanity may find expiation.

What if Iago were given command of a whaler, an Iago wounded by an Othello of a whale (Harold Bloom's thesis)? The negativity in Iago, his voiding of belief, combined with his manipulative skills, would give the reader an aspect of Ahab refracting the Satanic heroism of Milton's fallen angel. Shakespeare holds up a mirror. Attempting to smash it, Milton and Melville only fragment themselves, and the dimly reflective shards become the characters of *Paradise Lost* and *Moby-Dick*.

Ahab's Wounding: Indifference or Malice?

Besides Queequeg, Ishmael links Moby Dick to Shakespeare's Moor, the Othello who, having murdered Desdemona, announces his suicide by recalling how "in Aleppo once, / Where a malignant and a turbaned Turk / Beat a Venetian and traduced the state, / I took by th' throat the circumcised dog, / And smote him thus" (5.2.351–55). Othello then turns a dagger on himself. In the Syrian city of "Aleppo," a "Turk" beating "a Venetian" humiliated the Venetian state, as does Othello by murdering Desdemona. Having defended Venetian sovereignty against a "Turk," Othello, by his suicide, defends that "state" against himself as an Islamic enemy. Othello's violence defending sovereignty morphs into suicidal violence. For suicide, Ishmael substitutes the voyage. Having survived the *Pequod's* sinking, Ishmael depicts Ahab's wounding by Moby Dick in terms of Othello's suicide speech. But Ishmael references the biblical *topos* of all flesh being grass before echoing Othello's speech of self-slaughter: "[S]uddenly sweeping his sickle-shaped lower jaw beneath him, Moby Dick had reaped away Ahab's leg, as a mower a blade of grass in the field. No turbaned Turk, no hired Venetian or Malay, could have smote him with more seeming malice" (184). Ishmael's biblical and Shakespearean allusions contrast two divergent perspectives on the whale's wounding of Ahab. The first perspective casts the wounding as a mower's indifferent mowing of a "blade of grass," one "unnecessary duplicate" among numberless such blades (466). In this perspective, the mower cuts the blade of grass with surpassing indifference. In the second perspective, the wounding seems the malicious act of a ruthless enemy: a Turk (Venice's enemy), a Venetian mercenary (Othello), or a Malay (a piratical Islamic enemy of American whaling ships).

What implications does Ishmael produce by juxtaposing his allusion to Othello with the biblical flesh-as-grass *topos*? Occurring in the Hebrew Scriptures and the New Testament, this biblical commonplace parallels the transience of the flesh with the transience of glory. About the wicked, Psalm 37 states: "For they shall soon be cut down like the grass, and wither as the green herb" (2). Here, the grass and herb tropes imply the fault of the wicked brings on or at least hurries their being cut down. But in subsequent examples in the KJB, the trope encompasses all humanity, regardless of unworthiness or worthiness. In words and images resonant with Ecclesiastes, Psalm 103 reads: *"As for* man, his days *are* as grass: as a flower of the field, so he flourisheth. / For the wind passeth over it, and it is gone; and the place thereof shall know it no more" (15–16). The flower man resembles briefly flourishes, but then, blown on by the wind, the flower vanishes. Both the flourishing and the vanishing happen in a "place" which knows the flower then ceases to know the flower. However many flowers bloom and vanish in the place, the place remains. As Ecclesiastes teaches, like wisps of vapor wind readily disperses, every transient creature or created thing evaporates, yet the creation remains. In the beginning, God, calling out his word, let the elements of the creation be. Though these elements exhibit transience altogether, the word of God remains. Isaiah writes: "All flesh *is* grass, and all the goodliness thereof *is* as the flower of the field: The grass withereth, the flower fadeth: because the spirit of the Lord bloweth upon it: surely the people *is* grass. The grass withereth, the flower fadeth: but the word of our God shall stand for ever" (40.6–8). Flesh is grass, but the zenith, surpassing excellence, or "goodliness" of the flesh resembles the "flower of the field." In the New Testament, Peter gives the theme of flesh's transience succinct statement but changes "goodliness" to "glory" and so brings into the procession of the ephemeral such exaltations of self as Ahab pursues: "For all flesh *is* as grass, and all the glory of man as the flower of grass. The grass withereth, and the flower thereof falleth away: But the word of the Lord endureth for ever" (1 Peter 1.24–25). With Peter's variation, the flower of glory being of the grass becomes explicit. The biblical commonplace of the flesh as grass emphasizes the utter transience of the human and the complete impermanence of any "glory of man," while God's word goes on forever, as does the creation, like the sun shining on and on indifferently.

As Captain Boomer of the Enderby concedes to Ahab about Moby Dick, "There would be great glory in killing him" (441). Having lost an arm to Moby Dick, Boomer happily declines to seek this glory. Coveting the glory of killing the whale, Ahab declares to Boomer that, despite the risks, Moby Dick "will [...] be hunted" (441). The greatest strivings of Ahab for revenge and glory will pass into naught, and the sea will remain, the creation will remain, as indifferent to his life as to his death. This perspective Ishmael comes to uphold. Though Ishmael attempts to establish "The Honor and Glory of Whaling," eventually he rejects "the artificial fire" of an ambition antithetical to safety, comfort, and common happiness, and, extolling "the natural sun" ("the only true lamp—all others but liars!"), he decides "the truest of all books is Solomon's, and Ecclesiastes is the fine hammered steel of woe. 'All is vanity.' ALL" (424). All flesh is as grass. Ishmael's telling of Ahab's story ends by evoking how Ahab's place, the ocean, knows him no more: after Moby Dick tows Ahab into the depths and the Pequod sinks, "the great shroud of the sea rolled on as it rolled five thousand years ago," at the time of Noah's flood (572). The sea is a "great shroud," a burial shroud: the flood mows down and covers all flesh: "And, behold, I, even I, do bring a flood of waters upon the earth, to destroy all flesh, wherein *is* the breath of life, from under heaven; and every thing that *is* in the earth shall die" (Genesis 6.17). By reaping away Ahab's leg as a blade of grass, Moby Dick previews to Ahab his destiny to perish into oblivion.

Ahab worships fire, albeit by defying it, and, far from extolling the "natural sun," Ahab cries out, "I'd strike the sun if it insulted me" (164). The sun insults Milton's Satan by reminding him of the glory he has lost. Reaching Eden "inflam'd with rage," fierce to "wreck on innocent frail Man his loss / Of [his] first battle" with God, Satan addresses the sun: "O Sun, [...] how I hate thy beams / That bring to my remembrance from what state / I fell, how glorious once above thy sphere" (4.9, 11–12, 37–39). Describing the chaotic aftermath of a fatal encounter with Moby Dick, Ishmael asks the reader to consider "what pitches of inflamed, distracted fury" flare up in the "minds" of Moby Dick's "more desperate hunters" when, viewing destroyed whaleboats and the "sinking limbs of torn comrades," such a hunter swims out of range of "the white curds of the whale's direful wrath into the serene exasperating sunlight, that smiled on, as if at a birth or a bridal" (184). The hunter is Ahab, the scene is Ahab's first losing battle with Moby Dick, and the "exasperating sunlight" is the light of the creation indifferent to Ahab's striving. Milton's God, through his Son, mows the rebel angels down with the placidity of unrolling providence; Satan takes the loss personally. Othello promotes Cassio over Iago with prudent calculation, yet Iago suffers a wound to his pride. From a given perspective, Moby Dick may have bit off Ahab's leg with all the indifference of an anonymous force of nature, but, after that wounding, Ahab "cherished a wild vindictiveness against the whale" (184).

The words by which Ishmael offers a second perspective on Ahab's wounding speak to Ahab's sense of personal affront. Othello recounts how a "malicious" "turban'd Turk" "Beat" a Venetian. Othello then "smote" the "circumcised dog." Moby Dick humiliated Ahab by reaping away his leg: "No turbaned Turk, no hired Venetian or Malay, could have smote him with more seeming malice." Yet upon Ahab's wounding shone the "exasperating sunlight," the light of the creation, the indifferent light disclosing the vanity of all. Ahab's wounding: did this moment exemplify the vanity of all, or did this moment offer a motive for an all-consuming *agon?* The novel moves toward a culmination in which Ahab's *agon* reaches its climax only to have the sea swallow and cover all, the *Pequod,* Ahab, and the crew, in their transient vanity. This finale would give Ishmael the last word.

Ishmael Wants the Beginning

Ahab imagines himself an oppressively belated Adam carrying the burden of all the fallen human centuries accumulated since the expulsion from Paradise. Ishmael imagines himself a participant in an exalting earliness. Discussing the "Honor and Glory of Whaling," Ishmael claims to "push [his] researches up to the very spring-head of it," the very origin or beginning (361). In the process, he finds "many great demi-gods and heroes, prophets of all sorts" connected to whaling, suggesting the profession's "great honorableness and antiquity" (361). The farther back toward the origin, the greater the standing of those tied to whaling. Ishmael: "I am transported with the reflection that I myself belong, though but subordinately, to so emblazoned a fraternity" (361). When Ishmael imagines himself taking his place among the whalers, his transport becomes the exaltation of abiding in the now yet standing amidst a primeval beginning. To go whaling brings Ishmael to a "wonder-world," an "unwarped primal world" of the "antechronical" (7, 414, 456). Consider the following wonder: "[F]or six thousand years— and no one knows how many millions of ages before—the great whales [...] have been spouting all over the sea" (370). Over the centuries of whaling, whalers "have been close by the fountain of the whale, watching these sprinklings and spoutings" (370). Though myriad whalemen have closely observed them, whether "these spoutings are, after all, really water, or nothing but vapor" has remained a mystery "down to this blessed minute (fifteen and a quarter minutes past one o'clock P. M. of this sixteenth day of December, A. D. 1850)" (370). At the very moment of Ishmael's narrating, in the world of whaling, a phenomenon stands before the whaler as that phenomenon existed during the time of Adam, "six thousand years" ago, and even as it existed untold "millions of ages before" Adam. In whaling, in telling the story of whaling, Ishmael approaches, becomes ever so "close by," the primordial beginning. Consider a length of thread. Call the point just past one end of the thread point B, and call the point just past the other end point A. Call point B the now and point A the "antechronical." Call the thread the chronicle, the span of time separating the now from the beginning. To go whaling is to gather the chronicle through a narrow gate so point B verges on point A: the now verges on the antechronical. *Moby-Dick*'s prefatory "Extracts" begin with: "And God created great whales. *Genesis*" (xviii). These whales are among the creatures "the waters brought forth abundantly" (Gen. 1.21). These burgeoning waters partake of the waters that were there "In the beginning" (Gen. 1.1). From the point A of this Genesis extract, the subsequent extracts proceed in roughly chronological order, a list of whale-related quotations from works both famous and obscure. The extracts culminate in a point B, a *"Whale Song"*: "Oh, the rare old Whale, mid storm and gale / In his ocean home will be / A giant in might, where might is right, / And King of the boundless sea" (xxviii). The whale "will be" what he was in the beginning, the *"Whale Song"* as point B describing a chaos of waters such as the burgeoning waters participant of the beginning into which God brought forth whales. Again, point B verges on point A, with the intervening chronology metaleptically transumed, time overcome. The extract immediately prior to the *"Whale Song"* is a *"Nantucket Song"*: "So be cheery, my lads, let your hearts never fail, / While the bold harpooner is striking the whale!" (xxviii). On Ishmael's account, these whalers, approaching a whale, participate in a reversal of lateness into earliness, though the voyage of the *Pequod* ends with the ocean rolling on as in the time of Noah's flood. The closest Ishmael comes to the beginning will be an iteration or recreation or simulation of the beginning, just as the virtually all-consuming flood God brought staged a return to the beginning.

Should Ishmael suffer blockage from the voyage, should he be unable to transition from land to sea, he would freeze into the state of the latecomer, into such belatedness as burdens Ahab. When Ishmael's progress toward the whaling voyage stalls in New Bedford, at perhaps Ishmael's low point, Ishmael tramps late into the night along the icy streets in search of lodging. He wishes his body were not so vulnerable to the cold: "But it's too late to make any improvements now. The universe is finished; the copestone is on, and the chips were carted off a million years ago" (10). Later, during the voyage, this mood of belatedness manifests as a fear of insignificance: "And some certain significance lurks in all things, else all things are little worth, and the round world itself but an empty cipher, except to sell by the cartload, as they do hills about Boston, to fill up some morass in the Milky Way" (430). In winter, freezing New Bedford convinces Ishmael the creation is done with, the "copestone" in place, and the "chips" or rocky desiderata long having been "carted off." Art may decorate the stony refuse left over after the creation. In summertime New Bedford, plants whalers introduced flower abundantly on what would otherwise be plain, "bony" volcanic rock or "scraggy scoria": "So omnipotent is art; which in many a district of New Bedford has superinduced bright terraces of flowers upon the barren refuse rocks thrown aside at creation's final day" (33). But Ishmael desires more than a land-based decorative embellishment of belated, mute rocks left about like tombstone fragments commemorating a vital burgeoning long gone, as do the stone memorial plaques in the whaler's chapel. Leaving behind land and belated rockery and mute tombstones, Ishmael desires at sea to recapture and participate in the creation's first day, or really in the time before time of the beginning.

In New Bedford, after thinking the universe finished long ago, Ishmael imagines a homeless man freezing to death on the street to be Lazarus, and asks, "Would not Lazarus rather be in Sumatra than here? Would he not far rather lay him down lengthwise along the line of the equator; yea, ye gods! go down to the fiery pit itself, in order to keep out this frost?" (11). This Lazarus figures the fate of an Ishmael who never met his Queequeg, an Ishmael who lies freezing in New Bedford and who never will voyage to the tropics whaling ships frequent, where the waters burgeon as (did) those on which Noah sailed.

As the Pequod nears her fate, on the morning of the last day of the final three-day battle with Moby Dick, Ahab notes a pervading aura of earliness, of the time of the beginning: "What a lovely day again! were it a new-made world, and made for a summer-house to the angels, and this morning the first of its throwing open to them, a fairer day could not dawn upon that world" (563). Of course, the creation being a "summer-house to the angels" and "thrown open to them" hints at an episode in Genesis: the angels ("sons of God") enjoy a vacation in the new creation, have sex with the "daughters of men," and these sexual unions stir Yahweh to wrath and the decision to blot out the creation by a flood, sparing only Noah (6.1–8). When Ahab as lookout sights Moby Dick's spout for the last time, and the crewmen lower the whaleboats for the final encounter, Ahab explicitly identifies the ocean waters of his present moment with those of Noah: "But let me have one more good round look aloft here at the sea; there's time for that. An old, old sight, and yet somehow so young; aye, and not changed a wink since I first saw it, a boy, from the sand-hills of Nantucket! The same!—the same!—the same to Noah as to me" (565). The waters being "the same" to Ahab as to Noah implies the collapse or suspension of the intervening chronology, so the time of Ahab's final battle with Moby Dick becomes a fated repetition, and after the sinking of the *Pequod* the ocean seems a limitless flood recalling Noah's.

Ask of the oceans the *Pequod* travels: were these the waters there at the beginning? Ishmael wants to say yes, and Melville has Ishmael play out this desire over the course of the narrative. The novel's prefatory "Etymology" traces the south-sea island "*Erromangoan*" word for whale, "PEHEE-NUEE-NUEE," back through the European languages, back through Latin and Greek, to the Hebrew word for whale (xvi). The whales the Pequod hunts, as Leviathans, recall biblical creatures and swim in waters evocative of the waters there "In the beginning": "And the earth *was* without form, and void; and darkness was upon the face of the deep. And the Spirit of God moved upon the face of the waters" (Genesis 1.1–2). Or are the waters the Pequod travels those Noah traveled, waters in their chaotic, flooding boundlessness reversing (much of) the creation and so even more participant of the waters of the beginning? A vehicle for the logic of the "all-grasping western world," the prow of the *Pequod* cuts the leading edge of the chronological into the waves (380). So, in her sinking, the chronological goes down with the ship, leaving the waters as they were in the beginning, or so the narration's last sentence implies: "[T]hen all collapsed, and the great shroud of the sea rolled on as it rolled five thousand years ago" (572). Or rather, these waters recall that almost complete return to the beginning's void waste of waters Noah's flood achieved. The narrating Ishmael claims "Adam [...] died sixty round centuries ago" (37). After the Pequod sinks, "the sea rolled on as it rolled five thousand years ago," the time of Noah's flood. The destruction of the Pequod, with Ahab's and the crew's deaths, achieves the most all-encompassing of the upsurges of the beginning Ishmael seeks. Perhaps even more than Ahab's desire to realize his fate, Ishmael's desire for the beginning bears complicity with the *Pequod*'s going under. Ishmael's final biblical allusion (aside from those in the "Epilogue") casts the action of the narrative at large as ending in a return of the biblical flood that achieved a return to the beginning. This return to the beginning defines the sublime for Ishmael.

Ishmael's Transport

Ishmael narrates his transport, his exaltation of the sublime. This transport defines Ishmael's evocations of the wondrous grandeurs of whales and whaling as occurring in a moment of beginning, a moment when an atemporal and aspatial aboriginal flux yields to the creation's orderings of time and space. This transport toward wonder Ishmael discusses in relation to "Fossil Whales." Ishmael focuses on fossils that provide a link between the whales that existed before time and the biblical ancestors of the whales the *Pequod* hunts, that is, more generally, fossils providing a link "between the antechronical creatures, and those whose remote posterity are said to have entered the Ark" (456). Notice Ishmael's trope for his transport to the beginning ("by a flood"), as Ishmael will end his narrative by evoking Noah's flood:

> When I stand among these mighty Leviathan skeletons, skulls, tusks, jaws, ribs, and vertebrae, all characterized by partial resemblances to the existing breeds of sea-monsters; but at the same time bearing on the other hand similar affinities to the annihilated antechronical Leviathans, their incalculable seniors; I am, by a flood, borne back to that wondrous period, ere time itself can be said to have begun; for time began with man. (457)

These "pre-adamite" fossils transport Ishmael to another contemplation of the "wonder-world" as they provoke a transport that floods away time, and so "man," allowing Ishmael to encounter the atemporal (457). Marking the edge between an aboriginal atemporality and time (the correlate of "man"), these fossils give Ishmael sublime intimations of the chaos of waters prior to the creation: "Here Saturn's grey chaos rolls over me, and I obtain dim, shuddering glimpses into those Polar eternities; when wedged bastions of ice pressed hard upon what are now the Tropics; and in all the 25,000 miles of this world's circumference, not an inhabitable hand's breadth of land was visible" (457). Ishmael insists any skeletal remains of a whale barely hint at what encountering a whale *in situ* conveys, so the transport the fossils provide remains the wan dilution of the overwhelming transport rowing toward a whale at sea provides. In the cosmos Ishmael narrates, to cast a harpoon at a whale, or to row a whaleboat toward a whale, is to brush upon the all-pervading anonymous "existence" backgrounding and utterly indifferent to every human effort: "Ahab's harpoon had shed older blood than the Pharaohs'. Methuselah seems a schoolboy.

I look round to shake hands with Shem. I am horror-struck at this antemosaic, unsourced existence of the unspeakable terrors of the whale, which, having been before all time, must needs exist after all humane ages are over" (457). The "Leviathan comes floundering down upon us from the head-waters of the Eternities," and, "immortal in his species" however killable individually, the whale "swam the seas before the continents broke water," "despised Noah's ark," and "if ever the world is to be again flooded, [...] then the eternal whale will still survive [...] the equatorial flood" (459, 462). Encountering the whale, the whaler momentarily relinquishes all human-posited spatial-temporal orderings. The event of the whale-encounter assumes the dissolution of such orderings. Or the whale-encounter risks or puts at stake such orderings, giving moments of their evasion, yet the killing of a whale enacts the reassertion of such orderings. Discussing "The Mast-Head," the perch atop a mast where lookouts scan the ocean for whales, Ishmael notes, "your whales must be seen before they can be killed" (158). A hunt begins when a whaler sees a whale, and this gaze is made possible by and partakes of whale-hunting technology: the *Pequod*, whaleboats, and accoutrements the sailors deploy. Sighting a whale and reporting its location, the masthead stander initiates the hunt by a spatial-temporal ordering. The hunt ends with the detached observation of a dying whale, the whale's death correlating with the whale's assimilation to an object ordered in the human viewer's perspective. The chapter "Stubb Kills a Whale" ends with Stubb's pipe going out and the whale dying: "Stubb scattered the dead ashes over the water; and, for a moment, stood thoughtfully eyeing the vast corpse he had made" (286). Or again, in the chapter describing the harpooning technique known as "pitchpoling": "The agonized whale goes into his flurry; the tow-line is slackened, and the pitchpoler dropping astern, folds his hands, and mutely watches the monster die" (369). The whale swims in an aboriginal, atemporal, aspatial chaos of waters; the whale's death by harpooning corresponds to the whale's ordering into the human space and time of the "all-grasping western world." The moment of transport Ishmael seeks, the beginning, the time before time without man, implies the inexistence of whalers, of whaling, and of whale ships. No wonder atop the masthead Ishmael never sings out his sighting a whale, and no wonder the beginning's most complete return comes only after the sinking of the *Pequod*.

Ishmael's transport is specifically diluvian. The flood recovers the timeless time and spaceless space of the beginning: "I am, by a flood, borne back to that wondrous period, ere time itself can be said to have begun; for time began with man." This flood, like Noah's, transports Ishmael back to the beginning, when the wind swept over the face of the deep, before man, and before time and before space. With Noah's flood, Yahweh seeks to zero-out the creation and return to the beginning. A haven for creatures, Noah's ark contrasts to the *Pequod*, "[a] cannibal of a craft, tricking herself forth in the chased bones of her enemies" (70). Ishmael would approach a moment negating everything of man. His assertion of the vanity of "ALL" deeply resonates with this moment because by "vanity" Ecclesiastes implies the passing away of all, especially all the artifacts of human effort and of the humans who made the effort. All flesh is grass; the flood reaps away all flesh. "[A]s a mower a blade of grass in the field": this perspective on Moby Dick's taking of Ahab's leg belongs to Ishmael. "No turbaned Turk, no hired Venetian or Malay, could have smote him with more seeming malice": this perspective belongs to Ahab, who "piled upon the whale's white hump the sum of all the general rage and hate felt by his whole race from Adam down; and then, as if his chest had been a mortar, he burst his hot heart's shell upon it" (184). The moment of transport Ishmael would undergo would negate man. In futilely striving to bring death to Moby Dick, Ahab drives toward a moment of transport that would exalt man, "from Adam down," or at least the man Ahab, his personality.

Ahab's Transport

Should she exist, Ahab's personality, Ahab's inmost center, stands as a point of nothingness, without chronological duration, spatial extension, or sematic predication. This point would resemble the ever-receding center of a circle of ever-expanding circumference. Attributed to Empedocles: "The nature of God is a circle, of which the center is everywhere and the circumference is nowhere." When the Christian god dies, the expanding circle's center point becomes an actual nothing. The point has no content, as the horizon has no limit. Enacting a negation of semantic accretions, what Ahab calls his personality Harold Bloom might call *"an achieved dearth of meaning."*[18] Tumbling from a whaleboat and left adrift, Pip undergoes a voiding of center in being the lone point centering the ocean horizon that seems to expand limitlessly around him. Through this experience, Pip loses belief in his self, which for Pip goes missing. For Ahab, such a void defines his self and his belief.

In "The Dying Whale," Ahab speaks a soliloquy in which, apostrophizing the sea, he affirms his belief. This affirmation comes by way of an allusion to Satan's affirmation of his fate in *Paradise Lost*. Escaping by flight the lake of fire into which he fell, Satan seeks a place to "rest" and attains "dry land" (1.185, 227). Surveying the dark expanse of hell, Satan compares hell's gloom to heaven's light: "'Is this the Region, this the soil, the clime,' / Said then the lost Archangel; 'this the seat / That we must change for Heav'n, this mournful gloom / For that celestial light? Be it so [...]'" (1.242–45). Claiming to equal God in reason, and accusing God of vanquishing his "equals" only by "force," Satan welcomes hell as his own realm:

> Farewell happy fields
> Where joy forever dwells: hail horrors, hail
> Infernal world, and thou, profoundest Hell,
> Receive thy new possessor; one who brings
> A mind not to be chang'd by place or time.
>
> (1.249–53)

Concluding his meditation on a whale he had harpooned and now watches die, Ahab echoes Satan's hailing of hell: "Then hail, for ever hail, O sea, in whose eternal tossings the wild fowl finds his only rest. Born of earth, yet suckled by the sea; though hill and valley mothered me, ye billows are my foster-brothers!" (497). As Satan forsakes the light of heaven to hail the darkness visible of hell, Ahab turns from the "lovely sunset sea" toward the approaching night (496). The sunset's "inwreathing orisons" in the "rosy air" make the scene appear "as if far over from the deep green convent valleys of the Manilla isles, the Spanish land-breeze, wantonly turned sailor, had gone to sea, freighted with these vesper hymns" (496). This pious sunset "only soothed [Ahab] to a deeper gloom," and he turns from the sun to address the night (496). Ahab's turn from the sunset to the oncoming dark parallels how the whale, dying, faces toward the sun, only then to turn toward the darkness. About this whale Ahab declares, "He too worships fire; most faithful, broad, baronial vassal of the sun! [...] but see! no sooner dead, than death whirls round the corpse, and it heads some other way" (497). The "other way" toward which death turns the whale is away from the sun and toward the night. Turning toward the darkness, Ahab addresses his queen:

> Oh, thou dark Hindoo half of nature, who of drowned bones hast builded thy separate throne somewhere in the heart of these unverdured seas; thou art an infidel, thou queen, and too truly speakest to me in the wide-slaughtering Typhoon, and the hushed burial of its after calm. Nor has this thy whale sunwards turned his dying head, and then gone round again, without a lesson to me. (497)

Recall Ahab's exaltation of his "queenly personality," avatar of the Sin who anticipates her enthronement as Satan's queen and separate from God's realm. Ahab's queen establishes her "separate throne." And note how Ahab saying his queen speaks to him "in the wide-slaughtering Typhoon" suggests his queen speaks to him as would Athena, she of the storm-shield heralding slaughter and the "after calm." The "lesson" Ahab gains is that the whale, turning to "seek intercedings with yon all-quickening sun," does so vainly, for the sun "only calls forth life, but gives it not again" (497). In calling forth life, the sun takes on the generative voice of Genesis's Yahweh, who calls forth the whales. To hope for more life from the sun is a vanity. The dying whale petitioning the sun emits a "high aspiring, rainbowed jet": the whale presents to the sun a rainbow, a covenant sign promising more life (Genesis 9.11–13), but the whale "jetteth all in vain" (497). After the giving of life, there is no giving again, no resurrection after death. In contrast to the whale's "vain" faith, Ahab gains a "prouder" faith, a "darker faith," from his queen: "Yet dost thou, darker half, rock me with a prouder, if a darker faith. All thy unnamable imminglings float beneath me here; I am buoyed by breaths of once living things, exhaled as air, but water now" (497). The moist, exhaled breaths of the living, like all watery vapors, condense down into the ocean, its waters a vast collection of exhalations of the perishing, of last breaths. A darker faith indeed, a faith befitting a queen whose throne is made of the bones of the drowned. Pledging himself to his queen and her faith, Ahab cries out, "Then hail, for ever hail, O sea." If the sun resembles the generative word, John's Logos or Christ, Ahab denies Christological resurrection and embraces his Athena. On the last day of the climactic three-day battle with Moby Dick, in his last words, Ahab speaks of turning away from the sun and of spitting out his last breath. Then he hurls his harpoon. Possessed by Athena, Achilles hurls his spear at Hector. Possessed by his queenly personality, Ahab hurls his harpoon at Moby Dick.

Ahab Goes Under

Satan never battles God directly, and Milton finally reduces Satan to an abject hissing serpent. Just as in Ishmael Melville gives Desdemona the Othello she had hoped for, in Ahab Melville gives Satan a direct confrontation with his nemesis and a heroic end. Ahab finally confronts Moby Dick, if not quite face to face, then face to blank brow, and, like Achilles spearing Hector, Ahab spears the whale and precipitates his own fate of dying immediately thereafter. Ahab would cheer when Satan claims there is no one above him. In dissent, the Seraph Abdiel denounces Satan's "impious rage" and asks Satan if he is claiming equality with the "begotten Son," through whom, "As by His

Word the mighty Father made / All things, ev'n thee" (5.845, 835, 836–37). Abdiel insists Satan owes his existence to his despised Cassio, Christ the Word, who in turn owes his being to God. This assertion that Satan was made by what Satan calls "secondary hands" prompts Satan to declare: "We know no time when we were not as now; / Know none before us, self-begot, self-rais'd / By our own quick'ning power" (5.854, 859–61). Despite Satan's delusive pride of self-creation, if the reader is to believe Gabriel's angry statement to Satan, before God's command for all knees to bend to the Son, no one outdid Satan (then Lucifer) in the worship of God: "And thou sly hypocrite, who now wouldst seem / Patron of liberty, who more than thou / Once fawn'd, and cring'd, and servilely ador'd / Heav'n's awful Monarch?" (4.957–60).

Ahab once worshiped fire, say the fire of the sun, but to Starbuck's charge that seeking revenge on a "dumb brute" is "blasphemous," Ahab replies: "Talk not to me of blasphemy, man; I'd strike the sun if it insulted me […] Who's over me?" (163, 164). As the *Pequod's* Abdiel, Starbuck later thinks: "Horrible old man! Who's over him, he cries;—aye, he would be a democrat to all above; look, how he lords it over all below!" (169). Like Satan, Ahab acknowledges none his superior, even while deploying stirring rhetoric to suborn his crew to his purpose. And like Satan, Ahab claims to ever have been himself, declaring to Starbuck, "Ahab is for ever Ahab" (561). But Ishmael would convince the reader that the energy and ardency of Ahab in his quest to kill Moby Dick, rather than being forever the captain's self-quickening trait, only sprang into existence after Ahab's first confrontation with the whale.

The narrator Ishmael images Bulkington as the ship struggling away from the lee shore ("it fared with [Bulkington] as with the storm-tossed ship" [106]) and exclaims how, when this ship of the soul sinks, when Bulkington drowns, the sailor's soul will rise toward godhood: "Take heart, take heart, O Bulkington! Bear thee grimly, demigod! Up from the spray of thy ocean-perishing— straight up, leaps thy apotheosis!" (107). The implication is of the soul flying upward from the sinking body/ship. Yes, Ahab has a soul. But after his wounding by Moby Dick, Ahab's "torn body and gashed soul bled into one another; and so interfusing, made him mad" (185). And this soul-body would flee the will to revenge burning in Ahab, so much so that "the eternal, living principle or soul in him" occasionally takes advantage of sleep to cause Ahab, having fallen asleep in his hammock, "to burst from it in horror again" in a desperate attempt to "escape from the scorching contiguity of the frantic thing," from being contiguous with the "self-assumed, independent being" Ahab's "supreme purpose" had become "by its own sheer inveteracy of will" (202). This "frantic thing" "grimly live[s] and burn[s]," an "unbidden and unfathered birth" from which Ahab's body-soul or "common vitality" would flee (202). Bulkington has a soul; Ahab has an "unfathered" or self-quickening daemon. Ishmael imagines the "apotheosis" of Bulkington's "soul." The last exaltation Ahab achieves, the exaltation of his daemon, is another matter altogether. Ishmael imagines Bulkington's soul going up and away; in a daemonic ecstasy, Ahab goes out and down.

Ishmael imagines Ahab's "scorching" daemon as a demon, and this by way of the hell within Milton's Satan, the hell opening downward to ever deeper, more abyssal hells. When Ahab lies down in his hammock, in sleep he often suffers "intolerably vivid dreams": "a chasm seemed opening in him, from which forked flames and lightnings shot up, and accursed fiends beckoned him to leap down among them; when this hell in himself yawned beneath him, a wild cry would be heard through the ship; and with glaring eyes Ahab would burst from his state room" (201, 202). Ahab's soul would flee the hell within the captain, yet into that abyss Ahab's daemon would draw the captain, to hell's heart or void center.

Given the Miltonic provenance of Ahab's daemon, Ahab's final speech becomes a Satanic soliloquy. Ahab delivers this speech as the third and fatal day of the chase ends. Ishmael describes the *Pequod* as "the material counterpart of her monomaniac commander's soul" (423). Over the course of the chase's third day, Ahab repeatedly describes himself as a ship or as the *Pequod* itself, recalling Ishmael's comparison of Bulkington's soul to the *Pequod*. The "wild winds" "whip" Ahab's hairs "about [him] as the torn shreds of split sails lash the tossed ship they cling to" (563). The winds drive the *Pequod* forward; Ahab exclaims, "something so unchangeable, and full as strong, blow my keeled soul along!" (564). Addressing the ship, Ahab says, "we both grow old together; sound in our hulls, though, are we not, my ship?" (565). On the final day of the chase, Ahab's last day, Starbuck mans the ropes to lower Ahab in his whaleboat. In Ahab's last words to Starbuck, the captain describes his soul as a ship but his existence in dying as the ocean or a last cresting wave:

> "For the third time my soul's ship starts upon this voyage, Starbuck."
> "Aye, Sir, thou wilt have it so."
> "Some ships sail from their ports, and ever afterwards are missing, Starbuck!"
> "Truth, Sir: saddest truth."
> "Some men die at ebb tide; some at low water; some at the full of the flood;—and I feel now like a billow that's all one crested comb, Starbuck. I am old;—shake hands with me, man." (565–66)

The *Pequod* as Ahab's soul and Ahab's existence-toward-dying as a cresting wave: these analogies prepare the reader to receive Ahab's final speech. When Ahab compares his soul or his "common vitality" to the *Pequod*, the reader recalls Ishmael having underscored the split within Ahab between his soul-body and his daemon. This split finds dramatization in Ahab's final confrontation with the whale: as the *Pequod* sinks, as Ahab's ship or soul sinks or perishes, in Ahab's whaleboat the despairing yet exultant daemon named Ahab hurls his spear into Moby Dick.

On the third day, Ahab's end approaches: Moby Dick has battered the hull of the *Pequod,* and the ocean waters rush into the ship as Tashtego hammers one last flag of Ahab to the highest yet sinking mast. Viewing this scene from his whaleboat, Ahab speaks his final words:

> I turn my body from the sun. What ho, Tashtego! Let me hear thy hammer. Oh! ye three unsurrendered spires of mine; thou uncracked keel; and only god-bullied hull; thou firm

deck, and haughty helm, and Pole-pointed prow,—death-glorious ship! must ye then perish, and without me? Am I cut off from the last fond pride of meanest shipwrecked captains? Oh, lonely death on lonely life! Oh, now I feel my topmost greatness lies in my topmost grief. Ho, ho! from all your furthest bounds, pour ye now in, ye bold billows of my whole foregone life, and top this one piled comber of my death! Towards thee I roll, thou all-destroying but unconquering whale; to the last I grapple with thee; from hell's heart I stab at thee; for hate's sake I spit my last breath at thee. Sink all coffins and all hearses to one common pool! and since neither can be mine, let me then tow to pieces, while still chasing thee, though tied to thee, thou damned whale! *Thus,* I give up the spear! (571–72)

By sinking, the *Pequod* will "perish," says Ahab. But this ship Ahab has compared to his soul. Ahab looks on at the ship, at his soul, and he calls on the waves, the "bold billows of [his] whole foregone life," to "pour" into the ship. Ahab's soul had striven to flee Ahab's daemon, and now the two float distinct on the water: the sinking Pequod as Ahab's soul; Ahab as his "queenly personality" in his whaleboat. In this Turneresque tableau, Ahab in his whaleboat floating apart from the sinking *Pequod* allegorizes the ecstatic daemon standing outside of the static soul-body. Completely his daemon, his "personality," Ahab, standing in his whaleboat, strikes out at the whale from "hell's heart," from the point of void his self is. Othello in his quest for vengeance apprehends his selfhood as a dark cave, Satan his selfhood as a hell with always a deeper hell within: the void center of Ahab, his queenly personality, strikes out from "hell's heart."

Ahab evidences a ready enmity toward the sun from the voyage's very first days ("I'd strike the sun if it insulted me"), recalling Milton's Satan ("I hate thy beams" [4.37]). Ahab's last soliloquy begins with Ahab announcing his last and irreversible turn away from the sun and toward darkness: "I turn my body from the sun." Recall Ahab's interpretation of how whales, in their last living moments, turn toward the sun; then dying, death turns them away from the sun. Ahab's turn away from the sun would seem a turn from living and toward dying. Yet, seeing the sinking ship as perishing "without" him, and so as undergoing a "lonely death on lonely life," life here being the ocean on which the ship rests, Ahab then calls on all the waves of that life, of his "whole foregone life," to "pour" into the ship with the topmost wave, Ahab's "topmost grief," being the "one piled comber of [his] death," the death overtaking the "death-glorious ship," the ship Ahab thinks of as his soul, the soul interfused with his body through his initial wounding by Moby Dick. Willing the waves of his "whole foregone life" to flood the *Pequod*, culminating with the "one piled comber of [his] death," that is, the death of his soul-body the ship, Ahab turns from his death and toward Moby Dick as a wave distinct from his life and his death: "Towards thee I roll, thou all-destroying but unconquering whale." An Achilles whose Athena prompts his fateful spear throw, the daemonic Ahab in the whaleboat then proudly undergoes the despairing ecstasy of his fate: "*Thus,* I give up the spear!"

Despite Starbuck's final imploring of Ahab's soul, Ahab persists into the moment his daemon strives for, the confrontation with Moby Dick. Despite the apparent coming to pass of Fedallah's predictions that Ahab can only die on the voyage after seeing two hearses and Fedallah himself dead yet still going before Ahab as his pilot (hearse one, Moby Dick with the dead Fedallah bound by line to the whale and still piloting Ahab; hearse two, the sinking Pequod), Ahab without hesitation throws his harpoon. Despite Fedallah's warning to Ahab, "Hemp only can kill thee," Ahab without hesitation handles the most dangerous hemp, a tangled line pulled by a whale. After Ahab spears Moby Dick, the line Moby Dick speeds downward with becomes fouled in the boat. Ahab frees the line, but a tangle loops around his neck, muting the captain while instantaneously snatching him from his whaleboat. In his Platonic boasting of the soul's immortality in the whaleman's chapel, Ishmael foreshadows for the reader this fatal contingency: "Yes, there is death in this business of whaling—a speechlessly quick chaotic bundling of a man into Eternity" (37). But in the final confrontation with Moby Dick, before he throws his harpoon, and as prelude to doing so, Ahab turns from the sun and welcomes the death of his soul in the moment of his daemon's exaltation.

Ishmael would skirt his death, slipping through dying into a whaling afterlife. Or so his thoughts about the Pequod's blacksmith suggest. Ashore, after his alcoholism brought early demise to his family, the blacksmith decides to take to the ocean. Ishmael reads this as the blacksmith substituting for suicide a whaling voyage. The blacksmith, his family dead, could commit suicide, "but Death is only a launching into the region of the strange Untried; it is but the first salutation to the possibilities of the immense Remote, the Wild, the Watery, the Unshored" (486). Ishmael thinks of death as a gateway into the wondrous unknown, a shoreless ocean. And so, to those like the blacksmith "who still have left in them some interior compunctions against suicide, does the all-contributed and all-receptive ocean alluringly spread forth his whole plain of unimaginable, taking terrors, and wonderful, new-life adventures" (486). Or this vision of an ocean voyage as substituting for death, a death by suicide, is one "the thousand mermaids sing" to those such as the blacksmith (486). From the "hearts of infinite Pacifics," these mermaids sing:

> Come hither, broken-hearted; here is another life without the guilt of intermediate death; here are wonders supernatural, without dying for them. Come hither! bury thyself in a life which, to your now equally abhorred and abhorring, landed world, is more oblivious than death. Come hither! put up thy grave-stone, too, within the churchyard, and come hither, till we marry thee! (486)

Ishmael starts his narrative telling his readers his substitute for suicide is to take to the ocean. Ishmael imagines the whaling voyage will perform for him the function the mermaids suggest: by going whaling, Ishmael gives himself a substitute for suicide and enters a wonder world. After the first lowering's casual brush with mortality, Ishmael writes his will and thinks of himself as one who has died yet who continues spectrally on observing the wonders of whaling as if he were a ghost, there yet not there. And Ishmael wishes for the moment as the beginning, a moment when no one was there. In the final paragraphs of the novel, Ishmael narrates as if he had attained this wish. First he lets Death speak via an allusion to *Paradise Lost*, and then, in the final paragraph before the "Epilogue," as at the beginning, no one speaks.

After Ahab's disappearance, and as the *Pequod* finishes sinking while Tashtego continues to hammer the flag onto the mainmast, the novel's closing allusion to *Paradise Lost* boasts of the wresting of glory from heaven:

> But as the last whelmings intermixingly poured themselves over the sunken head of the Indian at the mainmast, leaving a few inches of the erect spar yet visible, together with long streaming yards of the flag, which calmly undulated, with ironical coincidings, over the destroying billows they almost touched;—at that instant, a red arm and a hammer hovered backwardly uplifted in the open air, in the act of nailing the flag faster and yet faster to the subsiding spar. A sky-hawk that tauntingly had followed the main-truck downwards from its natural home among the stars, pecking at the flag, and incommoding Tashtego there; this bird now chanced to intercept its broad fluttering wing between the hammer and the wood; and simultaneously feeling that etherial thrill, the submerged savage beneath, in his death-grasp, kept his hammer frozen there; and so the bird of heaven, with archangelic shrieks, and his imperial beak thrust upwards, and his whole captive form folded in the flag of Ahab, went down with his ship, which, like Satan, would not sink to hell till she had dragged a living part of heaven along with her, and helmeted herself with it. (572)

In shape and gesture proud ("his imperial beak thrust upwards"), the "bird of heaven" produces "archangelic shrieks" while held against the top of the once towering yet now almost submerged mainmast. The ship is "like Satan" and "sink[s] to hell." "Satan," in the form of the *Pequod*, carries a feminine pronoun, ships traditionally being female. Ahab's "ship, [...] like Satan, would not sink to hell till she had dragged a living part of heaven along with her." In *Paradise Lost*, having sunk to hell dragging with him a rebel crew and remnants of heavenly glory, Satan, or his archangelic "form," shines female: among his comrades, Satan "above the rest / In shape and gesture proudly eminent / Stood like a tow'r; his form had yet not lost / All her original brightness, nor appear'd / Less than Archangel ruin'd" (1.589–93). Though he and his god-bullied crew have fallen, Satan rallies himself and them, and then he commands his flag be flown, "[h]is mighty standard; that proud honor claim'd / Azazel as his right, a Cherub tall: / Who forthwith from the glittering staff unfurl'd / Th' imperial ensign, which full high advanc't / Shon like a meteor streaming to the wind" (1.533–37). In the midst of the final fight with Moby Dick, with two whale-broken boats hoisted aside the *Pequod* and crewmen wielding hammers to repair them, Ahab "saw all this; as he heard the hammers in the broken boats; far other hammers seemed driving a nail into his heart. But he rallied. And now marking that the vane or flag was gone from the main-mast-head, he shouted to Tashtego, who had just gained that perch, to descend again for another flag, and a hammer and nails, and so nail it to the mast" (568–69). Atop the sinking Satan-*Pequod*, this flag of Ahab enwraps the archangelic "sky-hawk," the living part of Milton's heaven Ahab's ship helmets itself with and only then sinks to hell. The triumph-in-defeat flag of Milton's Satan becomes the flag of the Ahab about to triumph in defeat, though in *Moby-Dick* no flag officer suffers betrayal or wounding, at least none who would wreak his drive for revenge amidst and upon unknowing mortals, whether a noble Moor and his bold love or Adam and his adventurous Eve.

Whose voice articulates this boastful allusion to *Paradise Lost*? Consider the allusion again. With the hammer he is using to nail Ahab's flag to the mainmast, the drowning Tashtego there pins the sky-hawk till then hovering and pecking at the flag:

> [A]nd so the bird of heaven, with archangelic shrieks, and his imperial beak thrust upwards, and his whole captive form folded in the flag of Ahab, went down with his ship, which, like Satan, would not sink to hell till she had dragged a living part of heaven along with her, and helmeted herself with it.

These words certainly make a general allusion to *Paradise Lost*, but more specifically they allude to words Death speaks to Satan. When Satan approaches the gates of hell, and Death moves to block him, Satan insultingly demands the "execrable shape" to move aside (2.681). In reply, Death asks Satan,

> Art thou that traitor Angel, art thou he,
> Who first broke peace in Heav'n and faith, till then
> Unbrok'n; and in proud rebellious arms,
> Drew after him the third part of Heav'n's sons,
> Conjur'd against the Highest; for which both thou
> And they outcast from God, are here condemn'd
> To waste eternal days in woe and pain? (2.689–95)

The sinking *Pequod*, as Satan, "dragged a living part of heaven along with her" downward "to hell." At hell's gate Death asks if the angel confronting him is the "traitor Angel" who "[d]rew after him the third part of Heav'n's sons" down to hell. Death's words ("Drew after him the third part") imply not only leading away from fidelity but also drawing downward. Death echoes Revelation: "And there appeared [...] in heaven [...] a great red dragon [...]. And his tail drew the third part of the stars of heaven, and did cast them to the earth" (12.3–4).

When the reader reaches the novel's final allusion to *Paradise Lost*, Ishmael's distinct narrative voice has been silent for some pages. The words voicing the final *Paradise Lost* allusion do so to describe a scene in which every single human succumbs to drowning, or so the reader reasonably assumes, being yet to learn of Ishmael's survival. This assumption and the *Paradise Lost* allusion would allow the novel's words to become Death's. This penultimate voicing of all-drowning death prepares for the narrative's ultimate paragraph and ultimate voicing, in which not even personified Death, but nothing and no one speaks.

The voyage starts with a silencing of Ishmael's voice as spoken aloud to others; the narrative proceeds with the reader listening to the post-voyage Ishmael in an unspecified location. How is the reader to imagine Ishmael's virtual disappearance as narrative persona while he narrates the three-day chase? The chase drives inexorably toward general disappearance. After Ahab vanishes in the blink of an eye, after the final allusion to *Paradise Lost,* after the waters close over the sinking *Pequod,* the ultimate paragraph of the narrative confronts the reader with an empty ocean scene, empty of man, and so without time, or so Ishmael would claim: "Now small fowls flew screaming over the yet yawning gulf; a sullen white surf beat against its steep sides; then all collapsed, and the great shroud of the sea rolled on as it rolled five thousand years ago" (572). To call this scene empty hints toward the dilemma of Ishmael: he would narrate a scene bereft of all narrators, a scene from which to say he is absent is to say too much, as the scene bears no memory of him. Here culminates Ishmael's drive to achieve the time-before-time of the beginning. Five thousand years ago, God inundated all life (except a remnant on Noah's ark), and so the sea became a "great shroud" covering the vast hosts of the drowned; this flood, undoing the creation, effects a return to the waste waters of the beginning: "In the beginning God created the heaven and the earth. / And the earth was without form, and void; and darkness *was* upon the face of the deep" (Genesis 1.1–2).

Ahab ends in fidelity to his belief in nothing, in his personality, in his daemon. In doing so, he follows his muse and acts in accordance with his fate. How does Ishmael bear out in his effort to speak nothing and attain the moment as the beginning? His tale's final paragraph describes a scene as a repetition of the beginning, the flood of Noah recapitulating the void waste of water there in the beginning. In relating this scene, Ishmael imagines himself gone, so the attainment of the moment of the beginning and his own absence, even the absence of his absence, would coincide. To say nothing, to think nothing, to be nothing, there at the beginning. An adherent of Ecclesiastes as Ishmael is might wish never to have been born, the state of uncompromised nonexistence Ecclesiastes recommends as complete felicity, though one unattainable for any reader of that text. Never to have been born would allow Ishmael inexistence without his having to die. The wish of the suicide is not to exist, to enter into inexistence. For Ishmael, the voyage substitutes for suicide. In narrating the return to the beginning as a moment of his inexistence, with the ocean recapitulating Noah's flood, Ishmael would grant himself his suicidal wish. Yet only as a fiction may Ishmael narrate the inexistence of Ishmael. And so his tale's last paragraph expresses an unattainable wish, or a wish attainable only in a fiction. Entering his irreversible moment, Ahab wills his own demise, achieves his fate, and does so with exaltation, however despairing. Ishmael's desired moment, the return to the beginning, Ishmael narrates in allusion to the repetition of the beginning Noah's flood performs. Desiring a moment full of his inexistence, a moment he imagines in speaking his tale's last paragraph but a moment undone by his return in the "Epilogue," where the Job quotation "And I only am escaped alone to tell thee" begins Ishmael's concession that in the moment he narrated as if he were inexistent he actually remained existent, Ishmael must always tell his story again to regain the epiphany of his inexistence toward which his entire tale drives (573). Thus, accosting whomever he can, Ishmael lives on like Coleridge's Ancient Mariner, telling his tale again and again, without end.

Seven

A Daemon Writes:
Florian's *The Tree of No*

> Thomas McFarland, formidably defending Coleridge
> against endlessly repetitive charges of plagiarism, has
> suggested that "plagiarism" ought to be added as a
> seventh revisionary ratio.
> —Harold Bloom, "Milton and His Precursors"

Before Milton's Adam and Eve walk hand in hand from Eden, and before their reception of grace, Eve considers suicide, despairing of the anxious hours spent shuffling toward death she and Adam have given themselves and all of oncoming humanity. Eve willed to garden away from Adam. The suicidal Eve would continue to exercise her will over her existence. She would act from her volition, her self, her "I." When Eve expresses her contemplation of suicide to Adam, he tells her she appears "sublime" to him in what he calls the "contempt" for "life and pleasure" her suicidal reasoning entails (10.1014, 1018, 1019). In *Paradise Lost,* the narrator Milton applies the term "sublime" to Adam, to the air, to angels, and to Christ soaring toward battle: all entities associated with a high, exalting flight in or toward God's realm. In the dream Satan gives Eve, he brings her the mirage of such flight, though her dream-flight's arc crests at the edge delimiting the sublunary from the celestial. For Adam to call Eve sublime acknowledges her potential membership in the exalted company of flyers, yet in the very sentence Adam offers this praise, he withdraws it:

Eve, thy contempt of life and pleasure seems
To argue in thee something more sublime
And excellent than what thy mind contemns;
But self-destruction therefore sought, refutes
That excellence thought in thee, and implies,
Not thy contempt, but anguish and regret
For loss of life and pleasure overlov'd.

                                                    (10.1013–19)

Adam manages to praise and to blame Eve simultaneously, with the blame taking away from Eve the sublimity the praise attributes to her. Adam explains to Eve how her excessive desire ("overlov'd") belies what she "seems": "sublime." So Adam qualifies his belated recognition of Eve as possessing a capacious "mind" open to transport. The "mind" of Eve "seems" to disdain "life and pleasure," and this appearance implies within her exists "something more sublime" than the life and pleasure her mind looks down upon as from a height. A reader of *Paradise Lost* and an exponent of sublimity, Immanuel Kant might claim in Eve supersensible Reason casts judgment on all the sensible.[1] Eve's apparent sublimity of mind resembles the stance toward the earth Raphael sought to teach Adam: to disdain earthly life and pleasure and aim toward heavenly life and pleasure. Adam's ability to do so would evidence his participation in the rationality God pinnacles, and Adam's prefall task was to educate Eve upward toward such rationality so she too could boast a mind fully human.

Eve cannot win for losing. Adam asserts her declaration for suicide "refutes / That [sublime] excellence" the unwary reader might find "in" her. No, rather than high-minded "contempt" for the earthly, Adam finds in Eve "anguish and regret / For loss of life and pleasure overlov'd." To seek an end declares a will, yet by her will Eve willed to walk away from Adam in the garden so she could work separately. By this will Eve earlier had willed to walk back to the lake, turning from the Adam she found less desirable than the image beckoning on the water. At the lake, first a voice, perhaps God's, tells Eve her desire only intends the image of her self, and then Adam, using words but also force, persuades

Eve to yield her desire. When Adam tells Eve her will to suicide "implies" not her "contempt" for "life and pleasure" but her errant "anguish" over the loss of what she loves too much, he is again pedantically chastising her desire.

Adam further argues to Eve that God would likely not allow them to find in self-caused death a refuge from punishment and pain. Rather, Adam proposes the two seek God's forgiveness. Adam again persuades Eve to give her will over; Eve renounces suicide when Adam persuades her to join him in prayer to beg God's forgiveness. Eve's renunciation of suicide and agreement to accept Adam's task of prayer signal the final eclipse of the willful Eve who insisted on gardening separately from Adam, the Eve whose desire always was troubling to the divine order.

Perhaps in walking away from Adam in Eden to garden independently, Eve intimates a pedestrian, horizontal, and earthbound sublime distinct from the sublime of vertical, heavenward flight. Imagine if, unmoved by Adam's persuasions to kneel and pray for forgiveness, the Eve who proposes suicide were to walk away from the trees of life and knowledge, taking her narrator Milton with her out from Eden to stroll down a road stretching beyond sight, an amble always foreshortening to a moment's step. Imagine Eve nicknaming her companion "Montgomery," perhaps after the British poet James Montgomery (1771–1854), author of *The World Before the Flood* (1812), ten cantos of heroic couplets on Adam, Eve, and their progeny post-Eden and pre-flood, or even more satirically, after the British poet Robert Montgomery (1807–1855), author of *Satan, or Intellect without God* (1830).[2] Imagine this mortal Eve somehow existing from the beginning to the end of time. Beginning, time begins ending, time being finite and through clocks a questionable prosthesis for parceling out the flashing moment. Imagine this willful, moment-hungry Eve telling her own story, from her first tryst with Adam in the Paradise of Genesis to her tour of the apocalypse of Revelation and on toward time's end.

Would this Eve answer to the interpellation "woman"? In *Paradise Lost*, the official line of Milton the narrator is that Eve, as the woman, should be subordinate to the man, Adam, or at least the narrator makes such statements by virtually quoting Paul, though without acknowledgement. Paul would spirit away the "I" in imitating Christ. By asserting herself in her wish to garden separately from Adam, Milton's Eve asserts her "I" and, walking away from Adam to garden alone, she walks away from the category "woman" the Pauline narrator Milton deploys. Besides the plants and trees, in the garden are: the man (Adam), the woman (Eve), and the beasts. The Eve who walks away may be unthinkable via the category "woman" Adam as the garden's supervisor recognizes. Or better: the willfully walking away Eve would be unthinkable by the category "man" as the designation by which Milton androcentrically names the prayerful Adam *and* Eve who would find and accept man's place in the hierarchy descending from God, to Christ, to man, to beast. The category "man" would move Adam above and away from the beastly. Imagine the Eve of self-assertion walking away from Adam to garden, encountering the serpent, eating the forbidden fruit, giving Adam the fruit to eat, laying with Adam lustily, and then rather than repenting, walking on, perambulating away from the garden altogether.

Such an unrepentant Eve would be very similar to the gender-anonymous first-person narrator of Sandy Florian's novel *The Tree of No*. Florian retells and rewrites the Biblical and Miltonic stories of the fall, taking her readers from Genesis to Revelation. The narrator of *The Tree of No* wakes to desire in a "scarlet garden, grounded by growth and considerable in size" (1). The narrator enjoys a tryst with Adam and then encounters one Montgomery, who is "celestially lying in the carved-out coffin" (2). This coffin rests "under the tree of no" (2). Having fallen in love with Montgomery while becoming subject to time, the narrator walks from the garden with Montgomery and undertakes deforestation to build roads and a city. *The Tree of No* ends with the narrator unpraying prayers and asserting the first-person pronoun: "It's Christmas at the introduction to our father who art in heaven, hallowed be thy name. Small turns. I am still waking. But the sin in me says I" (111).

Florian's narrator speaks the entire novel. Florian gives her narrator the chance to bypass the Miltonic gender system and speak in a language, an idiom of English, resistant to and even unknowable by the Logos or Son. In *Paradise Lost,* God explains to his son how, though Adam and Eve will fall, and all humanity will be born fallen, "Man shall not quite be lost, but sav'd who will; / Yet not of will in him, but grace in me" (3.173–74). Setting aside the "will," this grace shall "soft'n stony hearts / To pray, repent, and bring obedience due. / To prayer, repentance, and obedience due, / Though but endeavour'd with sincere intent, / Mine ear shall not be slow, mine eye not shut" (3.189–93). "To pray, repent, and bring obedience due": the prayers of repentance of the fallen and kneeling Adam and Eve imply their offer of obedience through their surrender of their wills. Rather than from any paradoxical will to abandon the will, their relinquishment of will comes through grace. This grace allows their prayers to become words without will and therefore worthy to appear before God. With grace spiriting away the will, the words become wholly without letter, sin, or flesh; the words become icons of spirit.

When Adam and Eve's prayers reach God by way of Christ's mediation, the first couple's words undergo in that mediation a transformation into iconic images of the kneeling supplicants. Christ or the Logos transubstantiates the words of the prayers into images of entire obedience in subordination. Through Christ, the redeemable spirit of the prayer-words separates out completely from their irredeemable, fleshly letters. Thus, when Christ presents the prayers to God, rather than reading letters, God sees icons. In the saying of these prayers as Christ mediates them and grace allows for them, the images of Adam and Eve enter Heaven, as if these images had achieved the long process of sublimation toward the capacity to eat heavenly food Raphael had suggested Adam and Eve undertake. This process Adam and Eve may have completed without Christ's mediation, the two being then as yet unfallen. Once fallen, only with the mediation of the Logos may the pair, or as yet their holograms, enter heaven. Christ sublimes Adam and Eve's prayers by a sublimation similar to the alchemical conversion of a solid into a gas, as when in Chaucer's *Canterbury Tales* the Canon's Yeoman mentions the "sublymyng" of solid substances into "eyr."[3] Prayers: the noun can refer to the persons praying or to the prayers the prayers pray. From the fallen flesh uttering the prayers Christ lifts the prayers up as spirit. The prayers' flesh remains earthbound as the prayers undergo sublimation, become sublime. The prayers as holographic images achieve the high flight to heaven, though only in the posture of kneeling. These images prefigure the selfless state to which Adam and Eve might attain after the apocalypse when all the beloved of God, through Christ, become one with God, Adam's self and especially Eve's undergoing decreation, to use Simone Weil's problematic term (*The Tree of No* gently wrestles Weil's *Gravity and Grace* to the ground).

For the eternal oneness, the entire wholeness, of the "all in all" to come about, all the differences God fleshed out in the beginning he, through Christ, must call back up and in, so "God shall be all in all," as if God were somehow to inhale in a single tremendous gasp all the breath he exhaled in the beginning to let the creation be, this inhalation reversing the contraction (the Kabbalist *tzimtzum*) of God by which he allowed for the creation as distinct from himself, an inhalation reinflating God so nothing other, nothing other than God, remains (3.341). This inhalation being then eternal, never again would any divine breathing occur. Never again would any beloved of God exist apart from God. All the apart, any part, would undergo entire sublimation into the whole the all in all promises to be, each part disappearing as a part that could ever be apart. As Milton's Christ says to his father: "Thou shalt be All in All, and I in thee / For ever, and in me all whom thou lov'st" (6.732–33). The first-person speaker, Christ, the second person addressee, the Father, and the third-person "all," the beloveds, shall become one, "All in All." Eve never again will be apart from Adam, who never will be apart from Christ, who never will be apart from the Father. Dissolving the grammatical differences of first, second, and third persons, collapsing the triad of desire, the all in all as limitlessly unitary wholeness or oneness would suspend desire, as if a Narcissus could love without his image echoing in any medium and without any Echo sounding to pine and ache for him.

In Milton's retelling of Echo and Narcissus, rather than there being a female voice echoing vainly to a male gazer who never leaves the water, Eve as Narcissus looks into the lake and a divine voice calls her away toward Adam. About this situation Florian's narrator dreams, but the dream weaves Eve's encounter with the serpent into the just-awakened Eve's encounter with the image in the lake:

> I was sitting at the edge of a kidney-shaped lake. I thought to myself, Where? then, Who? But I did not have the faculties of resolve. Sensing that my solitude had been intruded, I called out, and I heard a sharp reply. I looked around seeing no one but myself, so again I called out, and again I heard the sharp reply. My fear grew with the rustling of leaves. Then I thought to myself, this desolate awakening is infernal. This eternal echo, my destiny. (5)

Florian's narrator awakens to ask where and who the narrator is, yet where and who the narrator is precisely is the narrator's awakening self-consciousness. Rather than the divine voice Eve hears at the lake, the narrator hears "the rustling of leaves." In *Paradise Lost*, Satan in the serpent obliquely approaches the lone-gardening Eve and attempts to catch her eye. Eve hears but ignores the dead, fallen leaves the serpent causes to rustle: "[S]he busied heard the sound / Of rustling leaves, but minded not, as us'd / To such disport before her through the field, / From every beast, more duteous at her call, / Than at Circean call the herd disguis'd" (9.518–22). Florian's narrator senses an intrusion upon "solitude," calls out, hears an echoing reply, and looks for the source of the reply: "seeing no one but myself, [...] again I called out." Again the narrator receives "the sharp reply." And then the leaves rustle. In contrast, in *Paradise Lost*, the leaf-rustling Satan approaches the gardening-focused Eve absent her "Circean call": "He bolder now, uncall'd before her stood; / But as in gaze admiring" (9.523–24). Satan's admiring gaze echoes the gaze of Eve upon the image on the lake. Milton's Eve is "Circean" not only in that "every beast" obeys "her call" but also because her bewitching image arouses in Adam the desires Raphael says are common to beasts. Florian's "Circean" narrator calls out the beast in earth, air, and land creatures (118). At the lake in the dream, this narrator does call out, and "the rustling of leaves" increases the narrator's "fear," the narrator sensing something Satanic or infernal: "Then I thought to myself, this desolate awakening is infernal. This eternal echo, my destiny." In *Paradise Lost*, the image in the lake echoes Eve but a divine voice calls her to Adam. In *The Tree of No*, the narrator calls out and receives an echoing reply and in the entire absence of God's voice, the leaves rustle, and being as consciousness of self threatens to become the narrator's Satanic fate.

The narrator of *The Tree of No* awakens into an interminable consciousness: "In the beginning was the word, a cock, a cry, a bell, a blast, angels sing to manifest the dim undim unsetting sun, as the devil himself impels us onward. To a revolving ontology of consciousness" (4). Echoing the leaves Satan stirs in *Paradise Lost*, the dead and fallen leaves Florian's narrator hears rustle become emblematic of revolving thoughts: the narrator's "thoughts go round and round, like a little carousel with skeletal leaves" (7). Being, like Milton's Eve, a creature of shade, Florian's narrator describes the time most without shadows, noon, as hellish, as "the sun's high hell" (4). When consciousness predicates being, and being becomes without end as interminable consciousness, then the "sun" as an emblem of consciousness becomes "unsetting," and the awakening into consciousness without end becomes "infernal": "this desolate awakening is infernal" (5).

In the King James Bible, the phrase "world without end" appears twice and suggests everlasting salvation for Israel (Isaiah 45.17) and eternal glory for the diligent in Christ's cause (Ephesians 3.21). But in the medieval morality play *Everyman*, on God's orders, Death seeks out all persons to bring them to account, and Death turns the phrase "world without end" toward damnation. Death: "Every man will I beset that liveth beastly / Out of God's laws, and dreadeth not folly."[4] (74–75). The "beastly" who embrace "folly," those who "loveth riches," Death will "strike with [his] dart" and separate from "heaven" for an interminable residence in "hell" or an infernal world: "In hell for to dwell, world without end" (76, 77, 79). In *Paradise Lost*, to describe an interminable situation, the narrator Milton and other characters use the phrase "without end." With such beastliness as *Everyman* condemns and Raphael scorns, Florian's narrator begins: "Beastly, I fall at Adam under the shade" (1).

Paradise Lost anticipates God being all in all without end. Florian's narrator, who will favor the end over the beginning of the end, yet who will begin in the end, speaks from the position of the "not all." In *Paradise Lost,* the prayer-images of Adam and Eve Christ brings before God are silent. This becoming silent of the speech of prayer happens through Christ, the Logos, subliming the words of Adam and Eve from their bodies of sin. Rather than as the image of a wholeness (a holiness), of a body lifted up by the Logos and made whole or one, Florian's narrator speaks from a body Socrates would diagnose as marked by transgressions, Socrates in the *Gorgias* figuring transgressions' wounds to the soul as wounds on the body.[5] Florian has her narrator describe the narrator's own body as covered with wounds: "I realize in this new waking dream that I'm covered in all sorts of wounds. In bruises, gashes, lesions, slashes, and there's tumors on my cankerous tongue, until I open my brand new mouth and start screaming all over again" (3). Florian's narrator breaks with silence, screaming. Rather than cleansing prayers of postlapsarian earthiness for presentation to God, Florian's narrator ponders "transgressive speech and its relationship to the metropolis" (13). Of what is this speech the transgression, and how does this speech relate "to the metropolis"? To explore these questions requires asking another: how does the narrator first encounter Montgomery?

The narrator's fall into love with Montgomery and the garden's fall to the city are aspects of a single event. The narrator and Montgomery initially meet in their crossing from garden to metropolis. In this shift from an always already disappearing pastoral location to a city a complete necropolis shadows, the invention of tropes regarding the city happens out of a revision of the *topoi* or commonplaces of the pastoral and its fate. Harold Bloom asks, "Is a literary place, by pragmatic definition, a city?"[6] "However solitary a major writer is by vocation," in and through city encounters "he or she tends to find a closest friend in a contemporary literary artist" (x). Not only are cities "the essential requisite for literary relationships," but the "movement from garden to city" defines much of literature (x). Given these factors, Bloom heralds the city as *"the given* of literature" (x).

Consider Babylon a primordial metropolis of the literary, the Babylonian epic *Gilgamesh* being deep background to the Hebrew Bible and so to literature in English. The demoness Lilith, "the flying one," hails from Babylon. Or rather, her Babylonian associations partially come out of a Sumerian poem about her being driven from a garden tree. In an albeit disputable translation and interpretation, this Sumerian poem, a precursor to *Gilgamesh*, has Lilith making her home in the tree from which Gilgamesh's sister Inanna hopes to make a bed and a throne: "Then a serpent who could not be charmed / Made its nest in the roots of the *huluppu*-tree. / The *Anzu*-bird set his young in the branches of the tree. / And the dark maid Lilith built her home in the trunk."[7] The startled Inanna finds these creatures inhabiting the tree she cultivated to supply wood for the making of her city furniture. Gilgamesh helps Inanna rid her tree of these infestations. After Gilgamesh kills the serpent, "[T]he *Anzu*-bird flew with his young to the mountains; / And Lilith smashed her home and fled to the wild, uninhabited places" (9). Gilgamesh then uses wood from the tree to make a throne and a bed for Inanna (9). In effect, *Gilgamesh* and literature get a start with the chasing away of Lilith and the cutting down of the tree she had claimed as her home.

Driven from her tree, Lilith migrates into the Hebrew Bible. The prophet Isaiah describes how Yahweh dooms the kingdom of Edom to his wrath and destruction. Yahweh will bring such "chaos" that the "nobles" of Edom "shall name it No Kingdom There, and all its princes shall be nothing": "It shall be the haunt of jackals, an abode for ostriches. Wildcats shall meet with hyenas, goat-demons shall call to each other; there too Lilith shall repose, and find a place to rest" (34.11, 12, 13–14).[8] From the jackal-infested kingdom of "No," a desolate, anonymous "There," Lilith moves on to Jewish folklore, appearing in the satirical *Alphabet of Ben Sira* (c. 800 CE) as the first wife of Adam who, refusing his insistence he be on top in the missionary position, flies away to the sea where Yahweh's angels find her. The angels insist on dragging her back to Yahweh, but she refuses, and the angels threaten to drown her.

Lilith avoids this fate by agreeing that each day one hundred of her demon children shall die and that amulets bearing the names of her pursuing angels (Snvi, Snsvi, and Smnglof) will have the power to prevent her from harming newborns.[9]

In *The Tree of No*, a tapestry depicts the garden *topos* the novel's narrator must revise to invent tropes of the city she builds. The tapestry threatens to stifle this process. Florian has her narrator state, "My sentences appear to expect an actor or an actress," and the actress who steps forward is Lilith (62). Or rather, Lilith fights to step forward: "My actress struggles to make her appearance from behind her probable tapestry" (62). This tapestry stifling Lilith "displays the Garden of Eden" (62). Though the narrator's "sentences" "expect" an actress (or an actor), the "setting" of these sentences "clearly calls for a study" (62). The actress Lilith shuttles between a study and a city, yet: "Alone, she cannot invent a reason for what she has done in the city before she returns to the study" (62). What has she done in the city? Recall the narrator's concern with "the issue of transgressive speech and its relationship to the metropolis." In the city, speech transgresses, but this transgression depends on a break with the garden.

Before the narrator brings her forward as Lilith, the actress "stands impatiently waiting behind the tapestry [...] with bloodstains on her white chemise, knife dripping from her swollen hand" (62). For her act in the city she would, in the study, "invent" a "reason," yet she "cannot." This blockage of invention correlates to her struggle to step from behind the tapestry of the garden. Bloom takes the cherubim blocking the way back into Eden to emblematize the blocking element a poet must overcome to attain to sublimity.[10] For Florian's Lilith, the tapestry depicting Eden becomes that blocking entity, getting back to Eden not being the problem. Rather, Eden as stifling to Lilith is the problem.

In *Margins of Philosophy*, Derrida writes, "Not only is there no kingdom of *différance*, but *différance* instigates the subversion of every kingdom."[11] Where *différance* operates, there is no kingdom there. The force Yahweh brings to Edom, entirely dismantling any semantic order denoting a kingdom, quakes Edom into the "No Kingdom There" where Lilith may find rest with scandalous beasts. Such force operates in *The Tree of No*. After the narrator brings the actress forward to the reader as having "talons for feet," as having "wings," as having argued with Adam "in the bedroom," as "lodging in the middle of a tree trunk," as preying on "children and women enfeebled by pregnancy," and so on, that is, as being Lilith, the actress attains some solace: "But, now, behind the tapestry, my actress reposes perfectly, splendidly, without bloodstains on her clean chemise and acquires a perfect resting place in the white margins of my white pages" (62). In the "white margins" of *The Tree of No* Lilith finds "a perfect resting place." Though Lilith still stands behind the tapestry, the narrator takes the reading eye from the tapestry to the "white margins" of the narrator's "white pages" where Lilith finds repose, these margins becoming another "No Kingdom There." In reading the novel's very "sentences," the reader confronts these "white margins" of "white pages." In *The Tree of No,* contesting and evading the supervisory Logos, a tremendous revisionary force operates through a pervasive short-circuiting of semantic expectations to render the novel's English a "No Kingdom There" where invention burgeons and Lilith finds a place.

Florian's narrator speaks a language of and from the "beastly." This language neither answers to Christ the Logos nor seeks answerability to the Platonist *logos* without for all that eschewing logic or reason. The sentences the narrator produces pursue another logic, a logic other than the logic of the "all in all," of wholeness, of becoming one, of desire's suspension. The narrator's language requires of the reader some letting go. To read *The Tree of No,* the reader needs to learn again how to read. Part of this relearning involves instruction of the reader by the novel as to what a writerly consciousness may or may not be or even toward accepting a writerly consciousness or narrator so skeptical of and indifferent toward omniscience as to walk away from protocols of coherence insofar as such mask in the readerly endpoint of articulate meaning a subordination to and obligatory conjugation of oneness as a semantic ideal or a semantic unity inevitably implying a world behind or beyond "this world," behind or beyond these words, this world where the beasts are, the world where Paul says sin happens, the words in which sin happens.

Paradise Lost foregoes any moment such as that in *Ulysses* when Molly calls out to her author Joyce, "O Jamesy let me up out of this pooh sweets of sin."[12] When Milton's Eve prays to be forgiven and redeemed from the "sweets of sin," from the fallen world and death, the wages of sin, she addresses the absent Christ she and Adam took for God the Father when Christ came down from Heaven to Eden for the first couple's judgment. The narrator Milton speaks about Eve but never to her, even though his muse takes him to witness the events in Heaven and in Eden. Neither Sin nor Eve ever speaks to Milton. In *The Tree of No*, this situation undergoes a complex reversal: the narrator speaks about the novel's Milton, alias Montgomery, and the narrator reports the interactions and conversations the narrator has with Montgomery. Unlike Molly in relation to Joyce, Florian's narrator resists being at the mercy of Montgomery and strives to be a writer: "In a word, in irreverence for the god-like, no matter what, no matter how, a wretched writer" (64). The narrator wills to be a writer rather than an author, if authorship implies omniscience, the omnipotent locating of each word as a part wholly one with the whole.

Paradise Lost's narrator Milton calls Satan "the Author of all ill" (2.381). Sin says to Satan, "Thou art my father, thou my author, thou / My being gav'st me" (2.864–65). In Heaven, all the angels loyal to God ("No voice exempt, no voice but well could join / Melodious part, such concord is in Heav'n") declare God the "Author of all being" (3.370–71, 374). Milton calls Adam, the creaturely father to humankind, "[o]ur author" (5.397). Before eating the fruit, Eve says to Adam, "My author and disposer, what thou bidd'st, / Unargued I obey; so God ordains, / God is thy law, thou mine" (4.635–37). God angrily lumps "Man" in with the fallen angels as all being the "authors" of their own falls and revolts, yet nowhere in *Paradise Lost* does anyone ever call Sin or Eve the author of anything, even though both arguably are the authors of the crucial events of the epic, directly of Satan's fall and Adam's, and so indirectly of all the consequences, that is, the epic's story at large (3.130, 122). Or perhaps Sin and Eve more resemble writers in Barthes's sense of the term. Contemplating how Milton withholds the epithet "author" from them, Sin and Eve could each very justly arch a quizzical eyebrow. Wanting to be a writer "in irreverence for the god-like," Florian's narrator resembles, not the loyal angels uniformly subordinate to God, not the Eve who calls Adam her author, but the Satan who claims to be his own author, or perhaps Sin, who flatters Satan by calling him her author but who conceived herself in his head, willing herself into being more so than he ever does, more her own writer than he, a surprise to Satan but never to herself.

Whether rebelling or repentantly standing before Christ, thinking him God, author of all, the Eve of *Paradise Lost* knows nothing of Milton. Does Milton have the loyal angels call God the author of all being to distract readers from Milton's authorship of Eve? Yet is Eve simply of the realm of being? Perhaps Milton's God authors all being, and more potentially mortifying to Milton, he, Milton, perhaps authors precisely nothing, a lapse from being, an errance, or merely the will of Eve toward freedom, Eve being to Milton almost but not quite what Sin is to Satan. The will to freedom Milton grants Eve allows for the fiction of her unrepentantly walking out on her subordinate station in God's great *chain* of being. In this chain, the man, or Adam as erect, stands over Eve, as she exists in her place. Milton nobly writes of his God as the Holy Spirit that He "dost prefer / Before all temples th' upright heart and pure" (1.17–18). This uprightness, and Adam's erectness, hint toward immortality, as if, in the oneness with God, the "all in all," there will be neither beds nor coffins, nary a place for proneness, for sleep, for death. Milton died. Milton is dead. Whatever of him now existent rests prone entombed in St. Giles at Cripplegate, London. In 1793, one Verger Elizabeth Grant opened Milton's tomb and charged visitors for a peek.[13] What were the conditions of Milton's remains then, more than a century after his death? What are they now, with more than three centuries gone by since 1674? How far flat may bones settle into dust? Does the increasingly level proneness of Milton's remains over the centuries suggest the erosion of the hierarchical chain of being the narrator Milton adumbrates in *Paradise Lost?* Milton received a letter dated 6 June 1666, an auspiciously satanic (666) date: the letter reported the rumor of his death.[14] On 6 June 1966, Sandy Florian was born. Barthes believes "the birth of the reader must be at the cost of the death of the Author."[15] Yet since the claim to write death, to write as from beyond death, to write the death of the author, implies godlike authorial omnipotence, *The Tree of No* stages the death of the death of the author. As a reader of *Paradise Lost*, Florian thinks through the birth of her narrator as writer through the death of the death of an Author, here the coffin-bound yet still feisty Montgomery.

In *The Tree of No*, Montgomery appears prone in a coffin, while the upright narrator walks. The love of the narrator for Montgomery, the narrator's repeatedly falling in love with Montgomery, the narrator addresses as follows:

> If you press me to tell you why I love him, I feel that reason itself cannot be expressed, except by the echo, because it is he, because it is I, because it is he, because it is I. (2)

The emendation-minded reader might want to insert a "the" in the phrase "that reason itself," so that the narrator would be saying "that [the] reason itself" why the narrator loves Montgomery "cannot be expressed." However, this emendation would iron out an important ambiguity. Is the narrator suggesting that the "why" of the narrator's love for Montgomery, "that reason" for which the narrator does love him, is inexpressible, or is the narrator saying that "reason itself," reason in general, "cannot be expressed," and this inexpressibility of reason *per se* is at stake in any attempt to answer the question as to why the narrator loves Montgomery? This ambiguity allows the reader to realize that the inexpressibility of the specific reason why the narrator loves Montgomery is caught up in the inexpressibility of "reason itself." Readers of *The Tree of No* traverse a sublime literary defile where what reason is or might be is at stake.

The narrator tells the reader that the inexpressibility of the reason, or of reason in general, admits of an exception. The reason or reason in general may be expressed as follows: "because it is he, because it is I, because it is he, because it is I." In this "echo," the "it" serves as a placeholder alternatively for the "he" and for the "I." How should the reader think of the "it" each in turn is, "he" then "I"? The narrator's reason for loving Montgomery is logically prior to (even if existentially simultaneous with) the narrator's fall into love with Montgomery. The "it" marks how the reason for the love, the "because," comes down to the sheer contingent facticity of the "he" and the "I." In the passage in question, the pronoun "it" functions without any specific antecedent, referencing anonymous being. An encounter in this anonymity, awash in the bath of this anonymity, draws the lover-to-be world-ward, throws the lover downward and outward. The lover falls, inhabiting a world utterly drained of any aura of a world above or beyond, of any world besides the world there.

In the universe of *Paradise Lost,* an ultimate good, a *summum bonum,* orients all reasoning, that is, all obedience to God, as resulting ultimately in the obedient entering into oneness ("all in all") with God as mediated by Christ, by the Word or Logos. In this case, the final purpose of all reasoning, the *summum bonum* of oneness with God, corresponds with the highest being, God in his oneness and as the *summum genus* subsuming all beings. Florian's narrator states, "Absolute generic unity would be obtained if there were one summum genus under which all things could be subsumed. Beings and experiences are candidates for this position" (9). Let me underline the narrator's "if." This "if," along with the words of the rest of these two sentences, the narrator appropriates, almost verbatim, from William James's lecture "The One and the Many" in James's book *Pragmatism: A New Name for Some Old Ways of Thinking.*[16] In *Paradise Lost,* regarding the question whether a *summum* exists, there is no "if" involved, as "God supreme" fills "this position" (7.515). In *Paradise Lost,* Raphael advises Adam to rise (not fall) in love. Raphael urges Adam to love in Eve what may become man, or potentially fully human, that is, fully an image of God, of the one, of oneness. Such love would accord with reason, Raphael argues. The love and the reason together would lift Adam toward the one as Adam lifts Eve up from the beastly and toward man and the heavenly. What happens to reason and to love in a pragmatic world utterly disoriented from any *summum bonum* or *summum genus*?

Rather than rising in love with Montgomery, the narrator falls in love with Montgomery. Rather than love lifting the lovers toward an "all in all" or any "Absolute generic unity," toward any pinnacle of oneness serving to orient reason, the narrator in falling in love with Montgomery confronts an inexpressibility of reason. Just prior to stating the hypothetical condition of *"Absolute* generic unity," the existence of a *"summum genus,"* James ponders a world devoid of any *"generic unity"* whatsoever, devoid of the belonging of a thing to a "kind" or generic set (140, 139). Such belonging would allow reason to deduce from this belonging the traits of a particular example from the traits of the genre. A world devoid of *"generic unity"* would be a world where "every fact" remains "singular" (139). In this "world of singulars" James imagines, "logic would be useless" because logical deductions require the subsumption of particulars under genres: "With no two things alike in the world, we should be unable to reason from our past experiences to our future ones" (139, 140). James rejects such an absolute manyness, just as he rejects absolute oneness. James argues readers can still accept the phrase he places in quotation marks, "'The world is One,'" but: "It is neither a universe pure and simple nor a multiverse pure and simple" (148). This claim goes with a demotion of oneness from holding an absolute value. Between oneness and manyness, "[n]either is primordial or more essential or excellent than the other" (138). This refusal to embrace oneness to the exclusion of manyness or vice versa shows how, writes James, "pragmatism tends to *unstiffen* all our theories" (159). The parts gain a relative freedom from the whole, and this freedom challenges the Absolute, whether as *summum bonum* or *summum genus* or both:

> The One and All, first in the order of being and of knowing, logically necessary itself, and uniting all lesser things in the bonds of mutual necessity, how could it allow of any mitigation of its inner rigidity? The slightest suspicion of

> pluralism, the minutest wiggle of independence of any one
> of its parts from the control of the totality would ruin it.
> (159–60)

Should any part exhibit or retain "the most incipient nascency, or
the most residual trace, of a separation that is not 'overcome,'" then
"absolute monism is shattered" (161, 160). In effect, when Eve asks
to garden separately or apart from Adam, she asserts her relative
freedom as a part of the whole of God's creation. If a part exhibits
freedom from the whole, Absolutes go by the wayside, including
any *absolute* aesthetic oneness or unity: "*Absolute* aesthetic union is
thus another barely abstract ideal" (144).

In the "Addenda" to his novel *Watt*, Samuel Beckett offers
a relevant formulation: "limits to part's equality with whole."[17]
Beckett's incisive use here of the word "equality" speaks to Eve's
situation. As a part of the creation, she is to strive to become
Adam's equal insofar as Adam evidences reason and the rational
obedience that allows Adam to be in God's image and to, in
principle, become one with God, such as in the "all in all." Yet if
Eve were fully to attain this equality, she would disappear, her
distinct difference from Adam inhering in her desire, which has
no place in the "all in all." Wallace Stevens: "Both in nature and
in metaphor identity is the vanishing point of resemblance."[18]
The vanishing point of Eve approaches when her resemblance
to Adam, her increasing rationality, attains to identity: the final
realization of her equality with Adam would vanish her in
identity with him, as his completely imaging God through the
mediation of Christ would vanish Adam into God as "all in all."
Yet, in *Paradise Lost,* as long as Eve remains different than Adam,
she will be subordinate to Adam. Beckett is quite specific: there
are "limits" rather than a limit to the "part's equality with the
whole." One limit would be the part's disappearance into the
whole in being equal to or one with the whole, which would
vanish the relation of equality. Another limit to any equality of
the part with the whole would be the part's subordination to
the whole insofar as the part remains distinct from the whole.
And if the part only exists as a part insofar as some distinctness

from the whole persists, separation from the whole may happen as a contingency inherently available to the part as a part. This limit to the part's equality with the whole suggests the part's occurrence does not necessarily imply the whole's occurrence: the part may occur without the whole occurring. Eve may garden separately, may exist without implying the existence of the whole chain of being. Another example: a sentence from James's *Pragmatism* speculating on yet dismissing "Absolute generic unity," absolute wholeness, may occur in *The Tree of No* without the whole of *Pragmatism* reoccurring there in the novel, though James implicitly relinquishes in advance any claim to his work's absolute unity or original wholeness. A great many of the sentences, phrases, and even letters of *The Tree of No* are parts the narrator takes from various and sundry works. These parts occur in the novel without the whole of the works reoccurring. That is, these parts undergo a kind of liberation from their wholes, almost as when a thief or rebel says, "I liberated _____ from _____." However, reference to the works the narrator appropriates from remains active, allowing the liberated parts to imply various rich *hommages* to and myriad ironic statements about those works. The part offers an ironic perspective on the whole as the part bids the whole farewell. What the anxious pedant would call plagiarism becomes, through Florian's pen, a sublime exercise of what Bloom calls a revisionary ratio: the breaking in of feeling, thought, and wonder becomes all the more intense given the intensity of the ironic remarkings and hommagic reworkings taking place in the breaking of words out from the works of precursors. To an irreducible degree, the interpretation of *The Tree of No* then becomes a given reader's response to and assessment of the *hommages* and ironies resonant with that given reader's literacy. There will be as many *Trees of No* as there will be readers of the text yet with each reader reading the very same book, the book undergoing the intractable, irreversible singularity of itself and its fate. Florian's is as courageous an imagination as a reader could hope or dare to encounter.

The Tree of No solicits the occurrence of multiple and divergent readings, an occurrence James could only applaud, an occurrence both exemplifying James's notion of limited unity and taking James's thoughts elsewhere. *The Tree of No* exhibits numerous (yet how might a reader count them?) sentences, phrases, words, and, yes, letters, why not, the narrator takes and grafts onto or makes into the narrator's letters, words, phrases, sentences, and paragraphs. The novel engages in such grafting, thinks about grafting, lets the grafts articulate thoughts or perform significations straying from their sources like an Eve from her Adam, and poses the exegete with dilemmas. Any effort to read the novel toward some unity of meaning, affect, or thought becomes naïve and unknowing. If the reader claims to know, then the novel blithely poses knowledge as a problem.

Consider the following sentences from *The Tree of No:* "If it's true that one often needs the spur, it is also true that one often needs the curb. Sublimity is the echo of the great soul" (54). These sentences come from the W. Rhys Roberts translation of Longinus's *On the Sublime.* In that treatise, Longinus famously echoes himself by quoting his own line from a now lost work. To attain the "elevation of mind" necessary for sublimity,

> We must [...] nurture our souls (as far as that is possible) to thoughts sublime, and make them always pregnant, so to say, with noble inspiration. In what way, you may ask, is this to be done? Elsewhere I have written as follows: "Sublimity is the echo of a great soul." (81)

With fine equivocation, Longinus says "elevation of mind," or the quality of mind conducive to "thoughts sublime," is "an endowment" rather than "an acquirement" (81). Longinus seems to claim that a writer is capable of the sublime due to an inherited rather than an acquired trait, yet he states the soul receives "noble inspiration" as a woman becomes "pregnant." And then he impregnates himself or his own discourse with his own previously birthed thought. What exactly might the difference be between an "endowment" and an "acquirement," especially when Longinus acquires "elevation of mind" by endowing himself with his own sublime thought to "nurture" himself "to thoughts sublime"? Without hesitation, indeed with great gusto, Florian, or her narrator, appropriates the sentence "Sublimity is the echo of a great soul" and would usurp whatever "endowment" or "acquirement" of "sublime thoughts" that may accrue.

In *Paradise Lost* Milton lets myriad forerunners echo amidst sections of narration and dialog. The narrator of *The Tree of No* does so as well, except, like Longinus, the narrator echoes precursors by quoting them verbatim or almost verbatim. An ambitious yet mocking essay in poetics, the section of the novel (53–57) in which the echo-quote from Longinus's *On the Sublime* appears also quotes from or alludes to, among other works, Horace's *Art of Poetry*, Aristotle's *Poetics*, Plotinus's *Enneads* (those treating beauty), Boethius's *The Consolation of Philosophy*, and Sir Philip Sidney's *An Apology for Poetry* (also known as *The Defence of Poesy*). Winding its way through these authors' notions of the poet as a maker (poet, from the Latin *poēta*, from Greek *poiētēs*, maker, composer, from *poiein*, to create), this section ends by asking about the genesis of the poet or maker thought on the model of the god of Genesis:

> After all, who is the maker of the maker? Having made his own maker in his own likeness? Having set his maker in his likeness above and beyond the works of his own second and beastly nature? Whether it's by curse or by wisdom he has exalted his title. Marked it with the hard scope of science rather than by any partial allegation. (57)

In these words, Florian's narrator reworks passages from Sidney's *Apology*; a detour through the *Apology* will help to explicate how Florian's narrator both performs an *hommage* to and conducts an ironic commentary on Sidney.

In his *Apology*, Sidney catalogs, articulates, and exalts the traits of the poet and of poetry he gleans from Plato, Aristotle, Horace, and other exemplars. Sidney's *Apology* appeared posthumously in print in 1595 and was the major discourse on poetry written in English Milton read in the lead-up to his composition of *Paradise Lost*. Imagine for a moment the narrator of *The Tree of No* as the contemporary of Milton, even if in the odd era in which Florian's novel takes place: a time of *Paradise Lost* yet permeable to the time of Genesis, of Revelation, and of our contemporary world, but still within the horizon of Milton's epic and its recasting of Biblical times and time. Living out time with Montgomery, the narrator of *The Tree of No* would, like Milton, find Sidney's *Apology* to be a kind of latest epitome of poetry's defense. Yet, in the *Apology,* the narrator would also find Sidney invoking the story of Adam and Eve in a way that excludes Eve from being a poet, at least if a poet is a godlike maker who makes as Sidney's Platonic god makes. In full and irreversible commitment to poesy's pursuit, Florian's narrator proceeds in mockery: "In a word, in irreverence for the god-like, no matter what, no matter how, a wretched writer."

To work toward Sidney's abjection of the creation, of the creatural, of sexual difference, that is, of their exemplar Eve who discloses Adam as an exemplar of such, and to work toward Sidney's implicit barring of Eve from poethood and even from the realms of poetry, begin with Sidney's evocation of ancient names for poets. Attempting to define the sublime vocation of poetry by considering how the Greeks and Romans named poets, Sidney writes, "Among the Romans a poet was called *vates,* which is as much as a diviner, foreseer, or prophet."[19] This exalted title Sidney aligns with the Greek title for the writer of poetry:

> The Greeks called him "a poet," which name hath, as the most excellent, gone through other languages. It cometh of this word *poiein,* which is "to make": wherein, I know not whether by luck or wisdom, we Englishmen have met with the Greeks in calling him a *maker:* which name, how high and incomparable a title it is, I had rather were known by marking the scope of other sciences than by my partial allegation. (157)

By specifying the limits of the "other sciences" in their relationship to what Sidney calls "nature," which he personifies as a woman, Sidney would fully explicate the exaltation of poetry implicit in his following the Greeks to name the poet "a maker." Astronomy exemplifies how the arts and sciences take "the works of nature for [their] principal object, without which they could not consist, and on which they so depend, as they become actors and players, as it were, of what nature will have set forth" (157). Nature sets the scene and writes the script, and as "actors and players," the arts or sciences play out their allotted roles. Notice how, in Sidney's trope, nature becomes the container, the arts or sciences the contained: the arts or sciences act but only within the parameters of the scene nature establishes. These arts and sciences, studying what nature offers for inquiry, must follow her to avoid error, or thus insists the "moral philosopher" who observes humanity's "natural virtues, vices, and passions": "'follow nature,' (saith he) '[…] and thou shalt not err'" (157). Sidney puts a phrase from the 1560 Geneva Bible's translation of the Decalogue in the mouth of the "moral philosopher": "thou shalt not." The connotation of sin the word "err" carries, sin as error, will soon become relevant, though Sidney's "thou shalt not" already makes that connotation relevant. As artists or scientists studying some aspect of nature broadly conceived, the "lawyer," the "historian," the "grammarian," the "rhetorician," the "logician," the "physician," and even the "metaphysic[ian]" all must follow nature or fall into error (157). Though dealing with "abstract notions" and arguably with the "supernatural," the metaphysician still "build[s] upon the depth of nature," the supernatural being natural, however super (157). None of these nature-following artists or scientists merits the name "maker." They are explicators, and in their explications they ape nature. Their explications, however fine, are free of "error" only insofar as they faithfully follow nature's script within nature's scene.

Poetry alone exceeds nature's containment. What distinguishes poetry from the "other sciences," the various human arts, is that, while those arts all meekly follow nature and humbly operate in response to her logic and within the scope of her compass, "[o]nly the poet, disdaining to be tied to any such subjection, lifted up with the vigor of his own invention, doth grow in effect another nature, in making things either better than nature bringeth forth, or, quite anew, forms such as never were in nature, as the Heroes, Demigods, Cyclopes, Chimeras, Furies, and such like" (157). Following Boccaccio, Sidney denies poets are apes of nature, confined to servile imitation. While the other arts or sciences draw out and explicate the doings of nature, the poet, engaging in "invention," creates "another nature." As inventive, the poet rejects following nature yet does not therefore fall into error: "he goeth hand in hand, with nature, not enclosed within the narrow warrant of her gifts, but freely ranging only within the zodiac of his own wit" (157). Sidney's image of the male poet walking "hand in hand" with female nature presages for a reader of *Paradise Lost* Adam and Eve walking hand in hand out of Eden; *The Tree of No* prompts this association. Sidney's poet holds the hand of nature yet remains free, "disdaining […] subjection" to her. The astronomer must study the stars nature provides; the poet walks, "freely ranging only within the zodiac of his own wit," a second starry panoply within a second nature of the poet's own invention.

At this point, Sidney's poet seems an unfallen Adam, if, as Raphael argues, Adam's freedom consists in Adam disdaining any subjection to the beauteous Eve she might manage to impose through the desires and pleasures she and Adam share with the beasts. Adam criticizes Eve's suicidal anguish as a symptom not of any nature-transcending sublimity but of Eve's exorbitant love of "life and pleasure." Though Sidney never mentions Eve by name, he associates female nature, the over-loved earth, with a fallen "brazen" world and poets with an unfallen "golden" world: "Nature never set forth the earth in so rich tapestry as divers poets have done—neither with pleasant rivers, fruitful trees, sweet-smelling flowers, nor whatsoever else may make the *too much loved earth* more lovely. Her world is brazen, the poets only deliver a golden" (157, my emphasis). In *The Tree of No*, Lilith at first feels smothered by the poets' "rich tapestry" of a second nature, a "golden" rather than a "brazen" "earth" or Eden. This Lilith, or her narrator, wrestles Sidney with the ambition to say, in effect, "I am the necessary angel of earth, / Since, in my sight, you see the earth again, / Cleared of its stiff and stubborn, man-locked set."[20]

In *Works and Days*, Hesiod codified the tradition of naming the human ages by metals. Hesiod's golden age resembles Eden: oppressive work and aging are unknown, and trees' abundant fruit provides sustenance. Yet, in the brazen or bronze age, the arboreal turns from a demure provider of meals to the source of homicidal, suicidal, hell-bound giants. The brazen age ushers in a fallen "brazen race, sprung from ash-trees," war-like, self-destroying, and doomed to disappear anonymously into Hades.[21] The serpent in Milton's Eden has "brazen eyes" (7.496). Milton's Sin and perhaps Eve could merit the term "brazen." The "too-much-loved earth": Sidney's phrase and the judgment it bears Raphael would endorse, and Milton's Adam echoes Sidney in judging the suicidal Eve as pining over the "loss of life and pleasure overlov'd."

Sidney insists even in relation to man the poet outdoes nature, even if in bringing forth man "her uttermost cunning is employed" (157). Though nature's best efforts go into birthing man, the poet brings the ideal types of man into existence, albeit in fictions. Sidney asks: has nature "brought forth so true a lover as Theagenes, so constant a friend as Pylades, [...] so excellent a man every way as Virgil's Aeneas [?]" (157). The superiority of the poet over nature holds in the case of man, even though "the works of the one," nature, are "essential," while the works of "the other," the poet, consist of "imitation or fiction" (157). God and the poet, the Maker and the maker, work from a quasi-Platonic "idea" or eternal, unchanging blueprint: "the skill of the artificer standeth in that idea or fore-conceit of the work, and not in the work itself. And that the poet hath that idea is manifest, by delivering [his works] forth in such excellency as he hath imagined them" (157). While Sidney's Platonic god made nature from the ideal pattern of his "idea or fore-conceit," on her own Nature works more haphazardly and even brazenly, or so Adam would judge nature thought of as an Eve who insists on gardening without his rational supervision. There is vision, which only sees nature, and then there is supervision, which can see the "idea or fore-conceit." And so the "skill" of God or the poet manifests through God's or the poet's access to the perfect "idea or fore-conceit" of the creation God makes or of the poem the poet makes. The poem, the words in the world, always constitute a second-best and falling away from the "idea or fore-conceit." Similarly, God's "idea or fore-conceit" of the creation bears none of the fallenness possible in the creation or world. Notice: Sidney thinks of the deity of Genesis as a Platonist, and so the eternal, changeless "idea" of the creation precedes the turbulent, changeful, sexually desirous creation. To posit an eternal, changeless, Platonist "idea" of the creation as having preceded the creation of Genesis sets up the Genesis creation for devaluation precisely for exhibiting turbulence, change, and sexual desire.

In Sidney's account, the relation between maker and made may become involuted. Consider Cyrus the Great (c. 600–530 BCE), founder of the Persian Empire and immortalized, as Sidney might say, in the writings of the Greek historian and philosopher Xenophon (c. 430–354 BCE). Though nature may bring forth a Cyrus, Sidney's poet, in making manifest the ideal type, "bestow[s] a Cyrus upon the world, to make many Cyruses, if they will learn aright why and how that maker made him" (157–58). Nature makes a Cyrus, but the poet makes a Cyrus many natural men may and should emulate, as should perhaps the Cyrus nature made, were he to read a poem titled "Cyrus" and catch a glimpse in the poem of the ideal Cyrus, the poet's "idea, or fore-conceit." Suppose Cyrus the Great were a poet who in a poem manifested the "idea" or "fore-conceit" "Cyrus." The relation of the maker to the made, or of the maker Cyrus to the Cyrus he makes, becomes complex. Who then is the maker of the maker, if Cyrus as poet emulates the "idea" "Cyrus" he, the poet, makes, or makes manifest, in a poem?

Does Sidney straighten out or further tangle these relations in describing his Platonic-Protestant god as the maker who makes the maker the poet is? Sidney writes about his god, the poet, and nature:

> Neither let it be deemed too saucy a comparison to balance the highest point of man's wit with the efficacy of nature; but rather give right honor to the heavenly Maker of that maker, who, having made man to his own likeness, set him beyond and over all the works of that second nature: which in nothing he showeth so much as in poetry, when with the force of a divine breath he bringeth things forth far surpassing her doings, with no small argument to the

incredulous of that first accursed fall of Adam, since our erected wit maketh us know what perfection is, and yet our infected will keepeth us from reaching unto it. (158)

The Maker makes the maker "to his own likeness": just as the Maker presides over nature, so the maker presides over "second nature." Notice how Sidney here uses "man" as a synonym for "poet." Or: man most shows himself in God's image when man acts as a poet: godlike, "with the force of a divine breath," the poet creates, and the creations of the poet surpass by far "her doings," the doings of Nature. Made with reference to an ideal "fore-conceit," the poet's creations participate in perfection, a perfection readers can know in the poem but cannot reach in the world. Why can we not reach perfection? Sidney argues "our erected wit" can "know what perfection is," "yet our infected will," the artifact of Eve's transgression, or even just Eve herself as willful fruit eater, "keeps us from reaching unto" "perfection."

Did Milton pick up Sidney's association of the godlike poet with the erect ("erected wit")? When Satan first travels Eden, he views "all kind / Of living creatures," but then he sees "[t]wo of far nobler shape erect and tall, / Godlike erect" (4.286–87, 288–89). These two are Adam and Eve, though Eve, less "Godlike," is and becomes Adam's subversion. Narrating to Adam the process of the creation, Raphael explains how "Earth in her rich attire / Consummate lovely smil'd; air, water, earth, / By fowl, fish, beast, was flown, was swum, was walkt" (7.501–03). Milton's personification Earth seems very close to Sidney's personification of nature, realm of all the creatures. However, though some "of the sixth day yet remain'd," explains Raphael, "There wanted yet the master-work, the end / Of all yet done; a creature who not prone / And brute as other creatures, but endu'd / With sanctity of reason, might erect / His stature, and upright with front serene / Govern the rest, self-knowing" (7.504, 505–10). This "master-work" is man, man "not prone" like the "other creatures," man whose endowment of "reason" allows for his being "erect" and "self-knowing," so man can "[g]overn the rest" of the creatures, including the quasi-human creature Eve, this man as man being

Adam. Florian's narrator presents to the reader a Montgomery who is "prone," and this narrator contests the claim of man or his god to be "self-knowing." Upright and walking, Florian's narrator quests for self-knowledge. Milton distinguishes between the "upright heart" his god favors, such as displayed by Adam in his obedience, to Eve's will infected with the dreamy miasma of Satan's whisperings.

Sidney parallels God as the Maker of nature to the poet as the maker of a "second nature." As God stands above and beyond nature, so the poet stands above and beyond "second nature." In his sublime flight of invention, the poet exceeds any of nature's "doings." What is the difference between "nature" and "second nature"? Nature is "brazen," while second nature is "golden." The first is fallen, while the second is perfect. Brazen: bronze, yes, but also shameless and bold. With an "erected wit" knowing "perfection," Sidney's Adam would stand as an image of his maker. Yet, as displaying an "infected will," Sidney's Adam evidences his fall due to his seduction by Eve, his acquiescence to her errant will. For Sidney, in effect, Eve is the difference between the golden "second nature" partaking of perfection and brazen "nature" partaking of the fall. In *Paradise Lost,* after the fall, Adam angrily wishes God had never made Eve and had left nature devoid of the feminine. If we now can know yet not reach perfection, Eve's to blame.

In defending poetry and treating the perennial topics (imitation, invention, transport, eloquence, and so on) to exalt the poet, Sidney brings to a culmination the tradition of Plato, Aristotle, Horace, Plotinus, Boethius, Boccaccio, Scaliger, and so on. But Sidney's hyperbolic exaltation of the poet as a divine maker in the image of the Divine Maker proceeds by excluding Eve from being a poet and from the realm of poetry, "second nature." Or, because of Eve (the creatural, sexual difference, the "infected will"), none of us may reach unto the perfection of second nature though we can know that nature in poems. The despairing Adam of *Paradise Lost* wishes the creation had been made free of Eve, yet any such Eve-free creation would be a quasi-Platonic realm of forms rather than the burgeoning flux of Genesis.

In the Sidney-quoting section of *The Tree of No,* Florian has her narrator proceed by appropriating and modifying sentences and phrases about poetry and the poet from Horace, Longinus, Boethius, Boccaccio, and Scaliger, with topics from Plato and Aristotle thrown into the mix. This procedure to build up a discourse via echoes recalls and gently yet incisively mocks Sidney scribbling his essay into being by way of appropriations, paraphrases, and quotations from a quite similar panoply of sources. Florian's gesture of appropriating from Sidney and company underlines how Sidney, through his procedures to write his *Apology,* shows himself at least as much a borrower as a maker. Sidney wants his correlation of nature's Maker and the poet as the maker of second nature to warrant his claim "that the Greeks with some probability of reason gave him [the poet] the name above all names of learning" (158). Learners borrow, yet poets make: "The Greeks called him 'a poet,' which name hath, as the most excellent, gone through other languages. It comes of this word *poiein,* which is 'to make.'". The name "maker," "how high and incomparable a title it is."

The "other sciences" must limit their "scope" to the study of primary nature in its faulty and fallen corporeality: Sidney the Platonist implicitly though unthinkingly contrasts the dynamic flux of the Genesis creation with a changeless Platonic idea, what Sidney calls the "idea or fore-conceit of the work" as distinct from "the work itself," Sidney's deity having the ideal blueprint of the cosmos in mind before setting to work for six days. As distinct from Nature herself, the privilege of the poet in making a second nature is to voice such a blueprint forth in a poem intimating perfection. Sidney names his Platonic-Protestant deity as the Maker of the poet, who makes a second nature free of the faults of primary nature. The faultiness of primary nature, its errance from the Platonic blueprint, manifests the burgeoning flux of the Genesis creation, though only in abjection as fallen. Sidney's discourse correlates Adam as ideal man of erected wit with a Platonic notion of perfection while masking the Biblical creation as the deviance or error Sidney correlates with Adam as fallen via Eve. The Platonic blueprint becomes the unfallen ideal, and the Biblical creation becomes fallen nature, with Eve the agent of the fall, as if, absent Eve, the blueprint could manifest as an ideal universe, Adam's wish for a female-free creation. Sidney reads nature's faults as Eve's fault, Nature/Eve becoming the source of faults in her errant working on her own, again something Milton picks up. This scheme ends up locating in Eve the Genesis creation's desirous, tactile, prolific dynamism only in abjection as the beastly, as sin.

In *The Tree of No*, the narrator's appropriations of Horace and company culminate with a rewording of two passages from Sidney. Here are the Sidney passages: "give right honor to the heavenly Maker of that maker, who, having made man to his own likeness, set him beyond and over all the works of that second nature" and "I know not whether by luck or wisdom we Englishmen have met with the Greeks in calling him a *maker*: which name, how high and incomparable a title it is, I had rather were known by marking the scope of other sciences than by my partial allegation." Now here is the rewording of those passages in *The Tree of No*:

> After all, who is the maker of the maker? Having made his own maker in his own likeness? Having set his maker in his likeness above and beyond the works of his own second and beastly nature? Whether it's by curse or by wisdom he has exalted his title. Marked it with the hard scope of science rather than by any partial allegation.
>
> I have a war with history. (57)

A war indeed. These words and phrases appropriated from Sidney Florian's narrator uses to engage in a fine irreverence toward Sidney's godlike poet. Irreverence reveres, only playfully and satirically. Sidney would have the Maker make the maker or poet. Sidney would have this unitary, timeless quasi-Platonic deity float above and beyond primary nature just as the poet floats above and beyond second nature. Florian's narrator takes away Sidney's easy and confident capital-versus-lowercase distinction: Maker/maker. Did the poet make the poet's god? If so, what image does the poet have of himself as poet if the god the poet makes in his image floats "above and beyond" "beastly nature" just as the poet imagines himself to float "above and beyond the works of his own second nature"? Or did the god the poet made in turn make the poet, the Platonic image of the Protestant god the poet made in turn making the poet fashion himself toward the timeless, the placeless, the ideal in a quasi-Platonic sense, so the poet can only find in his ability to know yet not attain such perfection a symptom and allegory of Adam's fall and of the "infected will," "will" being a slang term for both the male and the female genitals in pre-penicillin Renaissance England?

"I have a war with history": the narrator of *The Tree of No* wars with the history of poetics insofar as advances in poesy have, in Sidney's account, implied advances in perfecting a second nature ever more exclusive of Eve, of the beastly, of earthbound desire. Milton's vision of Adam and Eve's prayers rising by the mediation of Christ the Logos to become sin-free speech, wholly clean holograms imaging Adam and Eve perfected into a second nature distinct from their fallen nature Eve brought about: this vision plays out a version of the logic Sidney articulates. Florian's narrator wars irreverently with Sidney's logic and with Milton's vision of Adam and Eve's prayers. Rather than straining to embody an ideal Platonic fore-conceit or to become through the redeeming Word a creature wholly iconic, the rogue textual beast titled *The Tree of No* works to let the narrator speak through a paratactic unbinding of words, phrases, and sentences from any discursive syntax attempting to stage parts as unifying absolutely with and so disappearing into wholes. *The Tree of No* walks away from the "all in all" endpoint toward which Milton has the Platonic-Christian Logos operate.

As *Paradise Lost* draws to an end, to pray, Adam and Eve return to the spot in Eden of their encounter with the Son, whom they took to be the Father. At the end of *The Tree of No*, in the penultimate page, to unpray prayers, the narrator also enacts a return: "We return to the city the way we also return to the tree, doubled over in his dilated eyes, the way dogs return to their vomit and sows are washed to wallow in mud" (110). Bending over Montgomery lying in his coffin, the narrator is "doubled over" in posture, but also "doubled over" as each of Montgomery's eyes reflect back the narrator's image. The pupils of Montgomery's eyes are "dilated": Is he dead? Sexually aroused? Intoxicated with hallucinogens? These states all involve pupil dilation, and, paradoxically, they all characterize Montgomery. Ken Russell's *Altered States* (1980), a film of hallucinogens, sex, and death, treats of *Paradise Lost* in its own oblique manner. About her motivations to rewrite *Paradise Lost* in *The Tree of No*, Florian states her dissatisfaction with Milton's language: "That's what prompted me to rewrite the text [*Paradise Lost*]. I wanted to give some of the most surreal biblical narratives the kind of acid-induced language they deserve."[22]

After stating "the day of death [is better] than the day of one's birth," Ecclesiastes claims: "Better *is* the end of a thing than the beginning thereof" (7.1, 8). Returning to the city, to Montgomery wide-eyed in his coffin, Florian's narrator rewrites this claim in a sentence exemplary of how *The Tree of No* holds opposites together to articulate contraries in a breath: "Far better is the end than the beginning of the end, prolonging its days like the shade" (110). The words after the comma rewrite Ecclesiastes 8.13: "But it shall not be well with the wicked, neither shall he prolong *his* days, *which are* as a shadow." "In the beginning," when God enacted creation, argues Altizer, God at once enacted his incarnation, his crucifixion, and his death: relinquishing infinite divine unity, God allows for the creation, something not-God, and accepts his subjection to necessity, a subjection his incarnation, crucifixion, and death play out.

Moving from the beginning, to the crucifixion, into necessity, and toward the culmination of irreversible finitude: at the novel's end, the narrator deftly sketches this march in the following paragraph while, toward the paragraph's end, echoing words from *Henry IV, Part 2* and from *The Tempest*. These words from Shakespeare treat a similar topic, humanity's irreversible finitude, yet the words treat this topic in contrary, antithetical manners: the narrator's juxtaposition of Shakespeare's words from these two plays achieves a devastating "wavering [of] the page" (Oventile par. 18):

In the beginning the word appeared, Presto, like a magic word so gently tragic. Like a crooked felon hung from branches. Like the Christmas tree and its metallic apples. We kneel in the bleachers and try to call back our words, recanto, retracto, denego, because it suddenly seems necessary that Shakespeare's deep word be realized. That darkness is the burier of the dead. That this instant is round with sleep. (110)

In *Henry IV, Part 2*, Northumberland envisions humanity seeking an end through universal murder ("That darkness is the burier of the dead"). In *The Tempest*, Prospero envisions humanity's end happening as universal melting away ("That this instant is round with sleep"). Florian's narrator brings these two visions together to illustrate "Shakespeare's deep word." To think about what Florian's narrator implies about "the word" (the Logos), about Shakespeare's "deep word," and about the *agon* between them, I need to explore the narrator's startling and uncanny juxtaposition of the words from *Henry IV, Part 2* and from *The Tempest*.

In *Henry IV, Part 2*, Northumberland learns of the death of his son in battle and that King Henry seeks to end Northumberland's life. In *Henry IV, Part 1*, Northumberland fakes arthritic illness to avoid battle. In *Part 2*, he will avoid battle again, but on receiving the news of his son Harry Percy's death, Northumberland thinks of himself as a sufferer of rheumatic fever or rheumatoid arthritis whose rage allows him to throw away his crutch and enter battle to revenge his son. Northumberland parallels the rheumatic fever to the rage. His rage at his son's death miraculously cures his limbs, his mournful rage becoming his rage for battle:

> And as the wretch whose fever-weak'ned joints,
> Like strengthless hinges, buckle under life,
> Impatient of his fit, breaks like a fire
> Out of his keeper's arms, even so my limbs,
> Weak'ned with grief, being now enrag'd with grief,
> Are thrice themselves. Hence therefore, thou nice crutch!
>
> (1.1.140–45)

His sudden overcoming of "rheumatic" illness (Mistress Quickly uses the word [2.4.57]) and his readiness for battle Northumberland attributes to his terrible grief at his son's death. One burning, the rheumatic fever, weakening his joints, he describes as being overcome by "fire." That is, the grief that, as rheumatic fever, weakens his joints, becoming "enraged," becomes a "fire" that heals his joints. And so Northumberland claims to be battle ready.

Yet he then goes on to imagine raging in battle in terms of raging rheumatic fever, that is, as a process that, in its inflammation, cures itself auto-destructively, grinding to a halt. Northumberland imagines the fratricidal murderousness of war that took his son raging generally and curing humanity of existence:

> Let heaven kiss earth! now let not Nature's hand
> Keep the wild flood confin'd! let order die!
> And let this world no longer be a stage
> To feed contention in a ling'ring act;
> But let one spirit of the first-born Cain
> Reign in all bosoms, that each heart being set
> On bloody courses, the rude scene may end,
> And darkness be the burier of the dead!
>
> (1.1.153–60)

Nature's collapse, the death of "order," "this world no longer" being the "stage" for humanity's "lingering act" of violent "contention" but fratricidal murder decimating all and so ending "the rude scene," humanity turning murderously on itself: this vision uncannily evokes the auto-immune dynamic of rheumatic conditions, in which the body attacks itself, and with "heaven" ruining onto "earth" ("heaven kisses earth"), this vision hints toward the destruction of the biosphere and the extinction of *homo sapiens*. After the "spirit of the first-born Cain" plays out completely, no one will be left to bury the dead but darkness. Northumberland's personification of night as Death the universal undertaker recalls lines from sonnet 73: "In me thou seest the twilight of such day / As after sunset fadeth in the west, / Which by and by black night doth take away, / Death's second self, that seals up all in rest" (5–8). Does Northumberland's vision of an arthritic Saint Vitus dance of universal homicide stiff-jointedly lurching toward a final paralysis of extinction image forth the "deep word" of Shakespeare Florian's narrator declares must necessarily attain realization?

Or does Prospero's gentler yet no less drastic vision of human transience image forth Shakespeare's "deep word"? To celebrate the betrothal of his daughter Miranda to Ferdinand, Prospero commands Ariel to summon the spirits Juno, Ceres, and Iris, who perform a masque. Iris calls in nymphs and reapers from the field to perform a dance. But then, suddenly remembering the "foul conspiracy / Of the beast Caliban and his confederates / Against [his] life," Prospero angrily halts the entertainment, commands the spirits to disperse, and, in response to Ferdinand's surprise at his "passion," states (4.1.139–41, 144):

> You do look, my son, in a mov'd sort,
> As if you were dismay'd; be cheerful, sir.
> Our revels now are ended. These our actors
> (As I foretold you) were all spirits, and
> Are melted into air, into thin air,
> And like the baseless fabric of this vision,
> The cloud-capp'd tow'rs, the gorgeous palaces,
> The solemn temples, the great globe itself,
> Yea, all which it inherit, shall dissolve,
> And like this insubstantial pageant faded
> Leave not a rack behind. We are such stuff
> As dreams are made on; and our little life
> Is rounded with a sleep.
>
> (4.1.146–58)

The dispersal of the spirits ("our actors") leads Prospero to a meditation on transience. Ecclesiastes figures everyone, everything, every thought, and every institution in creation as transient wisps of cloud. In the New Testament, James echoes Ecclesiastes: "For what is your life? It is even a vapour that appeareth for a little time, and afterward vanisheth away" (4.14, Geneva 1560). Prospero evidently keeps a Bible among his books.

Elaborating the Biblical trope of sunlight and wind dissolving cloud wisps into naught, Prospero considers how transience pervades all. Transience encompasses the play within the play the spirits stage, the Globe Theater ("the great globe"), and the entire "globe" or human world. All will "dissolve" as clouds do, "Leav[ing] not a rack behind," a rack being a thin, wind-driven wisp of cloud. All the dreams or figures gazers project onto clouds will likewise "dissolve." Like the spirits who stage the play by temporarily taking on visible and stable form, "We are [examples of] such [clouds]" upon which "dreams are made." Our dissolution is concomitant with the dissolution of the "fabric," stage, or institutional structure (tower, palace, or temple) that constitutes the *mise en scène* within which we define our selves, selves bounded by the decorum of our acts conforming to that scene. As the encircling horizon defining the scene is revealed to be a "baseless fabric," so the self at the center is revealed to be a "dream."

Prospero says "on" rather than "of." Images seen on clouds are not made *of* clouds: they are made *on* clouds. Such images are mere dreams because they are visions of stability and form projected upon such stuff as has neither, clouds. To say that dreams are made *of* clouds is to imply that the substance that the dreams are made of, cloud, participates in their form and stability, however fleeting the vision of form and stability may be. Fluidly supple beings, Iris and company may smoothly, serenely dislimn or dislimb. But the reader should not be too quick to think the Northumberland who envisions death as rigidity simply contrasts with a Prospero open to the wisdom of fluidity. After Isis and company disperse, Prospero, accompanied by Ariel and by spirits in the shape of hunting dogs, finds Caliban, Stephano, and Trinculo rifling through Prospero's possessions to steal the best. The thieving three flee. In an angry outburst, Prospero commands Ariel to give chase and set the spirit dogs on the pilfering trio. These dogs are to torment the trio's joints. Prospero to Ariel:

Go, charge my goblins that they grind their joints
With dry convulsions, shorten up their sinews

With aged cramps, and more pinch-spotted make them
Than pard or cat o' mountain.

                                                                (4.1.258–61)

That is, the dogs' bites are to manifest as symptoms of rheumatism
and arthritis. Perhaps this curse comes to Prospero's mind because
he suffers from some form of arthritis.

Florian wisely avoids having her narrator explicitly state
"Shakespeare's deep word" except through the startling
coincidentia oppositorum of Northumberland's and Prospero's
words. Yet Shakespeare's word displaces the Christian word
through the sudden understanding of the inevitable realization of
a dying uncannily mixing the most rigid, arthritic, lurching toward
inexistence with the most limber, fluid dissolving into oblivion.
The devastating juxtaposition of the words from Northumberland
and Prospero suggests a candidate for "Shakespeare's deep word"
would be "dying": dying attains realization necessarily. Another
candidate would be "nothingness": in their irreversible dying,
mortals realize their nothingness, both their destiny to lack
existence and, in their existence, to lack utterly any of the stability,
discrete semantic determination, or replicability of a thing. As Dr.
Seuss teaches, where thing one is, thing two is. What is a thing?
To answer, "a mortal," confuses a nothing, no-thing, for a thing.

To ward off the giving way on desire through repentant
prayer moving toward the "all in all" Eve accepts in *Paradise
Lost,* Florian's narrator reaches back to Shakespeare to counter
Milton's word or Logos with Shakespeare's "deep word." As
Paradise Lost ends, in prelude to their leaving Eden, the fallen
Adam and Eve pray in repentance and for forgiveness. Christ
the Logos mediates these prayers: the prayers appear before God
as if holograms of the kneeling supplicants. Christ washes from
the prayerful words of Adam and Eve contradiction, fleshliness,
error, sin: these words become silent images before God clean of
the "I," somehow enunciations become images of the enunciators
yet completely without the "I" enunciation presumes. The prayer
Eve utters becomes an image of Eve without her "I." Before God,
Adam and Eve kneel, except that some exceedingly fine tweezers

have reached into each and plucked out the "I" of each. These tweezers are Christ, the Logos, operating as grace. These without-I holograms exemplify the state of grace as Simone Weil conceives it: the decreation of the "I." Such would be the Adam and Eve eventually taken up into the "all in all": the believers in Christ, and Christ in God, and God all in all. In the "all in all," Eve's "I" would vanish, the separation she aspired to achieve would be overcome entirely in a limitless unity, a whole wholly subsuming, and so vanishing, any parts.

As *The Tree of No* ends, in prelude to the narrator's final assertion of the "I," the narrator would retract the prayers Milton's Adam and Eve make. These prayers, in their silence, gesture toward the ending of the world and of words in the Word, the Logos, Christ, God, all in all. In the final two pages of *The Tree of No*, the narrator seeks to unpray these prayers: "to call back our words, recanto, retracto, denego, because it suddenly seems necessary that Shakespeare's deep word be realized." In this effort, the realization of "Shakespeare's deep word" requires and supports the undoing of the narrator's words or prayers insofar as the logic of those Miltonic prayers governs the narrator's words. Milton's Adam and Eve find the spot in Eden where the Son, whom they took for the Father, judged them, and the two pray: "they forthwith to the place / Repairing where he judg'd them, / prostrate fell / Before him reverent" (10.1098–1100). They pray before the Son taken for the Father, as if the Son were taken for the Platonic sun Plato calls a father. Florian's narrator would unpray these prayers: "We unpray our prayers before the sun" (111). In a strange paradox, this unpraying would *let* or *allow* necessity to happen, the "necessary" realization of "Shakespeare's deep word."

Displacing the Word on the pedestal, the Christian-Miltonic word at a height reigning or surveying from above, "Shakespeare's deep word" tolls finitude. Yet this word also aligns with the delicious wisdom or sublime folly of unpraying prayers. The narrator seeks to unpray the prayers before the passing of the phenomenal world: "We kneel in bleachers, church pews, at the foot of our sleepless beds, unknotting and trying to unpray our prayers before the sun and the sky and the stars go dark and the clouds return ill with rain" (110). The last half of this sentence closely adapts Ecclesiastes, which urges the realization of desires here and now, because inevitably, Ecclesiastes warns, "desire shall fail" (12.5). Another word sounding within "Shakespeare's deep word" is "desire."

Question: which word tolls dying, nothingness, and desire as mutually inextricable yet mutually irreducible? Answer: "Shakespeare's deep word." This "deep word" and the words attendant on this word are words of the end, as distinct from the Logos or Christ, the Word of a beginning or beginning of the end. Florian's narrator would affirm the end yet is careful to suggest the inherence of the end in the beginning: "Far better is the end than the beginning of the end, prolonging its days like the shade." How and why for the narrator is "the end" "better" than "the beginning of the end"? Think of Achilles: a beginning of his end is the humiliation of Agamemnon taking Briseis. The long suffering of Achilles in his rage, his brooding in the camp away from the battle, prolongs this beginning, "prolonging its days like the shade." This existence is a kind of death in life for Achilles. His end, by contrast, his fate, becomes a moment of intense and antithetical life amidst dying. However the dragging days in the camp prolong themselves, Achilles's end or enactment of fate, though a punctual moment, is "better." In this sense, for the narrator of *The Tree of No*, the end is better than the beginning of the end. The novel's narrator aligns the beginning with the Son as the Word and the end with "Shakespeare's deep word."

In the section of the novel just prior to the last, the reader finds the following words: "We are saddling the narrow now" (107). To ride this horse, the "now," the moment, would resemble riding a chariot with Athena at the reigns, or riding a carriage with Emily Dickinson "the Day / [the poet] first surmised the Horses' Heads / Were toward Eternity." The "narrow now" resembles eternity in being without temporal duration, yet eternity, in *Paradise Lost*, as the "all in all," precludes the "I," especially the "I" of Milton's Eve insofar as Eve walks away from her subordination. As *The Tree of No* ends, the "narrow now" as horse allows the narrating "I" an irreversible ride, a transport earthbound, and this "before the sun and the sky and the stars go dark." How does this "now," this "instant" "round with sleep," relate to the "go[ing] dark," to the "darkness" which is "the burier of the dead"? While Christianity usually situates the resurrection after death, Bloom follows the Gnostics who locate resurrection before death, "before the sun and the sky and the stars go dark," before the great globe theater goes dark. Bloom quotes the gnostic Gospel According to Philip: "Those who say the lord first died and then arose are mistaken, for he first arose and then died."[23] This rising, Bloom explains, involves a knowing: "to know releases the spark, and one rises up from the body of this death. Ignorance falls away, one ceases to forget, one is again part of the Fullness" (188–89). The great and almost impassable difficulty of achieving such resurrection inheres in accepting the only sequel: dying. This resurrection only occurs before dying's completion, yet the occurrence of this resurrection opens to the complete realization of dying. "Shakespeare's deep word" sounds this realization and urges the achievement of such resurrection. The agonistic element in achieving such a rising entails the fierce struggle to abandon what *The Tree of No*'s narrator calls "prolonging," a word the narrator appropriates from Ecclesiastes. Rather than seeking to prolong the time of the beginning of the end, the narrator, "unhesitate to taste the waste," seeks the intensity of the moment (1). Nietzsche: "The love of life (*die Liebe zum Leben*) is almost the opposite of the love of long life. All love is concerned with the moment and with the eternal—but *never* with 'length.'"[24]

The resurrection prior to the sun, sky, and stars going dark resembles an irreversible crossing toward an orgasm become inevitable. Or mentioning this resemblance becomes necessary to explicate the Shakespearian eroticism prevalent in *The Tree of No*. The desire to realize desire before "desire shall fail": this sentiment from Ecclesiastes, and the wisdom Ecclesiastes offers about "the end," Florian cannily and uncannily plays against "the word" as the Logos at work "In the beginning." In the process, Wisdom herself, in her uncanny *coincidentia oppositorum* with Folly, perhaps returns to challenge or displace the Logos. Raphael shows himself a weak reader of Proverbs when he attempts simply to oppose Wisdom and Folly, and Adam too shows a weakness of thought in accepting this opposition.

The moment in question involves sensations heading toward saturation, sensations of an erotic tinge. The two sections of *The Tree of No* where the sentence "But the sin in me says I" appears deal with ending. The sentence appears in the last section, on the last page, as the last sentence, so the climactic word of the novel is "I." By this ending, the novel performs narratively the moment of the "I" existing without sequel: "I" then blank. Also containing "But the sin in me says I" are the pages immediately following the section titled "Psalms" (94). These pages give further insight into the dynamics of the moment the novel-ending iteration of the phrase performs. To call this moment the final one misconstrues it, this moment happening other than as one moment numerable in a sequence of moments. Nietzsche catches this innumerability at the start of *On the Genealogy of Morals* where he argues in the attempt to count our moments we always miscount because the moment of counting evades the enumeration, evades chronology. The sprinkling through the novel of the topic of counting addresses this distinction between the numerable and the innumerable.

How should a reader characterize the time of the beginning of the end? With Briseis taken, Achilles glimpses his end, and would act immediately, yet Athena checks him. Achilles then delays to reenter the battle and meet his fate. Satan, confronting Death, raises his spear, but Sin checks him. Satan then takes the long flight to Eden where Gabriel will show him the Homeric scales in the sky signaling his fate. Ahab first confronts Moby Dick, has his leg reaped, and then only after a journey of many months does he enter his final confrontation with the whale. This interval of delay Florian's narrator describes as "the beginning of the end" "prolonging its days like the shade." Rather than seeking to linger in this "prolonging," the narrator would be "unhesitate to taste the waste." This escape from or refusal of hesitation the narrator aligns with the "beastly." In *Moby-Dick*, Ishmael avers, "time began with man." For the narrator of *The Tree of No*, time begins with the cutting down of a tree:

Beastly, I, replete and eaten, sever the trunk of the tree to count its rings, one-one-thousand, two-one-thousand, weltering in the power of my consummate crime, like the yellower edges of guiltier graves. Time becomes my deputy. Time becomes my authority. As extending from the signal. And it's now that I begin to fall in love with Montgomery, celestially lying in the carved-out coffin. And it's now that I begin to fall in love with Montgomery, in the coffin under the tree of no. (2)

Consider the Eden of *Paradise Lost:* if a sojourner there were to cut down a tree, would the cross-section of trunk exhibit rings, and if so, would these mark the passing of time? Montgomery rests prone in a section of trunk carved out to be a coffin. This coffin rests "under the tree of no." Which tree, then, did the narrator cut down? Did the narrator cut down the tree of life or the tree of knowledge?

The time of the beginning of the end the end sloughs off. In this sloughing off, the "I" begins: "In the end, it's all endings always. In the end, it's all stones and doorways. In the end, I begin" (94). A threshold or moment without any chronological thickness whatsoever, this end hosts the "I," and in this threshold the "I" begins. To call this moment fleeting would be a misnomer insofar as fleeting implies brevity: the feeling of brevity belongs to the time of the beginning of the end. The notion of the fleeting or of brevity may imply the need to save time, yet the end precisely happens without salvation, without a savior, without the Word but with "Shakespeare's deep word." If salvation implies a reversal of loss, to cross into the end brings the narrator into the utterly irreversible yet with the loss of loss beckoning. This irreversibility suggests Nietzsche's "down going" or "going under."

Here the reader might murmur about how the novel ends with the pronoun "I" and begins: "Beastly, I fall at Adam under the shade." This appearance of the "I" at the end of the novel and at the beginning ("Beastly, I") does enact how "In the end, I begin." A reader could interpret this beginning in the end as the end of beginning by arguing the novel thus signals the eternal recurrence of its cosmos, with the narrator's unhesitant going under enacting the narrator's *amor fati*. Paul would escape the circling of sin, the perpetual return of an "I" to its constitutive sin. Putting Paul on hold ("Paul appeals to be freed. Liberty is postponed until the end of the war" [49]), *The Tree of No* ends with, "But the sin in me says I." The immediately preceding sentences evoke Christmas (the time one year ends and another begins) and the New Testament verses (Matthew 6.9–13, Luke 11.2–4) known as the Lord's Prayer. Florian's narrator steers the end of the novel ("I") toward the novel's beginning ("Beastly, I") by juxtaposing words from the Lord's Prayer with words from Simone Weil: "It's Christmas at the introduction to our father who art in heaven, hallowed be thy name. Small turns. I am still waking. But the sin in me says I." With these words, the narrator and the narrative end, and yet the narrator and the narrative begin ("In the end, I begin") in this confrontation between the traditional prayer and the narrator letting the sin within the narrator "say I." The version of the Lord's Prayer the Catholic liturgy uses derives from Matthew 6.9–13:

> Our Father who art in heaven,
> Hallowed be thy name.
> Thy kingdom come,
> Thy will be done,
> On earth as it is in heaven.
> Give us this day our daily bread;
> And forgive us our debts,
> As we also have forgiven our debtors;
> And lead us not into temptation,
> But deliver us from evil.

In the Mass, after the congregation and the priest recite the Lord's prayer, the priest elaborates on the deliverance from evil the prayer requests: "Deliver us, Lord, we pray, from every evil, graciously grant peace in our days, that, by the help of your mercy, we may be always free from sin." This hope, to be "free from sin," means for Weil to be free from the "I." There is the creation, and the "I" exists amidst the creation, yet as a function of the will or sin.

Milton's Adam and Eve pray, in shame of their earthly selves, and Christ mediates those prayers to spirit away those selves. Florian has her narrator seek to unpray these prayers through which grace suspends the "I." The contrary of such praying would be the saying by which the sin in the narrator says "I." The sin in the narrator enunciates the narrator's "I." In Luke, a disciple sees Jesus praying and asks, "Lord, teach us to pray, as John also taught his disciples" (11.1). Jesus then offers the Lord's Prayer. The disciple references John the Baptist, but Florian's concern is with how John Milton in *Paradise Lost* would teach his readers to pray in emulation of the repentant Adam and Eve. Milton's Adam and Eve, in praying, find ˙relief from selfhood, as by grace. Florian's narrator, through unpraying such Miltonic prayers, would achieve selfhood by delivering the self to the moment. When Florian has her narrator affirm, "But the sin in me says I," the narrator counters Paul's statements such as "ᴎot I, but the grace of God which was with me" or "I am crucified with Christ: nevertheless I live; yet not I, but Christ liveth in me" (1 Corinthians 15.10, Galatians 2.20).

In one of Shakespeare's palinodes to *Othello, The Winter's Tale,* Paulina uses clever stratagems and ruses to save Hermione from the murderous jealousy of her husband Leontes and indeed to stage Hermione's impossible return from the death Leontes believes he had brought to her. In *The Winter's Tale,* Paulina acts contrarily to Iago, the Paul who in *Othello* stokes the murderous jealousy of Othello and brings him to kill his wife Desdemona in the name of spirit. The narrator Milton in *Paradise Lost* often paraphrases Paul, and in *Moby-Dick* the narrator Ishmael identifies with Paul, and, before the final release of his daemon, weltering still on a breezeless ocean, Ahab hopes to meet Paul's ship and the breeze that ship will bring. Consider *Paradise Lost,* with the vision of the "all in all" and with the prayers of Adam and Eve cleansed of self, and *Moby-Dick,* with Ishmael's fiction of a final ocean scene empty of any "I": both works project an end without self, without an "I," whether of the narrator or the author. Neither the narrator Milton nor the narrator Ishmael says what Florian's narrator says: "In the end, I begin." To narrate an end void of any narrator, to tell of a time and a place void of the teller: in this gesture persists the presumptions of narrative omniscience and indeed omnipotence Florian's narrator mocks in the narrator's engagement with Sidney. With Montgomery prone in his coffin, *The Tree of No* proceeds assuming the death of the death of any such narrator claiming to narrate who and what are there without the narrator being there.

In "The Poems of Our Climate," Wallace Stevens speaks of "[t]he evilly compounded, vital I" and states: "The imperfect is our paradise."[25] Eden never was perfect, if Steven's word "imperfect" carries a reference to a Platonist distinction between, say, the form "tree," perfect, that is, one, intelligible, and changeless, and said form's exemplifications, imperfect, that is, changing, sensible, and various. About the "imperfect" being "our paradise," Stevens goes on to extol "delight": "Note that, in this bitterness, delight, / Since the imperfect is so hot in us, / Lies in flawed words and stubborn sounds" (22–24). A "hot" imperfection bearing "delight": the pronoun "I," turning idiomatic, emerges as the flawed word and stubborn sound *The Tree of No* voices. The novel's every page unfolds through and elaborates this "I." Ranging through "Beastly, I" and toward "But the sin in me says I," the singular *energeia* of the novel's usurped language becomes the narrator's signature.

Notes

Notes to Preface

1. Harold Bloom, introduction, *Till I End My Song: A Gathering of Last Poems,* ed. Harold Bloom (New York: Harper, 2010) xviii.

2. Quoted in Ann Shearer, *Athene: Image and Energy* (London: Viking Arkana, 1996) ix. In addition to Shearer, for informative discussions of Athena, see Susan Deacy, *Athena* (London: Routledge, 2008) and Karl Kerényi, *Athene: Virgin and Mother in Greek Religion,* trans. Murray Stein (Dallas: Spring, 1978).

3. Quoted in Henry Corbin, *Alone with the Alone: Creative Imagination in the Sūfism of Ibn 'Arabī,* trans. Ralph Manheim (Princeton: Princeton UP, 1998) 283.

4. See Plato, *Symposium,* trans. Robin Waterfield (Oxford: Oxford UP, 1994) 202d–203a. For discussion of the daemonic, see E. R. Dodds, *The Greeks and the Irrational* (Berkeley: U of California P, 1951) 39–43 and *Pagan and Christian in an Age of Anxiety* (Cambridge: Cambridge UP, 1965) 37–68.

5. Friedrich Nietzsche, *Thus Spoke Zarathustra: A Book for Everyone and Nobody,* trans. Graham Parkes (Oxford: Oxford UP, 2005) 14.

6. Brooks Haxton explains that the "fragment is often translated: 'Character is fate.' More literally, a man's *ethos* is his *daimon."* See *Heraclitus: Fragments,* trans. Brooks Haxton (New York: Penguin, 2001) 97, note to fragment 121.

7. See Ernst Robert Curtius, *European Literature and the Latin Middle Ages,* trans. Willard R. Trask (Princeton: Princeton UP, 1953) 235–46.

8. Henrik Ibsen, *The Master Builder: A Play in Three Acts,* trans. Edmund Gosse and William Archer (London: William Heinemann, 1893) 224. Hereafter references to this work are given in the text.

9. See Daniel Boyarin, *Border Lines: The Partition of Judeo-Christianity* (Philadelphia: U of Pennsylvania P, 2004).

Notes to Chapter One, Introduction

1. Henrik Ibsen, *The Lady from the Sea*, trans. Rolf Fjelde, *Henrik Ibsen: Four Major Plays*, vol. 2 (New York: Signet, 1970) 223–322.

2. Longinus, "On the Sublime," trans. W. R. Roberts, *Critical Theory Since Plato,* ed. Hazard Adams (New York: Harcourt, 1971) 92. Hereafter references to this work are given in the text.

3. Throughout the text, all quotations of Milton's poetry are

from John Milton, *English Poems*, ed. R. C. Browne, 2 vols. (Oxford: Clarendon, 1902–06).

4. Ibsen's title is *Bygmester Solness*. *Bygmester* means "master builder." In *Finnegans Wake*, Joyce introduces Finnegan as "Bygmester Finnegan, of the Stuttering Hand." Noting this introduction and the extensive echoes from *The Master Builder* in the novel, Marvin Carlson concludes, "Almost the entire story of the unhappy master builder can be found in *Finnegans Wake*." About the translation of "Appelsinia" as "Orangia," Carlson argues "Joyce must have been aware" of the Edenic "overtones" of "Appelsinia": "In Norwegian, 'orange' is 'appelsin' and the promised country 'Appelsinia,' suggesting strikingly the original fall of man, an underlying theme of *Finnegans Wake*, and the character of Hilda as temptress." See James Joyce, *Finnegans Wake* (1939; Oxford: Oxford UP, 2012) 4 and Marvin Carlson, "Henrik Ibsen and *Finnegans Wake*," *Comparative Literature* 12.3 (1960): 133, 134.

5. See Trausti Ólafsson, *Ibsen's Theatre of Ritualistic Visions: An Interdisciplinary Study of Ten Plays* (Oxford: Lang, 2008) 257.

6. Quoted in Catherine Clément, *Opera, or the Undoing of Women*, trans. Betsy Wing (Minneapolis: U of Minnesota P, 1988) 161.

7. Unless otherwise stated, biblical quotations are from *The Bible: Authorized King James Version with Apocrypha* (Oxford: Oxford UP, 1997). Verses and marginal glosses, with the spelling modernized, will be cited as Geneva, 1560 from *The Geneva Bible: A Facsimile of the 1560 Edition* (Peabody, MA: Hendrickson, 2007).

8. Henry James, *Essays in London and Elsewhere* (New York: Harper, 1893) 251.

9. On Ibsen's familiarity with Nietzsche's thought, and for that thought's influence on *The Master Builder*, see Michael W. Kaufman, "Nietzsche, Georg Brandes, and Ibsen's *Master Builder*," *Comparative Drama* 6.3 (1972): 169–86. Kaufman argues Ibsen distances himself finally from Nietzsche in the play. For a study of Ibsen, and especially *The Master Builder*, arguing for an extensive and sympathetic engagement with Nietzsche's thought and Nietzsche's logic of "going under," by Ibsen, see Theoharis C. Theoharis, *Ibsen's Drama: Right Action and Tragic Joy* (New York: St. Martin's, 1999).

10. Nietzsche ends his *Ecce Homo* as follows: "Have I been understood?—*Dionysus versus the Crucified.*—" See Friedrich Nietzsche, *Ecce Homo: How One Becomes What One Is*, trans. Walter Kaufmann, *Basic Writings of Nietzsche*, ed. Walter Kaufmann (New York: Modern Library, 1968) 791.

11. See Jacques Derrida, *The Gift of Death, Second Edition, and Literature in Secret*, trans. David Wills (Chicago: U of Chicago P, 2008).

12. And Knight describes *The Master Builder* as climaxing in such an episode. See G. Wilson Knight, *Henrik Ibsen* (New York: Grove, 1962) 11, 85–89.

13. See Thomas J. J. Altizer, *Genesis and Apocalypse: A Theological Voyage Toward Authentic Christianity* (Louisville: Westminster, 1990).

Notes to Chapter Two

1. Homer, *The Iliad,* trans. Robert Fagles (New York: Penguin, 1990) 4.597. Hereafter references to this work are given in the text.

2. See Ovid, *Metamorphoses,* trans. A. D. Melville (Oxford: Oxford UP, 1986) 5.269–74. Hereafter, references to this work are given in the text.

3. Boethius, *The Consolation of Philosophy,* trans. P. G. Walsh (Oxford: Oxford UP, 1999) 4. Hereafter references to the work are given in the text.

4. William Shakespeare, *Othello* (New Haven: Yale UP, 2005) 3.3.357. Hereafter references to this work are given in the text. All other works of Shakespeare will be quoted from G. Blakemore Evans, ed., *The Riverside Shakespeare* (Boston: Houghton, 1974) with references given in the text.

5. *The Anxiety of Influence,* the opening sentence of the chapter "Daemonization, or The Counter-Sublime," reads: "The strong new poet must reconcile in himself two truths: '*Ethos* is the *daimon*' and 'all things were made through him, and without him was not anything made that was made.'" In the poet, this struggle to reconcile Heraclitus's fragment with John's claim about the Logos proceeds not through a "dialectic between art and society" but through a "dialectic between art and art." See Harold Bloom, *The Anxiety of Influence: A Theory of Poetry* (London: Oxford UP, 1973) 99.

6. Samuel Beckett, *Krapp's Last Tape and Other Dramatic Pieces* (New York: Grove, 1960) 28. Hereafter references to this work are given in the text.

7. See Longinus, 77.

8. For a highly nuanced and sophisticated exploration of *ekphrasis,* see Murray Krieger, *Ekphrasis: The Illusion of the Natural Sign* (Baltimore: Johns Hopkins UP, 1992).

9. See James A. W. Heffernan, *Museum of Words: The Poetics of Ekphrasis from Homer to Ashbery* (Chicago: U of Chicago P, 1993) 6.

10. Alexander Pope, "An Essay on Criticism," *Critical Theory Since Plato,* ed. Hazard Adams (New York: Harcourt, 1971) 680. Hereafter references to this work are given in the text.

11. Emily Dickinson, "Because I could not stop for Death," *Final Harvest: Emily Dickinson's Poems* (Boston: Little, 1961) 17, 21–24. Hereafter references to this work are given in the text.

12. As Francis E. Peters explains, the "technical [philosophical] use of *energeia* is an Aristotelian innovation." Related to yet distinct from Aristotle's notion of *dynamis,* for Aristotle *energeia* "transcends [...] mere kinetics" as *kinesis* denotes a process in which the *kinesis* will cease once the process reaches its endpoint. In contrast, *energeia* is an "activity" in excess of reifying spatial-temporal kinetic limitations; thus the "eternal movement of the heavenly bodies [...] is pure *energeia.*" In his *Rhetoric,* Aristotle uses the term *energeia* to talk about words achieving a dynamic vividness. A dynamic burgeoning enters the words. This use of *energeia* by Aristotle in the *Rhetoric* is distinct from another term of Aristotle, *enargeia,* which denotes the use of language to represent an entity with pictorial exactitude and visual clarity. Though the two terms, being so close in spelling, are easily confusable, as Joseph Campana points out, the distinction between "vitality and visuality is critical." Lean toward *enargeia,* and the reader leans toward *ekphrasis* as static and pictorial. Lean toward *energeia,* and the reader leans toward Longinus and the ecstatic and dynamic. Quoting from *On the Sublime,* Campana states, "Longinus describes *energeia* as an immediacy of urgency in language that 'introduce[s] events in past time as happening in the present moment' and 'makes the audience feel themselves set in the thick of danger.'" See Francis E. Peters, *Greek Philosophical Terms: A Historical Lexicon* (New York: New York UP, 1967) 55–56; Aristotle, *Rhetoric,* trans. W. Rhys Roberts, *Aristotle: Rhetoric and Poetics* (New York: Modern Library, 1954) 3.11.1–2; and Joseph Campana, *The Pain of Reformation: Spenser, Vulnerability, and the Ethics of Masculinity* (New York: Fordham UP, 2012) 112.

13. See Harold Bloom, *The Anatomy of Influence: Literature as a Way of Life* (New Haven: Yale UP, 2011) 18.

14. Friedrich Nietzsche, *On the Genealogy of Morals: A Polemic,* trans. Douglas Smith (Oxford: Oxford UP, 1996) 3.

15. Harold Bloom, *Ruin the Sacred Truths: Poetry and Belief from the Bible to the Present* (Cambridge, MA: Harvard UP, 1989) 33. Hereafter references to this work are given in the text as *Ruin.*

16. Harold Bloom, *The Epic* (Philadelphia: Chelsea House, 2005) 25.

17. Sandy Florian, *The Tree of No* (Notre Dame, IN: Action Books, 2008) 111. Hereafter references to this work are given in the text.

18. *The Iliad of Homer,* trans. Richmond Lattimore (Chicago: U of Chicago P, 1951) 8.166.

19. Quoted in Beth Lau, *Keats's Paradise Lost* (Gainesville: UP of Florida, 1998) 32.

20. John Ruskin, *The Queen of the Air: Being a Study of the Greek Myths of Cloud and Storm* (New York: Wiley, 1872) 15. Hereafter references to this work are given in the text.

21. Eva Brann, *Homeric Moments: Clues to Delight in Reading the Odyssey and the Iliad* (Philadelphia: Dry, 2002) 143.

Notes to Chapter Three

1. See David Penchansky, *Twilight of the Gods: Polytheism in the Hebrew Bible* (Louisville: Westminster, 2005) 53–54. Hereafter references to this work are given in the text.

2. Søren Kierkegaard, *Philosophical Fragments: Johannes Climacus,* trans. and ed. Howard V. Hong and Edna H. Hong (Princeton: Princeton UP, 1985) 52.

3. William Blake, "Proverbs of Hell," *The Complete Poetry and Prose of William Blake,* ed. David V. Erdman (New York: Anchor, 1988) 18.

4. Quoted in *The Oxford Dictionary of Quotations,* ed. Elizabeth Knowles, 5th ed. (Oxford: Oxford UP, 1999) 418.

5. Cormac McCarthy, *The Road* (New York: Vintage, 2006) 56–57. Hereafter references to this work are given in the text.

6. For a catalog and discussion of these parallels, see Steven Charles Smith, "Jewish Wisdom and the Gospel of John," diss., Loyola U of Chicago, 2008.

7. Raymond E. Brown, *The Gospel According to John (I-XII),* Anchor Bible, vol. 29 (Garden City, NY: Doubleday, 1966) 13.

8. See Dale Moody, "God's Only Son: The Translation of John 3:16 in the Revised Standard Edition," *Journal of Biblical Literature* 72.4 (1953): 214–15.

9. Wayne A. Grudem, *Biblical Doctrine: Essential Teachings of the Christian Faith,* ed. Jeff Purswell (Grand Rapids, MI: Zondervan, 1999) 473.

10. Frank Kermode, "John," *The Literary Guide to the Bible,* ed. Robert Alter and Frank Kermode (Cambridge, MA: Harvard UP, 1987) 445. Hereafter references to this work are given in the text.

11. Robert Alter, *The Art of Biblical Narrative,* rev. ed. (New York: Basic, 2011) 60–73.

12. "Ptolemy's Version of the Gnostic Myth According to St. Irenaeus of Lyon, Against Heresies 1.1.1–1.8.5," trans. Bentley Layton, *The Gnostic Scriptures* (New York: Doubleday, 1987) 283. Hereafter references to this work are given in the text.

13. Euripides, *Helen,* trans. James Michie and Colin Leach (Oxford: Oxford UP, 1981) 173–92.

14. Plato, *The Republic of Plato,* trans. Allan Bloom (New York: Basic, 1968) 607a. Hereafter references to this work are given in the text.

15. *The Riverside Chaucer,* ed. Larry D. Benson (Oxford: Oxford UP, 1987) 398.

16. Elizabeth I, *Translations, 1592–1598,* ed. Janel Mueller and Joshua Scodel (Chicago: U of Chicago P, 2009) 76b.

17. Manlius Severinus Boethius, "*The Consolation of Philosophy:* From Book 1," trans. W. V. Cooper, *Critical Theory since Plato,* ed. Hazard Adams (New York: Harcourt, 1971) 115.

18. *Common Worship: Times and Seasons* (London: Church House, 2006) 58.

19. Boethius, *The Consolation of Philosophy,* trans. I.T., *Boethius: The Theological Tractates and The Consolation of Philosophy* (Cambridge, MA: Harvard UP, 1968) 291. Hereafter references to this work are given in the text as I.T.

20. Boethius, *Boethius's* In Ciceronis Topica, trans. Eleonore Stump (Ithaca, NY: Cornell UP, 1988) 119–20. Hereafter references to this work are given in the text.

21. See Kip Wheeler, "Medieval Literature," *Encyclopedia of Prostitution and Sex Work,* ed. Melissa Hope Ditmore, vol. 1 (Westport, CT: Greenwood, 2006) 296.

22. See Andrea Denny-Brown, *Fashioning Change: The Trope of Clothing in High- and Late-Medieval England* (Columbus: Ohio State UP, 2012) 28. Hereafter references to this work are given in the text.

23. See J. Burton, "Those are the High-Flying Cranes," *Journal of Semitic Studies* 15.2 (1970): 246–65.

24. On *shirk* and on the three daughters as a case of *shirk,* see G. R. Hawting, *The Idea of Idolatry and the Emergence of Islam: From Polemic to History* (Cambridge: Cambridge UP, 1999) 67–87 and 130–49.

25. The Qur'an, trans. M. H. Shakir (Elmhurst, NY: Tahrike Tarsile Qur'an, 1983) 53.2–3. Hereafter references to this work are given in the text.

26. See *Early Islamic Mysticism: Sufi, Qur'an, Mi'Raj, Poetic and Theological Writings,* trans. and ed. Michael A. Sells (New York: Paulist, 1996) 36–37.

27. Mohammed Shahab Ahmed, "The Satanic Verses Incident in the Memory of the Early Muslim Community: An Analysis of the Early Riwāyahs and Their Isnāds," diss., Princeton U, 1999, 41, 42. Ahmed presents his own translation of and then commentary on

each report of the Satanic verses incident. Hereafter references to this work are given in the text as Ahmed.

28. See Vassilios Christides, "Religious Syncretism in the Near East: Allāt-Athena in Palmyra," *Collectanea Christiana Orientalia* 1 (2003): 66. Hereafter references to this work are given in the text.

Notes to Chapter Four

1. By the verb "stone," Samuel Johnson reads Othello to mean Desdemona's unwillingness to admit her act hardens Othello's heart toward murder, while he had wanted to think of his killing her as an atoning sacrifice (quoted in Furness 300). In support of Johnson's reading, note how, to describe his resolution that Desdemona "shall not live," Othello had said to Iago, "my heart is turned to stone" (4.1.175). But with the phrase "stone my heart" might Shakespeare be alluding to the story of Jesus and the woman taken in adultery (John 8.3–11)? Othello would sacrifice a young woman he supposes taken in adultery, yet he imagines Desdemona stoning his heart. Being without sin, Desdemona can cast stones. Her ability to accept Jesus's invitation for anyone sinless to cast the first stone causes Othello to reevaluate his act not as a just sacrifice but as a murder.

2. Samuel Johnson, *Rasselas, Poems, and Selected Prose,* ed. Bertrand H. Bronson, 3rd ed. (San Francisco: Rinehart, 1971) 326.

3. Horace Howard Furness, ed., *Othello: A New Variorum Edition,* by William Shakespeare (Philadelphia: Lippincott, 1886) 300.

4. Desdemona: "That death's unnatural that kills for loving. / Alas, why gnaw you so your nether lip?" (5.2.43–44). Yet Othello wants death from Desdemona's loving. The nether lip—see the Lodovico comment of Emilia. Again, *Othello* is a play of lips and kissing, though Othello never ventures Desdemona's nether lips.

5. In *Hamlet,* standing in Ophelia's grave, Laertes calls for dirt to be mounded over him until "of this flat a mountain you have made / T' o'ertop old Pelion, or the skyish head / of blue Olympus" (5.1.252–54). The hidden Hamlet then reveals himself, leaps into the grave, and as the two fight, Hamlet tells Laertes, "if thou prate of mountains, let them throw / Millions of acres on us, til our ground, / Singeing his pate against the burning zone, / Make Ossa like a wart!" (5.1.280–83).

6. The spelling of Desdemona's name contains "demon," yet the name's pronunciation, especially in Italian, easily sounds "daemon."

7. To refer to the sky in chaotic storm, the second gentleman uses the word "heaven." Iago accuses Cassio of being familiar with only

"bookish theoric" (1.1.22). Something of this accusation resonates when Cassio says of the storm, "O let the heavens / Give [Othello] defense against the elements, / For I have lost him on a dangerous sea" (2.1.44–46). While the second gentleman uses "heaven" to refer to "the elements," the storm, Cassio invokes "the heavens" against the storm, heaven as a realm beyond, a heaven without storm, where storms could only be read of in books. As with his imagery of rocks and sands devoid of their "mortal" qualities, here the "heavens," the skies, exist as if without being skies, without being subject to weather. And consider: Cassio asks "Great Jove" to "guard" Othello by "swell[ing] his sail with [Jove's] own powerful breath," as if what a sailing vessel in a storm needs is more wind, as if there were a wind from a realm above somehow distinct from the winds of the storm (2.1.7, 8).

8. Chasseriau Théodore (1819–1856) attempts to draw the moment of Othello uttering, "O my fair warrior!" in his work titled *Othello de Shakespeare: "O ma belle guerrière!"* (Paris, musée du Louvre). The drawing shows Othello embracing Desdemona at the moment of uttering the phrase, his back mostly turned to the viewer and Desdemona's front mostly turned to the viewer yet with Othello's profile so intersecting hers that their faces are hidden from the viewer. The two share in secrecy the face-to-face moment when she is his warrior and he hers.

9. As Othello's ancient, Iago protects Othello's flag, the sign of Othello's warrior self. For the sea journey, Othello assigns Iago to protect Desdemona who, like Achilles's Briseis, also signifies his warrior status. But then the sign, landing in Cyprus first, usurps the referent. And is not the handkerchief a domestic version of the flag?

10. Desdemona's arrival at Cyprus as a blend of Aphrodite/Venus (Cassio's praise) and Athena/Minerva (Othello's praise) finds an analogue in Shakespeare's *Cymbeline.* A villain in the play is named Iachimo: "This name sounds like a diminutive of Iago, and the bearer resembles him in his way of thinking of men" (Horace Howard Furness, *Cymbeline: A New Variorum Edition,* by William Shakespeare [Philadelphia: Lippincott, 1913] 4). Toward the end of *Cymbeline,* the "Italian fiend" and soldier Iachimo mentions a statue of Minerva (5.5.210). The play begins with Cymbeline's discovery of his daughter Imogen's secret marriage to Posthumus (Othello hopes Desdemona will ease his becoming posthumous), whom Cymbeline banishes to Rome, where amidst the guests at a "feast," Posthumus sat "sadly," or so Iachimo recounts,

Hearing us praise our loves of Italy
For beauty that made barren the swell'd boast
Of him that best could speak; for feature, laming
The shrine of Venus, or straight-pight Minerva,
Postures beyond brief nature [...] (5.5.155, 160, 161–65)

In this praise contest, the participants praise their beloveds' "beauty" as exceeding praise and their "feature[s]" as making seem lame the statues of Venus and Minerva, whose "[p]ostures" outlast and transcend those found in nature. Posthumus, Iachimo explains, had then praised his wife Imogen's chastity, prompting Iachimo to bet Posthumus that he Iachimo could breach that chastity. Comic involutions of elements of *Othello* ensue: Iachimo manufactures "proof" of his conquest of Imogen, Posthumus seeks her murder, but she lives to be reunited with him. Within *Cymbeline,* as within *The Winter's Tale,* a kind of retraction and reversal of *Othello* occurs. Perhaps an aspect of Shakespeare wished never to have written *Othello.*

11. John Donne, *The Complete Poetry and Selected Prose of John Donne,* ed. Charles M. Coffin (New York: Modern Library, 1952) 488.

12. *Chapman's Homer: The Iliad and The Odyssey* (Ware: Wordsworth Editions, 2000) 9.300–01. Hereafter references to this work are given in the text.

13. Diana in ancient Rome was both a goddess of light (the moon) and of darkness (the forest), and a goddess of slaves, and in this capacity a rival to Christ. She was demonized by medieval Christianity and associated with witchcraft and magic. See Walter Stephens, *Demon Lovers: Witchcraft, Sex, and the Crisis of Belief* (Chicago: U of Chicago P, 2002) 128 and Ioan P. Couliano, *Eros and Magic in the Renaissance,* trans. Margaret Cook (Chicago: U of Chicago P, 1987) 79–84.

14. Quoted in Furness 311.

15. See Virginia Mason Vaughan, *Othello: A Contextual History* (Cambridge: Cambridge UP, 1994) 150.

16. Verdi's operas *Simon Boccanegra* (1857/1881) and *Otello* (1887) indirectly testify to how Shakespeare imagines Iago through Paul. In *Simon Boccanegra,* the Italian city of Genoa makes Simon its first doge or duke. The historical Simon had defeated Barbary pirates threatening the city and became doge. The Verdi opera makes Simon himself a former pirate, following its source, Antonio García Gutiérrez's play *Simón Bocanegra.* Though a close ally of Simon, the opera's villain Paolo, namesake of the apostle, betrays and eventually poisons Simon. The parallels between Paolo and Iago are evident,

and when Verdi wrote *Otello,* Verdi gave his Iago the same musical signature as Paolo.

17. Friedrich Nietzsche, *The Antichrist,* trans. Walter Kaufmann, *The Portable Nietzsche,* ed. Walter Kaufmann (New York: Penguin, 1982) 617.

18. Iago thinks via negation. Consider the dance of negations at work when, after Othello strikes Desdemona, Lodovico asks Iago if Othello is in his right mind, and Iago replies, "He's that he is. I may not breathe my censure / What he might be. If what he might, he is not, / I would to heaven he were!" (4.1.263–65).

19. See Maurice Blanchot, *The Space of Literature,* trans. Ann Smock (Lincoln: U of Nebraska P, 1982). Hereafter references to this work are given in the text as *Space.*

20. Friedrich Nietzsche, *The Will to Power,* trans. Walter Kaufmann and R. J. Hollingdale, ed. Walter Kaufmann (New York: Vintage, 1967) 270. Hereafter references to this work are given in the text as *Will.*

Notes to Chapter Five

1. John Milton, "From *Reason of Church-Government* (1642)," *The Riverside Milton,* ed. Roy Flannagan (Boston: Houghton, 1998) 924. Hereafter references to this work are given in the text.

2. Samuel Taylor Coleridge, "The Rime of the Ancient Mariner," *Coleridge: Poetical Works,* ed. Ernst Hartley Coleridge (Oxford: Oxford UP, 1989) 121–22.

3. "Melodious," *The Oxford English Dictionary,* 1933.

4. Sir Thomas Browne, *Hydriotaphia: Urne-Buriall, or, A Brief Discourse of the Sepulchrall Urnes Lately Found in Norfolk* (1658; New York: New Directions, 2010).

5. Moschus, "The Lament for Bion," trans. Andrew Lang, *Milton's "Lycidas" Edited to Serve as an Introduction to Criticism,* ed. Scott Elledge (New York: Harper, 1966) 25, 27.

6. William Wordsworth, "Ode: Intimations of Immortality from Recollections of Early Childhood," *Wordsworth: Poetical Works,* ed. Thomas Hutchinson (Oxford: Oxford UP, 1987) 64.

7. "Corrigenda," *Milton's Lycidas: The Tradition and the Poem,* ed. C. A. Patrides (Columbia: U of Missouri P, 1983) 58. Hereafter references to this work are given in the text.

8. Harold Bloom, "Preface: How to Read Milton's 'Lycidas,'" *A Map of Misreading* (Oxford: Oxford UP, 2003) xix.

9. Charles Lamb, "Oxford in the Vacation," *Essays of Charles Lamb,* ed. George Armstrong Wauchope (Boston: Ginn, 1904) 19, note 1.

10. Virginia Woolf, *A Room of One's Own,* ed. Mark Hussey (Orlando: Harcourt, 2005) 7. Hereafter references to this work are given in the text.

11. For this possible overlapping of the Heavenly Muse with the Holy Spirit, see Philip Edwards Phillips, *John Milton's Epic Invocations* (New York: Lang, 2000) 52, 104. Milton invites this overlapping when in his opening invocation he switches from invoking the "Heavenly Muse" to invoking the Holy Spirit: "And chiefly Thou, O Spirit! that dost prefer / Before all temples th' upright heart and pure, / Instruct me, for thou know'st; / Thou from the first / Wast present" (1.17–20).

12. John Milton, *Areopagitica, The Riverside Milton,* ed. Roy Flannagan (Boston: Houghton, 1998) 997. Hereafter references to this work are given in the text.

13. Francis Bacon, *The New Organon and Related Writings,* trans. James Spedding, Robert Leslie Ellis, and Douglas Denon Heath, ed. Fulton H. Anderson (Indianapolis: Bobbs-Merrill, 1960) 48, 56.

14. Percy Bysshe Shelley, *The Revolt of Islam, The Complete Poems of John Keats and Percy Bysshe Shelley* (New York: Modern Library, n. d.) 3390. Hereafter references to this work are given in the text.

15. T. S. Eliot, "The Wasteland," *The Wasteland and Other Poems* (New York: Harcourt, 1962) 60–63.

16. John Keats, "Ode to a Nightingale," *The Complete Poems,* ed. John Barnard (London: Penguin, 1988) 79–80.

17. Franz Kafka, *The Blue Octavo Notebooks,* trans. Ernst Kaiser and Eithne Wilkins, ed. Max Brod (Cambridge, MA: Exact Change, 1991) 15.

18. Simone Weil, *Gravity and Grace,* trans. Arthur Wills (1952; Lincoln: U of Nebraska P, 1997) 76. Hereafter references to this work are given in the text.

Notes to Chapter Six

1. Herman Melville, *Moby-Dick,* ed. Harrison Hayford, Hershel Parker, and G. Thomas Tanselle (1851; Evanston: Northwestern UP, 1988) 507. Hereafter references to this work are given in the text.

2. Ralph Waldo Emerson, "Circles," *Selections from Ralph Waldo Emerson,* ed. Stephen E. Whicher (Boston: Houghton, 1957) 168. In the same essay, Emerson claims, "Blessed be nothing" stands among the "proverbs which express the transcendentalism of common life" and then notes that "one man's wisdom [is] another's folly" (175).

3. Harold Bloom, *Shakespeare: The Invention of the Human* (New York: Riverhead, 1998) 436.

4. Herman Melville, *Pierre, or The Ambiguities,* ed. Harrison Hayford, Hershel Parker, and G. Thomas Tanselle (1852; Evanston: Northwestern University Press, 1971) 217.

5. And Ishmael only pronounces his name aloud once, and that before the voyage, in his alarm that Queequeg has locked himself in a room at the Try-Pots inn in which a previous whaler guest has committed suicide: "'Queequeg,' said I softly through the key-hole:—all silent. 'I say, Queequeg! why don't you speak? It's I—Ishmael'" (82). Before and during the voyage, Ishmael will occasionally report his interior, silent thoughts, addressing himself by his supposed name. For example: "If then, Sir William Jones, who read in thirty languages, could not read the simplest peasant's face, in its profounder and more subtle meanings, how may unlettered Ishmael hope to read the awful Chaldee of the Sperm Whale's brow?" (347).

6. Sir Walter Scott, *Tales of Grandfather,* vol. 2 (Philadelphia: Desilver, 1836) 64.

7. See Joseph Addison, *Cato: A Tragedy* (London: Longman, 1808) 58–59.

8. *Bohn's Classical Library: The Works of Plato,* vol. 1, trans. Henry Cary (1848; London: George Bell & Sons, 1881) 326 [250c]. Melville likely consulted the Bohn Plato in writing *Moby-Dick.* See Merton M. Sealts, Jr., *Pursuing Melville 1940–1980* (Madison: The U of Wisconsin P, 1982) 299.

9. *Bohn's,* vol. 1, 118 [109c–e].

10. Socrates asserts his truly philosophic friends will follow him into death ASAP, but without violating the suicide taboo (*Bohn's,* vol. 1, 58–60 [61b–62c]). One may only kill oneself when the sovereign gods signal that doing so enacts their will, even if they signal through the problematic sovereignty implicit in an Athenian death sentence.

11. Sealts (301–02) notes the combined allusion.

12. See Maurice Blanchot, *The Book to Come,* trans. Charlotte Mandell (Stanford: Stanford UP, 2003) 7–8.

13. Robin Grey and Douglas Robillard, "Melville's Milton: A Transcription of Melville's Marginalia in His Copy of *The Poetical Works of John Milton," Melville and Milton: An Edition and Analysis of Melville's Annotations of Milton,* ed. Robin Grey (Pittsburgh: Duquesne UP: 2004) 158. In Melville's copy of *The Poetical Works of John Milton,* the 1836 two-volume collection edited by John Mitford, Melville's markings and annotations interpret Milton as an author who professes Christianity yet spurns Christian gatherings, harbors abyssal doubts, and may even be of the Devil's party despite masking as the Christian god's defender. Melville marked Mitford's

paraphrase of a biographer's statement that Milton's "wanderings in religious belief" took Milton "from Puritanism to Calvinism, from Calvinism to an esteem for Arminius, and finally [...] to a dereliction of every denomination of Protestants" (120). About these "wanderings" Melville comments: "He who thinks for himself never can remain of the same mind. I doubt not that darker doubts crossed Milton's soul, than ever disturbed Voltaire. And he was more of what is called an Infidel" (121). While the deist Voltaire may be more fitly "called an Infidel" than Milton, Voltaire's rationalistic deism lends itself to a relative serenity of belief compared to the "darker doubts" restless and free thought brought to the professedly Christian Milton.

The Mitford edition of Milton includes Andrew Marvell's poem "On *Paradise Lost.*" Melville marked the following lines in which Marvell wonders whether Milton may, in *Paradise Lost,* be seeking to dissolve the aura of extra-literary authority Christians commonly grant their Bible: "the argument / Held me awhile misdoubting his intent, / That he would ruine (for I saw him strong) / The sacred truths to Fable and old song"; Melville annotated Marvell's lines thus: "It is still 'misdoubted' by some. First impressions are generally true, too, Andrew" (122). Though Marvell's poem goes on to suggest *Paradise Lost* does indeed justify the ways of God to men, Melville suggests Marvell should have followed his first impression and realized that the poem may very well have a more ambiguous "intent." In an annotation, Melville writes: "There is a basis for the doubt expressed by A. Marvell in his lines to Milton on the publication of the P. Lost. There was a twist in Milton" (187).

14. Herman Melville, *Correspondence,* ed. Lynn Horth (Evanston: Northwestern UP, 1993) 196.

15. Quoted in Hershel Parker, *Herman Melville: A Biography, Volume 2: 1851–1891* (Baltimore: Johns Hopkins UP, 2002) 300.

16. Walt Whitman, "Aboard at a Ship's Helm," *Leaves of Grass and Selected Prose* (San Francisco: Rinehart, 1962) 218.

17. William Ernest Henley, *Poems* (London: Nutt, 1919) 119.

18. Harold Bloom, "The Breaking of Form," *Deconstruction and Criticism* (New York: Continuum, 1979) 12.

Notes for Chapter Seven

1. Though the example is *Samson Agonistes,* for the contemplation of suicide as a Kantian moment of relinquishing all of the sensible as a motive only to then take up duty as a motive, see Sanford Budick, *Kant and Milton* (Cambridge, MA: Harvard UP, 2010) 208.

2. See James Montgomery, *The World Before the Flood, The Poetical Works of James Montgomery,* vol. 1 (Boston: Houghton, 1858) 1–134 and Robert Montgomery, *Satan, or Intellect without God, The Poetical Works of Robert Montgomery* (London: Chapman, 1854) 323–85.

3. Geoffrey Chaucer, "The Canon's Yeoman's Prologue and Tale," *The Tales of Canterbury,* ed. Robert A. Pratt (Atlanta: Houghton, 1974) 770, 767.

4. *Everyman, Everyman and Medieval Miracle Plays,* ed. A. C. Cawley (Dent: Everyman's Library, 1986) 74–75. Hereafter references to this work are given in the text.

5. See Plato, *Gorgias,* trans. Robin Waterfield (Oxford: Oxford UP, 1994) 524c–525a.

6. Harold Bloom, "Cities of the Mind," *Bloom's Literary Places: New York,* by Jesse Zuba (Philadelphia: Chelsea House, 2005) ix. Hereafter references to this work are given in the text.

7. Diane Wolkstein and Samuel Noah Kramer, *Inanna: Queen of Heaven and Earth: Her Stories and Hymns from Sumer* (New York: Harper, 1983) 6.

8. *The New Oxford Annotated Bible, Third Edition: New Revised Standard Version,* ed. Michael D. Coogan (Oxford: Oxford UP, 2001).

9. See "The Alphabet of Ben Sira," *Rabbinic Fantasies: Imaginative Narratives from Classical Hebrew Literature,* ed. David Stern and Mark Jay Mirsky (New Haven: Yale UP, 1990) 183–84.

10. Harold Bloom, "The Covering Cherub or Poetic Influence," *Poetics of Influence: New and Selected Criticism,* ed. John Hollander (New Haven: Schwab, 1988) 94.

11. Jacques Derrida, *Margins of Philosophy,* trans. Alan Bass (Chicago: U of Chicago P, 1982) 22.

12. James Joyce, *Ulysses,* ed. Hans Walter Gabler (New York: Vintage, 1986) 633.

13. See Paul Middleton and Leigh Hatts, *London City Churches* (London: Bankside, 2003) 46.

14. Barbara K. Lewalski, *The Life of John Milton* (Malden, MA: Blackwell, 2003) 450.

15. Roland Barthes, *Image–Music–Text,* trans. Stephen Heath (New York: Hill, 1977) 148.

16. William James, *Pragmatism: A New Name for Some Old Ways of Thinking* (New York: Longmans, 1909) 140. Hereafter references to this work are given in the text.

17. Samuel Beckett, *Watt,* ed. C. J. Ackerley (London: Faber, 2009) 215.

18. Wallace Stevens, *The Necessary Angel* (New York: Vintage, 1951) 72.

19. Sir Philip Sidney, *An Apology for Poetry, Critical Theory since Plato,* ed. Hazard Adams (New York: Harcourt, 1971) 156. Hereafter references to this work are given in the text.

20. Wallace Stevens, "Angel Surrounded by Paysans," *Collected Poetry and Prose,* ed. Frank Kermode and Joan Richardson (New York: Library of America, 1997) 11–13. This angel appears only "for a moment" (19).

21. Hesiod, "The Five Ages," trans. H. G. Evelyn-White, *The Portable Greek Reader,* ed. W. H. Auden (New York: Penguin, 1976) 56–57.

22. Robert Savino Oventile, "An Interview with Sandy Florian," *COIN* (2011): 45 pars., web, 20 March 2011. Hereafter references to this work are given in the text.

23. Harold Bloom, *Omens of Millennium: The Gnosis of Angels, Dreams, and Resurrection* (New York: Riverhead, 1996) 189. Hereafter references to this work are given in the text.

24. Quoted in James I. Porter, "Nietzsche and the Impossibility of Nihilism," *Nietzsche, Nihilism, and the Philosophy of the Future,* ed. Jeffrey Metzger (London: Continuum, 2009) 143.

25. Wallace Stevens, "The Poems of Our Climate," *Collected Poetry and Prose,* ed. Frank Kermode and Joan Richardson (New York: Library of America, 1997) 13, 21. Hereafter references to this work are given in the text.

Works Cited

Addison, Joseph. *Cato: A Tragedy*. London: Longman, 1808.

Ahmed, Mohammed Shahab. "The Satanic Verses Incident in the Memory of the Early Muslim Community: An Analysis of the Early Riwāyahs and Their Isnāds." Diss. Princeton U, 1999.

"The Alphabet of Ben Sira." *Rabbinic Fantasies: Imaginative Narratives from Classical Hebrew Literature*. Ed. David Stern and Mark Jay Mirsky. New Haven: Yale UP, 1990. 167–202.

Alter, Robert. *The Art of Biblical Narrative*. Rev. ed. New York: Basic, 2011.

Altizer, Thomas J. J. *Genesis and Apocalypse: A Theological Voyage Toward Authentic Christianity*. Louisville: Westminster, 1990.

Aristotle. *Rhetoric*. Trans. W. Rhys Roberts. *Aristotle: Rhetoric and Poetics*. New York: Modern Library, 1954. 1–218.

Bacon, Francis. *The New Organon and Related Writings*. Trans. James Spedding, Robert Leslie Ellis, and Douglas Denon Heath. Ed. Fulton H. Anderson. Indianapolis: Bobbs-Merrill, 1960.

Barthes, Roland. *Image–Music–Text*. Trans. Stephen Heath. New York: Hill, 1977.

Beckett, Samuel. *Krapp's Last Tape and Other Dramatic Pieces*. New York: Grove, 1960.

———. *Watt*. Ed. C. J. Ackerley. London: Faber, 2009.

The Bible: Authorized King James Version with Apocrypha. Oxford: Oxford UP, 1997.

Blake, William. *The Complete Poetry and Prose of William Blake*. Ed. David V. Erdman. New York: Anchor, 1988.

Blanchot, Maurice. *The Book to Come*. Trans. Charlotte Mandell. Stanford: Stanford UP, 2003.

———. *The Space of Literature*. Trans. Ann Smock. Lincoln: U of Nebraska P, 1982.

Bloom, Harold. *The Anatomy of Influence: Literature as a Way of Life*. New Haven: Yale UP, 2011.

———. *The Anxiety of Influence: A Theory of Poetry*. London: Oxford UP, 1973.

———. "The Breaking of Form." *Deconstruction and Criticism*. New York: Continuum, 1979. 1–37.

———. "Cities of the Mind." *Bloom's Literary Places: New York*, by Jesse Zuba. Philadelphia: Chelsea House, 2005. vii–xi.

———. "The Covering Cherub or Poetic Influence." *Poetics of Influence: New and Selected Criticism*. Ed. John Hollander. New Haven: Schwab, 1988. 77–99.

———. *The Epic*. Philadelphia: Chelsea House, 2005.

———. Introduction. *Till I End My Song: A Gathering of Last Poems*. Ed. Harold Bloom. New York: Harper, 2010. xvii–xxviii.

———. *Omens of Millennium: The Gnosis of Angels, Dreams, and Resurrection*. New York: Riverhead, 1996.

———. "Preface: How to Read Milton's Lycidas." *A Map of Misreading*. Oxford: Oxford UP, 2003. xiii–xxiii.

———. *Ruin the Sacred Truths: Poetry and Belief from the Bible to the Present*. Cambridge, MA: Harvard UP, 1989.

———. *Shakespeare: The Invention of the Human*. New York: Riverhead, 1998.

Boethius. *Boethius's* In Ciceronis Topica. Trans. Eleonore Stump. Ithaca, NY: Cornell UP, 1988.

———. *The Consolation of Philosophy*. Trans. I.T. *Boethius: The Theological Tractates and The Consolation of Philosophy*. Cambridge, MA: Harvard UP, 1968. 128–411.

———. *The Consolation of Philosophy*. Trans. P. G. Walsh. Oxford: Oxford UP, 1999.

———. "*The Consolation of Philosophy*: From Book 1," trans. W. V. Cooper, *Critical Theory since Plato*, ed. Hazard Adams (New York: Harcourt, 1971) 115.

Bohn's Classical Library: The Works of Plato. Vol. 1. 1848. Trans. Henry Cary. London: George Bell & Sons, 1881.

Boyarin, Daniel. *Border Lines: The Partition of Judeo-Christianity*. Philadelphia: U of Pennsylvania P, 2004.

Brann, Eva. *Homeric Moments: Clues to Delight in Reading the Odyssey and the Iliad*. Philadelphia: Dry, 2002.

Brown, Raymond E. *The Gospel According to John (I-XII)*. Anchor Bible. Vol. 29. Garden City, NY: Doubleday, 1966.

Browne, Sir Thomas. *Hydriotaphia: Urne-Buriall, or, A Brief Discourse of the Sepulchrall Urnes Lately Found in Norfolk*. 1658. New York: New Directions, 2010.

Budick, Sanford. *Kant and Milton*. Cambridge, MA: Harvard UP, 2010.

Burton, J. "Those are the High-Flying Cranes." *Journal of Semitic Studies* 15.2 (1970): 246–65.

Campana, Joseph. *The Pain of Reformation: Spenser, Vulnerability, and the Ethics of Masculinity*. New York: Fordham UP, 2012.

Carlson, Marvin. "Henrik Ibsen and *Finnegans Wake*." *Comparative Literature* 12.3 (1960): 133–41.

Chapman's Homer: The Iliad and The Odyssey. Ware: Wordsworth Editions, 2000.

Chaucer, Geoffrey. "The Canon's Yeoman's Prologue and Tale." *The Tales of Canterbury*. Ed. Robert A. Pratt. Atlanta: Houghton, 1974. 454–77.

Christides, Vassilios. "Religious Syncretism in the Near East: Allāt-Athena in Palmyra." *Collectanea Christiana Orientalia* 1 (2003): 65–81.

Clément, Catherine. *Opera, or the Undoing of Women*. Trans. Betsy Wing. Minneapolis: U of Minnesota P, 1988.

Coleridge, Samuel Taylor. "The Rime of the Ancient Mariner." *Coleridge: Poetical Works*. Ed. Ernst Hartley Coleridge. Oxford: Oxford UP, 1989. 186–209.

Common Worship: Times and Seasons. London: Church House, 2006.

Corbin, Henry. *Alone with the Alone: Creative Imagination in the Sūfism of Ibn 'Arabī*. Trans. Ralph Manheim. Princeton: Princeton UP, 1998.

"Corrigenda." *Milton's Lycidas: The Tradition and the Poem*. Ed. C. A. Patrides. Columbia: U of Missouri P, 1983. 12–13.

Couliano, Ioan P. *Eros and Magic in the Renaissance*. Trans. Margaret Cook. Chicago: U of Chicago P, 1987.

Curtius, Ernst Robert. *European Literature and the Latin Middle Ages*. Trans. Willard R. Trask. Princeton: Princeton UP, 1953.

Deacy, Susan. *Athena*. London: Routledge, 2008.

Denny-Brown, Andrea. *Fashioning Change: The Trope of Clothing in High- and Late-Medieval England*. Columbus: Ohio State UP, 2012.

Derrida, Jacques. *The Gift of Death, Second Edition, and Literature In Secret*. Trans. David Wills. Chicago: U of Chicago P, 2008.

———. *Margins of Philosophy*. Trans. Alan Bass. Chicago: U of Chicago P, 1982.

Dickinson, Emily. "Because I could not stop for Death." *Final Harvest: Emily Dickinson's Poems*. Boston: Little, 1961. 177–78.

Dodds, E. R. *The Greeks and the Irrational*. Berkeley: U of California P, 1951.

———. *Pagan and Christian in an Age of Anxiety*. Cambridge: Cambridge UP, 1965.

Donne, John. *The Complete Poetry and Selected Prose of John Donne*. Ed. Charles M. Coffin. New York: Modern Library, 1952.

Early Islamic Mysticism: Sufi, Qur'an, Mi`Raj, Poetic and Theological Writings. Trans. and Ed. Michael A. Sells. New York: Paulist, 1996.

Eliot, T. S. "The Wasteland." *The Wasteland and Other Poems*. New York: Harcourt, 1962. 28–54.

Elizabeth I. *Translations, 1592–1598*. Ed. Janel Mueller and Joshua Scodel. Chicago: U of Chicago P, 2009.

Emerson, Ralph Waldo. "Circles." *Selections from Ralph Waldo Emerson*. Ed. Stephen E. Whicher. Boston: Houghton, 1957. 168–78.

Euripides. *Helen*. Trans. James Michie and Colin Leach. Oxford: Oxford UP, 1981.

Evans, G. Blakemore, ed. *The Riverside Shakespeare*. Boston: Houghton, 1974.

Everyman. *Everyman and Medieval Miracle Plays*. Ed. A. C. Cawley. Dent: Everyman's Library, 1986. 205–34.

Florian, Sandy. *The Tree of No*. Notre Dame, IN: Action Books, 2008.

Furness, Horace Howard, ed. *Cymbeline: A New Variorum Edition*, by William Shakespeare. Philadelphia: Lippincott, 1913.

———. *Othello: A New Variorum Edition*, by William Shakespeare. Philadelphia: Lippincott, 1886.

The Geneva Bible: A Facsimile of the 1560 Edition. Peabody, MA: Hendrickson, 2007.

Grey, Robin and Douglas Robillard. "Melville's Milton: A Transcription of Melville's Marginalia in His Copy of *The Poetical Works of John Milton*." *Melville and Milton: An Edition and Analysis of Melville's Annotations of Milton*. Ed. Robin Grey. Pittsburgh: Duquesne UP: 2004. 115–203.

Grudem, Wayne A. *Biblical Doctrine: Essential Teachings of the Christian Faith*. Ed. Jeff Purswell. Grand Rapids, MI: Zondervan, 1999.

Hawting, G. R. *The Idea of Idolatry and the Emergence of Islam: From Polemic to History*. Cambridge: Cambridge UP, 1999.

Heffernan, James A. W. *Museum of Words: The Poetics of Ekphrasis from Homer to Ashbery*. Chicago: U of Chicago P, 1993.

Henley, William Ernest. *Poems*. London: Nutt, 1919.

Heraclitus: Fragments. Trans. Brooks Haxton. New York: Penguin, 2001.

Hesiod. "The Five Ages." Trans. H. G. Evelyn-White. *The Portable Greek Reader*. Ed. W. H. Auden. New York: Penguin, 1976. 55–58.

Homer. *The Iliad*. Trans. Robert Fagles. New York: Penguin, 1990.

Ibsen, Henrik. *The Lady from the Sea*. Trans. Rolf Fjelde. *Henrik Ibsen: Four Major Plays*. Vol. 2. New York: Signet, 1970. 223–322.

———. *The Master Builder: A Play in Three Acts*. Trans. Edmund Gosse and William Archer. London: William Heinemann, 1893.

The Iliad of Homer. Trans. Richmond Lattimore. Chicago: U of Chicago P, 1951.

James, Henry. *Essays in London and Elsewhere*. New York: Harper, 1893.

James, William. *Pragmatism: A New Name for Some Old Ways of Thinking*. New York: Longmans, 1909.

Johnson, Samuel. *Rasselas, Poems, and Selected Prose*. Ed. Bertrand H. Bronson. 3rd ed. San Francisco: Rinehart, 1971.

Joyce, James. *Finnegans Wake*. Oxford: Oxford UP, 2012.

———. *Ulysses*. Ed. Hans Walter Gabler. New York: Vintage, 1986.

Kafka, Franz. *The Blue Octavo Notebooks*. Trans. Ernst Kaiser and Eithne Wilkins. Ed. Max Brod. Cambridge, MA: Exact Change, 1991.

Kaufman, Michael W. "Nietzsche, Georg Brandes, and Ibsen's *Master Builder*." *Comparative Drama* 6.3 (1972): 169–86.

Keats, John. "Ode to a Nightingale." *The Complete Poems*. Ed. John Barnard. London: Penguin, 1988. 346–48.

Kerényi, Karl. *Athene: Virgin and Mother in Greek Religion*. Trans. Murray Stein. Dallas: Spring, 1978.

Kermode, Frank. "John." *The Literary Guide to the Bible*. Ed. Robert Alter and Frank Kermode. Cambridge, MA: Harvard UP, 1987. 440–66.

Kierkegaard, Søren. *Philosophical Fragments: Johannes Climacus*. Trans. and Ed. Howard V. Hong and Edna H. Hong. Princeton: Princeton UP, 1985.

Knight, G. Wilson. *Henrik Ibsen*. New York: Grove, 1962.

Krieger, Murray. *Ekphrasis: The Illusion of the Natural Sign*. Baltimore: Johns Hopkins UP, 1992.

Lamb, Charles. "Oxford in the Vacation." *Essays of Charles Lamb*. Ed. George Armstrong Wauchope. Boston: Ginn, 1904. 15–23.

Lau, Beth. *Keats's Paradise Lost*. Gainesville: UP of Florida, 1998.

Lewalski, Barbara K. *The Life of John Milton*. Malden, MA: Blackwell, 2003.

Longinus. *On the Sublime*. Trans. W. R. Roberts. *Critical Theory since Plato*. Ed. Hazard Adams. New York: Harcourt, 1971. 76–102.

McCarthy, Cormac. *The Road*. New York: Vintage, 2006.

"Melodious." *The Oxford English Dictionary*. 1933.

Melville, Herman. *Correspondence*. Ed. Lynn Horth. Evanston: Northwestern UP, 1993.

———. *Moby-Dick*. 1851. Ed. Harrison Hayford, Hershel Parker, and G. Thomas Tanselle. Evanston: Northwestern UP, 1988.

———. *Pierre, or The Ambiguities*. 1852. Ed. Harrison Hayford, Hershel Parker, and G. Thomas Tanselle. Evanston: Northwestern University Press, 1971.

Middleton, Paul and Leigh Hatts. *London City Churches*. London: Bankside, 2003.

Milton, John. *Areopagitica*. *The Riverside Milton*. Ed. Roy Flannagan. Boston: Houghton, 1998. 997–1024.

———. *English Poems*. Ed. R. C. Browne. 2 vols. Oxford: Clarendon, 1902–06.

———. "From *Reason of Church-Government* (1642)." *The Riverside Milton*. Ed. Roy Flannagan. Boston: Houghton, 1998. 902–25.

Montgomery, James. *The World Before the Flood*. *The Poetical Works of James Montgomery*. Vol. 1. Boston: Houghton, 1858. 1–134.

Montgomery, Robert. *Satan, or Intellect without God, The Poetical Works of Robert Montgomery.* London: Chapman, 1854. 323–85.

Moody, Dale. "God's Only Son: The Translation of John 3:16 in the Revised Standard Edition." *Journal of Biblical Literature* 72.4 (1953): 213–219.

Moschus. "The Lament for Bion." Trans. Andrew Lang. *Milton's "Lycidas" Edited to Serve as an Introduction to Criticism.* Ed. Scott Elledge. New York: Harper, 1966. 25–30.

The New Oxford Annotated Bible, Third Edition: New Revised Standard Version. Ed. Michael D. Coogan. Oxford: Oxford UP, 2001.

Nietzsche, Friedrich. *The Antichrist.* Trans. Walter Kaufmann. *The Portable Nietzsche.* Ed. Walter Kaufmann. New York: Penguin, 1982. 565–656.

———. *Ecce Homo: How One Becomes What One Is.* Trans. Walter Kaufmann. *Basic Writings of Nietzsche.* Ed. Walter Kaufmann. New York: Modern Library, 1968. 656–791.

———. *On the Genealogy of Morals: A Polemic.* Trans. Douglas Smith. Oxford: Oxford UP, 1996.

———. *Thus Spoke Zarathustra: A Book for Everyone and Nobody.* Trans. Graham Parkes. Oxford: Oxford UP, 2005.

———. *The Will to Power.* Trans. Walter Kaufmann and R. J. Hollingdale. Ed. Walter Kaufmann. New York: Vintage, 1967.

Ólafsson, Trausti. *Ibsen's Theatre of Ritualistic Visions: An Interdisciplinary Study of Ten Plays.* Oxford: Lang, 2008.

Oventile, Robert Savino. "An Interview with Sandy Florian." *COIN* (2011): 45 pars. Web. 20 March 2011.

Ovid. *Metamorphoses.* Trans. A. D. Melville. Oxford: Oxford UP, 1986.

The Oxford Dictionary of Quotations. Ed. Elizabeth Knowles, 5th ed. Oxford: Oxford UP, 1999.

Parker, Hershel. *Herman Melville: A Biography, Volume 2: 1851–1891.* Baltimore: Johns Hopkins UP, 2002.

Penchansky, David. *Twilight of the Gods: Polytheism in the Hebrew Bible.* Louisville: Westminster, 2005.

Peters, Francis E. *Greek Philosophical Terms: A Historical Lexicon.* New York: New York UP, 1967.

Phillips, Philip Edwards. *John Milton's Epic Invocations.* New York: Lang, 2000.

Plato. *Gorgias*. Trans. Robin Waterfield. Oxford: Oxford UP, 1994.

———. *The Republic of Plato*. Trans. Allan Bloom. New York: Basic, 1968.

———. *Symposium*. Trans. Robin Waterfield. Oxford: Oxford UP, 1994.

Pope, Alexander. "An Essay on Criticism." *Critical Theory Since Plato*. Ed. Hazard Adams. New York: Harcourt, 1971. 277–286.

Porter, James I. "Nietzsche and the Impossibility of Nihilism." *Nietzsche, Nihilism, and the Philosophy of the Future*. Ed. Jeffrey Metzger. London: Continuum, 2009. 143–57.

"Ptolemy's Version of the Gnostic Myth According to St. Irenaeus of Lyon, Against Heresies 1.1.1–1.8.5." Trans. Bentley Layton, *The Gnostic Scriptures* (New York: Doubleday, 1987) 283.

The Qur'an. Trans. M. H. Shakir. Elmhurst, NY: Tahrike Tarsile Qur'an, 1983.

The Riverside Chaucer. Ed. Larry D. Benson. Oxford: Oxford UP, 1987.

Ruskin, John. *The Queen of the Air: Being a Study of the Greek Myths of Cloud and Storm*. New York: Wiley, 1872.

Scott, Sir Walter. *Tales of Grandfather*. Vol. 2. Philadelphia: Desilver, 1836.

Sealts, Merton M., Jr. *Pursuing Melville 1940–1980*. Madison: U of Wisconsin P, 1982.

Shakespeare, William. *Othello*. New Haven: Yale UP, 2005.

Shearer, Ann. *Athene: Image and Energy*. London: Viking Arkana, 1996.

Shelley, Percy Bysshe. *The Revolt of Islam*. *The Complete Poems of John Keats and Percy Bysshe Shelley*. New York: Modern Library, n. d. 33–176.

Sidney, Sir Philip. *An Apology for Poetry*. *Critical Theory since Plato*. Ed. Hazard Adams. New York: Harcourt, 1971. 154–77.

Smith, Steven Charles. "Jewish Wisdom and the Gospel of John." Diss. Loyola U of Chicago, 2008.

Stephens, Walter. *Demon Lovers: Witchcraft, Sex, and the Crisis of Belief*. Chicago: U of Chicago P, 2002.

Stevens, Wallace. *Collected Poetry and Prose*. Ed. Frank Kermode and Joan Richardson. New York: Library of America, 1997.

———. *The Necessary Angel*. New York: Vintage, 1951.

Theoharis, Theoharis C. *Ibsen's Drama: Right Action and Tragic Joy*. New York: St. Martin's, 1999.

Vaughan, Virginia Mason. *Othello: A Contextual History*. Cambridge: Cambridge UP, 1994.

Weil, Simone. *Gravity and Grace*. Trans. Arthur Wills. 1952. Lincoln: U of Nebraska P, 1997.

Wheeler, Kip. "Medieval Literature." *Encyclopedia of Prostitution and Sex Work*. Ed. Melissa Hope Ditmore. Vol. 1. Westport, CT: Greenwood, 2006. 294–99.

Whitman, Walt. "Aboard at a Ship's Helm." *Leaves of Grass and Selected Prose*. San Francisco: Rinehart, 1962. 217–18.

Wolkstein, Diane and Samuel Noah Kramer. *Inanna: Queen of Heaven and Earth: Her Stories and Hymns from Sumer*. New York: Harper, 1983.

Woolf, Virginia. *A Room of One's Own*. Ed. Mark Hussey. Orlando: Harcourt, 2005.

Wordsworth, William. "Ode: Intimations of Immortality from Recollections of Early Childhood." *Wordsworth: Poetical Works*. Ed. Thomas Hutchinson. Oxford: Oxford UP, 1987. 460–62.

Index

Made in the USA
San Bernardino, CA
16 April 2014